AF837281

ECONOMIC ISSUES, PROBLEMS AND PERSPECTIVES

FROM SURPLUS TO DEFICIT

THE IMPACT OF LEGISLATION ON THE FEDERAL BUDGET

ECONOMIC ISSUES, PROBLEMS AND PERSPECTIVES

Additional books in this series can be found on Nova's website under the Series tab.

Additional E-books in this series can be found on Nova's website under the E-books tab.

ECONOMIC ISSUES, PROBLEMS AND PERSPECTIVES

FROM SURPLUS TO DEFICIT

THE IMPACT OF LEGISLATION ON THE FEDERAL BUDGET

VANESSA C. SIBHOAN
EDITOR

Nova Science Publishers, Inc.
New York

Copyright © 2011 by Nova Science Publishers, Inc.

All rights reserved. No part of this book may be reproduced, stored in a retrieval system or transmitted in any form or by any means: electronic, electrostatic, magnetic, tape, mechanical photocopying, recording or otherwise without the written permission of the Publisher.

For permission to use material from this book please contact us:
Telephone 631-231-7269; Fax 631-231-8175
Web Site: http://www.novapublishers.com

NOTICE TO THE READER

The Publisher has taken reasonable care in the preparation of this book, but makes no expressed or implied warranty of any kind and assumes no responsibility for any errors or omissions. No liability is assumed for incidental or consequential damages in connection with or arising out of information contained in this book. The Publisher shall not be liable for any special, consequential, or exemplary damages resulting, in whole or in part, from the readers' use of, or reliance upon, this material. Any parts of this book based on government reports are so indicated and copyright is claimed for those parts to the extent applicable to compilations of such works.

Independent verification should be sought for any data, advice or recommendations contained in this book. In addition, no responsibility is assumed by the publisher for any injury and/or damage to persons or property arising from any methods, products, instructions, ideas or otherwise contained in this publication.

This publication is designed to provide accurate and authoritative information with regard to the subject matter covered herein. It is sold with the clear understanding that the Publisher is not engaged in rendering legal or any other professional services. If legal or any other expert assistance is required, the services of a competent person should be sought. FROM A DECLARATION OF PARTICIPANTS JOINTLY ADOPTED BY A COMMITTEE OF THE AMERICAN BAR ASSOCIATION AND A COMMITTEE OF PUBLISHERS.

Additional color graphics may be available in the e-book version of this book.

LIBRARY OF CONGRESS CATALOGING-IN-PUBLICATION DATA

From surplus to deficit : the impact of legislation on the federal budget /
editors, Vanessa C. Sibhoan.
p. cm.
Includes index.
ISBN 978-1-61728-927-9 (hardcover)
1. Budget deficits--United States. 2. Budget deficits--United
States--Forecasting. I. Sibhoan, Vanessa C.
HJ2051.F76 2010
336.73--dc22

2010035855

Published by Nova Science Publishers, Inc. † New York

CONTENTS

PREFACE

The annual federal budget deficit is the amount by which federal government outlays exceed revenues for a given fiscal year, with surpluses generated when revenues exceed outlays. Budget deficits or surpluses are often used to gauge national fiscal health, as budget balances over time determine levels of federal debt held by the public, and corresponding net interest payments required for debt service. During an economic downturn, budget deficits could be viewed as effective fiscal policy, with lawmakers enacting tax cuts and increasing federal spending to simulate economic activity. This book examines to what extent major legislative changes from 2001 to 2009 caused the budget to move from surplus to deficit.

Chapter 1- After recording a fiscal year (FY) 2000 federal budget surplus of $236.2 billion, the Congressional Budget Office (CBO) in January 2001 projected continued surpluses throughout the decade. However, enactment of major legislation during the 107th to 111th Congresses, in combination with changing economic conditions, altered the federal budget outlook for the decade dramatically. In FY2002, the budget recorded a deficit for the first time since 1997, and the federal government has run a deficit in each subsequent year.

This report examines to what extent major legislative changes from 2001 to 2009 caused the budget to move from surplus to deficit. Legislative actions taken in 2009 increased the FY2009 deficit by $509 billion, whereas legislative actions taken between 2001 and 2008 increased the FY2009 deficit by $903 billion. Furthermore, legislative changes have cumulatively increased federal budget deficits over FY2001 to FY2009 by $5.4 trillion.

Chapter 2- The Congressional Budget Office (CBO) projects that if current laws and policies remained unchanged, the federal budget would show a deficit of about $1.3 trillion for fiscal year 2010 (see Summary Table 1). At 9.2 percent of gross domestic product (GDP), that deficit would be slightly smaller than the shortfall of 9.9 percent of GDP ($1.4 trillion) posted in 2009. Last year's deficit was the largest as a share of GDP since the end of World War II, and the deficit expected for 2010 would be the second largest. Moreover, if legislation is enacted in the next several months that either boosts spending or reduces revenues, the 2010 deficit could equal or exceed last year's shortfall.

The large 2009 and 2010 deficits reflect a combination of factors: an imbalance between revenues and spending that predates the recession and turmoil in financial markets, sharply lower revenues and elevated spending associated with those economic conditions, and the costs of various federal policies implemented in response to those conditions.

In: From Surplus to Deficit: The Impact of Legislation on the... ISBN: 978-1-61728-927-9
Editor: Vanessa C. Sibhoan © 2011 Nova Science Publishers, Inc.

Chapter 1

THE IMPACT OF MAJOR LEGISLATION ON BUDGET DEFICITS: 2001 TO 2009

Marc Labonte and Andrew Hanna

SUMMARY

After recording a fiscal year (FY) 2000 federal budget surplus of $236.2 billion, the Congressional Budget Office (CBO) in January 2001 projected continued surpluses throughout the decade. However, enactment of major legislation during the 107th to 111th Congresses, in combination with changing economic conditions, altered the federal budget outlook for the decade dramatically. In FY2002, the budget recorded a deficit for the first time since 1997, and the federal government has run a deficit in each subsequent year.

This report examines to what extent major legislative changes from 2001 to 2009 caused the budget to move from surplus to deficit. Legislative actions taken in 2009 increased the FY2009 deficit by $509 billion, whereas legislative actions taken between 2001 and 2008 increased the FY2009 deficit by $903 billion. Furthermore, legislative changes have cumulatively increased federal budget deficits over FY2001 to FY2009 by $5.4 trillion.

Several major tax laws passed by Congress reduced federal government revenues, including the Economic Growth and Tax Relief Reconciliation Act of 2001 (P.L. 107-16), the Jobs and Growth Tax Relief Reconciliation Act of 2003 (P.L. 108-27), and the Working Families Tax Relief Act of 2004 (P.L. 108-311). On an aggregated basis, estimates by CBO and the Joint Committee on Taxation (JCT) at the time of legislative enactment placed the total anticipated cost for these three laws at $1.76 trillion for FY2001 to FY2011.

The Medicare Prescription Drug, Improvement, and Modernization Act of 2003 (P.L. 108-173) established a new Medicare Part D prescription drug benefit, which CBO originally projected would cost $552.2 billion over 10 years. However, the Boards of Trustees for Medicare estimated in May 2009 that Part D expenditures would total $381.3 billion for this same period.

Funding for "Global War on Terror" operations has been provided primarily through emergency supplemental appropriations law. For FY2001 to FY2009, Congress approved legislation appropriating about $943.8 billion for military operations in Iraq and Afghanistan, with $887.8 billion of this amount allocated to the Department of Defense.

On September 6, 2008, the Federal Housing Finance Agency exercised authority provided under the Housing and Economic Recovery Act of 2008 (P.L. 110-289) to place Fannie Mae and Freddie Mac into conservatorship. In August 2009, CBO estimated net subsidy costs related to Fannie Mae and Freddie Mac at $291 billion for FY2009. The Emergency Economic Stabilization Act of 2008 (Division A of P.L. 110-343) established the Troubled Asset Relief Program (TARP). In January 2010, CBO projected TARP would increase budget deficits by $99 billion over the complete duration of the program.

In response to significant weakness in the U.S. economy, the Economic Stimulus Act of 2008 (P.L. 110-185) provided a refundable individual income tax rebate. JCT estimated in February 2008 that P.L. 110-185 would increase federal budget deficits by approximately $124.5 billion for FY2008 to FY2018. To provide additional economic stimulus, Congress enacted the American Recovery and Reinvestment Act of 2009 (P.L. 111-5) on February 17, 2009. In January 2010 CBO estimated that P.L. 111-5 will increase federal budget deficits by $862 billion over 10 years.

The annual federal budget deficit is the amount by which federal government outlays exceed revenues for a given fiscal year (FY), with surpluses generated when revenues exceed outlays.[1] Budget deficits or surpluses are often used to gauge national fiscal health, as budget balances over time determine levels of federal debt held by the public, and corresponding net interest payments required for debt service.[2] During an economic downturn, budget deficits could be viewed as effective fiscal policy, with lawmakers enacting tax cuts and increasing federal spending to simulate economic activity. However, recurring deficits can generate serious longer-term macroeconomic consequences, including a reduction in national saving and investment, and a decreased rate of capital accumulation.[3] This report examines to what extent major legislative changes from 2001 to 2009 caused the budget to move from surplus to deficit.

FEDERAL BUDGET DEFICITS: 2001 TO 2009

After recording a FY2000 federal budget surplus of $236.2 billion, the Congressional Budget Office (CBO) in January 2001 projected continued surpluses throughout the decade, with a $710 billion positive budget balance expected for FY2009.[4] However, enactment of major legislation during the past decade, in combination with changing economic conditions, altered the long-term federal budget outlook dramatically. In FY2002, the budget recorded a deficit for the first time since 1997, and the federal government has run a deficit in each subsequent year. Most recently, the FY2009 deficit was $1.4 trillion, a $2.1 trillion negative change in budget balance from the $710 billion FY2009 surplus projected by CBO in 2001.[5]

The broad reason the budget moved from surplus to deficit is because Congress chose an overall level of spending that exceeded chosen revenue levels. However, the budget is the sum of its parts, so no single spending or tax decision can be taken in isolation and be said to have "caused" the deficit in an absolute sense.

Furthermore, some determinants of spending and revenues are not directly controlled by Congress. When economic conditions change, spending and revenues automatically change without any change in law. For example, when economic growth slows, the growth of taxable income slows, so that less revenue is collected at a given tax rate than previously. Likewise, if a slowdown in economic growth causes unemployment to rise, spending on unemployment insurance and other means-tested mandatory spending programs will also increase without any change in law. Economists refer to these changes as "automatic stabilizers" because they automatically cause the deficit to rise when the economy slows, thereby helping to offset the slowdown in growth because of the deficit's expansionary effects on aggregate spending. It should also be noted that when economic growth is strong, the opposite effects occur, with levels of taxable income increasing and outlays on mandatory spending for unemployment insurance and other economic support programs decreasing.

For a detailed examination of why the budget moved from surplus to deficit, it is necessary to have a benchmark against which the actual deficit can be compared. One benchmark would be to compare the 2009 deficit to the 2001 surplus, but this approach would be fraught with several difficulties. For one thing, spending and revenues are expected to increase over time because of inflation and economic growth, among other factors, so that $1 spent in 2009 is not comparable to $1 spent in 2001. In addition, the economy in 2009 is not at the same level of production or in the same position in the business cycle as the economy in 2001, so the economy's effect on the budget is not the same either. Finally, the same law yields different levels of spending or revenue over time. For example, entitlement spending can increase automatically if the number of beneficiaries increases. Therefore, comparing spending or revenue levels from one year to the next could give the false impression that policy had changed when it had not.

This report uses a different benchmark: it compares the actual budget balance in the past nine years to CBO's January 2001 baseline projection of the surplus for each of those years. Generally speaking, the baseline is a projection of the future path of government spending and revenues under current policy assuming no changes in the law. The purpose of baseline construction by CBO is to provide a neutral foundation for which to assess policy options, and it is not intended to predict future changes in revenue and spending legislation.[6] The Deficit Control Act of 1985 (P.L. 99-177) established specific rules for CBO to follow in calculating baseline projections, and additional information about budgetary baselines as it relates specifically to mandatory spending, federal revenues, and discretionary spending will be provided later in this discussion. CBO projected in 2001 that if policy had not changed, the surplus would have grown each year.[7] Any year could have been chosen as the benchmark; this report uses CBO's 2001 baseline as the benchmark because estimated 10-year surpluses peaked in this projection. In subsequent reports, the surplus projections would be continually adjusted downward, as CBO became progressively more pessimistic about the future path of deficits. Thus, the results that follow are partly a function of the benchmark chosen.

Table 1 shows the differences between CBO's January 2001 baseline projections and the actual budget balance for FY2001 to FY2009, attributing deficit increases to the legislative, economic, and technical categories. Legislative changes refer to enacted laws affecting revenue, mandatory spending, or discretionary spending. Along with spending increases and revenue reductions implemented by the enactment of new laws, legislative changes have also increased the national debt and the cost of debt servicing. The combined change in debt servicing attributed to the enactment of new legislation is reported separately in Table 1. Over the past 10 years, legislative changes have increased federal budget deficits by approximately $5.4 trillion. Each year since 2003, legislative changes that increased the deficit were larger than the annual surplus projected by CBO in January 2001.

Table 1. Differences between 2001 Baseline Projections and Actual Budget Balance, FY2001-FY2009 (in billions of dollars)

	2001	2002	2003	2004	2005	2006	2007	2008	2009	Cumulative Total: 2001-2009
Baseline Surplus Projection in Jan. 2001[a]	**281**	**313**	**359**	**397**	**433**	**505**	**573**	**635**	**710**	**4,206**
Legislative Changes	-81	-150	-363	-519	-543	-632	-721	-1,005	-1,361	**-5,375**
Revenue	-74	-81	-186	-272	-218	-199	-233	-381	-370	**-2,014**
Nondefense Discretionary Spending	0	-12	-35	-49	-65	-93	-83	-89	-135	**-561**
Defense Spending	0	-38	-84	-122	-155	-177	-205	-245	-283	**-1,309**
Mandatory Spending	-7	-14	-43	-41	-41	-72	-72	-118	-345	**-753**
TARP[b]	0	0	0	0	0	0	0	0	-152	**-152**
Other Mandatory Spending	-7	-14	-43	-41	-41	-72	-72	-118	-193	**-601**
Debt Service	0	-5	-15	-37	-60	-93	-131	-175	-227	**-743**
Economic Changes	-37	-121	-113	-59	2	15	20	1	-143	**-345**
Technical Changes	-35	-201	-259	-231	-206	-137	-34	-86	-614	**-1,897**
Fannie Mae/ Freddie Mac[c]	0	0	0	0	0	0	0	0	-291	**-291**
Other Technical Changes	-35	-201	-259	-231	-206	-137	-34	-86	-417	**-1,606**
Total Changes	-153	-471	-737	-810	-751	-753	-736	-1,090	-2,124	**-7625**
Actual Budget Surplus (+) / Deficit (-)	**128**	**-158**	**-378**	**-413**	**-319**	**-248**	**-163**	**-455**	**-1,414**	**-3,420**

Source: Congressional Research Service. Data compiled from Congressional Budget Office, *The Budget and Economic Outlook* (January 2001 to January 2010); and Congressional Budget Office, *An Analysis of the President's Budgetary Proposals* (May 2001 to March 2009).

Notes: Negative numbers indicate an increase in the deficit. Columns may not be additive due to rounding.

a. In the January baseline, CBO does not report changes to the previous year deficit that occurred since the August baseline. Therefore, any changes between the actual deficit and the baseline deficit projected in August have been apportioned evenly between economic and technical changes.

b. With regards to the Troubled Asset Relief Program (TARP), CBO in January 2009 projected mandatory outlays at $184 billion for FY2009. Revised estimates of TARP budgetary impact were provided in March and August 2009 through the technical changes category. However, all TARP spending in this table is accounted for as mandatory spending. It should also be noted that in

January 2010 CBO projected a negative outlay level for TARP in FY2010 to reflect changes in economic and market conditions occurring since the actual FY2009 figure of $152 billion was recorded. This change is included in the total for technical changes.

[c.] CBO has accounted for Fannie Mae and Freddie Mac as federal operations since January 2009. In August 2009, CBO estimated Fannie Mae and Freddie Mac FY2009 subsidy costs at $291 billion, which is the amount presented in this table. However, due to budgetary rules, when CBO released new baseline projections in January 2010, the actual FY2009 budgetary impact for these entities was scored as the level of Treasury Department cash infusions, which was $91 billion in FY2009. This change is included in the total for technical changes.

At the same time, independent of new legislation passed by Congress, economic variables such as inflation, the unemployment rate, and interest rates have affected both outlays and federal receipts, and CBO classifies these as economic changes. In addition, differences between budget projections and the actual annual deficit or surplus were also caused by modifications to CBO technical assumptions. For example, if more beneficiaries took up an entitlement benefit than projected, or if fewer taxpayers claimed a tax credit than projected, there would be a technical change to CBO's projections.

In 2009, legislative changes accounted for about $1.36 trillion of the shift from surplus to deficit that has occurred since the 2001 projection. Economic changes to the projection were small relative to legislative and technical changes. Although there was a severe recession not anticipated in the 2001 projection, the actual level of GDP in 2009 was still fairly close to what CBO had projected in 2001. Technical changes made up an estimated $614 billion of this shift to deficit, although almost half of those changes were due to CBO's decision to move Fannie Mae and Freddie Mac on budget after the Treasury took them into conservatorship in 2008. Although CBO did not consider this to be a legislative change, it can be thought of as a policy change because it resulted in these entities receiving large-scale direct federal support.

Mandatory Spending and Federal Revenues: 2001 to 2009

Mandatory Spending

Mandatory spending (also referred to as direct spending) consists primarily of outlays on benefit programs such as Social Security, Medicare, and Medicaid. The level of spending dedicated to entitlement programs is determined by established rules of eligibility and benefit formulas. Consequently, mandatory spending outlays are allocated automatically and are not subject to the annual discretionary appropriations process. In regards to budgetary treatment of mandatory programs, CBO follows baseline construction rules specified in the Deficit Control Act of 1985 (P.L. 99-177), where direct spending authorizations scheduled to expire by law are assumed to continue if outlays exceed $50 million, and the program under consideration was established prior to enactment of the Balanced Budget Act of 1997 (P.L. 105-33).[8]

Mandatory spending outlays have accounted for a significant proportion of both federal spending and overall economic activity during the past decade (see Table 2).[9] In particular, mandatory outlays have grown from 9.9% of GDP in FY2001 to 14.7% in FY2009. Among the key drivers of entitlement growth for FY2001 to FY2009, a cumulative $4.8 trillion was spent on Social Security benefits and $3.2 trillion was allocated for Medicare.[10]

Although mandatory spending has contributed significantly to increasing federal budget deficits over the past 10 years, much of this entitlement outlay growth stems from programs established before 2001.[11] Consequently, because this report examines the budgetary impact of major laws enacted during the past five legislative sessions of Congress, mandatory programs such as Social Security, Medicare (Part A, Part B and Part C), and Medicaid will not be addressed in detail.

It should also be noted that while direct spending outlays have increased in recent years, much of this entitlement growth was projected by CBO at the beginning of the decade when future budget surpluses were projected. As Table 2 indicates, CBO's January 2001 budget baseline assumed mandatory outlay levels that exceeded actual amounts for every year from FY2001 to FY2007, with significant underestimation of actual direct spending only occurring for FY2009, when new mandatory spending on the Troubled Asset Relief Program (TARP), activities related to Fannie Mae and Freddie Mac, and other economic stabilization and economic stimulus initiatives were implemented largely in response to the U.S. financial crisis. Consequently, the expansion in entitlement spending was not a major determinant of the decade long shift from projected budget surpluses to actual budget deficits.

Federal Revenues

Similar to mandatory spending, the level of federal receipts is not directly determined by law. Instead, enacted revenue legislation specifies tax rates and various other features of the tax system, which in combination with economic conditions determine the actual level of revenues collected. The enactment of the Economic Growth and Tax Relief Reconciliation Act of 2001 (EGTRRA; P.L. 107-16), the Jobs and Growth Tax Relief Reconciliation Act of 2003 (JGTRRA; P.L. 108-27), and other tax legislation impacted the level of federal revenue collected over the past 10 years, and will be discussed later in this report. In contrast to the budgetary treatment of mandatory spending, the CBO baseline assumes that most current tax provisions will expire as scheduled.[12]

With respect to both total collections and as a share of the overall economy, federal receipts fluctuated between FY2001 to FY2009. Table 3 illustrates total federal revenues as a proportion of GDP peaked in FY2001 at 19.5%, declined to 16.1% by FY2004, before rebounding to a 18.5% share of economic activity in FY2007. By FY2009, however, federal receipts reached their lowest level of the decade—14.8% of GDP. In dollar terms, revenue traced a similar trajectory, with receipts decreasing from $2.0 trillion in FY2001 to $1.8 trillion for FY2004, before increasing to a peak level of $2.6 trillion for FY2007, followed by two years of revenue decline. Individual income taxes, historically the largest source of federal revenue, peaked as proportion of GDP in FY2001 at 9.7%, before declining to 6.9% of GDP in FY2004. Individual income receipts increased during FY2005 to FY2007, but then declined to a decade low of 6.4% of GDP by FY2009.[13]

Table 2. Mandatory Spending Outlays, FY2001-FY2009

	2001		2002		2003		2004		2005		2006		2007		2008		2009	
	% GDP	**$ Billions**	**% GDP**	**$ Billions**	**% GDP**	**$ Billions**	**% GDP**	**$ Billions**	**% GDP**	**$ Billions**	**% GDP**	**$ Billions**	**% GDP**	**$ Billions**	**% GDP**	**$ Billions**	**% GDP**	**$ Billions**
Social Security	4.2	429.4	4.3	452.1	4.3	470.5	4.2	491.5	4.2	518.7	4.1	543.9	4.2	581.4	4.2	612.1	4.8	677.7
Medicare	2.3	237.9	2.4	253.7	2.5	274.2	2.5	297.2	2.7	332.6	2.8	373.6	3.1	436.0	3.2	456.0	3.5	499.0
Medicaid	1.3	129.4	1.4	147.5	1.5	160.7	1.5	176.2	1.5	181.7	1.4	180.6	1.4	190.6	1.4	201.4	1.8	250.9
Income Security	1.1	114.7	1.2	129.1	1.3	141.0	1.6	189.9	1.6	196.1	1.5	199.2	1.5	202.4	1.8	259.9	2.4	348.5
Other Retirement / Disability	0.9	93.0	0.9	96.1	0.9	99.9	0.9	104.0	0.9	111.8	0.9	113.5	0.9	122.9	0.9	129.4	1.0	138.1
Other Programs	0.9	91.8	1.1	117.2	1.2	135.9	0.7	87.3	0.9	106.4	1.1	141.4	0.7	95.0	0.9	129.2	2.6	374.5
Offsetting Receipts	-0.9	-88.7	-0.9	-89.9	-0.9	-100.6	-0.9	-109.0	-1.0	-127.8	-1.1	-140.5	-1.3	-177.6	-1.3	-193.1	-1.4	-194.7
Total Mandatory Spending (Actual)	**9.9**	**1,007.4**	**10.5**	**1,105.7**	**10.8**	**1,181.4**	**10.6**	**1,237.2**	**10.6**	**1,319.5**	**10.7**	**1,411.8**	**10.4**	**1,450.7**	**11.0**	**1,595.0**	**14.7**	**2,093.9**
Memorandum																		
Total Mandatory Spending (Jan. 2001 Baseline Projection)	10.5	1,089	10.6	1,157	10.6	1,219	10.7	1,296	10.9	1,378	10.8	1,441	10.9	1,520	11.0	1,614	11.2	1,713

Source: Congressional Budget Office, *The Budget and Economic Outlook: Fiscal Years 2010 to 2020* (Tables F-9 and F-10), January 2010.

Notes: Columns may not be additive due to rounding. In the context of mandatory spending, offsetting receipts are fees and other charges recorded by CBO as negative budget authority and outlays.

Table 3. Revenues by Major Source, FY2001-FY2009

	2001		2002		2003		2004		2005		2006		2007		2008		2009	
	% GDP	**$ Billions**	**% GDP**	**$ Billions**	**% GDP**	**$ Billions**	**% GDP**	**$ Billions**	**% GDP**	**$ Billions**	**% GDP**	**$ Billions**	**% GDP**	**$ Billions**	**% GDP**	**$ Billions**	**% GDP**	**$ Billions**
Individual Income Taxes	9.7	994.3	8.1	858.3	7.2	793.7	6.9	809.0	7.5	927.2	7.9	1,043.9	8.4	1,163.5	7.9	1,145.7	6.4	915.3
Corporate Income Taxes	1.5	151.1	1.4	148.0	1.2	131.8	1.6	189.4	2.2	278.3	2.7	353.9	2.7	370.2	2.1	304.3	1.0	138.2
Social Insurance Taxes	6.8	694.0	6.6	700.8	6.5	713.0	6.3	733.4	6.4	794.1	6.3	837.8	6.3	869.6	6.2	900.2	6.3	890.9
Excise Taxes	0.6	66.2	0.6	67.0	0.6	67.5	0.6	69.9	0.6	73.1	0.6	74.0	0.5	65.1	0.5	67.3	0.4	62.5
Estate and Gift Taxes	0.3	28.4	0.3	26.5	0.2	22.0	0.2	24.8	0.2	24.8	0.2	27.9	0.2	26.0	0.2	28.8	0.2	23.5
Custom Duties	0.2	19.4	0.2	18.6	0.2	19.9	0.2	21.1	0.2	23.4	0.2	24.8	0.2	26.0	0.2	27.6	0.2	22.5
Miscellaneous Receipts	0.4	37.8	0.3	33.9	0.3	34.5	0.3	32.6	0.3	32.8	0.3	44.6	0.3	47.6	0.3	50.0	0.4	51.7
Total Revenues	**19.5**	**1,991.1**	**17.6**	**1,853.1**	**16.2**	**1,782.3**	**16.1**	**1,800.1**	**17.3**	**2,153.6**	**18.2**	**2,406.9**	**18.5**	**2,568.0**	**17.5**	**2,524.0**	**14.8**	**2,104.6**

Source: Congressional Budget Office, *The Budget and Economic Outlook: Fiscal Years 2010 to 2020,* Tables F-3 and F-4, January 2010.

Notes: Columns may not be additive due to rounding.

IMPACT OF MAJOR LEGISLATION ON BUDGET DEFICITS: 2001 TO 2009

The following sections review legislation enacted from 2001 to 2009 with budgetary impact greater than $50 billion over 10 years. Most laws examined include key provisions that directly affect mandatory spending or federal revenues, but supplemental appropriations legislation related to "Global War on Terror" programs and 2005 Hurricane emergency relief is also covered. Annual appropriations providing for non-defense discretionary spending is discussed separately at the end of this report. It should also be noted that the measured impact of legislation does not include resulting increases in debt service costs.

Table 4. Budgetary Effects of Legislative Changes by Year of Enactment, FY2001-FY2009 ($ in billions)

	2001	2002	2003	2004	2005	2006	2007	2008	2009	Cumulative Total: 2001-2009
2001 Legislation	-81	-52	-107	-131	-138	-174	-201	-221	-241	**-1,346**
2002 Legislation	0	-98	-131	-127	-113	-99	-103	-112	-121	**-904**
2003 Legislation	0	0	-125	-259	-212	-159	-164	-182	-189	**-1,290**
2004 Legislation	0	0	0	-2	-40	-82	-105	-116	-128	**-473**
2005 Legislation	0	0	0	0	-40	-52	-15	-3	3	**-107**
2006 Legislation	0	0	0	0	0	-66	-106	-85	-92	**-349**
2007 Legislation	0	0	0	0	0	0	-27	-36	-32	**-95**
2008 Legislation	0	0	0	0	0	0	0	-250	-103	**-353**
2009 Legislation	0	0	0	0	0	0	0	0	-458	**-458**
Total Legislative Changes (2001-2009)	**-81**	**-150**	**-363**	**-519**	**-543**	**-632**	**-721**	**-1,005**	**-1,361**	**-5,375**

Source: Congressional Research Service. Data compiled from Congressional Budget Office, *The Budget and Economic Outlook* (January 2001 to January 2010); and *An Analysis of the President's Budgetary Proposals* (May 2001 to March 2009).

Notes: Negative numbers indicate an increase in the deficit. Columns may not be additive due to rounding. On a subsidy basis, conservatorship of Fannie Mae and Freddie Mac added $291 billion to the deficit in 2009. This amount is not included in the Table because CBO classifies it as a technical, as opposed to legislative, change.

Table 4 presents the budgetary effect of legislative changes occurring from 2001 to 2009 relative to CBO's January 2001 baseline projections. Laws passed by Congress in 2001 and 2003, notably the Economic Growth and Tax Relief Reconciliation Act of 2001 (EGTRRA; P.L. 107-16) and the Jobs and Growth Tax Relief Reconciliation Act of 2003 (JGTRRA; P.L. 108-27), generated the largest 10-year increases in budget deficits, about $1.7 trillion. Legislation enacted in FY2009, including the Emergency Economic Stabilization Act (EESA; P.L. 110-343) and the American Recovery and Reinvestment Act of 2009 (ARRA; P.L. 111-5), caused the 2009 deficit to increase by $509 billion, while legislative changes from 2001 to 2008 caused the 2009 deficit to increase by an additional $903 billion. For the decade as whole, it can be estimated that legislative changes have increased deficits, relative to the 2001 baseline projections, by about $5.4 trillion.

EGTRRA, JGTRRA and Other Major Tax Legislation

From 2001 to 2006, several laws were enacted under the Bush Administration that reduced federal government revenues. However, since the Joint Committee on Taxation (JCT) and CBO typically measure the budgetary effect of revenue policy only when legislation is under consideration by Congress, the actual ex-post impact of specific laws on budget deficits can be difficult to determine.[14] Consequently, in this section all CBO and JCT data on legislative cost is accompanied by both the approximate date of the estimate, as well as any needed clarification about the point in the legislative process when the estimate was performed.

Economic Growth and Tax Relief Reconciliation Act of 2001

On June 7, 2001, President Bush signed into law the Economic Growth and Tax Relief Reconciliation Act of 2001 (EGTRRA; P.L. 107-16). EGTRRA established a new 10% regular income tax bracket, gradually reduced various income tax rates through 2006, and increased the child tax credit to $1,000 over 10 years. Additionally, the law phased-in an increase in the basic standard deduction for married couples filing joint returns in order to provide marriage penalty relief, raised the annual limit on contributions to education individual retirement accounts (IRAs), and phased-in an increase in the unified credit exemption amount and a reduction of tax rates for estate and generation-skipping transfer taxes (including a complete repeal of estate and generation-skipping transfer taxes for 2010).[15] To comply with the Congressional Budget Act of 1974, most provisions in EGTRRA are scheduled to sunset at the end of calendar year 2010.[16]

In May 2001, JCT estimated that EGTRRA, as cleared by Congress, would have a negative budgetary impact of $1.35 trillion for FY2001 to FY2011. Among the key components of the cost estimate, JCT expected the marginal rate reduction provisions to decrease government revenues by $874.9 billion over 10 years, and for the expanded child tax credit to cost $171.8 billion during the same timeframe.[17]

Jobs and Growth Tax Relief Reconciliation Act of 2003

The second major tax cut under the Bush Administration, the Jobs and Growth Tax Relief Reconciliation Act of 2003 (JGTRRA; P.L. 108-27), was enacted on May 28, 2003 and accelerated many of the tax reductions previously implemented by EGTRRA. In particular, for 2003 and 2004 the increase in the child tax credit was raised to $1,000, and the basic standard deduction amount for married taxpayers filing a joint return was increased to twice the basic standard deduction amount for single individuals. Additional EGTRRA provision accelerations implemented by JGTRRA included an expansion of the 15% rate bracket for married couples filing joint returns, and an acceleration of the regular income tax rate reductions scheduled for 2004 and 2006. JGTRRA also contained tax incentives for businesses such as a first-year depreciation allowance equal to 50% for certain property acquired after May 5, 2003, and before January 1, 2005, and provided for significant reductions in taxes on capital gains and dividends received prior to January 1, 2009.[18]

In May 2003, JCT and CBO projected that JGTRRA, as enacted, would increase federal budget deficits by $349.7 billion for FY2003 to FY2013. The acceleration of previously enacted tax reductions was expected to cost $171.4 billion over the next five years, with new reductions in taxes on dividends and capital gains estimated to decrease government receipts by another $148.1 billion. [19]

Other Tax Legislation with Budgetary Impact: 2004 to 2006

In the 108th and 109th Congress, several laws were passed that extended and in some cases modified revenue reduction provisions previously enacted under EGTRRA and JGTRRA. The Working Families Tax Relief Act of 2004 (WFTRA; P.L. 108-311), signed into law on October 4, 2004, extended tax relief for married taxpayers filing a joint return through 2008, maintained the $1,000 child tax credit through 2009, and extended the 10% income tax bracket through 2010. In September 2004, JCT and CBO estimated WFTRA would decrease federal revenues by $122.2 billion over FY2005 to FY2014, while raising direct spending (mostly from increased outlays for refundable tax credits) by $23.8 billion over the same period, for a combined 10-year budgetary impact of $145.9 billion.[20]

On May 17, 2006, another tax cut extension was signed into law, the Tax Increase Prevention and Reconciliation Act of 2005 (TIPRA; P.L. 109-222).[21] TIPRA extended the reduced tax rates on capital gains and dividends through 2010 and extended the exception for active financing income for controlled foreign corporations, among other provisions. In June 2006, JCT projected that the conference agreement for TIPRA would reduce federal revenues by $69.1 billion for FY2006 to FY2015.[22]

The Pension Protection Act of 2006 (PPA; P.L. 109-280), signed into law on August 17, 2006, provided comprehensive reform of U.S. pension law.[23] PPA included several provisions that reduced federal government revenues, such as making permanent increases in limits on contributions to pension plans or IRAs first enacted under EGTRRA, and extending a non-refundable credit available to low-income individuals contributing to either a 401(k) savings plan or an IRA (EGTRRA's "Saver's Credit"). In August 2006, JCT estimated that PPA, as cleared by Congress, would reduce federal revenues by $72.9 billion for FY2007 to FY20016, and CBO estimated that the legislation would decrease outlays on direct spending by $5.0 billion over 10 years, for a total 10-year budgetary effect of $67.9 billion. [24]

In addition to legislation related to EGTRRA and JGTRRA, Congress routinely extends other expiring tax provisions. Among these tax extenders laws, only the Tax Relief and Health Care Act of 2006 (TRHCA; P.L. 109-432) meets the criteria of budgetary effect exceeding $50 billion specified above. TRHCA implemented numerous changes to tax law, including an extension through 2007 of the research and development credit, the deduction for state and local taxes, and the deduction for qualified tuition and related expenses. TRHCA also extended several expiring energy tax provisions through 2008 and made changes to rules governing Health Savings Accounts. [25] In December 2006, JCT and CBO estimated that the law would decrease federal government revenues by $40.0 billion for FY2007 to FY2016.[26] In addition, CBO projected that direct spending provisions in TRHCA related to the Medicare payments for physicians' fee services and other programmatic changes were expected to increase mandatory outlays by $10.5 billion, and thus in combination TRHCA was estimated to raise deficits by $50.5 billion over 10 years.

Table 5 shows JCT and CBO estimated increases in federal budget deficits related to EGTRRA, JGTRRA, WFTRA, TIPRA, PPA and TRHCA. For each bill, the projected budgetary impact is presented over both a 5-year and 10-year budget window.

Table 5. Estimated Budget Effects of Major Tax Cuts, 107th to 109th Congress ($ in billions)

Legislation	5-Year Budget Window	Net Budgetary Effect[a]	10-Year Budget Window	Net Budgetary Effect[a]
Economic Growth and Tax Relief Reconciliation Act of 2001[b]	FY2001-FY2006	-552.5	FY2001-FY2011	-1,348.5
Jobs and Growth Tax Relief Reconciliation Act of 2003[b]	FY2003-FY2008	-342.9	FY2003-FY2013	-349.7
Working Families Tax Relief Act of 2004[b]	FY2005-FY2009	-132.8	FY2005-FY2014	-145.9
Tax Increase Prevention and Reconciliation Act of 2005[b]	FY2006-FY2010	-70.0	FY2006-FY2015	-69.1
Pension Protection Act of 2006	FY2007-FY2011	-5.9	FY2007-FY2016	-67.9
The Tax Relief and Health Care Act of 2006[c]	FY2007-FY2011	-41.0	FY2007-FY2016	-50.5
Total		**-1,145.1**		**-2,031.6**

Source: CBO and JCT Cost Estimates for EGTRRA, JGTRRA, WFTRA, TIPRA, PPA and TRHCA.

Notes: Negative numbers indicate an increase in the deficit. Columns may not be additive due to rounding.

a. All budgetary effects were estimated by CBO and JCT at the time of legislative enactment.

b. Budgetary effects reported for the Economic Growth and Tax Relief Reconciliation Act of 2001, the Jobs and Growth Tax Relief Reconciliation Act of 2003, the Working Families Tax Relief Act of 2004, and the Tax Increase Prevention and Reconciliation Act of 2005 include provisions related to the Alternative Minimum Tax (AMT).

c. For the Tax Relief and Health Care Act of 2006, budgetary effects for both revenue provisions, and direct spending provisions related to Medicare and other programs are reported in this table.

The Alternative Minimum Tax: Increases in the Basic Exemption and Other Structural Modifications

An alternative minimum tax (AMT) is intended to ensure that taxpayers with significant income pay a minimum amount of tax. An add-on minimum tax was originally passed by Congress through the Tax Reform Act of 1969 (P.L. 91-72), and the first AMT was enacted as part of the Tax Equity and Fiscal Responsibility Act of 1982 (P.L. 97-248).[27] Provisions of the AMT have been modified numerous times since 1982, including through the Tax Reform Act of 1986 (P.L. 99-514), and the Omnibus Budget Reconciliation Act of 1993 (P.L. 103-66).[28] Under present law, the AMT is determined by subtracting a basic exemption amount from an individual's calculated AMT tax base (computed by adding back various tax adjustments and preferences), with the remaining tax base assessed under a two-tiered rate structure of 26% for all income up to $175,000, and 28% on any income above this amount.[29]

Over the past decade, the combined effects of inflation and new legislative reductions in federal income tax have increased concern in Congress about the growing number of taxpayers that might be affected by the AMT. In response, lawmakers have implemented numerous increases in the AMT basic exemption during the 107th to 111th Congresses.[30] The enactment of EGTRRA in 2001 temporarily raised the AMT exemption level to $49,000 for joint returns and $35,750 for unmarried individuals effective through 2004. JGTRRA increased the basic AMT exemption amount for 2003 and 2004 to $58,000 for joint returns and $40,250 for unmarried individuals. WFTRA extended the AMT patches provided in JGTRRA for 2005, and TIPRA increased the AMT exemption amount for 2006 to $62,550 for joint returns and $42,500 for unmarried individuals. Other recent AMT patches were enacted through the Tax Extenders and Alternative Minimum Tax Relief Act of 2008 (TEAMTRA; Division C of P.L. 110-343), and the American Recovery and Reinvestment Act of 2009 (ARRA; P.L. 111-5).

Along with the periodic increases in the AMT patch passed by Congress, revenue legislation signed into law over the past 10 years has also modified other components of the AMT that reduced federal government revenues. For instance, EGTRRA allowed various nonrefundable personal tax credits to fully offset AMT tax liability for 2001 to 2003, a provision extended in later years by WFTRA, TIPRA, the Tax Increase Prevention Act of 2007 (TIPA; P.L. 110-166), TEAMTRA and ARRA.

Table 6 reports the expected budgetary impact for all AMT provisions contained in EGTRRA, JGTRRA, WFTRA, TIPRA, TIPA, TEAMTRA and ARRA. It should be noted that the presented legislative costs are aggregated amounts including both the increases in the AMT basic exemption, along with all other AMT structural modifications.

Agricultural Policy: 2002 and 2008 Farm Bills

The Farm Security and Rural Investment Act of 2002 (2002 farm bill; P.L. 107-171) was signed into law on May 13, 2002, reauthorizing the major federal farm programs administered by the U.S. Department of Agriculture for FY2002 to FY2007. As mentioned in the above discussion on mandatory spending, under baseline construction rules direct spending programs are assumed to continue even after expiration of current law. Thus, the impact of the 2002 farm bill on federal budget deficits was not measured in terms of the total mandatory outlays to be spent on agricultural programs covered by the legislation, but instead as compared to the level of March 2002 baseline direct spending that would have occurred during the budgetary window under provisions of the previous farm bill, the Federal Agriculture Improvement and Reform Act of 1996 (1996 farm bill; P.L. 104-127), as amended.

In May 2002, CBO estimated that the 2002 farm bill would increase federal budget deficits by $49.2 billion over FY2002 to FY2007, bringing total spending on federal farm programs to $470.5 billion over six years when baseline spending is included.[31] Among the largest expenditures, CBO expected the 2002 farm bill to increase direct spending on commodity support programs by $37.6 billion over six years, and to increase outlays on agricultural conservation programs by $6.5 billion during the same period.

In the 110th Congress, the main agricultural policies contained in P.L. 107-171 were reauthorized through the Food, Conservation, and Energy Act of 2008 (2008 farm bill; P.L. 110-246).[32] Similar to P.L. 107-171, financing for most programs covered in the 2008 farm bill only extend through a limited number of years, FY2008 to FY2012. Relative to CBO's March 2008 baseline projection of $301.4 billion in federal farm program direct spending over five years, the 2008 farm bill was projected in May 2008 to increase mandatory spending by another $5.6 billion for FY2008 to FY2012, while raising $5.0 billion in federal revenues.[33] Consequently, although P.L. 110-246 is estimated to cover approximately $307.0 billion in spending over FY2008 to FY2012, the increase in federal deficits scored by CBO is only $0.6 billion.

Table 6. Estimated Revenue Effects for AMT Legislative Changes, 107th to 111th Congresses ($ in billion)

Legislation	Fiscal Years with Revenue Effect	Net Budgetary Effect[a]
Economic Growth and Tax Relief Reconciliation Act of 2001	2001-2005	-13.9
Jobs and Growth Tax Relief Reconciliation Act of 2003	2003-2005	-17.8
Working Families Tax Relief Act of 2004	2005-2006	-22.6
Tax Increase Prevention and Reconciliation Act of 2005	2006-2007	-33.9
Tax Increase Prevention Act of 2007	2008	-50.6
Tax Extenders and Alternative Minimum Tax Relief Act of 2008	2009-2010	-64.1
American Recovery and Reinvestment Act of 2009	2009-2011	-69.8
Total		**-272.7**

Source: JCT Cost Estimates for EGTRRA, JGTRRA, WFTRA, TIPRA, TIPA, TEAMTRA and ARRA

Notes: Negative numbers indicate an increase in the deficit. Columns may not be additive due to rounding.

[a.] All budgetary effects were estimated by JCT at the time of legislative enactment

As estimated by CBO at the time of legislative enactment, the 2002 and 2008 farm bills combined generate federal budget deficits of $49.8 billion for their authorized time windows. However, due to the five-month gap between the scheduled expiration of mandatory program authorization under P.L. 107-171 and the enactment of P.L. 110-246, the actual increase in federal budget deficits is likely greater than this combined level. Further, it should be noted that if the 2008 farm bill was scored against CBO's March 2002 baseline, which assumed continuation of the 1996 farm bill, the 2008 reauthorization would have increased budget deficits by $38.7 billion for FY2008 to FY2012. Thus the combined budgetary effect of the 2002 and 2008 farm bills would be $87.9 billion if scored collectively against the March 2002 baseline.

Funding for Military Operations in Afghanistan, Iraq and Other Global War on Terror Programs

Over the past 10 years, Congress enacted legislation financing military operations in Afghanistan, Iraq, and other countries, generating significant long-term budgetary effects. From FY2001 to FY2009, support for Global War on Terror (GWOT) operations has been provided primarily through emergency supplemental appropriations law.[34] Some funds for war programs have also been made available through regular annual appropriations legislation, such as the Department of Defense Appropriations Act, 2005 (P.L. 108-287) and the Foreign Operations, Export Financing, and Related Programs Appropriations Act, 2006 (P.L. 109-102).

Table 7. Defense Department, Foreign Operations Funding, and Veterans Affairs Medical Funding for Iraq, Afghanistan and Other Global War on Terror Operations, FY2001-FY2009 ($ in billions)

	DOD Funds	Foreign Aid Embassy	VA Medical	Total Cost
2001 Emergency Supplemental Appropriations Act for Recovery from and Response to Terrorist Attacks on the United States (P.L. 107-38)	14.0	0.3	0.0	14.3
Department of Defense Appropriations Act, 2003 (P.L. 107-248)	7.1	0.0	0.0	7.1
Department of Defense and Emergency Supplemental Appropriations for Recovery from and Response to Terrorist Attacks on the United States Act, 2002 (P.L. 107-117)	3.4	0.0	0.0	3.4
2002 Supplemental Appropriations Act for Further Recovery From and Response to Terrorist Attacks on the United States (P.L. 107-26)	13.8	0.4	0.0	14.1
Foreign Operations, Export Financing, and Related Programs Appropriations Act, 2002 (P.L. 107-115)	0.0	0.2	0.0	0.2
Consolidated Appropriations Resolution, 2003 (P.L. 108-7)	10.0	0.4	0.0	10.4

Table 7. (Continued)

Legislation		Foreign		
	DOD Funds	Aid Embassy	VA Medical	Total Cost
Emergency Wartime Supplemental Appropriations Act, 2003 (P.L. 108-11)	62.6	3.4	0.0	66.0
Department of Defense Appropriations Act, 2004 (P.L. 108-87)	-3.5	0.0	0.0	-3.5
Emergency Supplemental Appropriations Act for Defense and for the Reconstruction of Iraq and Afghanistan, 2004 (P.L. 108-106)	64.9	21.2	0.0	86.1
Consolidated Appropriations Act, 2004 (P.L. 108-199)	0.0	0.5	0.0	0.5
Department of Defense Appropriations Act, 2005, Titles IX and X (P.L. 108-287)	25.0	0.7	0.0	25.7
Department of Defense Appropriations Act, 2005 (P.L. 108-287)	2.1	0.0	0.0	2.1
Consolidated Appropriations Act, 2005 (P.L. 108-447)	0.0	1.0	0.0	1.0
Emergency Supplemental Appropriations Act for Defense, the Global War on Terror, and Tsunami Relief, 2005 (P.L. 109-13)	75.9	3.1	0.0	79.0
Department of the Interior, Environment, and Related Agencies Appropriations Act, 2006 (P.L. 109-54)	0.0	0.0	0.2	0.2
Foreign Operations, Export Financing, and Related Programs Appropriations Act, 2006 (P.L. 109-102)	0.0	1.0	0.0	1.0
Science, State, Justice, Commerce, and Related Agencies Appropriations Act, 2006 (P.L. 109-108)	0.0	0.1	0.0	0.1
Military Quality of Life and Veterans Affairs Appropriations Act, 2006 (P.L. 109-114)	0.0	0.0	0.4	0.4
Department of Defense, Emergency Supplemental Appropriations to Address Hurricanes in the Gulf of Mexico, and Pandemic Influenza Act, 2006, Title IX (P.L. 109-148)	50.0	0.0	0.0	50.0
Department of Defense, Emergency Supplemental Appropriations to Address Hurricanes in the Gulf of Mexico, and Pandemic Influenza Act, 2006 (P.L. 109-148)	0.8	0.0	0.0	0.8
Emergency Supplemental Appropriations Act for Defense, the Global War on Terror, and Hurricane Recovery, 2006 (P.L. 109-234)	66.0	3.2	0.0	69.2
Department of Defense Appropriations Act, 2007 (P.L. 109-289)	70.5	0.0	0.0	70.5
Revised Continuing Appropriations Resolution, 2007 (P.L. 110-5)	0.0	1.3	0.6	1.8
U.S. Troop Readiness, Veterans' Care, Katrina Recovery, and Iraq Accountability Appropriations Act, 2007 (P.L. 110-28)	94.5	3.8	0.4	98.7

Legislation	DOD Funds	Foreign Aid Embassy	VA Medical	Total Cost
FY2008 Continuing Resolution (P.L. 110-92)	5.2	0.0	0.0	5.2
Department of Defense Appropriations Act, 2008 (P.L. 110-116)	12.2	0.0	0.0	12.2
Consolidated Appropriations Act, 2008 (P.L. 110-161)	70.0	2.1	0.9	73.0
Supplemental Appropriations Act, 2008 (P.L. 110-252)	160.2	3.1	0.4	163.6
Supplemental Appropriations Act, 2009 (P.L. 111-32)	73.3	5.2	1.3	79.8
Subtotal	877.4	51.8	4.2	933.4
Unidentified Transfers	2.0	0.0	0.0	2.0
FY2003 Transfers	1.2	0.0	0.0	1.2
FY2004 Transfers	5.7	0.0	0.0	5.7
FY2005 Transfers	1.5	0.0	0.0	1.5
Subtotal Transfers	10.4	0.0	0.0	10.4
Total Enacted (w/transfers)	887.8	51.8	4.2	943.8

Source: Adapted from "Table C-1. Defense Department, Foreign Operations Funding, and VA Medical Funding for Iraq, Afghanistan and Other Global War on Terror Activities, FY2001-2009", presented in CRS Report RL33110, *The Cost of Iraq, Afghanistan, and Other Global War on Terror Operations Since 9/11*, by Amy Belasco.

Notes: Columns may not be additive due to rounding. See Table C-1 in CRS Report RL33110, *The Cost of Iraq, Afghanistan, and Other Global War on Terror Operations Since 9/11*, for details on CRS calculations of funds transferred from DOD regular appropriations in FY2003 to FY2005.

Table 7 shows all legislation enacted during the 107th to 111th Congresses supporting GWOT operations through the end of FY2009. Appropriations for each law are reported for the following three expenditure types: Defense Department, Foreign Operations Funding, and Veterans Affairs Medical Funding. In total, Congress has approved legislation appropriating $943.8 billion for military operations Iraq, Afghanistan, and other countries for FY2001 to FY2009, with $887.8 billion of this amount allocated to the Defense Department.

Another way to view the cost of military operations in Iraq, Afghanistan, and related GWOT activities is to examine the amount of funding appropriated for each major operation. **Table 8** presents the FY2001 to FY2009 aggregated spending levels for Operation Enduring Freedom (OEF), which covers ongoing operations in Afghanistan, the Philippines, Somalia and other nations; Operation Iraqi Freedom (OIF); and Operation Noble Eagle (ONE), which provides additional security for U.S. military bases and for homeland security purposes. Of the $943.8 billion in allocated funds for FY2001 to FY2009, approximately $682.8 billion has been approved for OIF, $226.7 billion allocated for OEF, and $28.5 billion appropriated for ONE.

Table 8. Estimated War Funding by Operation, FY2001-FY2009 ($ in billions)

Operation	2001-2002	2003	2004	2005	2006	2007	2008	2009	Cumulative Total: 2001-2009
Operation Enduring Freedom	20.8	14.7	14.5	20.0	19.0	39.1	43.4	55.2	226.7
Operation Iraqi Freedom	0.0	53.0	75.9	85.5	101.6	130.8	141.1	94.8	682.8
Enhanced Security	13.0	8.0	3.7	2.1	0.8	0.5	0.1	0.2	28.5
Unallocated	0.0	5.5	0.0	0.0	0.0	0.0	0.0	0.0	5.5
Total	**33.8**	**81.1**	**94.1**	**107.6**	**121.4**	**171.0**	**184.8**	**150.4**	**943.8**
Memorandum:	38	84	122	155	177	205	245	283	1,309[a]
Legislative Changes In Defense Spending Relative to the Jan. 2001 Baseline Projection									

Source: Adapted from "Table 1. Estimated War Funding by Operation: FY2001-FY2010 War Request", presented in CRS Report RL33110, *The Cost of Iraq, Afghanistan, and Other Global War on Terror Operations Since 9/11*, by Amy Belasco.

Notes: Columns may not be additive due to rounding. Positive numbers in the table represent an increase in spending, which increases the deficit.

[a] For the memorandum, the total includes war spending.

Funding for GWOT operations has been provided primarily through supplemental appropriations, whereas other changes in national defense policy have been implemented through regular defense appropriations law. As shown in **Table 8**, relative to CBO's January 2001 baseline, which held projected military outlays for FY2001 to FY2009 constant in inflation-adjusted terms, annual national defense spending (including both regular and supplemental appropriations) has increased by about $1.3 trillion over the past nine years.

Sustainable Growth Rate System: Medicare Physician Payment Updates

Since the establishment of the Medicare program in 1965, various methods have been used to determine physician payment rates for covered medical services.[35] In an effort to better control Medicare's outlays for physician services, the Balanced Budget Act of 1997 (P.L. 105-33) implemented the current Sustainable Growth Rate (SGR) system, which sets target levels for health expenditures, and adjusts payment rates to account for differences between cumulative Medicare spending and spending goals. Under the SGR system, when actual spending does not exceed the expenditure targets, the annual physician fee schedule updates are calculated as determined in statue based on the annual change in the Medicare economic index (MEI), changes in the Medicare population, and other factors.[36] Although expenditures did not begin to exceed SGR targets until 2002, this discrepancy between actual costs and payment limits has grown larger in each subsequent year.

The cumulative difference between allowed and actual expenditures from 1996 to 2008 is shown in Figure 1. For the second quarter of 2002, actual physician service expenditures exceeded allowed levels under SGR by $0.6 billion. However, this cumulative difference grew to $24.4 billion by the start of 2005, and has expanded rapidly to an estimated $63.6 billion difference by the last quarter of 2008.

To avoid the reductions in physician fee schedules that have been mandated since 2003 under SGR, Congress has passed several legislative overrides. The Consolidated Appropriations Resolution of 2003 (P.L. 108-7) replaced the scheduled 4.4% payment rate reduction with a 1.6% increase in rates for 2003. The Medicare Prescription Drug, Improvement, and Modernization Act of 2003 (MMA; P.L. 108-173) replaced rate reductions in 2004 and 2005 with increases of 1.5% for both years. More recently, legislative overrides to physician fee payment decreases mandated under SGR were enacted through the Tax Relief and Health Care Act of 2006 (TRHCA; P.L. 109-432), the Medicare, Medicaid, and SCHIP Extension Act of 2007 (MMSEA; P.L. 110-173), the Medicare Improvement for Patients and Providers Act of 2008 (MIPPA; P.L. 110-275), and the Temporary Extension Act of 2010 (P.L. 111-144). Table 9 reports the legislative overrides to scheduled cuts in Medicare physician fees signed into law during the 108th to 111th Congresses.

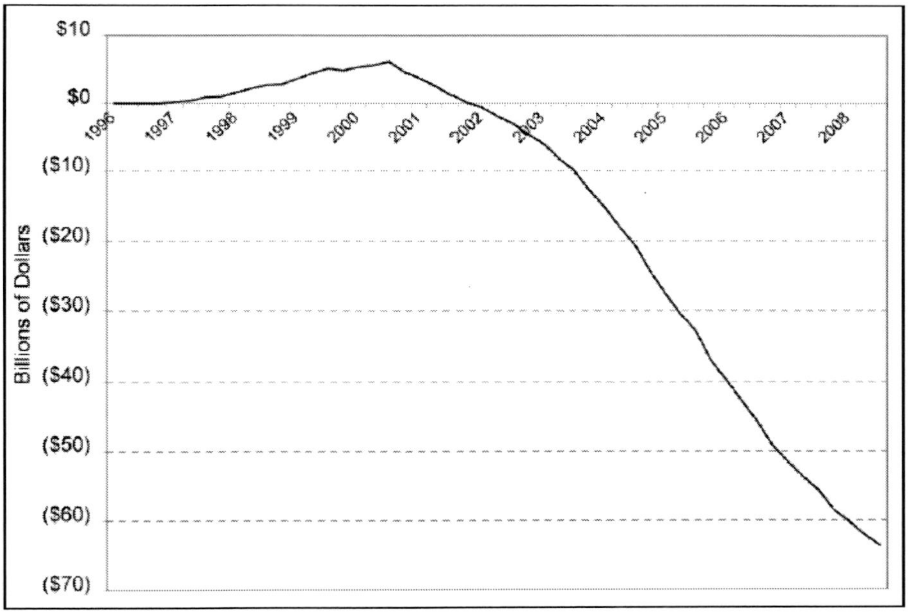

Source: "Figure 1. Difference Between Cumulative Allowed and Actual Expenditures for Physician Services Under the SGR System", CRS Report R40907, *Medicare Physician Payment Updates and the Sustainable Growth Rate (SGR) System*, by Jim Hahn.

Notes: Positive numbers shown in this figure indicate that actual expenditures did not exceed target expenditures allowed under the SGR system for 1996 to 2001. Negative numbers indicate that actual expenditures exceeded the SGR targets beginning in 2002.

Figure 1. Difference Between Allowed and Actual Expenditures for Physician Services Under the SGR System 1996-2008.

Table 9. Legislative Overrides to Medicare Physician Payment Reductions Mandated Under the Sustainable Growth Rate System, 108th to 111th Congresses

Year	Formula Update	Actual Update	Legislation
2003	-4.4%	1.6%	Consolidated Appropriations Resolution of 2003 (P.L. 108-7)
2004	-4.5%	1.5%	Medicare Modernization Act of 2003 (P.L. 108-173)
2005	-3.3%	1.5%	P.L. 108-173
2006	-4.4%	0.2%	Deficit Reduction Act of 2005 (P.L. 109-171)
2007	-5.0%	0%	Tax Relief and Health Care Act of 2006 (P.L. 109-432)
Jan-Jun 2008	-10.1%	0.5%	Medicare, Medicaid, and SCHIP Extension Act of 2007 (P.L. 110-173)
Jul-Dec 2008	-10.6% reduction from June 2008 level	0% (0.5% from 2007 level)	Medicare Improvement for Patients and Providers Act of 2008 (P.L. 110-275)
2009		1.1%	P.L. 110-275
2010		0%	Temporary Extension Act of 2010 (P.L. 111-144)

Source: Adapted from "Table 1. Summary of Updates and Legislative Activity: 2002-2009", presented in CRS Report R40907, *Medicare Physician Payment Updates and the Sustainable Growth Rate (SGR) System*, by Jim Hahn. Information on budgetary impact for all laws was obtained from CBO cost estimates.

Medicare Part D Prescription Drug Benefit

On December 8, 2003, President Bush signed into law the Medicare Prescription Drug, Improvement, and Modernization Act of 2003 (MMA; P.L. 108-173). The legislation established a voluntary Medicare prescription drug benefit effective January 1, 2006, under a new Part D of Title XVIII of the Social Security Act. MMA specified that drug coverage be delivered to beneficiaries through either a private prescription drug plan, or prescription drug coverage integrated into Medicare Part C, with all plan providers offering at a minimum "standard coverage," or alternative coverage with actuarially equivalent benefits.[37] Another key provision of MMA was the establishment of the Medicare Advantage (MA) program under Part C, which replaced Medicare+Choice. In addition, the legislation provided for Medicare cost containment initiatives and changes to Medicare's fee-for-service program.

Table 10 shows that CBO's original calculation projected net Medicare Part D outlays to increase federal budget deficits by approximately $552.2 billion over the next decade. In particular, CBO estimated that for FY2004 to FY2013 Medicare Part D would require $771.3 billion in payments for benefits and mandatory administrative costs. However, during this same 10-year budget window CBO also anticipated these expenditures to be partially offset by $130.6 billion in premiums paid by beneficiaries, and another $88.5 billion in payments made by states.[38] In addition, other provisions of MMA, including $12.5 billion in savings from changes to Medicare Part A and Part B, and $144.7 billion in expected savings from reduced spending on Medicaid and other federal programs was originally projected by CBO to reduce the total cost of the legislation to $395.0 billion over 10 years.

Since the 2003 enactment of MMA, the Boards of Trustees of the Federal Hospital Insurance and Federal Supplementary Medical Insurance Trust Funds have included updated information on Part D expenditures in their annual reports to Congress. As presented in **Table 10**, the Medicare Trustees 2009 report showed total spending on the prescription drug benefit for FY2004 to F2008 at about $105.9 billion, which was lower than the $147.0 billion amount originally projected by CBO over the same budget window.[39] Further, this most recent Medicare Trustees report also projects Part D expenditures for FY2009 to FY2013 at $275.4 billion, which is also lower than the $405.2 billion outlay level originally estimated by CBO for this time period. It should be noted that other provisions of MMA that were originally anticipated to create budgetary savings through changes in Medicare Part A and Part B, and reduced Medicaid spending are challenging to quantify in terms of actual expenditures, and are not included in the annual Medicare Trustees reports.

Table 10. Estimated Cost of the Medicare Part D Prescription Drug Benefit, ($ in billions)

	2004	2005	2006	2007	2008	2009	2010	2011	2012	2013	2004-2013
CBO Original Cost Estimate	0.6	1.5	32.1	52.9	59.9	65.7	72.6	79.5	88.5	98.9	552.2
2009 Medicare Trustees Report	0.2	1.2	27.7	41.5	35.3	43.8	52.2	59.3	55.0	65.1	381.3
Memorandum:	3.8	6.0	27.5	40.2	44.0	46.5	49.8	53.0	58.7	65.5	395.0
CBO Original Cost Estimate for all provisions of P.L. 108-173											

Source: Congressional Budget Office, *Projection of Spending for the Medicare Part D Benefit: Letter to the Honorable William "Bill" M. Thomas*, February 9, 2005; and The Boards of Trustees of the Federal Hospital Insurance and Federal Supplementary Medical Insurance Trust Funds, *2009 Medicare Trustees Report* (Table V.E8.), May 12, 2009.

Notes: Columns may not be additive due to rounding. Positive numbers indicate an increase in mandatory spending, and thus reflect a net increase in the deficit. Medicare Part D cost is measured as total expenditures less premium income and transfers from states.

Deficit Reduction Act of 2005

The Deficit Reduction Act of 2005 (DRA; P.L. 109-171), signed into law by President Bush on February 8, 2006, stipulated significant reductions in mandatory spending for a variety of government programs. In regards to student loan programs, DRA mandated lower payments to education lenders, an increase in the interest rate charged on loans to parents of students, and decreased insurance reimbursements for lenders, among other changes. DRA also impacted Medicaid by permitting states to charge beneficiaries higher premiums, while also reducing Medicaid payments for outpatient prescription drugs. P.L. 109-171 also included provisions that decreased Medicare spending, increased collections from spectrum license auctions administered by the Federal Communication Commission, and raised premiums paid by private companies to the Pension Benefit Guaranty Corporation.

As part of CBO's March 2006 analysis of the President's FY2007 Budget, it was estimated that DRA would reduce mandatory spending by approximately $106 billion for FY2007 to FY2016.[40] Included in this cost projection, the programmatic changes to Medicaid and Medicare were expected to decrease net federal spending respectively by $40 billion and $21 billion over 10 years, whereas student loan program provisions were anticipated to generate net budgetary savings of about $30 billion over this time period.

Emergency Funding in Response to 2005 Hurricanes: Katrina, Rita, and Wilma

In the aftermath of Hurricanes Katrina, Rita, and Wilma, several emergency supplemental appropriations laws were enacted during the 109th and 110th Congresses, adding significantly to federal budget deficits.[41] In September 2005, Congress passed two bills related to Hurricane Katrina emergency relief and recovery efforts, P.L. 109-61 and P.L. 109-62, providing a combined $62.3 billion in supplemental funds.[42] Department of Defense appropriations measure in 2006 (P.L. 109-148) provided $29.0 billion to fund the restoration of federal facilities damaged by the three hurricanes, and another $20.0 billion was made available through a emergency supplemental appropriations law (P.L. 109-234), which supported recovery assistance performed by the Department of Agriculture and the Natural Resources Conservation Service, among others.[43] The 2007 emergency supplemental bill financing military operations in Iraq and Afghanistan (P.L. 110-28) included an estimated $6.9 billion for the Department of Homeland Security, the U.S. Army Corps of Engineers, and other agencies to provide Gulf Coast relief, and another supplemental law (P.L. 110-239) allocated $2.9 billion for ongoing disaster relief related to the 2005 Hurricanes.[44]

Table 11 shows all appropriations legislation enacted during the 109th and 110th Congresses to support emergency relief efforts related to Hurricanes Katrina, Rita, and Wilma. In total, Congress has approved legislation increasing federal budget deficits by $134.1 billion for Gulf Coast recovery over FY2005 to FY2008.

Additionally in the 109th Congress, tax legislation related to 2005 Hurricane recovery was enacted, reducing federal government revenues over several years. The Katrina Emergency Tax Relief Act of 2005 (P.L. 109-73) contained various types of tax relief, including a temporary suspension of limitations for qualified corporate and individual charitable contributions, and an extension of the replacement period for non-recognition of gain for property located in the Hurricane Katrina disaster area. In late September 2005, JCT estimated that P.L. 109-73 would reduce federal revenues by $6.3 billion for FY2006 and FY2007.[45] The Gulf Opportunity Zone Act of 2005 (P.L. 109-135) offered numerous tax incentives related to business activities in the Gulf Cost, and was estimated by JCT to reduce government revenues by $8.7 billion for FY2006 to FY2015.[46]

Table 11. Supplemental Appropriations for Emergency Response to Hurricanes Katrina, Rita and Wilma, 109th and 110th Congress ($ in billions)

Legislation	Public Law No.	Date Enacted	Total Cost
Emergency Supplemental Appropriations Act to Meet Immediate Needs Arising From the Consequences of Hurricane Katrina, 2005	P.L. 109-61	Sept. 2, 2005	10.5
Second Emergency Supplemental Appropriations Act to Meet Immediate Needs Arising From the Consequences of Hurricane Katrina, 2005	P.L. 109-62	Sept. 8, 2005	51.8
Department of Defense, Emergency Supplemental Appropriations to Address Hurricanes in the Gulf of Mexico, and Pandemic Influenza Act, 2006	P.L. 109-148	Dec. 30, 2005	29.0
Emergency Supplemental Appropriations Act for Defense, the Global War on Terror, and Hurricane Recovery, 2006	P.L. 109-234	June 15, 2006	20.0
U.S. Troop Readiness, Veterans' Care, Katrina Recovery, and Iraq Accountability Appropriations Act, 2007	P.L. 110-28	May 25, 2007	6.9
Department of Defense Appropriations Act, 2008	P.L. 110-116	Nov. 13, 2007	5.9
Supplemental Appropriations Act, 2008	P.L. 110-252	June 30, 2008	7.0
Consolidated Security, Disaster Assistance, and Continuing Appropriations Act, 2009	P.L. 110-329	Sept. 30, 2008	2.9
Total			**134.1**

Source: Adapted from "Table 3. FY2005-FY2008 Supplemental Disaster Appropriations After Hurricanes Katrina, Rita, and Wilma", presented in CRS Report R40708, *Disaster Relief Funding and Emergency Supplemental Appropriations*, by Bruce R. Lindsay and Justin Murray.

Notes: Columns may not be additive due to rounding. See Table 3 in CRS Report R40708, *Disaster Relief Funding and Emergency Supplemental Appropriations*, for details on rescissions related to P.L. 109-234. These recissions are included in the $20.0 billion level of appropriations reported in this table.

Financial Crisis of 2008

Federal Conservatorship of Fannie Mae and Freddie Mac

The Housing and Economic Recovery Act of 2008 (HERA; P.L. 110-289), signed into law on July 30, 2008, implemented numerous changes in federal housing policy. Among other provisions, HERA authorized the Treasury Secretary to purchase obligations and other securities issued by government-sponsored enterprises (GSEs) involved in the mortgage market, and established the Federal Housing Finance Agency (FHFA) as the new single regulator for these GSEs.

On September 6, 2008, the Director of FHFA exercised authority provided under HERA to place two GSEs, the Federal National Mortgage Association (Fannie Mae) and the Federal Home Loan Mortgage Corporation (Freddie Mac), into conservatorship. FHFA defines conservatorship as "the legal process in which a person or entity is appointed to establish control and oversight of a Company to put it in a sound and solvent condition. In a conservatorship, the powers of the Company's directors, officers, and shareholders are transferred to the designated Conservator." [47] At the same time, the Treasury Department contracted with Fannie Mae and Freddie Mac to make direct cash infusions to maintain their solvency and liquidity. Specifically, Treasury pledged to purchase senior preferred shares in Fannie Mae and Freddie Mac paying 10% annual dividends, and mortgage-backed securities issued by the firms. In return, Treasury received $1 billion of senior preferred shares and warrants for 79.9% of these GSEs' common shares.[48]

Because of this high level of government control, CBO concluded that Fannie Mae and Freddie Mac were now effectively federal operations and has accounted for the mortgages owned or guaranteed by these entities as loans and loan guarantees of the federal government since January 2009.[49] Treatment of GSE cost by CBO is similar to the budgetary consideration of federal credit programs under the Federal Credit Reform Act of 1990, in which the budget records a subsidy cost for federal loan commitments, with total budgetary impact calculated by discounting future loan cash flows by interest rates on Treasury securities with comparable maturity. However, in the case of Fannie Mae and Freddie Mac, CBO replaces the Treasury discount rates with rates reflecting the market risk associated with the GSEs' credit obligations.[50]

In August 2009, CBO estimated that the operations of Fannie Mae and Freddie Mac would increase the FY2009 federal deficit by $291 billion. Included in this estimate was the $248 billion subsidy cost for the GSEs' assets and liabilities at the beginning of the conservatorship, along with another $43 billion in subsidy costs associated with new business undertaken by Fannie Mae and Freddie Mac in FY2009. Additionally, CBO projected that the activities of these entities would add $99 billion to federal budget deficits for FY2010 to FY2019. **Table 12** presents the estimated budgetary effect of Fannie Mae and Freddie Mac conservatorship, as reported in CBO's January and August 2009 baseline projections.

Since CBO determined Fannie Mae and Freddie Mac should be accounted for in the federal budget, the Treasury cash infusions are considered intragovernmental payments, and thus have no effect on federal budget deficits. In contrast to CBO, the Office of Management and Budget (OMB) continues to treat Fannie Mae and Freddie Mac as nongovernmental entities for federal budgeting purposes. Consequently, OMB does not include GSE subsidy costs in its budget estimates, but instead scores the Treasury cash infusions as the total budgetary effect of federal government operations related to these two entities. **Table 13** shows the estimated levels of Treasury Department GSE cash infusions, as included in CBO's January and August 2009 baseline projections.

Table 12. CBO Projections of Subsidy Costs for Federal Conservatorship of Fannie Mae and Freddie Mac ($ in billions)

Date of CBO Baseline Budget Projection	FY2009	FY2010-FY2019
January 2009	238	71
August 2009	291	99

Sources: Congressional Budget Office, *Budget and Economic Outlook* (January 2009 and August 2009).

Note: Positive numbers indicate an increase in mandatory spending, and thus reflect a net increase in the deficit.

Table 13. Projections of Treasury Department Cash Infusions for Fannie Mae and Freddie Mac ($ in billions)

Date of CBO Baseline Budget Projection	2009	2010-2019
January 2009	18	78
August 2009	112	51
January 2010	96	NA

Source: Congressional Budget Office, *Budget and Economic Outlook* (January 2009, August 2009 and January 2010).

Notes: In January 2010, CBO recorded $91 billion in net outlays related to Fannie Mae and Freddie Mac for FY2009. This reflects $96 billion in Treasury cash infusions offset moderately by over $4 billion in dividends from Fannie Mae and Freddie Mac stock. At this time, no projections were offered about Treasury GSE cash infusions for FY2010 to FY2019.

Because of budgetary rules, when CBO released new baseline projections in January 2010, the actual FY2009 budgetary impact for Fannie Mae and Freddie Mac was scored as the level of net outlays from Treasury cash infusions, and not as the net subsidy cost associated with federal conservatorship. In particular, CBO recorded a value of $91 billion for the two GSEs in FY2009, reflecting almost $96 billion in cash infusions offset moderately by more than $4 billion in dividends on Fannie Mae and Freddie Mac stock.[51] At the same time, as part of this January 2010 estimate, CBO projected GSE future budgetary impact for FY2010 to FY2020 in terms of subsidy costs, and not as net outlays on Treasury cash infusions.

Emergency Economic Stabilization Act of 2008

The Emergency Economic Stabilization Act of 2008 (EESA; Division A of P.L. 110-343) was signed into law on October 3, 2008, establishing the Troubled Asset Relief Program (TARP).[52] Under TARP, the Treasury Secretary is authorized to purchase or insure up to $700 billion of mortgage related assets, or any other assets the Secretary, in consultation with the Chairman of the Federal Reserve, determine would be required to promote stability in the financial markets.[53] Among the major TARP initiatives, the Capital Purchase Program has been used by the Treasury to purchase senior preferred shares from U.S. financial institutions. In addition, Treasury has invested $20 billion in both Bank of America and Citigroup through the Targeted Investment Program, provided loans and equity investments to General Motors, GMAC, Chrysler, and Chrysler Financial under the Automotive Industry Financing Program, and offered various forms of financial assistance to the American International Group.

Similar to CBO's budgetary treatment of Fannie Mae and Freddie Mac, Section 123 of EESA stipulates that accounting for the budgetary impact of TARP must be conducted under procedures outlined in the Federal Credit Reform Act of 1990, but with an adjustment for market risk. In particular, CBO is not recording the gross cash disbursement of Treasury purchases initiated under TARP, but is instead estimating the government's net subsidy costs on a present value basis. Generally speaking, CBO calculates the subsidy costs for the TARP program by subtracting the purchase cost from the estimated market of the value acquired assets, discounted at a rate reflecting market risk.[54]

The expected effect of EESA on federal budget deficits has been revised numerous times. In January 2009, CBO estimated that subsidy costs for TARP transactions would total $184 billion for FY2009 and $5 billion for FY2010. However, in March 2009, changes in market conditions and increased subsidy costs attributed to new Treasury Department transactions prompted CBO to increase its projected cost to $336 billion for FY2009 and $20 billion for FY2010. Because of improved market conditions, CBO in August 2009 once again revised the estimated budgetary impact of TARP, reducing projected outlays to $133 billion for FY2009, but increasing anticipated subsidy costs to $108 billion for FY2010 to FY2019. In January 2010, CBO provided another revision to TARP subsidy costs, recording an actual FY2009 subsidy of $152 billion. As circumstances have changed since the recording of this figure, a credit re-estimate was provided for FY2010 through a projected negative outlay of $67 billion. (The negative outlay of $67 billion does not reflect TARP spending that will take place in 2010.) Consequently, as of January 2010, CBO estimates a budgetary impact of $99 billion for the full duration of the TARP program.[55]

Table 14 presents TARP cost estimates as reported in CBO's January 2009, March 2009, August 2009, and January 2010 baseline projections.

Economic Stimulus

In response to the deep and long recession that began in December 2007, two major bills were enacted to stimulate the economy.

Economic Stimulus Act of 2008

On February 13, 2008, President Bush signed into law the Economic Stimulus Act of 2008 (P.L. 110-185). The key provision in P.L. 110-185 was a refundable tax rebate which equaled 10% of an individual's first $6,000 of taxable income ($12,000 for couples), with a minimum rebate of $300 ($600 for couples) and a maximum of $600 ($1,200 for couples). This rebate was phased-out at a 5% rate for income over $75,000 for individuals ($150,000 for couples), with a full phase-out at $87,000 ($174,000 for couples).[56] Further, a $300 rebate was available to individuals with no tax liability provided that earned income, Social Security benefits, and veterans disability payments totaled at least $3,000. Along with the rebate for individuals, P.L. 110-185 also included two business tax deductions. One provision allowed businesses to deduct 50% of investments made in 2008 on certain equipment, and another provision increased deductions permitted for small businesses under Section 179 of the Internal Revenue Code for purchases of certain types of property.

In February 2008, JCT projected that P.L. 110-185 would increase federal budget deficits by approximately $124.5 billion over FY2008 to FY2018.[57] Most significantly, the individual tax rebate was expected to reduce federal government revenues by $106.7 billion in FY2008 and by $10 billion in FY2009. Additionally, the 50% bonus depreciation on certain equipment placed in service in 2008 was estimated to reduce federal government revenues by $43.9 billion in FY2008, and by $5.6 billion in FY2009. However, since this business tax provision involved bringing the deduction forward in time, JCT estimated that the provision would effectively increase revenue by $42.1 billion over FY2010 to FY2018, with a net 10-year effect of a $7.4 billion revenue decrease.

Table 15 presents the budgetary effect of all major provisions of P.L. 110-185, estimated by JCT in February 2008.

Table 14. Estimated Budgetary Effects of the Troubled Asset Relief Program ($ in billion)

Date of CBO Baseline Budget Projection	FY2009	FY2010	FY2011-FY2014
January 2009	184	5	0
March 2009	336	20	0
August 2009	133	80	28
January 2010	152	-67	14

Source: Congressional Budget Office, *Budget and Economic Outlook* (January 2009, August 2009, and January 2010); and *An Analysis of the President's Budgetary Proposals* (March 2009).

Note: Positive numbers indicate an increase in mandatory spending, and thus reflect a net increase in the deficit.

Table 15. Estimated Budgetary Effects of the Economic Stimulus Act of 2008 ($ in billions)

Provision	FY2008	FY2009	FY2008-FY2018
Rebates for Individuals	-106.7	-10.0	-116.7
Appropriations to Carry Out Rebates	-0.2	-0.1	-0.3
Increase Section 179 Expensing and Phase-out Amounts for 2008	-0.9	-0.6	-0.1
50% Bonus Depreciation	-43.9	-5.6	-7.4
Total	**-151.7**	**-16.3**	**-124.5**

Source: Joint Committee on Taxation, *Estimated Budget Effects of the "Economic Stimulus Act of 2008", as Passed by the House of Representatives and the Senate on February 7, 2008 (JCX-17-08),* February 8, 2008.

Notes: Negative numbers indicate an increase in the deficit. Columns may not be additive due to rounding. All budgetary effects were estimated by JCT at the time of legislative enactment.

American Recovery and Reinvestment Act of 2009

In response to significant weakness in the U.S. economy, President Obama signed into law the American Recovery and Reinvestment Act of 2009 (ARRA; P.L. 111-5) on February 17, 2009. Division A of ARRA provided discretionary spending authority for a broad range of agencies, programs, and activities, including major authorizations for the State Fiscal Stabilization Fund and energy and water development initiatives.[58] Division B of ARRA contained numerous direct spending provisions that offered fiscal relief to states under the Medicaid program, increased benefits for the Temporary Assistance for Needy Families program, extended unemployment compensation, and provided subsidies for COBRA health insurance premiums. Division B of ARRA also contained several tax provisions including the Making Work Pay tax credit, which was a temporary refundable tax credit of up to $400 for individuals and $800 for married couples for tax years 2009 and 2010. Further, ARRA expanded the Hope education tax credit for 2009 and 2010, modified and extended the first-time homebuyer tax credit, and expanded certain rules related to net operating losses for businesses.[59]

CBO and JCT estimated in February 2009 that ARRA would increase federal budget deficits by $787.2 billion over FY2009 to FY2019.[60] For Division A, CBO projected discretionary spending outlays of $34.8 billion in FY2009, $110.7 billion for FY2010, with discretionary outlays totaling $308.3 billion over FY2009 to FY2019. With respect to direct spending provisions in Division B of ARRA, CBO estimated federal budget deficit increases of $85.3 billion in FY2009, $108.6 billion for FY2010, with mandatory outlays totaling $267.0 billion over 10 years. Finally, JCT estimated that Division B tax provisions would decrease federal government revenues by $64.8 billion in FY2009, $180.1 billion in FY2010, and by $211.8 billion over FY2009 to FY2019.

Table 16 presents the budgetary impact of discretionary spending, mandatory spending, and revenue provisions of ARRA, as estimated by CBO and JCT in February 2009.

In January 2010, CBO released a revised projection for the budgetary impact of ARRA, anticipating that the law would now increase deficits by $75 billion above the original cost estimate, to $862 billion over FY2009 to FY2010.[61] The modification to CBO's cost projection for ARRA is attributed in part to increased outlays on unemployment compensation, which as of January 2010, were calculated to be approximately $21 billion greater than initially anticipated for 2009 and 2010. In addition, the Build America Bond program, a tax credit bond option for state and local governments established under ARRA, experienced participation levels significantly exceeding the original expectations of CBO and JCT. Consequently, CBO's January 2010 revision to the ARRA cost estimate projects an additional $26 billion in outlays for the program over FY2010 to FY2019. CBO's revised ARRA cost projection also included new estimates related to Medicaid spending and the Making Work Pay tax credit.

Table 16. Budgetary Impact of the American Recovery and Reinvestment Act of 2009: Estimated by CBO and JCT in February 2009 ($ in billions)

	2009	2010	2011	2012	2013	2014	2015	2016	2017	2018	2019	2009-2019
Discretionary Spending[a]												
(Division A)												
Estimated Outlays	34.8	110.7	76.3	38.1	22.9	12.8	7.0	3.1	1.6	0.8	0.1	308.3
Mandatory Spending[a]												
(Division B)												
Estimated Outlays	85.3	108.6	49.9	8.1	7.4	15.1	4.7	-4.7	-4.1	-1.9	-1.4	267.0
Revenues[b]												
(Division B)												
Estimated Outlays	-64.8	-180.1	-8.2	10.0	2.7	5.5	7.1	5.8	5.1	5.0	0.1	-211.8
Net Impact on the Deficit[a]												
	184.9	**399.4**	**134.4**	**36.1**	**27.6**	**22.4**	**4.7**	**-7.3**	**-7.5**	**-6.1**	**-1.4**	**787.2**

Source: Congressional Budget Office, *Cost Estimate for the Conference Agreement for H.R. 1: American Recovery and Reinvestment Act of 2009*, February 13, 2009.

Notes: Columns may not be additive due to rounding. All budgetary effects were estimated by CBO and JCT at the time of legislative enactment.

a. For figures on discretionary spending, mandatory spending, and net impact on the deficit, positive numbers indicate an increase in the deficit.

b. For figures on revenues, negative numbers reflect an increase in the deficit.

CHANGES IN NON-DEFENSE DISCRETIONARY SPENDING: 2001 TO 2009

Discretionary spending supports a variety of defense, domestic and international federal government operations, with the latter two categories comprising non-defense discretionary spending. Domestic discretionary spending funds numerous federal agencies and programs, including education, law enforcement, and energy, while discretionary spending on international programs includes financing for diplomatic missions and foreign aid. In relative terms, domestic outlays comprised about 93% of total annual non-defense discretionary spending during FY2001 to FY2009, while international outlays made up the remaining 7%. With regards to legislation, annual appropriations laws provides the budget authority for discretionary spending, which can be granted both for a single year or over a longer time horizon.

Table 17 shows non-defense discretionary spending over the past decade, both in nominal and constant dollars, and as a percentage of GDP. Adjusted for inflation, domestic and international outlays increased from $391.0 billion in FY2001 to approximately $477.4 billion in FY2006 (in FY2005 dollars). After declining in constant dollars in 2007, non-defense discretionary spending reached its peak for the decade in FY2009 at $516.2 billion, due in large part to economic stimulus initiatives related to the 2008 financial crisis. Compared with the size of the economy as a whole, non-defense discretionary spending equaled 3.4% of GDP in FY2001, comprised approximately 3.8% of GDP for FY2003 to FY2006, and has risen to 4.1% of GDP for FY2009.[62]

Unlike mandatory spending or revenue provisions that are authorized permanently or for several years at a time, appropriation levels are determined annually. This means that there is no straightforward way to project spending levels under current policy in the future, and hence no straightforward way to estimate discretionary policy changes over time. Under the Deficit Control Act of 1985 (P.L. 99-177), CBO is required to project future discretionary spending as the level of budget authority for the current fiscal year, adjusted using the employment cost index and the GDP deflator. Consequently, one way to measure policy changes in non-defense discretionary spending over the past decade is to compare the baseline level of constant spending adjusted for inflation projected by CBO in January 2001, against actual non-defense discretionary outlays for FY2001 to FY2009. Under this approach, which is illustrated in Figure 2, actual FY2002 non-defense discretionary spending was $17 billion above the level estimated by CBO in January 2001 and $81 billion above constant spending in FY2006. Due largely to economic stimulus spending implemented by the American Recovery and Reinvestment Act of 2009 (ARRA; P.L. 111-5), actual non-defense discretionary spending for FY2009 was $135 billion above this constant spending benchmark.

Another way to benchmark current policy for non-defense discretionary outlays is to keep spending constant as a share of GDP. This benchmark could be justified on the grounds that non-defense discretionary spending has stayed relatively constant as a percentage of GDP over the past 25 years. Figure 2 compares actual non-defense discretionary outlays during this time period to outlays fixed at the FY2001 non-defense discretionary spending share of GDP, which was 3.4%. Because GDP tends to grow faster than inflation, this benchmark typically yields smaller estimates of legislative changes to discretionary spending than the inflation-adjusted benchmark. Under this approach, actual non-defense outlays in FY2002 were $31.4 billion above the benchmark and $103.1 billion above the benchmark for FY2009.

Table 17. Non-Defense Discretionary Spending, FY2001 to FY2009 ($ in billions)

Year	Nominal $	Constant FY2005 $	% GDP
2001	343.3	391.0	3.4
2002	385.4	429.4	3.7
2003	420.5	455.2	3.8
2004	441.4	461.0	3.8
2005	474.8	474.8	3.8
2006	496.7	477.4	3.8
2007	493.0	458.3	3.5
2008	522.3	469.2	3.6
2009	581.0	516.2	4.1

Source: Office of Management and Budget, *Budget of the U.S. Government: Fiscal Year 2011 (Historical Tables 8-7. and 8.8)*, February 2010; and Congressional Budget Office, *The Budget and Economic Outlook: Fiscal Years 2010 to 2020* (Table F-8), January 2010.

Note: Non-defense discretionary spending figures present the aggregated total of all domestic and international discretionary spending for the given fiscal year.

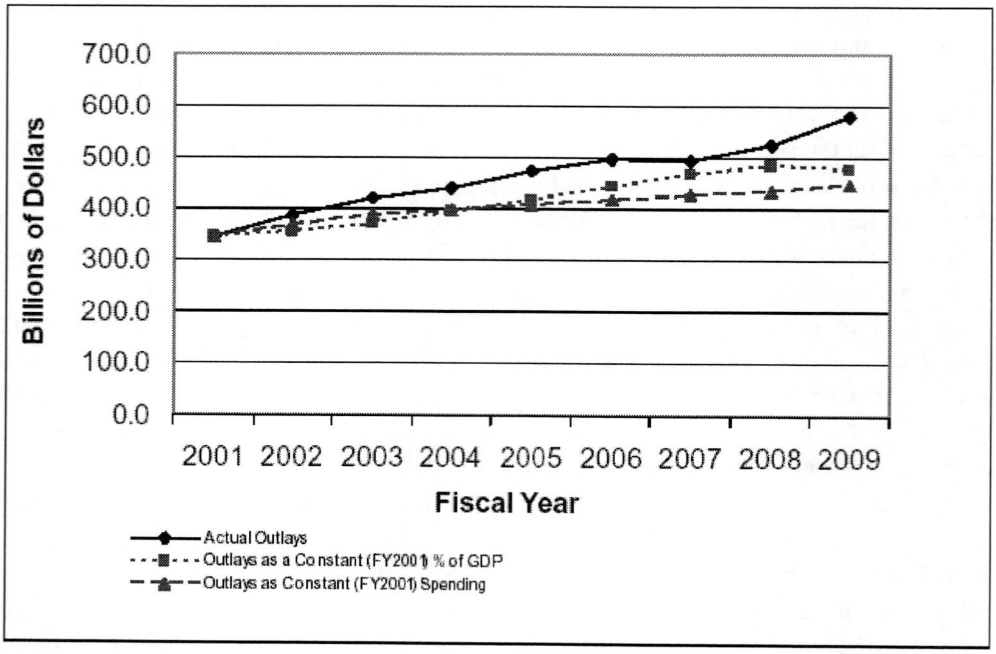

Source: Office of Management and Budget, Budget of the U.S. Government: Fiscal Year 2011 (Historical Tables 8-7. and 10.1)

Figure 2. Non-defense Discretionary Spending, FY2001-FY2009.

End Notes

1 The federal budget includes both on-budget and off-budget components. The Balanced Budget and Emergency Deficit Control Act of 1985 (P.L. 99-177) moved revenues and outlays of the two Social Security Trust Funds off-budget, and the Postal Service was moved off-budget by the Omnibus Reconciliation Act of 1989. All annual federal budgetary figures presented in this report use combined on-budget and off-budget totals. For more information, see CRS Report RS20350, *Off-Budget Status of Federal Entities: Background and Current Proposals*, by Bill Heniff Jr.

2 See CRS Report RL31235, *The Economics of the Federal Budget Deficit*, by Brian W. Cashell.

3 See CRS Report R40088, *The Federal Budget: Current and Upcoming Issues*, by D. Andrew Austin and Mindy R. Levit.

4 Congressional Budget Office, *The Budget and Economic Outlook: Fiscal Years 2002-2011,* Table 1-2, January 2001, available at http://www.cbo.gov/ftpdocs/27xx/doc2727/entire-report.pdf.

5 Congressional Budget Office, *The Budget and Economic Outlook: Fiscal Years 2010 to 2020*, Table 1-3, January 2010, available at http://www.cbo.gov/ftpdocs/108xx/doc10871/01-26-Outlook.pdf.

6 See CRS Report 98-560, *Baselines and Scorekeeping in the Federal Budget Process*, by Bill Heniff Jr.

7 See CRS Report RL31414, *Baseline Budget Projections: A Discussion of Issues*, by Marc Labonte. For an alternative evaluation, see Alan Auerbach et al., "New Estimates of the Budget Outlook," Brookings Institution, *Issues in Economic Policy #3*, February 2006.

8 For CBO's description of mandatory spending in the context of P.L. 99-177, see Congressional Budget Office, *The Budget and Economic Outlook: Fiscal Years 2010 to 2020*, January 2010.

9 For a discussion of historical trends in mandatory spending, see CRS Report RL33074, *Mandatory Spending Since 1962*, by D. Andrew Austin and Mindy R. Levit.

10 Data on mandatory spending for FY2001 to FY2009 was collected from Congressional Budget Office, *The Budget and Economic Outlook: Fiscal Years 2010 to* 2020, Tables F-9 and F-10, January 2010.

11 For instance, the Social Security Act (P.L. 74-271) was signed into law in 1935, and the Social Security Amendments (P.L. 89-97), which created Medicare and Medicaid, were enacted in 1965.

12 For further discussion of CBO's budgetary treatment of revenue legislation, see Congressional Budget Office, *The Budget and Economic Outlook: Fiscal Years 2010 to 2020 (Box 4.1 Effect of Expiring Tax Provisions on CBO's Revenue Baseline*), January 2010.

13 Data on federal revenues for FY2001 to FY2009 was collected from Congressional Budget Office, *The Budget and Economic Outlook: Fiscal Years 2010 to 2020 (Tables F-3 and F-4*), January 2010.

14 For a CBO discussion about the difficulties in measuring the budgetary impact of EGTRRA and JGTRRA, see Congressional Budget Office, *The Budgetary Costs of EGTRRA and JGTRRA Compared with Projected Deficits*, July 20, 2007, available at http://www.cbo.gov/ftpdocs/83xx/doc8337/07-20-EGTRRA-JGTRRA_and_Deficits.pdf.

15 For analysis of EGTRRA and a comparison of House, Senate and Administration proposals prior to enactment of the law, see CRS Report RL30973, *2001 Tax Cut: Description, Analysis, and Background*, by David L. Brumbaugh et al.

16 In contrast to the budgetary treatment of authorization legislation for mandatory programs, CBO assumes that most current tax provisions will expire as scheduled. Consequently, CBO projected in January 2010 projected that expiring tax provisions under EGTTRA, JGTRRA, and other legislation would increase revenues by 2.7% of GDP for FY2010 to FY2012.

17 Joint Committee on Taxation, *Estimated Budget Effects of the Conference Agreement for H.R. 1836,* JCX-51-01, May 26, 2001, available at http://www.jct.gov/publications.html?func=startdown&id=2001.

18 For analysis of JGTRRA, see CRS Report RL32034, *The Jobs and Growth Tax Relief Reconciliation Act of 2003 and Business Investment*, by Gary Guenther.

19 Congressional Budget Office, *Cost Estimate for H.R. 2, Jobs and Growth Tax Relief Reconciliation Act of 2003*, May 23, 2003, available at http://www.cbo.gov/ftpdocs/42xx/doc4249/hr2.pdf.

20 Congressional Budget Office, *Cost Estimate for H.R. 1308, Working Families Tax Relief Act of 2004*, September 30, 2004, available at http://www.cbo.gov/ftpdocs/58xx/doc5868/hr1308pg.pdf.

21 For a discussion of TIPRA in the context of other reconciliation legislation effecting budget deficits, see CRS Report RS22098, *Deficit Impact of Reconciliation Legislation Enacted in 1990, 1993, 1997, and 2006*, by Robert Keith.

22 Joint Committee on Taxation, *Estimated Revenue Effects of the Conference Agreement for the "Tax Increase Prevention and Reconciliation Act of 2005,* JCX-18-06, May 9, 2006, available at http://www.jct.gov/publications.html?func=startdown&id=1502.

23 See CRS Report RL33703, *Summary of the Pension Protection Act of 2006*, by Patrick Purcell.

24 Congressional Budget Office, *Cost Estimate of H.R. 4, Pension Protection Act of 2006*, August 16, 2006, available at http://www.cbo.gov/ftpdocs/74xx/doc7493/hr4pgo.pdf.

[25] See CRS Report RS22551, *Tax Provisions in the Tax Relief and Health Care Act of 2006 (H.R. 6111)*, by Erika K. Lunder.

[26] Congressional Budget Office, *Cost Estimate for H.R. 6111, Tax Relief and Health Care Act of 2006*, December 28, 2006, available at http://www.cbo.gov/ftpdocs/77xx/doc7714/hr6111pgo.pdf.

[27] See Joint Committee on Taxation, *Present Law and Background Relating to the Individual Alternative Minimum Tax (JCX-38-07)*, June 25, 2007, available at http://www.jct.gov/x-38-07.pdf.

[28] For a description of various legislative changes made to the individual AMT, see CRS Report RL30149, *The Alternative Minimum Tax for Individuals*, by Steven Maguire.

[29] See CRS Report RL33899, *Modifying the Alternative Minimum Tax (AMT): Revenue Costs and Potential Revenue Offsets*, by Jane G. Gravelle.

[30] For a discussion about the AMT in the context of the federal budget, see Congressional Budget Office, *The Individual Alternative Minimum Tax*, January 15, 2010, available at http://www.cbo.gov/ftpdocs/108xx/doc10800/01-15-AMT_Brief.pdf.

[31] Congressional Budget Office, *Cost Estimate for H.R. 2646, Farm Security and Rural Investment Act of 2002*, May 22, 2002, available at http://www.cbo.gov/ftpdocs/34xx/doc3468/hr2646omb.pdf.

[32] See CRS Report RL34696, *The 2008 Farm Bill: Major Provisions and Legislative Action*, coordinated by Renée Johnson.

[33] Congressional Budget Office, *Cost Estimate for H.R. 2419, Food, Conservation, and Energy Act of 2008*, May 13, 2008, available at http://www.cbo.gov/ftpdocs/92xx/doc9230/hr2419conf.pdf.

[34] CRS reports reviewing all of these laws are available, including CRS Report RL31406, *Supplemental Appropriations for FY2002: Combating Terrorism and Other Issues*, by Amy Belasco and Larry Nowels; CRS Report RL32783, *FY2005 Supplemental Appropriations for Iraq and Afghanistan, Tsunami Relief, and Other Activities*, by Amy Belasco and Larry Nowels; and CRS Report R40531, *FY2009 Spring Supplemental Appropriations for Overseas Contingency Operations*, coordinated by Stephen Daggett and Susan B. Epstein.

[35] For a review of historical changes to the system for determining physician payment rates under Medicare, see Congressional Budget Office, *The Sustainable Growth Rate Formula for Setting Medicare's Physician Payment Rates*, September 6, 2006, available at http://www.cbo.gov/ftpdocs/75xx/doc7542/09-07-SGR-brief.pdf.

[36] See CRS Report R40907, *Medicare Physician Payment Updates and the Sustainable Growth Rate (SGR) System*, by Jim Hahn.

[37] In 2010, the standard coverage includes a $310 deductible, 25% coinsurance costs up to an initial coverage limit of $2,830, and no coverage until out-of-pocket costs exceeded $6,440.00. For more information on current features of the Medicare Part D prescription drug benefit. See CRS Report R40611, *Medicare Part D Prescription Drug Benefit*, by Patricia A. Davis.

[38] See Congressional Budget Office, *Projection of Spending for the Medicare Part D Benefit: Letter to the Honorable William "Bill" M. Thomas*, February 9, 2005, available at http://www.cbo.gov/ftpdocs/60xx/doc6076/ThomasLtr2-9-05.pdf.

[39] The Boards of Trustees of the Federal Hospital Insurance and Federal Supplementary Medical Insurance Trust Funds, *2009 Medicare Trustees Report* (*Table V.E8.*), May 12, 2009, available at http://www.cms.hhs.gov/ReportsTrustFunds/downloads/tr2009.pdf.

[40] Congressional Budget Office, An Analysis of the President's Budgetary Proposals for Fiscal Year 2007 (Appendix A: Changes to CBO's Baseline Since January 2006), March 2006, available at http://www.cbo.gov/ftpdocs/70xx/ doc7069/03-14-PresidentsBudget.pdf.

[41] For an assessment by CBO on the cost of federal efforts related to the 2005 Hurricanes, see Congressional Budget Office, *The Federal Government's Spending and Tax Actions in Response to the 2005 Gulf Coast Hurricanes*, August 1, 2007, available at http://www.cbo.gov/ftpdocs/85xx/doc8514/08-07-Hurricanes_Letter.pdf.

[42] See CRS Report R40708, *Disaster Relief Funding and Emergency Supplemental Appropriations*, by Bruce R. Lindsay and Justin Murray.

[43] Both P.L. 109-148 and P.L. 109-234 included rescissions designed to partially offset the costs of the emergency supplemental appropriations. For a discussion of rescissions in P.L. 109-148, see CRS Report RL32153, *Across-the-Board Spending Cuts in End-of-Session Appropriations Acts*, by Robert Keith.

[44] See CRS Report RL34711, *Consolidated Appropriations Act for FY2009 (P.L. 110-329): An Overview*, by Robert Keith.

[45] Joint Committee on Taxation, Estimated Revenue Effects of H.R. 3768, The "Hurricane Katrina Tax Relief Act of 2005", As Amended by the Senate on September 15, 2005 (JCX-66-05 R), September 20, 2005, available at http://www.jct.gov/publications.html?func=startdown&id=1549.

[46] Joint Committee on Taxation, Estimated Revenue Effects of H.R. 4440, The "Gulf Opportunity Zone Act of 2005", As Passed by the House of Representatives and Senate on December 16, 2005 (JCX-89-05), December 20, 2005, available at http://www.jct.gov/publications.html?func=startdown&id=1526.

[47] For a review of new programs introduced and other actions taken by the Treasury, Federal Reserve, and Federal Deposit Insurance related to the 2008 financial crisis, see CRS Report R41073, *Government Interventions in Response to Financial Turmoil*, by Baird Webel and Marc Labonte.

[48] Treasury Department, *Statement by Secretary Henry M. Paulson, Jr. on Treasury and Federal Housing Finance Agency Action to Protect Financial Markets and Taxpayers*, September 7, 2008, available at http://www.treas.gov/ press/releases/hp1129.htm.

[49] For an explanation by CBO of the accounting of these GSEs as federal government operations, see Congressional Budget Office, *The Budget and Economic Outlook: An Update,* August 2009, available at http://www.cbo.gov/ftpdocs/ 105xx/doc10521/08-25-BudgetUpdate.pdf.

[50] For information on CBO's methodology for estimating subsidy costs related to Fannie Mae and Freddie Mac, see Congressional Budget Office, *CBO's Budgetary Treatment of Fannie Mae and Freddie Mac,* January 2010, available at http://www.cbo.gov/ftpdocs/108xx/doc10878/01-13-FannieFreddie.pdf.

[51] Congressional Budget Office, *The Budget and Economic Outlook: Fiscal Years 2010 to 2020*, January 2010.

[52] For an overview of EESA, see CRS Report RL34730, *Troubled Asset Relief Program: Legislation and Treasury Implementation*, by Baird Webel and Edward V. Murphy.

[53] The Helping Families Save Their Homes Act (P.L. 111-22) was enacted on May 20, 2009, reducing TARP mandatory authorization by $1.24 billion.

[54] For information on CBO's methodology for estimating subsidy costs related to TARP, see Congressional Budget Office, *The Troubled Asset Relief Program: Report on Transactions Through June 17, 2009,* June 2009, available at http://www.cbo.gov/ftpdocs/100xx/doc10056/06-29-TARP.pdf.

[55] Congressional Budget Office, *The Budget and Economic Outlook: Fiscal Years 2010 to 2020 (Box 1-2: Recent Activity in the Troubled Asset Relief Program*, January 2010.

[56] For an overview of P.L. 110-185, see CRS Report RS22850, *Tax Provisions of the 2008 Economic Stimulus Package*, by Jane G. Gravelle.

[57] Joint Committee on Taxation, Estimated Budget Effects of the "Economic Stimulus Act of 2008", as Passed by the House of Representatives and the Senate on February 7, 2008 (JCX-17-08), February 8, 2008, available at http://www.jct.gov/publications.html?func=startdown&id=1323.

[58] See CRS Report R40537, *American Recovery and Reinvestment Act of 2009 (P.L. 111-5): Summary and Legislative History*, by Clinton T. Brass et al.

[59] See CRS Report RL34664, *The First-Time Homebuyer Tax Credit*, by Carol A. Pettit.

[60] Congressional Budget Office, *Cost Estimate for the Conference Agreement for H.R. 1, American Recovery and Reinvestment Act of 2009*, February 13, 2009, available at http://www.cbo.gov/ftpdocs/99xx/doc9989/ hr1conference.pdf.

[61] Congressional Budget Office, *The Budget and Economic Outlook: Fiscal Years 2010 to 2020*, January 2010.

[62] Data on non-defense discretionary spending for FY2001 to FY2009 was collected from Office of Management and Budget, *Budget of the U.S. Government: Fiscal Year 2011 (Historical Tables 8-7. and 10.1)*; and Congressional Budget Office, *The Budget and Economic Outlook: Fiscal Years 2010 to 2020* (*Tables F-3 and F-4*), January 2010.

In: From Surplus to Deficit: The Impact of Legislation on the... ISBN: 978-1-61728-927-9
Editor: Vanessa C. Sibhoan © 2011 Nova Science Publishers, Inc.

Chapter 2

THE BUDGET AND ECONOMIC OUTLOOK: FISCAL YEARS 2010 TO 2020

Congressional Budget Office

SUMMARY

The Congressional Budget Office (CBO) projects that if current laws and policies remained unchanged, the federal budget would show a deficit of about $1.3 trillion for fiscal year 2010 (see Summary Table 1). At 9.2 percent of gross domestic product (GDP), that deficit would be slightly smaller than the shortfall of 9.9 percent of GDP ($1.4 trillion) posted in 2009. Last year's deficit was the largest as a share of GDP since the end of World War II, and the deficit expected for 2010 would be the second largest. Moreover, if legislation is enacted in the next several months that either boosts spending or reduces revenues, the 2010 deficit could equal or exceed last year's shortfall.

The large 2009 and 2010 deficits reflect a combination of factors: an imbalance between revenues and spending that predates the recession and turmoil in financial markets, sharply lower revenues and elevated spending associated with those economic conditions, and the costs of various federal policies implemented in response to those conditions.

The deep recession that began two years ago appears to have ended in mid-2009. Economic activity picked up during the second half of last year, with inflation-adjusted GDP and industrial production both showing gains. Still, GDP remains roughly 6½ percent below CBO's estimate of the output that could be produced if all labor and capital were fully employed (that difference is called the output gap), and the unemployment rate, at 10 percent, is twice what it was two years ago.

Economic growth in the next few years will probably be muted in the aftermath of the financial and economic turmoil. Experience in the United States and in other countries suggests that recovery from recessions triggered by financial crises and large declines in asset prices tends to be protracted. Also, although aggressive action on the part of the Federal Reserve and the fiscal stimulus package enacted in early 2009 helped moderate the severity of the recession and shorten its duration, the support coming from those sources is expected to wane. Furthermore, spending by households is likely to be constrained by slow growth of income, lost wealth, and limits on their ability to borrow, and investment spending will be slowed by the large number of vacant homes and offices.

Under current law, the federal fiscal outlook beyond this year is daunting: Projected deficits average about $600 billion per year over the 2011–2020 period. As a share of GDP, deficits drop markedly in the next few years but remain high—at 6.5 percent of GDP in 2011 and 4.1 percent in 2012, the first full fiscal year after certain tax provisions originally enacted in 2001, 2003, and 2009 are scheduled to expire. Thereafter, deficits are projected to range between 2.6 percent and 3.2 percent of GDP through 2020.

Those accumulating deficits will push federal debt held by the public to significantly higher levels. At the end of 2009, debt held by the public was $7.5 trillion, or 53 percent of GDP; by the end of 2020, debt is projected to climb to $15 trillion, or 67 percent of GDP. With such a large increase in debt, plus an expected increase in interest rates as the economic recovery strengthens, interest payments on the debt are poised to skyrocket. CBO projects that the government's annual spending on net interest will more than triple between 2010 and 2020 in nominal terms, from $207 billion to $723 billion, and will more than double as a share of GDP, from 1.4 percent to 3.2percent (see Summary Figure 1).

Moreover, CBO's baseline projections understate the budget deficits that would arise under many observers' interpretation of current policy, as opposed to current law. In particular, the projections assume that major provisions of the tax cuts enacted in 2001, 2003, and 2009 will expire as scheduled and that temporary changes that have kept the alternative minimum tax (AMT) from affecting many more taxpayers will not be extended. The baseline projections also assume that annual appropriations rise only with inflation, which would leave discretionary spending very low relative to GDP by historical standards. If the tax cuts were made permanent, the AMT was indexed for inflation, and annual appropriations kept pace with GDP, the deficit in 2020 would be nearly the same, historically large, share of GDP that it is today, and debt held by the public would equal nearly 100 percent of GDP.

The Budget Outlook

In 2010, under an assumption that no legislative changes occur, CBO estimates that federal spending will total $3.5 trillion and revenues will total $2.2 trillion. The resulting deficit of about $1.3 trillion would be just $65 billion less than last year's shortfall and more than three times the size of the deficit recorded in 2008. Total outlays are projected to increase by just $5 billion, while revenues are projected to rise by $70 billion. The deficit for this year is on track to be about as large as last year's because an expected decline in federal aid to the financial sector will be offset by increases in other outlays, particularly spending from last year's stimulus legislation and outlays for income support programs, health care programs, Social Security, and net interest. At the same time, revenues are projected to increase only modestly primarily because of the slow pace of economic recovery forecast by CBO and the lagged effect of the recession on tax receipts.

Summary Table 1. CBO's Baseline Budget Outlook

	Actual 2009	2010	2011	2012	2013	2014	2015	2016	2017	2018	2019	2020	Total, 2011-2015	Total, 2011-2020
	In Billions of Dollars													
Total Revenues	2,105	2,175	2,670	2,964	3,218	3,465	3,625	3,814	3,996	4,170	4,352	4,563	15,941	36,836
Total Outlays	3,518	3,524	3,650	3,613	3,756	3,940	4,105	4,335	4,521	4,712	5,000	5,250	19,065	42,883
Total Deficit (-) or Surplus	**-1,414**	**-1,349**	**-980**	**-650**	**-539**	**-475**	**-480**	**-521**	**-525**	**-542**	**-649**	**-687**	**-3,124**	**-6,047**
On-budget	-1,551	-1,434	-1,076	-757	-659	-608	-619	-659	-659	-669	-765	-793	-3,719	-7,263
Off-budget[a]	137	86	96	108	120	133	139	138	134	127	116	107	595	1,216
Debt Held by the Public at the End of the Year	7,544	8,797	9,785	10,479	11,056	11,556	12,055	12,595	13,133	13,678	14,329	15,027	n.a.	n.a.
	As a Percentage of Gross Domestic Product													
Total Revenues	14.8	14.9	17.8	18.8	19.3	19.7	19.7	19.8	19.9	20.0	20.1	20.2	19.1	19.6
Total Outlays	24.7	24.1	24.3	23.0	22.5	22.4	22.3	22.6	22.6	22.6	23.1	23.3	22.9	22.8
Total Deficit	**-9.9**	**-9.2**	**-6.5**	**-4.1**	**-3.2**	**-2.7**	**-2.6**	**-2.7**	**-2.6**	**-2.6**	**-3.0**	**-3.0**	**-3.7**	**-3.2**
Debt Held by the Public at the End of the Year	53.0	60.3	65.3	66.6	66.3	65.6	65.4	65.5	65.5	65.7	66.1	66.7	n.a.	n.a.
Memorandum:														
Gross Domestic Product (Billions of dollars)	14,236	14,595	14,992	15,730	16,676	17,606	18,421	19,223	20,036	20,823	21,667	22,544	83,425	187,719

Source: Congressional Budget Office.

Note: n.a. = not applicable.

[a] Off-budget surpluses comprise surpluses in the Social Security trust funds and the net cash flow of the Postal Service.

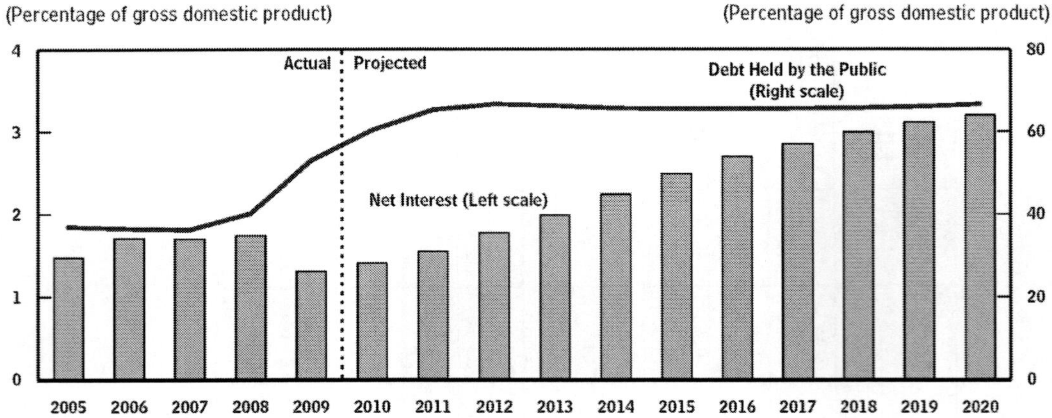

Source: Congressional Budget Office.

Summary Figure 1. Debt Held by the Public and Net Interest.

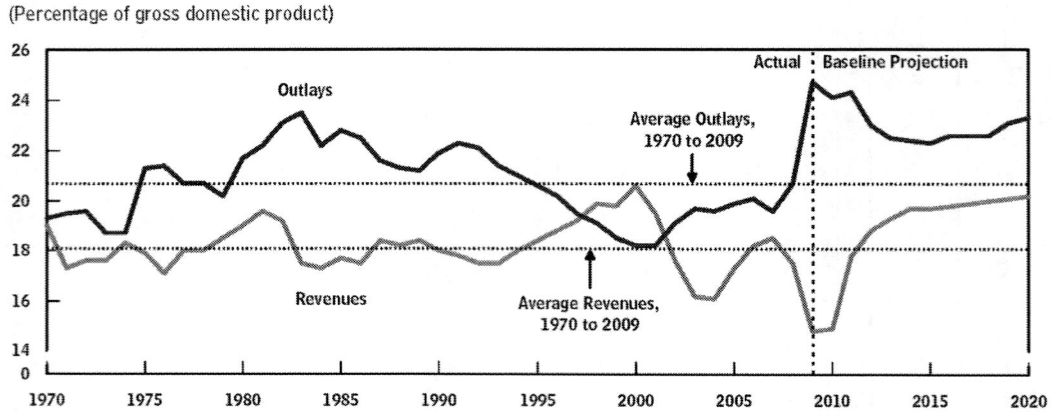

Source: Congressional Budget Office.

Summary Figure 2. Total Revenues and Outlays.

In 2011, according to CBO's baseline projections, the deficit falls to $980 billion, or 6.5 percent of GDP, as the economy improves, certain tax provisions expire as scheduled, and spending related to the economic downturn abates. Revenues are projected to rise by about $500 billion, an increase of 23 percent, while outlays are projected to increase by $126 billion, or 4 percent.

Looking beyond 2011, CBO's baseline projections show outlays remaining between 22.3 percent and 23.3 percent of GDP (compared with 24.1 percent in 2010) (see Summary Figure 2). Continued economic growth will allow payments for unemployment compensation and other benefit programs to subside, and discretionary spending is assumed to increase slowly. However, the retirement of more members of the baby-boom generation and rising health care spending per person will cause outlays for Medicare, Medicaid, and Social Security to continue to grow fairly rapidly.

The baseline projections show revenues rising to 20.2 percent of GDP by 2020 (compared with 14.9 percent in 2010), with most of the increase stemming from individual income tax receipts. Almost half of the increase in those receipts relative to the size of the economy can be attributed to the expiration of provisions originally enacted in the Economic Growth and Tax Relief Reconciliation Act of 2001, the Jobs and Growth Tax Relief Reconciliation Act of 2003, and the American Recovery and Reinvestment Act (ARRA), as well as other expiring tax provisions; the remainder is due to the economic recovery and structural features of the individual income tax system.

The Economic Outlook

Severe economic downturns often sow the seeds of robust recoveries. During a slump in economic activity, consumers defer purchases, especially for housing and durable goods, and businesses postpone capital spending and try to cut inventories. Once demand in the economy picks up, the disparity between the desired and actual stocks of capital assets and consumer durable goods widens quickly, and spending by consumers and businesses can accelerate rapidly. Although CBO expects that the current recovery will be spurred by that dynamic, in all likelihood, the recovery will also be dampened by a number of factors. Those factors include the continuing fragility of some financial markets and institutions; declining support from fiscal policy as the effects of ARRA wane and tax rates increase because of the scheduled expiration of key tax provisions; and slow wage and employment growth, as well as a large excess of vacant houses.

In CBO's forecast, real GDP increases by 2.1 percent between the fourth quarter of 2009 and the fourth quarter of 2010 and by 2.4 percent in 2011 (see Summary Table 2). Given CBO's estimate of growth in potential output, those GDP growth rates will narrow the difference between actual output and potential output (the output gap) only slightly. Growth of real GDP will accelerate after 2011, spurred by stronger business investment and residential construction. For 2012 through 2014, CBO projects that real GDP will increase by an average of 4.4percent per year, which would close the output gap completely by the end of 2014.

Even though economic activity began to increase again during the second half of 2009, the unemployment rate continued to rise, finishing the year at 10.0 percent. Hiring usually lags behind output during the initial stages of a recovery because firms tend to increase output first by boosting productivity and by raising the number of hours that existing employees work; adding employees tends to occur later. CBO expects that the unemployment rate will average slightly above 10 percent in the first half of 2010 and then turn downward in the second half of the year (see Summary Figure 3). As the economy expands further, the rate of unemployment is projected to continue declining until, in 2016, it reaches 5 percent, which is equal to CBO's estimate of the rate of unemployment consistent with the usual rate of job turnover in U.S. labor markets.

Reflecting the large amount of slack in the economy, inflation will decrease further from its already low level in 2009, CBO forecasts. The core price index for personal consumption expenditures (that is, the PCE price index excluding the prices of food and energy) will rise by about 1 percent (on a fourth-quarter-to-fourth-quarter basis) in 2010 and by 0.9 percent in 2011. The overall PCE price index will rise by 1.4 percent in 2010 and 1.1 percent in 2011.

CBO's forecast anticipates slower growth in 2010 and 2011 than does the forecast of the *Blue Chip* consensus (reflecting the views of about 50 private-sector economists). Most private forecasters probably assume that the Congress will not allow previous tax cuts to expire as scheduled. If CBO assumed, in contrast with the assumption of its baseline, that all of the expiring tax provisions were extended beyond 2010, the agency's forecast of the level of real GDP at the end of 2011 would be in line with the forecast of the *Blue Chip* consensus (although real GDP in later years would be diminished relative to the baseline projection by the greater accumulation of government debt). CBO's forecast for inflation is roughly in line with that of the *Blue Chip* consensus in 2010 but significantly lower in 2011.

Summary Table 2. CBO's Economic Projections for Calendar Years 2009 to 2020

	Estimated 2009	Forecast		Projected Annual Average	
		2010	2011	2012–2014	2015–2020
	Fourth Quarter to Fourth Quarter (Percentage change)				
Real GDP	-0.4	2.1	2.4	4.4	2.4
GDP Price Index	0.9	1.0	0.9	1.2	1.7
PCE Price Index	1.4	1.4	1.1	1.2	1.8
Core PCE Price Index[a]	1.5	1.0	0.9	1.1	1.7
Consumer Price Index[b]	1.7	1.6	1.1	1.3	1.9
Core Consumer Price Index[a]	2.0	1.1	0.9	1.2	1.9
	Calendar Year Average				
Nominal GDP					
Billions of dollars	14,253	14,706	15,116	17,816 [c]	22,770 [d]
Percentage change	-1.3	3.2	2.8	5.6	4.2
Unemployment Rate (Percent)	9.3	10.1	9.5	6.5	5.0
Interest Rates (Percent)					
Three-Month Treasury bill rate	0.1	0.2	0.7	2.9	4.6
Ten-Year Treasury note rate	3.2	3.6	3.9	4.5	5.5

Sources: Congressional Budget Office; Department of Commerce, Bureau of Economic Analysis; Department of Labor, Bureau of Labor Statistics; Federal Reserve Board.

Note: GDP = gross domestic product; PCE = personal consumption expenditure.

a. Excludes prices for food and energy.

b. The consumer price index for all urban consumers.

c. Level in 2014.

d. Level in 2020.

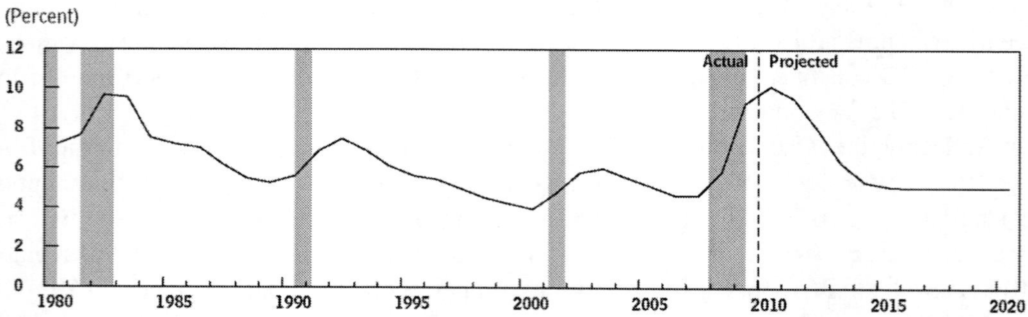

Source: Congressional Budget Office.

Summary Figure 3. Unemployment Rate.

1. THE BUDGET OUTLOOK

The Congressional Budget Office (CBO) projects that if current laws and policies remained unchanged, the federal budget would show a deficit of $1.35 trillion for fiscal year 2010 (see Table 1-1). At 9.2 percent of gross domestic product (GDP), that deficit would be slightly smaller than the shortfall of 9.9 percent of GDP posted in 2009. Last year's deficit was the largest as a share of GDP in nearly 65 years, and the deficit expected for 2010 would be the second-largest shortfall over that period. Moreover, if legislation is enacted in the next several months that either boosts spending or reduces revenues, the 2010 deficit could equal or exceed last year's shortfall.

The large 2009 and 2010 deficits reflect a combination of factors: an imbalance between revenues and spending that predates the recession and the recent turmoil in financial markets; sharply lower revenues and elevated spending associated with those economic conditions; and the costs of various federal policies implemented in response to the conditions. Such policies include the fiscal stimulus legislation enacted in February 2009; aid for the financial, housing, and automotive sectors of the economy; and the expansion and extension of unemployment insurance benefits.

CBO's estimates for 2010—and the projections that make up its 10-year budgetary baseline—reflect an assumption that no further legislation affecting the budget will be enacted. Accordingly, the projections exclude the effects of potential policy changes to spending or revenues, including any steps that lawmakers may take in the future to boost employment, provide additional funding for military operations in Afghanistan, or reform the health care system. CBO estimates that under that assumption, total outlays will change little from 2009 to 2010, but revenues will increase by 3.3 percent.

Under current law, the federal fiscal outlook beyond this year is daunting: Projected deficits average about $600 billion per year over the 2011–2020 period despite an anticipated economic recovery, albeit a slow and tentative one. (CBO's outlook for the economy is described in detail in Chapter 2.) In the baseline projections, deficits drop markedly in the next few years but remain high—at 6.5 percent of GDP in 2011 and 4.1 percent in 2012, the first full fiscal year after certain tax provisions originally enacted in 2001, 2003, and 2009 are scheduled to expire.[1] Thereafter, deficits in CBO's baseline are projected to range between 2.6 percent and 3.2 percent of GDP through 2020 (see Figure 1-1).

Those accumulating deficits will push total federal debt held by the public to significantly higher levels. In 2009, debt held by the public jumped from $5.8 trillion to $7.5 trillion. CBO projects that by the end of 2010, that figure will rise to $8.8 trillion—at 60 percent of GDP, the highest level since 1952. Under the assumptions of the baseline, federal debt is projected to continue its upward climb, reaching $15 trillion (67 percent of GDP) by the end of 2020. With such a large increase in debt, plus an expected rise in interest rates as the economic recovery strengthens, interest payments on the debt are likely to skyrocket. CBO projects that the government's annual net interest spending will more than triple between 2010 and 2020 in nominal terms (from $207 billion a year to $723 billion) and will more than double as a share of GDP (from 1.4 percent to 3.2 percent).[2]

Table 1-1. Projected Deficits and Surpluses in CBO's Baseline

(Billions of dollars)	Actual 2009	2010	2011	2012	2013	2014	2015	2016	2017	2018	2019	2020	Total, 2011-2015	Total, 2011-2020
On-Budget Deficit	-1,551	-1,434	-1,076	-757	-659	-608	-619	-659	-659	-669	-765	-793	-3,719	-7,263
Off-Budget Surplus[a]	137	86	96	108	120	133	139	138	134	127	116	107	595	1,216
Total Deficit	**-1,414**	**-1,349**	**-980**	**-650**	**-539**	**-475**	**-480**	**-521**	**-525**	**-542**	**-649**	**-687**	**-3,124**	**-6,047**
Memorandum:														
Total Deficit as a Percentage of GDP	-9.9	-9.2	-6.5	-4.1	-3.2	-2.7	-2.6	-2.7	-2.6	-2.6	-3.0	-3.0	-3.7	-3.2
Debt Held by the Public as a Percentage of GDP[b]	53.0	60.3	65.3	66.6	66.3	65.6	65.4	65.5	65.5	65.7	66.1	66.7	n.a.	n.a.

Source: Congressional Budget Office.

Note: GDP = gross domestic product; n.a. = not applicable.

[a] Off-budget surpluses comprise surpluses in the Social Security trust funds and the net cash flow of the Postal Service.

[b] Debt held at the end of the year.

CBO's baseline projections are not intended to be a forecast of future budgetary outcomes; rather they serve as a neutral benchmark that legislators and others can use to assess the potential effects of policy decisions. Under the current-law assumptions of the baseline, various tax provisions are assumed to expire as scheduled, boosting revenues substantially. Similarly, the baseline projections reflect the assumption that cuts in Medicare's payments for physicians' services will occur as scheduled under current law. In addition, spending for discretionary programs is generally assumed to continue at the levels most recently enacted by the Congress, with annual adjustments only for inflation.

Future discretionary appropriations are likely to differ from the amounts assumed in the baseline, and lawmakers will almost certainly enact changes to spending and tax policies. Although CBO's baseline does not incorporate such potential changes, this chapter shows how some alternative policy assumptions would affect the budget over the next 10 years. For example, if all of the tax provisions that are set to expire in the coming decade were extended and the alternative minimum tax (AMT) was indexed for inflation, annual revenues would average 16 percent of GDP through 2020 rather than the 19.5 percent projected in the baseline, and the total deficit for the 2011–2020 period would be more than $7 trillion higher. Under that scenario, the deficits from 2011 to 2020 would average about 7 percent of GDP, and debt held by the public would reach 98 percent of GDP by the end of 2020, the highest level since 1946. In the other direction, if funding for the wars in Iraq and Afghanistan and related activities was assumed to fall rapidly through 2013 rather than grow at the rate of inflation, the total deficit for the 2011–2020 period would be $1.1 trillion lower than the amount projected in the baseline.

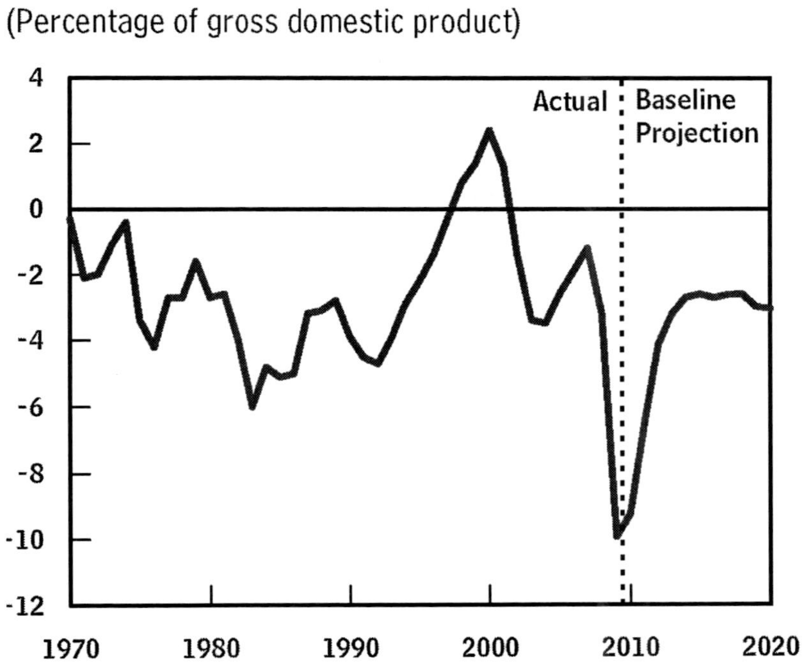

Source: Congressional Budget Office.

Figure 1-1. The Total Deficit or Surplus, 1970 to 2020.

Throughout the coming decade, spending on the government's health care and retirement programs will increasingly strain the federal budget. In CBO's baseline, outlays for Medicare and Medicaid (excluding funding provided by the 2009 stimulus legislation) are projected to increase at an average rate of about 7 percent a year between 2011 and 2020. Moreover, as growing numbers of baby boom-ers become eligible for Social Security retirement benefits, costs for that program will rise significantly. Although low inflation will restrain Social Security's growth in the short term, future cost-of-living adjustments to benefits and increases in the number of beneficiaries will help boost the annual growth rate of Social Security spending from just over 3 percent this year to an estimated 6 percent in 2020.

Those trends will accelerate after the 10-year projection period. Under current law, federal health care costs are likely to keep growing faster than GDP—as they have for the past 40 years. In addition, the share of the population age 65 or older will continue to expand rapidly. As a consequence, the growth of spending for Medicare, Medicaid, and Social Security will speed up from its already rapid rate. To keep annual deficits and total federal debt from reaching levels that would substantially harm the economy, lawmakers would have to increase revenues significantly as a percentage of GDP, decrease projected spending sharply, or enact some combination of the two.[3]

A Review of 2009

The budget deficit surged to $1.4 trillion in 2009, the largest shortfall on record in dollar terms and nearly $1trillion greater than the deficit recorded the previous year. As a percentage of GDP, the deficit more than tripled in 2009 to 9.9 percent, its highest level since the end of World War II. Revenues fell to their lowest level as a percentage of GDP since 1950 (14.8 percent), and outlays climbed to their highest share of GDP since 1946 (24.7percent).

Revenues in 2009

Last year, every major category of revenues declined (see Table 1-2). As a result, total revenues plunged by 17 percent, or nearly $420 billion, to $2.1 trillion.

The deep recession that began in December 2007 caused substantial drops in corporate profits and taxable personal income. Consequently, receipts from corporate income taxes fell by 55 percent ($166 billion) in 2009, and receipts from individual income taxes declined by 20 percent ($230 billion). Even revenues from social insurance taxes (primarily the payroll taxes for Social Security and Medicare) decreased by 1 percent ($9 billion), the first decline since 1946.

Revenues from the remaining, smaller, sources fell by almost 8 percent ($14 billion) in 2009, following an average annual increase of nearly 3 percent over the preceding 10 years. Declines in receipts from excise taxes, estate and gift taxes, and customs duties were only slightly offset by small increases in the amount of money that the Federal Reserve System remitted to the Treasury and in receipts from miscellaneous fees and fines. The declines in those taxes and duties resulted from the recession, decreases in wealth, and a jump in excise tax credits taken for alcohol-fuel mixtures. (For more details about past and future revenues, see Chapter 4.)

Table 1-2. Average Annual Rates of Growth in Revenues and Outlays since 1999 and as Projected in CBO's Baseline

(Percent)	Actual		Projected[a]		
	1999–2008	2009	2010	2011	2012–2020
Revenues					
Individual income taxes	3.3	-20.1	3.3	33.0	7.7
Corporate income taxes	4.9	-54.6	6.1	81.6	5.1
Social insurance taxes	4.6	-1.0	-1.4	6.4	4.7
Other revenues[b]	2.7	-7.8	27.5	3.1	3.3
Total Revenues	**3.9**	**-16.6**	**3.3**	**22.7**	**6.1**
Outlays					
Mandatory[c]	6.4	31.3	-7.1	5.1	4.4
Discretionary	7.5	9.0	10.9	*	1.1
Net interest	0.5	-25.9	10.3	13.0	13.4
Total Outlays	**6.1**	**18.0**	**0.2**	**3.6**	**4.1**
Total Outlays Excluding Net Interest	**6.8**	**22.0**	**-0.4**	**3.0**	**3.2**
Memorandum:					
Consumer Price Index	2.8	-0.3	2.4	1.4	1.7
Nominal Gross Domestic Product	5.2	-1.4	2.5	2.7	4.6

Source: Congressional Budget Office.

Note: * = between -0.05 percent and zero.

a. When constructing its baseline, CBO uses the employment cost index for wages and salaries to inflate discretionary spending related to federal personnel and the gross domestic product price index to adjust other discretionary spending.

b. Includes excise taxes, estate and gift taxes, customs duties, and miscellaneous receipts.

c. Includes offsetting receipts (funds collected by government agencies from other government accounts or from the public in businesslike or market-oriented transactions that are recorded as offsets to outlays).

Outlays in 2009

Federal spending rose even faster last year than revenues fell—by 18 percent ($536 billion), to a total of $3.5 trillion. That rate of increase was nearly three times the average growth rate of federal outlays over the previous 10 years (see Table 1-2).

Mandatory Outlays. Much of the rise in outlays in 2009 came from mandatory programs. After growing by an average of about 6 percent a year from 1999 to 2008, mandatory spending (excluding net interest) soared by 31percent ($499 billion) last year, to $2.1 trillion. Three initiatives accounted for nearly two-thirds of that increase. Outlays recorded for the Troubled Asset Relief Program (TARP) totaled $152 billion in 2009; net payments to Fannie Mae and Freddie Mac accounted for another $91 billion; and fiscal stimulus legislation, the American Recovery and Reinvestment Act of 2009 (ARRA), increased mandatory outlays by $80 billion (largely for Medicaid, unemployment benefits, payments to Social Security beneficiaries, and supplemental nutrition assistance).

Outlays for Social Security, Medicaid, and Medicare grew at a combined rate of 13 percent (or by $154 billion) in 2009, with nearly one-third of the increase coming from ARRA funding. With that stimulus funding excluded, Social Security outlays rose by 9 percent ($53 billion) last year, primarily because the 5.8 percent cost-of-living adjustment that took effect in January 2009 was the largest annual adjustment since 1982. Medicaid spending (excluding stimulus funding) increased by 9 percent ($18billion) in 2009—exceeding its 7 percent average annual growth rate of the previous 10 years—largely because higher unemployment boosted enrollment in the program. Medicare outlays (including an offset for premium payments) also rose at a faster rate than the average of the past decade, growing by 10 percent ($39 billion).

In addition, payments for unemployment benefits rose by $76 billion in 2009, pushing outlays for that program to more than double the level recorded in 2008. The jump was caused by substantially higher unemployment as well as increased and extended benefits to unemployed workers ($27 billion from ARRA and $17 billion from other legislation). As a whole, all other mandatory spending rose by 5 percent ($17 billion) in 2009. (For a more detailed discussion of spending programs, see Chapter 3.)

Discretionary Outlays. On the discretionary side of the budget, outlays grew last year by 9 percent ($102 billion). Spending for defense rose by a total of $43 billion; of that increase, $15 billion was for operations and maintenance (which grew by 6 percent), $12 billion was for procurement (which grew by 10 percent), and $7 billion was for personnel (which grew by 6 percent). CBO estimates that roughly one-third of the total increase in discretionary outlays for defense in 2009 was associated with military operations in Iraq and Afghanistan. (Funding for those operations is discussed in more detail in Box1-1.)

Nondefense discretionary outlays rose by $59 billion in 2009. Slightly more than half of that increase resulted from funding that lawmakers provided in ARRA. The new State Fiscal Stabilization Fund (which provides money to state and local governments, primarily for their education expenses) spent more than $12 billion in 2009. Additional ARRA funding boosted outlays for student financial aid by more than $6 billion. Outlays for ground transportation programs rose by a total of $7 billion in 2009, with $3 billion of the increase coming from ARRA funds. (For a detailed breakdown of ARRA spending in 2009 and projections for 2010 through 2020, see AppendixA.)

Some other categories of discretionary spending saw large increases in outlays unrelated to stimulus funding. They included veterans' affairs (which increased by $6 billion, primarily for medical care) and international affairs (which rose by $5 billion, primarily for global health programs and international peacekeeping).

Net Interest. Partly offsetting those increases in outlays, net interest payments declined by 26 percent ($65 billion) last year, despite the fact that federal debt held by the public grew by $1.7 trillion. The government's net interest spending fell mainly because of lower short-term interest rates and lower costs for inflation-indexed securities.

CBO's Baseline Projections for 2010

Under the assumptions of CBO's baseline, the budget deficit will decline in 2010 by $65 billion (or by 0.7 percent of GDP). Total outlays are projected to remain virtually the same as last year, increasing by just $5 billion, and revenues are projected to rise by $70 billion (see Table 1-3).

Given the economic and financial turmoil that existed in 2009 and the improvement anticipated for 2010, why is the deficit projected for this year not significantly smaller? The short answer is that an expected decline in federal aid to the financial sector in 2010 will be offset by increases in other outlays—particularly spending from last year's stimulus legislation; outlays for income support programs, health care programs, and Social Security; and net interest spending. At the same time, revenues are expected to increase only modestly this year, primarily because of the slow projected pace of the economic recovery and the lagged effect of the recession on revenues.

Revenues in 2010

Under the assumption that current laws and policies remain unchanged, revenues are projected to rise by $70 billion, or roughly 3 percent, in 2010. Relative to the size of the economy, the increase is slight: from 14.8 percent of GDP in 2009 to 14.9 percent in 2010. More than $40 billion of the projected rise in revenues this year stems from remittances to the Treasury by the Federal Reserve System, which are expected to increase sharply as a result of the Federal Reserve's recent actions to support the economy. Together, receipts from individual income taxes and social insurance taxes will grow by $18 billion in 2010, and receipts from corporate income taxes will rise by $9 billion. With remittances from the Federal Reserve excluded, projected revenues increase by only 1 percent.

Outlays in 2010

Because the financial system is stabilizing, CBO anticipates that the federal outlays recorded for programs to aid that sector of the economy will fall in 2010. Many financial institutions that received federal assistance through the TARP have already repaid their funding, and it appears that the program will not use the full $700 billion authority it was originally granted to buy so-called troubled assets. As a result, total outlays over the life of the program are now expected to be substantially lower than previously anticipated. Because of those lower costs, CBO estimates that outlays for the TARP will be $218 billion lower in 2010 than they were last year. In addition, net spending on federal deposit insurance is expected to drop by $27 billion this year. And although the housing sector remains weak, CBO estimates that outlays for Fannie Mae and Freddie Mac will be lower as well.[4]

Spending in other areas, however, is expected to rise noticeably in 2010. In particular, outlays resulting from ARRA will grow by $112 billion as more of the funding provided in the legislation is spent. Furthermore, outlays (excluding ARRA spending) for unemployment compensation are expected to continue growing from their record level of 2009 because of the lagged effect of the recession on unemployment and because of legislation extending emergency benefits. As a result, outlays for regular unemployment benefits will increase from $75 billion last year to $82 billion this year, CBO projects, and emergency benefits will boost spending in 2010 by another $3 billion. Excluding the effects of ARRA, outlays for the Supplemental Nutrition Assistance Program will rise from $51 billion in 2009 to $60 billion in 2010 as a result of increased enrollment.

Box 1-1. Funding for Operations in Iraq and Afghanistan and for Related Activities

Since September 2001, lawmakers have provided a total of nearly $1.1 trillion in budget authority for operations in Iraq and Afghanistan and related activities. That amount includes funding for military and diplomatic operations in Iraq, Afghanistan, and other regions; for some veterans' benefits and services; and for related activities of the Department of Justice (see the table at right). Appropriations specifically designated for those activities averaged about $100 billion a year from 2003 through 2006, rose to $187 billion in 2008, and then declined to $155 billion last year. So far, lawmakers have appropriated $130 billion for such activities for 2010, although further appropriations may be needed later this year as a result of the Administration's decision to increase U.S. forces in Afghanistan.

Estimated Appropriations Provided for U.S. Operations in Iraq and Afghanistan and for Other War-Related Activities, 2001 to 2010 (Billions of dollars of budget authority)

	2001	2002	2003	2004	2005	2006	2007	2008	2009	2010	Total, 2001-2010
Military Operations and Other Defense Activities											
Iraq[a]	0	0	46	68	53	89	113	134	91	61	654
Afghanistan and other[b]	14	18	34	21	18	22	39	42	49	63	319
Subtotal	**14**	**18**	**80**	**88**	**71**	**111**	**152**	**175**	**140**	**123**	**973**
Indigenous Security Forces[c]											
Iraq	0	0	0	5	5	3	6	3	1	0	23
Afghanistan	0	0	0	0	1	2	7	3	6	7	26
Subtotal	**0**	**0**	**0**	**5**	**7**	**5**	**13**	**6**	**7**	**7**	**49**
Diplomatic Operations and Foreign Aid[d]											
Iraq	0	0	3	15	1	3	3	2	2	0	29
Other	*	2	5	2	2	1	2	2	6	0	21
Subtotal	*	**2**	**8**	**17**	**3**	**4**	**5**	**4**	**8**	**0**	**51**
Other Services and Activities[e]											
Iraq	0	0	0	0	*	*	1	1	*	0	2
Other	0	0	0	0	*	*	*	*	*	0	1
Subtotal	**0**	**0**	**0**	**0**	*	*	**1**	**2**	*	**0**	**2**
Total Budget Authority[f]	**14**	**19**	**88**	**111**	**81**	**120**	**171**	**187**	**155**	**130**	**1,075**

Source: Congressional Budget Office.

Note: * = between zero and $500 million.

a. CBO estimated funding provided for Operation Iraqi Freedom by allocating funds on the basis of information in budget justification materials from the Department of Defense and in monthly reports on its obligations.

[b] Includes Operation Enduring Freedom (in and around Afghanistan), Operation Noble Eagle (homeland security missions, such as combat air patrols, in the United States), the restructuring of Army and Marine Corps units, classified activities other than those funded by appropriations for the Iraq Freedom Fund, efforts to increase the size of the Army and Marine Corps, and other operations. (For 2005 through 2009, funding for Operation Noble Eagle has been intermingled with regular appropriations for the Department of Defense; that funding is not included in this table.)

[c] Funding for indigenous security forces—which was appropriated in accounts for diplomatic operations and foreign aid (budget function 150) in 2004 and in accounts for defense (budget function 050) since 2005—is used to train and equip local military and police units in Iraq and Afghanistan.

[d] In 2010, funding for diplomatic operations in, and foreign aid to, countries assisting the United States in fighting terrorism is in regular appropriations and cannot be separated from appropriations for activities unrelated to those operations.

[e] Includes funding for some veterans' benefits and services and for certain activities of the Department of Justice. Excludes about $5 billion in spending by the Department of Veterans Affairs (VA) for medical care, disability compensation, and survivor benefits for veterans of operations in Iraq and Afghanistan and related activities that CBO estimates has been spent from regular appropriations for the VA but was not explicitly appropriated for war-related expenses.

[f] The appropriations for 2010 shown here were considered by the House and Senate before the President announced that the number of U.S. troops in Afghanistan would increase. Additional appropriations may be provided for 2010.

Of the nearly $1.1 trillion in budget authority provided between 2001 and 2010, funding for military operations and related defense activities totals $973 billion, most of which has gone to the Department of Defense (DoD). Lawmakers have also provided more than $49 billion to train and equip indigenous security forces in Iraq and Afghanistan.[1] Thus, a total of $1,022 billion has been appropriated since September 2001 for military operations in Iraq and Afghanistan and for other war-related activities. In addition, $51 billion has been provided for diplomatic activities and aid to Iraq, Afghanistan, and various countries that are assisting the United States in fighting terrorism.

DoD reports that in 2009, obligations for operations in Iraq and Afghanistan and related activities averaged slightly more than $11 billion per month—about $2 billion less than the monthly average in 2008. Operation Iraqi Freedom accounted for about 65 percent of those obligations (down from 80 percent in 2008 and 85 percent in 2007). Operation Enduring Freedom (in and around Afghanistan) accounted for another 35 percent in 2009. Additional security missions that have taken place in the United States since the terrorist attacks of September 11, 2001—such as combat air patrols over Washington, D.C., and New York City, known as Operation Noble Eagle—accounted for less than 1 percent in 2009.

Because most appropriations for operations in Iraq and Afghanistan and for related activities appear in the same budget accounts as appropriations for DoD's other functions, it is impossible to determine precisely how much of the funding provided for those activities has actually been spent. The Congressional Budget Office (CBO) estimates that budget authority for military operations in Iraq and Afghanistan and for related defense activities resulted in outlays of about $730 billion through 2009 ($155 billion of which occurred in 2009). Of the budget authority appropriated for international affairs activities related to the war efforts, about $40 billion was spent through 2009 ($5 billion in 2009), CBO estimates. In all, outlays for operations in Iraq and Afghanistan amounted to about $160 billion last year. On the basis of appropriations to date, outlays in 2010 could total roughly $165 billion, in CBO's estimation, although outlays will be higher if further appropriations for war-related activities are provided later in the year.

[1.] The $49 billion includes $5 billion provided for Iraqi security forces in 2004 in an appropriation for the State Department's Iraq Relief and Reconstruction Fund.

Spending for Social Security, Medicare, and Medicaid (excluding outlays resulting from ARRA funding) will continue to grow faster than the economy as a whole, rising by $78 billion, or nearly 6 percent, this year for the three programs combined. In addition, outlays for retirement, disability, and education benefits for veterans will grow by $8 billion, or 16 percent. Together, outlays for all other mandatory programs are projected to increase by $14 billion, or 6 percent, in 2010.

Discretionary outlays (excluding those stemming from ARRA) are projected to grow by $67 billion, or about 6 percent. Nondefense discretionary outlays rise by nearly 7 percent, slightly above their average growth rate of the previous 10 years, whereas defense outlays increase by less than 5 percent, well below their average growth rate over the past decade. Outlays for net interest (excluding the effects of ARRA) are expected to be $16 billion higher this year than last year, largely because of additional government borrowing.

Because of the rules that govern CBO's baseline, the projections for 2010 may omit a significant amount of spending that will occur if other legislation is enacted during the remainder of the fiscal year. Under current law, emergency unemployment benefits will not be available to people who exhaust their regular benefits after February. Such benefits have been extended or enhanced regularly since they were first enacted in June 2008, and they could be continued again. Similarly, fees paid for physicians' services under Medicare are scheduled to be reduced by 21 percent beginning in March, although cuts in such payments have been delayed several times in the past. Moreover, additional funding for the war in Afghanistan may be provided to support the troop increase there. Whether any such increases in spending will be offset by reductions elsewhere in the budget is uncertain.

CBO's Baseline Projections for 2011 to 2020

If various tax provisions enacted in the past decade expire as scheduled and other spending and revenue policies are also unchanged, the budget deficit will fall from 9.2 percent of GDP this year to 3.2 percent by 2013, CBO projects. That drop in baseline deficits occurs because the expiration of those tax provisions will boost revenues substantially, the economy is expected to improve, and spending related to the economic downturn will abate. Thereafter, the deficit is projected to remain between 2.6 percent and 3.0 percent of GDP each year through 2020 (see Table 1-3). By comparison, the deficit has averaged 2.6 percent of GDP over the past 40 years.

Table 1-3. CBO's Baseline Budget Projections

	Actual 2009	2010	2011	2012	2013	2014	2015	2016	2017	2018	2019	2020	Total, 2011-2015	Total, 2011-2020
	In Billions of Dollars													
Revenues														
Individual income taxes	915	946	1,258	1,434	1,595	1,729	1,854	1,969	2,091	2,199	2,316	2,448	7,870	18,894
Corporate income taxes	138	147	266	318	350	394	365	387	393	401	403	416	1,693	3,693
Social insurance taxes	891	878	934	993	1,056	1,115	1,165	1,212	1,260	1,310	1,361	1,416	5,263	11,822
Other revenues	160	204	211	219	218	227	241	246	252	261	271	282	1,115	2,427
Total Revenues	**2,105**	**2,175**	**2,670**	**2,964**	**3,218**	**3,465**	**3,625**	**3,814**	**3,996**	**4,170**	**4,352**	**4,563**	**15,941**	**36,836**
On-budget	1,451	1,533	1,997	2,253	2,463	2,668	2,789	2,943	3,088	3,225	3,369	3,539	12,170	28,335
Off-budget	654	642	673	711	754	797	836	871	908	945	982	1,024	3,771	8,501
Outlays														
Mandatory spending	2,094	1,946	2,045	1,989	2,077	2,188	2,272	2,414	2,524	2,638	2,838	3,008	10,572	23,994
Discretionary spending	1,237	1,371	1,371	1,344	1,346	1,357	1,373	1,402	1,426	1,450	1,486	1,518	6,792	14,074
Net interest	187	207	233	280	333	396	459	519	572	624	676	723	1,701	4,816
Total Outlays	**3,518**	**3,524**	**3,650**	**3,613**	**3,756**	**3,940**	**4,105**	**4,335**	**4,521**	**4,712**	**5,000**	**5,250**	**19,065**	**42,883**
On-budget	3,001	2,968	3,073	3,010	3,122	3,276	3,409	3,602	3,747	3,894	4,134	4,332	15,889	35,598
Off-budget	517	556	577	603	634	665	697	733	774	818	866	917	3,176	7,285
Deficit (-) or Surplus	**-1,414**	**-1,349**	**-980**	**-650**	**-539**	**-475**	**-480**	**-521**	**-525**	**-542**	**-649**	**-687**	**-3,124**	**-6,047**
On-budget	-1,551	-1,434	-1,076	-757	-659	-608	-619	-659	-659	-669	-765	-793	-3,719	-7,263
Off-budget	137	86	96	108	120	133	139	138	134	127	116	107	595	1,216
Debt Held by the Public	7,544	8,797	9,785	10,479	11,056	11,556	12,055	12,595	13,133	13,678	14,329	15,027	n.a.	n.a.
Memorandum:														
Gross Domestic Product	14,236	14,595	14,992	15,730	16,676	17,606	18,421	19,223	20,036	20,823	21,667	22,544	83,425	187,719

Table 1-3. (Continued)

	Actual 2009	2010	2011	2012	2013	2014	2015	2016	2017	2018	2019	2020	Total, 2011-2015	Total, 2011-2020
	As a Percentage of Gross Domestic Product													
Revenues														
Individual income taxes	6.4	6.5	8.4	9.1	9.6	9.8	10.1	10.2	10.4	10.6	10.7	10.9	9.4	10.1
Corporate income taxes	1.0	1.0	1.8	2.0	2.1	2.2	2.0	2.0	2.0	1.9	1.9	1.8	2.0	2.0
Social insurance taxes	6.3	6.0	6.2	6.3	6.3	6.3	6.3	6.3	6.3	6.3	6.3	6.3	6.3	6.3
Other revenues	1.1	1.4	1.4	1.4	1.3	1.3	1.3	1.3	1.3	1.3	1.3	1.3	1.3	1.3
Total Revenues	**14.8**	**14.9**	**17.8**	**18.8**	**19.3**	**19.7**	**19.7**	**19.8**	**19.9**	**20.0**	**20.1**	**20.2**	**19.1**	**19.6**
On-budget	10.2	10.5	13.3	14.3	14.8	15.2	15.1	15.3	15.4	15.5	15.6	15.7	14.6	15.1
Off-budget	4.6	4.4	4.5	4.5	4.5	4.5	4.5	4.5	4.5	4.5	4.5	4.5	4.5	4.5
Outlays														
Mandatory spending	14.7	13.3	13.6	12.6	12.5	12.4	12.3	12.6	12.6	12.7	13.1	13.3	12.7	12.8
Discretionary spending	8.7	9.4	9.1	8.5	8.1	7.7	7.5	7.3	7.1	7.0	6.9	6.7	8.1	7.5
Net interest	1.3	1.4	1.6	1.8	2.0	2.2	2.5	2.7	2.9	3.0	3.1	3.2	2.0	2.6
Total Outlays	**24.7**	**24.1**	**24.3**	**23.0**	**22.5**	**22.4**	**22.3**	**22.6**	**22.6**	**22.6**	**23.1**	**23.3**	**22.9**	**22.8**
On-budget	21.1	20.3	20.5	19.1	18.7	18.6	18.5	18.7	18.7	18.7	19.1	19.2	19.0	19.0
Off-budget	3.6	3.8	3.8	3.8	3.8	3.8	3.8	3.8	3.9	3.9	4.0	4.1	3.8	3.9
Deficit (-) or Surplus	**-9.9**	**-9.2**	**-6.5**	**-4.1**	**-3.2**	**-2.7**	**-2.6**	**-2.7**	**-2.6**	**-2.6**	**-3.0**	**-3.0**	**-3.7**	**-3.2**
On-budget	-10.9	-9.8	-7.2	-4.8	-3.9	-3.5	-3.4	-3.4	-3.3	-3.2	-3.5	-3.5	-4.5	-3.9
Off-budget	1.0	0.6	0.6	0.7	0.7	0.8	0.8	0.7	0.7	0.6	0.5	0.5	0.7	0.6
Debt Held by the Public	53.0	60.3	65.3	66.6	66.3	65.6	65.4	65.5	65.5	65.7	66.1	66.7	n.a.	n.a.

Source: Congressional Budget Office.

Note: n.a. = not applicable.

Revenues in the 2011–2020 Period

Revenues jump substantially in 2011 and 2012 in CBO's -baseline projections as a number of tax provisions enacted in the past decade expire as scheduled and the economic recovery continues. Under those assumptions, revenues would rise by 23 percent next year and by another 11 percent in 2012, CBO projects. At that point, revenues would equal 18.8 percent of GDP, 3.9 percentage points higher than in 2010.

The effects of expiring tax provisions account for about two-thirds of the projected increase in revenues relative to GDP over the next two years. The rest of the increase stems largely from the effects of continued improvement in economic conditions. CBO expects that as economic activity accelerates and prices of financial assets rise, wages and salaries, corporate profits, and other taxable income will grow more rapidly than GDP. Other factors, related to the timing of tax payments, will also help to raise revenues.

In the baseline, revenues edge up each year as a percentage of GDP from 2013 through the end of the projection period, reaching 20.2 percent in 2020. Virtually all of that increase comes from growth in individual income tax receipts, mainly because the structure of the income tax tends to cause revenues to rise faster than GDP over time.

Outlays in the 2011–2020 Period

CBO constructs its baseline in accordance with the provisions set forth in the (now expired) Balanced Budget and Emergency Deficit Control Act of 1985 and the Congressional Budget and Impoundment Control Act of 1974. Under the Deficit Control Act, projections for most mandatory programs assume that present laws continue unchanged.[5] Thus, CBO's baseline projections for mandatory programs reflect expected changes in the economy, demographics, and other factors that affect the implementation of laws that govern those programs. For discretionary spending, the baseline assumes that the most recent year's budget authority, including any supplemental appropriations, is provided in each future year, with adjustments for projected inflation (as measured by specified indexes) and certain other factors. Using that methodology, CBO projects that total outlays will remain relatively stable as a share of GDP over the next decade, ranging between 22.3 percent and 24.3 percent—well above the average of 20.7 percent of GDP over the past 40 years.

Mandatory spending (including offsetting receipts) is projected to grow by slightly more than 5 percent in 2011 and then decrease by nearly 3 percent the following year, in part because of a shift in the timing of certain benefit payments from 2012 into 2011. Without that shift, outlays would increase by less than 4 percent in 2011 and remain essentially flat in 2012 as spending from ARRA dropped markedly. For the rest of the baseline period, mandatory spending is projected to grow at an average rate of about 5 percent annually, ending the decade at 13.3 percent of GDP, similar to the level projected for this year.

Under the assumptions of the baseline, discretionary outlays are projected to decline over the next two years, to 8.5 percent of GDP in 2012 (slightly below the 2009 level). Thereafter, because discretionary budget authority is assumed simply to keep pace with expected inflation, outlays are projected to grow at an average rate of 1.5 percent a year through 2020 (less than one-third the projected growth rate of nominal GDP). In stark contrast to that baseline projection, actual discretionary spending grew by an average of 7.5 percent a year between 1999 and 2008.

Table 1-4. Changes in CBO's Baseline Projections of the Deficit Since August 2009

(Billions of dollars)	2010	2011	2012	2013	2014	2015	2016	2017	2018	2019	Total, 2010-2014	Total, 2010-2019
Total Deficit as Projected in August 2009	-1,381	-921	-590	-538	-558	-558	-620	-626	-622	-722	-3,988	-7,137
Changes												
Legislative												
Revenues	-44	4	7	8	26	-14	5	5	3	1	1	*
Outlays[a]	31	10	2	-2	-7	-8	-9	-10	-11	-10	34	-15
Subtotal, legislative	-75	-6	5	10	33	-5	14	15	14	11	-33	16
Economic												
Revenues	51	46	25	30	62	76	79	81	75	74	214	598
Outlays[a]	-5	-1	5	-5	-12	-11	-9	-2	2	10	-18	-28
Subtotal, economic	56	47	21	35	74	87	88	83	73	63	233	626
Technical												
Revenues	-96	-97	-79	-41	-25	-15	-7	3	12	17	-338	-327
Outlays[a]	-147	3	7	4	-2	-11	-4	*	18	18	-134	-113
Subtotal, technical	51	-100	-86	-45	-23	-3	-3	3	-6	-1	-204	-214
Total Effect on the Deficit[b]	32	-59	-60	*	83	78	99	100	80	74	-4	427
Total Deficit as Projected in January 2010	-1,349	-980	-650	-539	-475	-480	-521	-525	-542	-649	-3,992	-6,709

Source: Congressional Budget Office.

Notes: More details about changes in CBO's projections since August 2009 are presented in Appendix B.

* = between -$500 million and $500 million.

a. Includes net interest payments.

b. Negative numbers represent an increase in the deficit; positive numbers represent a decrease in the deficit.

Changes in CBO's Baseline since August 2009

CBO's current estimate of the deficit for 2010 is slightly smaller—by $32 billion, or 2.3 percent—than the one it published in August in *The Budget and Economic Outlook: An Update* (see Table 1-4). Both the outlay and revenue projections for this year have been reduced since August, by $121 billion and $89 billion, respectively. The largest change to projected outlays is a $147 billion decrease in the estimated cost of the Troubled Asset Relief Program. (For more details about recent changes in the TARP, see Box 1-2.) Revenue projections for this year have been reduced mainly because recent receipts from individual and corporate income taxes have been smaller than expected.

Since August, CBO has also pared $427 billion from its baseline projection of the total deficit for the 2010–2019 period. Changes in CBO's outlook for the economy (discussed in detail in Chapter 2) more than account for that improvement in the bottom line, reducing the projected 2010–2019 deficit by $626 billion, on net:

- Economic changes, particularly higher projections of growth in corporate profits and wages and salaries, have added $598 billion to baseline revenues over that 10-year period.
- Lower anticipated interest rates and other revisions to the economic outlook have caused CBO to reduce its estimate of net interest payments through 2019 by $415 billion.
- In the other direction, higher estimates of inflation, increases in projected unemployment rates, and other economic changes have boosted estimates for outlays other than net interest spending by a total of $388 billion.

New legislation enacted since August has had only a small effect on the budget outlook, cutting $16 billion from the total deficit projected for the 2010–2019 period.

Technical factors (things not directly related to new legislation or revisions to the economic outlook) have increased the projected 10-year deficit by $214 billion. On the revenue side, lower-than-expected income tax receipts in recent months and other factors have reduced revenue projections, primarily for the early years of the projection period. Together, those technical factors decrease projected revenues by $327 billion over 10 years. At the same time, technical changes have reduced outlay projections—mostly for net interest payments and the TARP—by $113 billion over the 2010–2019 period. (Changes to CBO's baseline projections since August are described in greater detail in AppendixB.)

Uncertainty and Budget Projections

Actual budgetary outcomes will almost certainly differ from CBO's baseline projections because of future legislative actions, unanticipated changes in economic conditions, and many other factors that affect federal spending and revenues. The full range of potential changes is impossible to determine. However, examining some potential changes shows how sensitive CBO's current-law projections are to changes in the assumptions underlying them.

BOX 1-2. RECENT ACTIVITY IN THE TROUBLED ASSET RELIEF PROGRAM

Much has changed over the past few months in the Troubled Asset Relief Program (TARP). Many institutions have left the program sooner than expected, certain initiatives have gotten off to a slow start or been reduced in scope, and some efforts have been abandoned. As a result, it appears that the costs of the program will be much lower than initially expected.

The largest part of the TARP was the Capital Purchase Program, which gave direct support to financial institutions by purchasing preferred stock from them. That program has now been completed, having disbursed $205 billion over the previous 14 months (see the table at right). As of the end of December 2009, seven of the eight original recipients had repurchased their preferred stock; the only exception was Citi-group, which converted its preferred shares to common stock. Nearly $85 billion of the total disbursements under that initiative remain outstanding.

CBO's Baseline Estimates of Federal Funding for the TARP (As of mid-December 2009) (Billions of dollars)

	Amount Disbursed or Committed	Maximum Assumed To Be Used	Cost or Earnings (-) Over the Life of the Program
Capital Purchase Program	205	84 [a]	-3
Additional Assistance to Citigroup			
Targeted Investment Program	20	0	-2
Citigroup asset guarantee	5	5	*
Subtotal	25	5	-2
Additional Assistance to Bank of America			
Targeted Investment Program	20	0	-1
Bank of America asset guarantee	0	0	*
Subtotal	20	0	-2
Assistance to American International Group	70	70	9
Assistance to the Automotive Industry	81	79 [a]	47
Term Asset-Backed Securities Loan Facility	20	20	1
Public-Private Investment Program	30	30	3
Home Affordable Modification Program	50	20	20
Remaining TARP Funds[b]	198	50	25
Total[c]	**699**	**357**	**99**

Sources: Congressional Budget Office; Department of the Treasury.

Notes: The legislation that created the Troubled Asset Relief Program (TARP) requires that the federal budget display the costs of purchasing or insuring troubled assets using procedures similar to those specified in the Federal Credit Reform Act but adjusting for market risk (in a manner not reflected in that law). In particular, the federal budget should not record the gross cash disbursement for the purchase of a troubled asset (or the cash receipt for its eventual sale); instead, the number recorded in the budget should reflect an estimate of the government's net cost for the purchase. Broadly speaking, the net cost is the purchase price minus the present value (calculated using an appropriate discount factor that reflects the riskiness of the asset) of any estimated future earnings from holding the asset and the proceeds from the eventual sale of the asset.

CBO's January 2010 baseline was completed in mid-December 2009; after that, the Treasury disbursed another $3.8 billion to GMAC (the financing arm of General Motors) and converted some previous purchases of GMAC's preferred stock to common stock.

* = between -$500 million and zero.

[a] Amount outstanding as of mid-December 2009.

[b] Reflects CBO's assessment that of the funds remaining under the original authority for the TARP, a maximum of $50 billion will be disbursed at a subsidy rate of 50 percent.

[c] Authority for the TARP was originally set at a maximum of $700 billion outstanding at one time; that total was reduced by nearly $1.3 billion in the Helping Families Save Their Homes Act of 2009 (Public Law 111-22).

In addition to support under the Capital Purchase Program, Bank of America and Citigroup both received another $20 billion from the TARP and a commitment to guarantee certain assets. Both institutions have now repaid the additional funding and terminated the guarantees. (The guarantee agreement with Bank of America was never implemented.)

The American International Group (AIG) has also received substantial funding from the TARP. In November 2008, the Treasury purchased $40 billion in preferred stock from AIG, and in April 2009, it created a $30 billion line of credit for the company. Approximately $5 billion of that credit line was outstanding as of the end of December.

Besides helping financial institutions, the TARP has provided significant assistance to the U.S. automotive industry—specifically, General Motors (GM), GMAC (GM's financing company), Chrysler, Chrysler Financial, and various suppliers. The loans to Chrysler Financial have been repaid, as has a small portion of the funding for GM, Chrysler, and the suppliers. As of the middle of December, about $79 billion of that assistance (currently in the form of equity, loans, and preferred stock) was outstanding.

Three other programs are currently active in the TARP: the Term Asset-Backed Securities Loan Facility (TALF), the Public-Private Investment Program (PPIP), and the Home Affordable Modification Program (HAMP). The Treasury has allocated $20 billion to cover potential losses from the TALF, which provides financing to investors who buy highly rated securities backed by assets such as auto loans, credit card loans, student loans, and business loans guaranteed by the Small Business Administration. The PPIP is planning to use $30 billion (plus $10 billion provided by private investors) to purchase highly rated commercial mortgage-backed securities (MBSs) as well as residential MBSs not backed by Fannie Mae or Freddie Mac that were issued before 2009. The Treasury has committed $50 billion for the HAMP for direct payments to mortgage servicers to help homeowners avoid foreclosure. Through December, the HAMP had disbursed less than $15 million, and the TALF and PPIP had not declared any losses.

All told, the Congressional Budget Office now estimates that the total cost of the TARP will be $99 billion (excluding administrative costs) over the life of the program. Most of that cost is projected to stem from the assistance to the automotive industry, payments from the HAMP, and potential costs for future activities.

Uncertainty About Future Legislative Actions

To illustrate how different fiscal policies might affect the baseline, CBO estimated the budgetary impact of some alternative actions that lawmakers could take. Examples include drawing down U.S. forces in Iraq and Afghanistan at different rates in coming years, increasing or freezing future discretionary appropriations, extending tax provisions that are due to expire, and indexing the alternative minimum tax for inflation (see Table 1-5 on page 16). The discussion below focuses on how those policy actions would directly affect revenues and outlays. Such changes, however, would also have an impact on the projected costs of servicing the federal debt; those costs are shown separately in Table 1-5.

War-Related Discretionary Spending. CBO's projections of discretionary spending for the next 10 years include outlays for the wars in Iraq and Afghanistan and for related activities. The outlays projected in the baseline come from budget authority provided for those purposes in 2009 and prior years, from the $130 billion in budget authority already provided for 2010, and from the $1.4 trillion that is projected to be appropriated over the 2011–2020 period, under the assumption that funding each year matches the $130 billion level for 2010 plus adjustments for inflation. (Additional funding may be needed in 2010, however, because of the decision to increase U.S. forces in Afghanistan.)

In coming years, the annual funding required for war-related activities may eventually be smaller than the amounts in the baseline if the number of deployed troops and the pace of operations diminish over time. Considerable uncertainty exists about future military operations. To illustrate it, CBO has formulated two alternative budget scenarios involving the deployment of U.S. forces to Iraq, Afghanistan, or future military actions elsewhere in the world. (Many other scenarios—some costing more and some less—are also possible.)

In 2009, the number of U.S. active-duty, reserve, and National Guard personnel deployed for war-related activities averaged about 220,000, CBO estimates. Under one of the alternative scenarios, that average would fall by 9 percent in 2010; under the other, it would rise by 7 percent. (In both cases, an increase in personnel deployed to Afghanistan this year would be offset to varying degrees by a reduction in personnel deployed to Iraq.) After 2010, total troop levels would decline in both scenarios, but at different rates and to different sustained levels. (Those levels could represent various allocations of forces between Iraq, Afghanistan, and other regions.)

In the first scenario, average troop levels would drop significantly over a three-year period—from roughly 200,000 this year to 150,000 in 2011, 65,000 in 2012, and 30,000 by the beginning of 2013.[6] The number of deployed troops in 2013 would be maintained through 2020, although not necessarily in Iraq and Afghanistan. This scenario also assumes that additional supplemental appropriations will be provided this year for the troop increase in Afghanistan. Under those assumptions about troop levels and funding, outlays would be $4 billion higher in 2010 than CBO currently projects, but annual outlays would be lower than the amounts in the baseline starting in 2011. Over the 2011–2020 period, total outlays for such military operations would be about $900 billion less than the amount projected in the baseline.

In the second scenario, the number of troops deployed for war-related purposes would rise to an average of about 235,000 in 2010 and then decline more gradually and to a higher sustained level than in the first scenario.[7] The average number of military personnel deployed overseas for such purposes would be reduced to 230,000 in 2011, 195,000 in 2012, 135,000 in 2013, 80,000 in 2014, and 60,000 in 2015 and thereafter. This scenario also assumes that further supplemental appropriations will be provided this year for the war in Afghanistan. Under this scenario, outlays would be higher than the baseline projections between 2010 and 2012 but lower than those projections beginning in 2013. Total discretionary outlays over the 2011–2020 period would be about $550 billion less than the amount in the baseline.

Other Discretionary Spending. Many alternative assumptions are possible about the future growth of discretionary spending. For example, if appropriations (excluding those for operations in Iraq and Afghanistan) were assumed to grow each year through 2020 at the same rate as nominal GDP—instead of at the rate of inflation—the total discretionary spending projected for that period would be $1.8 trillion higher than in the baseline. In contrast, if lawmakers did not increase appropriations after 2010 to account for inflation, total discretionary outlays would be $1.1 trillion lower during that 10-year period than in the baseline. Under that scenario (sometimes referred to as a freeze in appropriations), total discretionary spending would fall from 9.4 percent of GDP this year to 5.7 percent in 2020—the lowest level in 50 years.

Revenues. Under the rules that govern CBO's baseline, major provisions of the Economic Growth and Tax Relief Reconciliation Act of 2001, the Jobs and Growth Tax Relief Reconciliation Act of 2003, and the American Recovery and Reinvestment Act of 2009 are assumed to expire as scheduled at the end of calendar year 2010. Those expirations will increase net revenues by raising tax rates, eliminating the 10 percent tax bracket, reducing the child tax credit, discontinuing the Making Work Pay credit, reinstating the estate tax with a lower effective exemption amount, and raising tax rates on capital gains and dividends. Under a scenario in which the expiring provisions were extended, projected revenues would be lower than the amounts in the baseline. For example, if all expiring tax provisions (except those related to the exemption amount for the AMT) were extended, total revenues over the 2011–2020 period would be $4.5 trillion lower, according to estimates by the Joint Committee on Taxation and CBO.[8] Under that scenario, the effect of reducing the amount of regular tax that people owed would be partly offset by an increase in the number of taxpayers subject to the AMT.

Another policy change that would affect revenues involves modifying the AMT. The exemption amount and brackets for that alternative tax do not automatically increase with inflation, as the parameters of the regular individual income tax do. Consequently, as people's income rises over time, more taxpayers become subject to the AMT. That phenomenon is expected to cause the impact of the AMT to grow sharply in coming years. If, instead, the tax was indexed for inflation after 2009 (starting from the 2009 exemption amount), with no other changes to the tax code, federal revenues over the next 10 years would be $558 billion lower than the amount in the baseline, according to CBO and the Joint Committee on Taxation.

Table 1-5. Budgetary Effects of Selected Policy Alternatives Not Included in CBO's Baseline

(Billions of dollars)													
	2010	**2011**	**2012**	**2013**	**2014**	**2015**	**2016**	**2017**	**2018**	**2019**	**2020**	**Total, 2011-2015**	**Total, 2011-2020**
	Policy Alternatives That Affect Discretionary Outlays												
Reduce the Number of Troops Deployed for Military Opera-tions in Iraq and Afghanistan and for Other War-Related Activities to 30,000 by 2013[a]													
Effect on the deficit[b]	-4	2	32	68	92	105	114	118	121	124	126	299	902
Debt service	*	*	*	2	6	11	17	24	32	40	49	19	182
Reduce the Number of Troops Deployed for Military Opera-tions in Iraq and Afghanistan and for Other War-Related Activities to 60,000 by 2015[c]													
Effect on the deficit[b]	-8	-20	-21	3	36	65	85	95	100	103	106	63	552
Debt service	*	*	-1	-1	-1	1	5	9	15	21	27	-2	76
Increase Regular Discretionary Appropriations at the Rate of Growth of Nominal GDP[d]													
Effect on the deficit[b]	0	-9	-37	-82	-129	-170	-207	-244	-279	-315	-352	-426	-1,823
Debt service	0	*	-1	-3	-9	-15	-26	-39	-54	-73	-94	-27	-314
Freeze Total Discretionary Appropriations at the Level Provided for 2010													
Effect on the deficit[b]	0	10	24	42	63	88	116	145	175	207	239	227	1,108
Debt service	0	*	*	2	5	8	14	21	31	42	56	15	180
		Policy Alternatives That Affect the Tax Code[e]											
Extend EGTRRA and JGTRRA[f]													
Effect on the deficit[b]	-3	-115	-216	-243	-257	-269	-277	-285	-293	-302	-311	-1,099	-2,567
Debt service	*	-1	-5	-14	-29	-43	-61	-78	-99	-121	-144	-91	-594
Extend Other Expiring Tax Provisions[g]													
Effect on the deficit[b]	-46	-145	-202	-204	-204	-200	-199	-198	-201	-205	-211	-955	-1,969
Debt service	*	-2	-6	-15	-28	-39	-53	-67	-83	-99	-116	-90	-508
Index the AMT for Inflation[h]													
Effect on the deficit[b]	-7	-69	-31	-35	-39	-44	-50	-58	-66	-77	-88	-219	-558
Debt service	*	-1	-2	-4	-6	-9	-12	-16	-20	-25	-31	-22	-125

(Billions of dollars)													
	2010	**2011**	**2012**	**2013**	**2014**	**2015**	**2016**	**2017**	**2018**	**2019**	**2020**	**Total, 2011-2015**	**Total, 2011-2020**
Memorandum:													
Interactive Effect of Extending EGTRRA and JGTRRA and Indexing the AMT													
Effect on the deficit[b]	0	-13	-43	-48	-53	-59	-64	-71	-78	-85	-93	-215	-606
Debt service	0	*	-1	-2	-5	-8	-12	-16	-21	-27	-33	-17	-126
Total Discretionary Outlays in CBO's Baseline	1,371	1,371	1,344	1,346	1,357	1,373	1,402	1,426	1,450	1,486	1,518	6,792	14,074
Total Outlays for Operations in Iraq and Afghanistan in CBO's Baseline	164	150	139	137	137	136	139	141	143	146	149	699	1,417
Total Deficit in CBO's Baseline	-1,349	-980	-650	-539	-475	-480	-521	-525	-542	-649	-687	-3,124	-6,047

Sources: Congressional Budget Office; Joint Committee on Taxation.

Note: GDP = gross domestic product; EGTRRA = Economic Growth and Tax Relief Reconciliation Act of 2001; JGTRRA = Jobs and Growth Tax Relief Reconciliation Act of 2003; AMT = alternative minimum tax; * = between -$500 million and $500 million.

[a] This alternative does not extrapolate the $130 billion in budget authority for military operations and associated costs in Iraq and Afghanistan provided for 2010. However, it incorporates the assumption that an additional $16 billion in budget authority will be provided in 2010 to carry out operations in those two countries. Future funding for operations in Iraq, Afghanistan, or elsewhere would total $121 billion in 2011, $69 billion in 2012, $40 billion in 2013, and about $25 billion a year from 2014 on—for a total of $395 billion over the 2011–2020 period.

[b] Excluding debt service.

[c] This alternative does not extrapolate the $130 billion in budget authority for military operations and associated costs in Iraq and Afghanistan provided for 2010. However, it incorporates the assumption that an additional $36 billion in budget authority will be provided in 2010 to carry out operations in those two countries. Future funding for operations in Iraq, Afghanistan, or elsewhere would total $158 billion in 2011, $143 billion in 2012, $108 billion in 2013, $71 billion in 2014, $51 billion in 2015, and about $40 billion a year from 2016 on—for a total of $746 billion over the 2011–2020 period.

[d] Under this alternative, appropriations for 2010 for operations in Iraq and Afghanistan are extrapolated according to the rules that govern CBO's baseline.

[e] The Joint Committee on Taxation's estimates for these tax policy alternatives are preliminary and will be updated later.

[f] These estimates do not include the effects of extending the increased exemption amount or the treatment of personal credits for the AMT that expired at the end of 2009. The effects of that alternative are shown separately.

[g] The estimates include the effects of extending several expiring provisions that were enacted or modified in the American Recovery and Reinvestment Act of 2009, such as the Making Work Pay tax credit, the American Opportunity tax credit, and the exclusion from taxable income of certain amounts of unemployment benefits. The estimates also include the impact of extending other expiring provisions that have been in effect for a number of years.

[h] This alternative incorporates the assumption that the exemption amount for the AMT (which was increased through 2009) is extended at its higher level and, together with the AMT tax brackets, is indexed for inflation after 2009. In addition, the treatment of personal credits against the AMT (which was also continued through the end of 2009) is assumed to be extended. The estimates shown are relative to figures under current law. If this alternative was enacted together with the extension of the expiring tax provisions, an interactive effect would occur after 2010 that would make the combined revenue loss through 2020 greater than the sum of the two separate estimates.

The number of taxpayers who are subject to the AMT, however, will depend on whether the expiring tax provisions enacted in the past decade remain in effect. If those provisions were extended and the AMT was indexed for inflation, the combination of the two changes would reduce revenues by more than the sum of the two policy alternatives considered separately. The interaction of those two policy changes would lower revenues by an additional $606 billion between 2011 and 2020. Thus, the total impact of extending all of the tax provisions that are set to expire in the next 10 years and indexing the AMT for inflation would be to reduce revenues over the 2011–2020 period by $5.7 trillion.

Other Sources of Uncertainty

In addition to being affected by future legislative actions, the federal budget is sensitive to economic and technical factors that are difficult to forecast. When CBO constructs its baseline, it must make projections of such economic variables as interest rates, inflation, and the growth of GDP. Discrepancies between those projections and actual economic conditions can make budgetary outcomes differ significantly from the baseline. For instance, CBO's economic forecast anticipates that real GDP will grow by 2.2 percent in calendar year 2010, by 1.9 percent in 2011, by an average of 4.4 percent a year from 2012 to 2014, and by 2.4 percent annually from 2015 to 2020. If the actual growth rate of real GDP was 0.1 percentage point higher or lower each year, the cumulative deficit projected for the 2011–2020 period would be higher or lower by about $300 billion. (For further discussion of how various economic assumptions affect budget projections, see AppendixC.)

Uncertainty also surrounds technical factors that affect CBO's baseline projections. For example, spending per enrollee in Medicare and Medicaid—which has generally grown faster than GDP—is hard to predict, but it will have a large impact on the costs of those two programs in coming years. If per capita costs grew 1 percentage point faster or slower per year over the next decade than CBO has projected, total outlays for Medicare and Medicaid would be about $700 billion higher or lower over that period. In another example, CBO's baseline projections depend on assumptions about prices and crop yields for agricultural commodities, all of which are volatile and strongly affect how much the government will pay farmers under price- and income-support programs.

Projections of revenues are particularly sensitive to technical uncertainty. Forecasting the total amount of future income is part of CBO's economic projections, but forecasting the amount of revenue that the government will collect from a given amount of total income requires technical assumptions about the distribution of income and about many subtle aspects of taxpayers' behavior. Differences between those assumptions and actual outcomes can lead to significant deviations from CBO's baseline revenue projections.

Federal Debt Held by the Public

Debt held by the public consists of debt securities that the Treasury issues to raise cash to fund the operations and pay off the maturing liabilities of the federal government. (Other measures of debt are discussed in Appendix D.) The Treasury borrows money from the public by selling securities in the capital markets; that debt is purchased by various buyers in the United States and by private investors and central banks in other countries.

Holders of Federal Debt

Of the $7.5 trillion in federal debt held by the public that was outstanding at the end of 2009, domestic investors owned 52 percent ($4.0 trillion) and foreign investors held 48 percent ($3.6 trillion). Individual households and the Federal Reserve System are the largest U.S. holders of Treasury debt, each accounting for about 10 percent of the total (see Table 1-6). Other U.S. investors that purchase Treasury debt include mutual funds, state and local governments, and pension funds. Among foreign investors, those in China and Japan have the largest holdings of Treasury securities.[9] Together, central banks and private entities in those two countries hold about one-fifth of U.S. Treasury debt.

Table 1-6. Holders of Federal Debt Held by the Public, 2004 and 2009

	2004		2009	
	Billions of Dollars	Percentage of Total	Billions of Dollars	Percentage of Total
U.S. Holders				
Individuals	436	10.2	802	10.6
Federal Reserve System	700	16.3	769	10.2
Mutual funds	256	6.0	643	8.5
State and local governments	379	8.8	503	6.7
Pension and retirement funds	281	6.5	501	6.6
Other	394	9.2	742	9.8
Subtotal, U.S. holders	2,447	57.0	3,960	52.5
Foreign Holders[a]				
China	209	4.9	799	10.6
Japan	699	16.3	751	10.0
United Kingdom	62	1.4	249	3.3
Major oil-exporting countries	57	1.3	185	2.5
Caribbean banking institutions	82	1.9	173	2.3
Other	739	17.2	1,427	18.9
Subtotal, foreign holders	1,849	43.0	3,584	47.5
Total Public Debt	**4,296**	**100.0**	**7,544**	**100.0**

Source: Congressional Budget Office based on Board of Governors of the Federal Reserve System, *Flow of Funds Accounts of the United States,* Table L.209 (for domestic holders and total foreign holders), and the Federal Reserve Board's Treasury International Capital Survey, January 2010 (for individual foreign holders).

a. Numbers for foreign countries include holdings by individuals, businesses, and government entities. The numbers for individual foreign holders were estimated by the Federal Reserve on the basis of its surveys of holdings.

Trends in Debt Held by the Public

The amount of federal debt held by the public has fluctuated markedly over the past few decades. After peaking at nearly 50 percent of GDP in 1993, it fell to 33 percent by 2001 following a string of years with brisk economic growth and with budget surpluses rather than deficits (see Figure 1-2). Debt soon began increasing again relative to GDP, reaching 41 percent in 2008 and 53 percent in 2009. Under the assumptions of the baseline (in particular, that tax provisions expire as scheduled and that discretionary spending grows at the rate of inflation), debt held by the public is projected to rise to 60 percent of GDP this year and 65 percent next year and then remain at about that percentage through 2020 (see Table 1-7). Such levels of debt relative to GDP would be the highest recorded since the early 1950s.

Changes in policy would produce different amounts of publicly held debt. For example, if the number of U.S. troops involved in war-related activities declined to 30,000 by 2013 (the first alternative scenario discussed above and shown in Table 1-5) but all other policies were consistent with those assumed in the baseline, debt held by the public at the end of 2020 would be $1.1 trillion lower than the $15.0 trillion projected in the baseline. By contrast, if all of the tax provisions that are set to expire over the next 10 years were extended through the projection period, and if the exemption amount and brackets for the AMT were indexed for inflation from their 2009 levels, debt held by the public would be $7 trillion higher in 2020 than the baseline projection. Under that scenario, debt held by the public would equal 98 percent of GDP in 2020.

Why Changes in Debt Held by the Public Do Not Equal Deficits

In many years, the amount of money that the Treasury borrows by selling securities (net of the amount of maturing securities that it redeems) roughly equals the annual budget deficit. However, a number of factors—which are collectively labeled "other means of financing" and are not directly included in budget totals—also affect the government's need to borrow from the public. Those factors include reductions (or increases) in the government's cash balances and the cash flows reflected in the financing accounts used for federal credit programs.

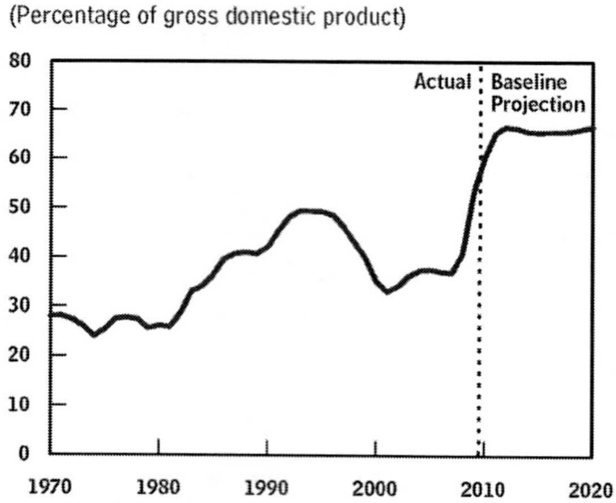

Source: Congressional Budget Office.

Note: Data are for debt held by the public at the end of the year.

Figure 1-2. Federal Debt Held by the Public, 1970 to 2020.

For 2009, federal borrowing was $328 billion greater than the size of the deficit, mainly because of funding for the TARP, purchases of mortgage-backed securities by the Treasury, and financing for student loans. In 2010, other means of financing are expected to cause Treasury borrowing to be $96 billion smaller than the deficit (thus reducing publicly held debt by that amount). After 2010, other means of financing will raise the Treasury's borrowing needs relative to the size of deficits, CBO projects.

The Treasury is likely to reduce cash balances considerably in the next few years. Specifically, it is expected to have about $200 billion less in cash at the end of 2010 than at the end of 2009, primarily because of the conclusion of the Supplementary Financing Program, which held $165 billion in cash at the Federal Reserve at the end of last year.[10] In addition to that program, the Treasury's regular cash holdings are projected to decline by $35 billion in 2010 and by the same amount in 2011 before stabilizing at a total balance of $40 billion at the end of each subsequent year.

Credit financing accounts have a large impact on the government's borrowing. Direct student loans, the Advanced Technology Vehicles Manufacturing Loan Program, rural housing programs, loans made by the Small Business Administration, and other direct loan programs require the government to disburse money up front in anticipation of repayment later. Those initial disbursements are not counted as budget outlays (such outlays reflect only the programs' estimated costs for subsidies, defaults, and other items). Each year from 2010 to 2020, the amount of loans disbursed will generally be larger than the amount of repayments and interest collected, CBO projects. Thus, the government's annual borrowing needs will be $43 billion greater, on average, because of such programs than the annual budget deficits would indicate.

The Treasury will also need to borrow in 2010 to finance some activities of the TARP, final purchases of mortgage-backed securities from the public (under a program that expired at the end of December), and cash payments to Fannie Mae and Freddie Mac. Cash flows for such activities will require the Treasury to borrow nearly $60 billion more this year than CBO's estimate of the deficit would imply. In later years, those cash flows are likely to be more modest and to have less effect on the Treasury's borrowing needs.

The Long-Term Budget Outlook

The severe economic downturn and nearly unprecedented turmoil in the financial system over the past few years—combined with federal policies implemented in response to those conditions—have caused deficits to climb dramatically. However, even after the economy has recovered and the budgetary costs of associated federal policies have waned, the budget outlook will remain daunting. If tax provisions expire as scheduled and discretionary spending grows at the rate of inflation each year (as assumed in CBO's baseline), budget deficits averaging almost 3 percent of GDP will persist between 2013 and 2020. Federal debt held by the public will reach 67 percent of GDP by 2020, the largest share since the early 1950s. Moreover, if expiring tax provisions are extended or spending grows faster than is assumed in the baseline, those deficits—and the corresponding debt that will result—may be much larger.

Beyond the 10-year projection period, rising health care costs and the aging of the U.S. population will continue to exacerbate the fiscal challenges facing the nation. Recurring large deficits and the resulting increases in federal debt over time will reduce national saving and investment relative to what would otherwise occur, and the reduced pace of capital accumulation, in turn, will lower the long-term growth of productivity, output, wages, and income.

Table 1-7. CBO's Baseline Projections of Federal Debt

(Billions of dollars)												
	Actual 2009	**2010**	**2011**	**2012**	**2013**	**2014**	**2015**	**2016**	**2017**	**2018**	**2019**	**2020**
Debt Held by the Public at the Beginning of the Year	5,803	7,544	8,797	9,785	10,479	11,056	11,556	12,055	12,595	13,133	13,678	14,329
Changes to Debt Held by the Public												
Deficit	1,414	1,349	980	650	539	475	480	521	525	542	649	687
Other means of financing	328	-96	8	44	38	25	19	18	14	3	2	12
Total	**1,741**	**1,253**	**989**	**694**	**577**	**501**	**499**	**539**	**539**	**545**	**650**	**699**
Debt Held by the Public at the End of the Year	7,544	8,797	9,785	10,479	11,056	11,556	12,055	12,595	13,133	13,678	14,329	15,027
Memorandum:												
Debt Held by the Public at the End of the Year as a Percentage of GDP	53.0	60.3	65.3	66.6	66.3	65.6	65.4	65.5	65.5	65.7	66.1	66.7
Debt Held by the Public Net of Financial Assets[a]												
In billions of dollars	6,540	7,960	8,939	9,584	10,116	10,585	11,105	11,630	12,152	12,687	13,360	14,037
As a percentage of GDP	45.9	54.5	59.6	60.9	60.7	60.1	60.3	60.5	60.6	60.9	61.7	62.3

Source: Congressional Budget Office.

Note: GDP = gross domestic product.

[a] Subtracts from debt held by the public the value of financial assets (such as preferred stock) purchased from institutions participating in the Troubled Asset Relief Program, holdings of preferred stock in Fannie Mae and Freddie Mac, the Treasury's purchases of mortgage-backed securities, cash balances, and other financial instruments.

The single greatest threat to budget stability is the growth of federal spending on health care—pushed up both by increases in the number of beneficiaries of Medicare and Medicaid (because of the aging of the population) and by growth in spending per beneficiary that outstrips growth in per capita GDP. For the nation's fiscal situation to be sustainable in future decades, growth in such spending will have to be reduced relative to its historical trend and to CBO's projected path. Today, outlays for Medicaid and Medicare combined (excluding offsetting receipts) equal about 5.5 percent of GDP. Under current law, spending for those two programs is expected to keep growing faster than the economy, reaching 6.6 percent of GDP by 2020 and potentially reaching 10 percent by 2035.[11] Without changes to federal fiscal policy—involving some combination of lower spending and higher revenues than the amounts projected under current law—those rising costs will rapidly drive the size of federal debt held by the public well beyond the 67 percent of GDP projected for 2020.

2. The Economic Outlook

The deep recession that began two years ago appears to have ended in mid-2009. Economic activity picked up during the second half of the year, with real (inflation-adjusted) gross domestic product and industrial production both posting gains. Still, GDP remains roughly 6½ percent below the Congressional Budget Office's estimate of the output that could be produced if all labor and capital were fully employed (so-called potential output), and the unemployment rate—at 10 percent—is twice what it was two years ago.

CBO expects that the pace of the economic recovery in the next few years will be slower than might be anticipated on the basis of previous recoveries from deep recessions, for several reasons:

- Economic growth will probably be restrained by the aftermath of the financial and economic turmoil. Experience in the United States and in other countries suggests that recovery from recessions triggered by financial crises and large declines in asset prices tends to be protracted.
- Although aggressive action on the part of the Federal Reserve and the fiscal stimulus package enacted in early 2009 helped moderate the severity of the recession and shorten its duration, the support coming from those sources is expected to wane. In addition, under the assumption that current laws and policies remain unchanged—an assumption that is reflected in CBO's forecast—tax rates will increase in 2011, further hampering growth.
- Household spending is likely to be dampened by slow income growth, lost wealth, and constraints on households' ability to borrow. Investment spending will be slowed by the large number of vacant homes and offices.

In CBO's forecast, real GDP increases by 2.1 percent between the fourth quarter of 2009 and the fourth quarter of 2010 and by 2.4 percent in 2011 (see Table 2-1). Given CBO's estimate of growth in potential output, those GDP growth rates will narrow the difference between actual output and potential output (the output gap) only slightly. Growth in real GDP will accelerate after 2011, spurred by stronger business investment and residential construction. From 2012 through 2014, real GDP will increase by an average of 4.4 percent per year, CBO projects, which would close the output gap completely by the end of 2014 (see Figure 2-1).

Table 2-1. CBO's Economic Projections for Calendar Years 2009 to 2020

	Estimated 2009	Forecast		Projected Annual Average	
		2010	2011	2012–2014	2015–2020
	Year to Year (Percentage change)				
Nominal GDP (Billions of dollars)	14,253	14,706	15,116	17,816 [a]	22,770 [b]
Nominal GDP	-1.3	3.2	2.8	5.6	4.2
Real GDP	-2.5	2.2	1.9	4.4	2.4
GDP Price Index	1.2	0.9	0.9	1.1	1.7
PCE Price Index[c]	0.2	1.9	1.1	1.2	1.7
Core PCE Price Index[d]	1.5	1.2	1.0	1.1	1.7
Consumer Price Index[e]	-0.2	2.4	1.3	1.2	1.9
Core Consumer Price Index[f]	1.8	1.5	1.0	1.1	1.9
	Calendar Year Average (Percent)				
Unemployment Rate	9.3	10.1	9.5	6.5	5.0
Three-Month Treasury Bill Rate	0.1	0.2	0.7	2.9	4.6
Ten-Year Treasury Note Rate	3.2	3.6	3.9	4.5	5.5
Tax Bases (Billions of dollars)					
Domestic economic profits	990	1,263	1,307	1,487 [a]	1,588 [b]
Wages and salaries	6,329	6,517	6,671	8,061 [a]	10,365 [b]
Tax Bases (Percentage of GDP)					
Domestic economic profits	6.9	8.6	8.6	8.6	7.3
Wages and salaries	44.4	44.3	44.1	45.0	45.4
	Fourth Quarter to Fourth Quarter (Percentage change)				
Nominal GDP	0.5	3.1	3.3	5.7	4.1
Real GDP	-0.4	2.1	2.4	4.4	2.4
GDP Price Index	0.9	1.0	0.9	1.2	1.7
PCE Price Index[c]	1.4	1.4	1.1	1.2	1.8
Core PCE Price Index[d]	1.5	1.0	0.9	1.1	1.7
Consumer Price Index[e]	1.7	1.6	1.1	1.3	1.9
Core Consumer Price Index[f]	2.0	1.1	0.9	1.2	1.9
Unemployment Rate[g]	10.1	10.0	9.1	5.2	5.0

Sources: Congressional Budget Office; Department of Commerce, Bureau of Economic Analysis; Department of Labor, Bureau of Labor Statistics; Federal Reserve.

Notes: Economic projections for each year from 2009 to 2020 appear in Appendix E.

GDP = gross domestic product; PCE = personal consumption expenditure.

a. Level in 2014.

b. Level in 2020.

c. The personal consumption expenditure price index.

d. The personal consumption expenditure price index excluding prices for food and energy.

e. The consumer price index for all urban consumers.

f. The consumer price index for all urban consumers excluding prices for food and energy.

g. Values are fourth-quarter averages.

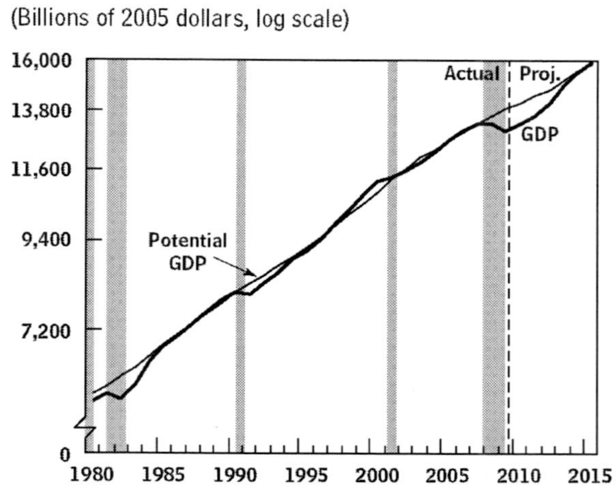

Sources: Congressional Budget Office; Department of Commerce, Bureau of Economic Analysis.
Notes: Real gross domestic product is GDP adjusted for inflation. Potential GDP is CBO's estimate of the output the economy would produce if its resources—capital and labor—were fully employed. Data are annual and are plotted through 2015.

Figure 2-1. Real Gross Domestic Product.

Even though output began to grow during the second half of 2009, the unemployment rate continued to rise, reaching 10.1 percent in October and finishing the year at 10.0 percent (see Figure 2-2). Since the beginning of this recession, payroll employment has fallen by more than 7 million, reflecting both the rise in unemployment and a drop in labor force participation; payroll employment has not yet begun to increase again. Although new claims for unemployment insurance have fallen substantially since early 2009, they remain well above prerecession levels. Moreover, hiring rates are still very low, and they show only faint signs of recovery.

This pattern of labor market activity is typical of recent recessions, in which the unemployment rate continued to rise for more than a year after real GDP began to grow. Hiring usually lags behind output during the initial stages of a recovery because firms tend to increase output first by boosting productivity and by raising the number of hours that existing employees work; adding employees tends to occur later. Moreover, the unemployment rate often rises for a few quarters after employment begins to recover, because the perception of improved job prospects encourages workers who had dropped out of the labor force during the recession to reenter the labor force. CBO expects that the unemployment rate will average slightly above 10 percent in the first half of 2010 and then turn downward in the second half of the year. As the economy expands further, the rate of unemployment is projected to continue declining until, in 2016, it reaches 5 percent; that figure is equal to CBO's estimate of the natural rate of unemployment (which reflects, in part, the difficulty of making immediate matches between job seekers and jobs).[12] In CBO's forecast, the persistently elevated level of unemployment depresses labor income in 2010. Beyond 2010, CBO expects labor income to grow more rapidly than GDP (as conditions in labor markets improve) and, by 2020, to approach the share of GDP that prevailed, on average, between 1979 and 2008.

Reflecting the large amount of slack in the economy, inflation will decrease further from its already low level in 2009, CBO forecasts. The core price index for personal consumption expenditures (that is, the PCE price index excluding the prices of food and energy) will rise by about 1 percent (on a fourth-quarter-over-fourth-quarter basis) in 2010 and 0.9 percent in 2011.[13] Overall inflation is also expected to remain quiescent; the PCE price index rises by 1.4 percent in 2010 and 1.1 percent in 2011 in CBO's forecast. The consumer price index for all urban consumers (CPI-U), a measure more closely related to the budget than is the PCE price index, rises by 1.6 percent and 1.1 percent in those years. Over the following three years, inflation, as measured by any of those indexes, is projected to average 1.5 percent or less.

Short-term interest rates will remain at very low levels through the middle of next year and then rise slowly as the recovery progresses, in CBO's estimation. As part of its aggressive easing of monetary policy in response to the financial crisis, the Federal Reserve reduced the target federal funds rate—the overnight interest rate at which depository institutions borrow and lend monetary reserves—to near zero in late 2008 and held it at that level throughout 2009. If inflation stays low and the recovery is gradual, as CBO anticipates, then the Federal Reserve is likely to keep its target interest rate low for some time. As economic activity strengthens more noticeably by the end of 2011, CBO expects that the Federal Reserve will begin raising the federal funds rate rapidly. Interest rates on short-term federal borrowing generally follow the funds rate closely. In CBO's forecast, the yield on the 3-month Treasury bill averages 0.2 percent in 2010 and 0.7 percent in 2011. By late 2014, when the economy strengthens further, the yield will rise to 4 percent, CBO projects. Based on that path for short-term rates, CBO assumes that the rate on 10-year Treasury notes will rise gradually from an average of 3.6 percent in 2010 to 4.9 percent in 2014.

CBO expects that output will reach its potential level by 2014. For the following five years, CBO projects growth in GDP averaging 2.4 percent, the same rate as that of potential output. The unemployment rate is projected to average 5 percent between 2015 and 2020, and consumer price inflation as measured by the PCE price index will average 1.7 percent during that period. From 2015 through 2020, the interest rates on three-month Treasury bills and 10-year Treasury notes will average 4.6 percent and 5.5 percent, respectively.

CBO's current economic projections are similar to its previous projections, which were issued in August 2009. In this forecast, real growth is expected to be slightly faster during the first half of 2010 but slightly slower during the rest of 2010 and in 2011. (For the 2010–2020 period as a whole, the projection for real growth is almost unchanged.) The rate of unemployment is expected to be somewhat higher, on average, reflecting an upward revision to the estimate of the natural rate of unemployment. Interest rates remain low for longer than in the previous forecast. The projection for inflation is somewhat higher than it was last August. The lower interest rates and higher inflation (the latter through its effect on the projection of federal receipts) are the primary reasons for the improved budget outlook. Altogether, the changes in economic projections reduce the federal deficit by an estimated $626 billion over the 2010–2019 period (see AppendixB for more details).

CBO's forecast anticipates slower growth in 2010 and 2011 than do the forecasts of the *Blue Chip* consensus (reflecting the views of about 50 private-sector economists) and the forecasts of most participants in last November's meeting of the Federal Open Market Committee of the Federal Reserve System (reported as the "central tendency" of their forecasts).[14] That difference probably stems, at least in part, from divergent assumptions about fiscal policy.

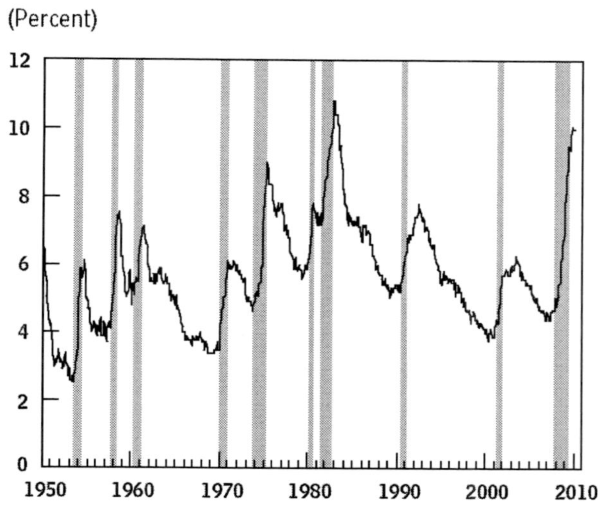

Sources: Congressional Budget Office; Department of Labor, Bureau of Labor Statistics.
Note: Data are monthly and are plotted through December 2009.

Figure 2-2. Unemployment Rate.

CBO's current-law forecast reflects the assumption that the tax cuts enacted in 2001 and 2003 will expire as scheduled at the end of 2010 and that the exemption amounts for the alternative minimum tax will fall back this year to the amounts they would have been in the absence of the regular "patches" (temporary adjustments). By contrast, private forecasters and the Federal Reserve probably expect that the Congress will extend some or all of those provisions, and they may expect that other stimulative fiscal measures will be enacted as well. If CBO assumed that all of the expiring tax provisions were extended beyond 2010 and no other stimulative fiscal measures were passed, the agency's forecast of the level of real GDP at the end of 2011 would be in line with the forecast of the *Blue Chip* consensus and near the lower end of the central tendency of the Federal Reserve's forecasts. (However, the greater accumulation of government debt that would result would diminish real GDP in later years.) CBO's inflation forecast calls for inflation that is roughly in line with that of the *Blue Chip* consensus in 2010 but significantly lower in 2011, and it is at the lower end of the central tendency of the Federal Reserve's forecasts for 2010 and 2011.

All economic projections are subject to a substantial degree of uncertainty, but turning points in the business cycle are particularly difficult to assess. Several risks appear to be especially important now:

- The Congress, the Federal Reserve, the Treasury, and other government agencies instituted a series of substantial and innovative policy actions during the financial crisis and recession. Determining the degree to which those initiatives will support output and employment as they wind down in the next few years is not straightforward.
- Business-cycle recoveries from recessions caused by financial crises and declines in asset prices (in the United States and abroad) have tended to be muted. However, it is uncertain to what degree this recovery will follow that historical pattern.

- The outlook for inflation is particularly uncertain in this recovery because of the unusual amount of excess capacity in the economy and because of the unprecedented nature of the actions taken by the Federal Reserve during the financial crisis.

Factors Affecting Economic Growth Through 2014

Severe economic downturns often sow the seeds of robust recoveries. During a slump in economic activity, consumers defer purchases, especially for housing and durable goods, and businesses postpone capital spending and try to cut inventories. Once demand in the economy picks up, the disparity between the desired and actual stocks of capital assets and consumer durable goods widens quickly, and spending by consumers and businesses can accelerate rapidly. For example, following the deep recession of 1981 to 1982, during which the output gap exceeded 7 percent, real GDP surged by nearly 8 percent in 1983 and by roughly 6 percent in 1984, led by spending on consumer durable goods, housing, and business investment.

Although CBO expects that the current recovery will be spurred by that dynamic, in all likelihood the recovery will also be dampened by continued financial weakness, a lessening of fiscal and monetary stimulus, a subpar recovery in the housing market, and the likelihood that employment growth will lag output growth, thus holding back the recovery in workers' incomes.

Financial Markets and Institutions

Conditions in many financial markets improved substantially during the second half of 2009, but continuing problems in the financial sector will slow the pace of the recovery. Improving market conditions have allowed policymakers to begin withdrawing the support provided during the financial crisis; in particular, financial institutions have greatly reduced their reliance on the Federal Reserve's emergency liquidity facilities. Nevertheless, loan losses continue to mount in the banking sector, and activity remains subdued in the once-vibrant private markets for mortgage- and asset-backed securities—markets that have been a major source of funds for lending in recent years.

The risk of further deterioration in many financial markets has diminished, although it has not disappeared.

Improvements are particularly apparent in the money market (in which financial institutions and banks obtain short-term financing), as the perceived riskiness of lending in that market has fallen significantly. Indeed, the cost to banks of borrowing from other banks has fallen sharply from its peak during the crisis to a level that is well below its precrisis average, suggesting that banks' access to short-term credit is near normal levels. In some cases, businesses' cost of short-term borrowing in the market for commercial paper has fallen to unprecedented levels. For highly rated businesses, for instance, the interest rate on 3-month commercial paper—which during the crisis had reflected a high risk premium—declined in late 2009 to about 20 basis points, implying that the perceived riskiness of such lending is close to its average level. (Lower-rated borrowers continue to pay higher rates, but those rates have also dropped markedly.)

Conditions for longer-term borrowing and in equity markets have improved as well. By lowering the cost of capital for businesses, those improvements should provide support for renewed investment activity, although firms dependent on bank financing may face greater constraints. Interest rates on corporate debt fell sharply last year, reflecting a reduction in financial markets' assessment of the risk of such lending. As a consequence, corporations issued $1.3 trillion in new debt securities in 2009—40 percent more than they issued in 2008. Equity prices also have increased—the Standard & Poor's 500 index climbed by nearly 60 percent from its low in March 2009—as prospects for economic growth in the United States and in the rest of the world improved.

Although conditions have returned to normal in many financial markets, they have yet to recover in others—especially in the banking sector and in securitization markets.

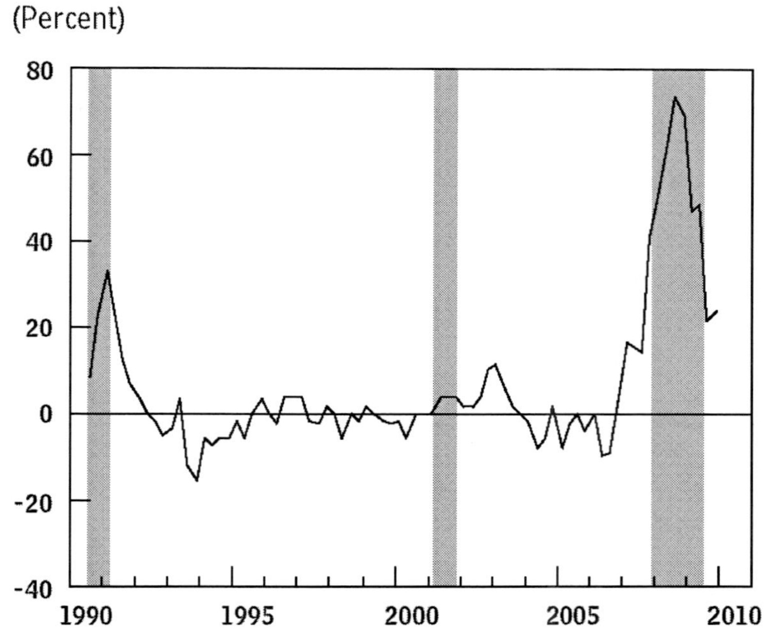

Sources: Congressional Budget Office; Federal Reserve.

Notes: The figure shows the net percentage of respondents to the Federal Reserve's October 2009 *Senior Loan Officer Opinion Survey on Bank Lending Practices* who reported tightening lending standards. Similar movements were reported in the lending standards for other loans and credit cards.

Data are quarterly; the final data point represents the third quarter of 2009.

Data on mortgages before the first quarter of 2007 cover all mortgage loans; data after that point cover only prime mortgage loans (those made to creditworthy borrowers and thus with a relatively small risk of default).

The net percentage who reported tightening standards for nonprime mortgages after the first quarter of 2007 has been greater than the percentage so reporting for prime mortgages.

Figure 2-3. Tightening of Standards for Home Mortgage Loans from Commercial Banks.

Banks. The financial situation of many banks remains fragile, and their losses on loans continue to mount. The net percentage of loans written off as losses (charged off) by banks through the third quarter of 2009 increased to 2.9 percent (on an annual basis) from 1.5

percent one year earlier. CBO expects losses on bank loans to persist for some time because improvements in loan performance tend to lag those in the overall economy. The magnitude of loan losses has led to a sharp increase in the number of bank failures, and CBO expects more failures over the next few years.

Lending by banks remains weak—loans outstanding at commercial banks decreased by about $500 billion during 2009—reflecting both a lower supply of loans from banks and a lower demand for loans by businesses and consumers. Supply fell because banks became concerned about loan losses and acted to preserve their capital. According to the Federal Reserve's October 2009 survey of senior loan officers, banks have progressively tightened their lending standards, although the rate of tightening has declined (see Figure 2-3). Demand for loans fell because good investment opportunities were scarce and the ability to service debts declined with income in the recession. Small businesses, for example, report to the National Federation of Independent Business that they see tighter-than-usual credit conditions, but their main concern remains a lack of sales rather than an inability to borrow as much as they wish.

An important and continuing source of exposure for banks is loans they made on commercial real estate. Weak economic conditions are likely to boost losses on those loans and on securities backed by commercial real estate. Of the approximately $3.5 trillion in debt associated with commercial real estate that was outstanding in mid-2009, about $1.7 trillion was held on the books of banks and thrifts, and about 8 percent of those loans were considered delinquent, almost double the level of a year earlier. Defaults on commercial real estate loans seem likely to mount as refinancing for many of the almost $500 billion of loans maturing during 2010 and 2011 may be difficult to obtain.[15]

Securitization Markets. In the past two decades, securitization—the process of bundling loans into asset-backed securities and selling the securities to investors in the open market—has become an important source of funding for many types of consumer and commercial credit and for commercial and residential mortgages. During the recent crisis, unexpected losses on what were highly rated asset-backed securities shook investors' confidence in those products, and activity in certain segments of the market disappeared entirely. The market for securities backed by commercial real estate was hit particularly hard, and almost no securitization of residential mortgages has occurred in the past two years without the backing of the federal government (see Figure 2-4).

Monetary Policy

CBO expects that the Federal Reserve will use monetary policy to continue to support the nascent recovery until it perceives that the risks of significantly higher inflation outweigh the risks that the economy will fall back into recession. That calculation will probably suggest a lessening of monetary stimulus beginning next year.

During the recession, the Federal Reserve turned to nontraditional means to provide monetary stimulus. It lowered its target for the federal funds rate to nearly zero to stimulate economic activity, but because of the magnitude of the disruptions to the financial system, it also saw a need for additional actions.[16] To put downward pressure on medium-term interest rates (those on securities with terms to maturity of between 2 years and 10 years) in the mortgage and debt markets, the Federal Reserve purchased a large amount of mortgage-backed securities and other medium- and long-term debt in the open market. It also created a number of emergency facilities, most of which have now largely wound down, to restore liquidity and confidence in the markets, and it provided financing to several "systemically important institutions." As a consequence, the Federal Reserve's asset holdings at the end of last year were more than twice as large as they were before the financial crisis. Although the effects of those nontraditional policy actions are hard to quantify, CBO believes that they have provided a significant amount of stimulus—mitigating the impact of the financial crisis on the broader economy and moderating the depth of the recession.

Those nontraditional policy actions have complicated the outlook for monetary policy, however. CBO expects that, beginning next year, the Federal Reserve will seek to withdraw the monetary stimulus in a way that supports the recovery yet avoids creating inflationary pressures. (That outlook is based in part on the expectations of financial market participants and in part on CBO's forecast for economic growth.) Before the financial crisis, if the Federal Reserve had wanted to remove monetary stimulus, it would have done so by raising the federal funds rate. Now, however, to remove stimulus, the Federal Reserve can undertake different combinations of raising the federal funds rate and reducing its holdings of assets. Because the Federal Reserve has not faced that choice before, it is difficult for it and for outside forecasters to accurately project the interplay between traditional and nontraditional policy tools during the coming years. In CBO's forecast, the Federal Reserve keeps its target rate very low through the middle of 2011 and begins to raise that rate only as clear signs of improving economic activity and labor market conditions emerge.

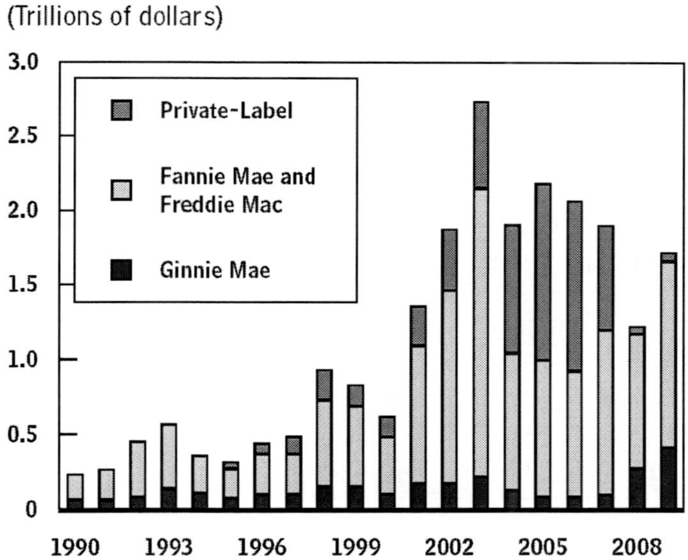

Source: Congressional Budget Office based on data through 2008 from Inside Mortgage Finance, *The 2009 Mortgage Market Statistical Annual*, vol. 2, *The Secondary Market* (Bethesda, Md.: Inside Mortgage Finance Publications, 2009).

Note: Data for 2009 are estimated.

Figure 2-4. Issuance of Mortgage-Backed Securities.

Many economists worry that inflation could increase if monetary stimulus provided by the Federal Reserve is not removed in a timely manner. One particular concern is that the Federal Reserve may be constrained from decreasing its holdings of mortgage-related assets while the housing market remains fragile. However, there is also a risk that the Federal Reserve will sell assets or raise the funds rate too quickly, in which case the economic recovery may be even more muted than CBO anticipates.

Fiscal Policy

Federal fiscal policy supported economic activity in 2009, both through the effects of legislation (especially the American Recovery and Reinvestment Act) and through the effects of the automatic fiscal stabilizers—automatic changes in federal revenues and outlays caused by the ups and downs of business cycles.[17] Fiscal policy will boost output and employment to an even greater extent in 2010, according to CBO's estimates, but its impact will decline in subsequent years. In addition, increases in tax rates scheduled in current law will begin to restrain economic activity in 2011.

CBO expects that the direct and indirect economic effects of ARRA will peak in the first half of 2010 and then diminish, adding to demand by progressively smaller amounts in the second half of 2010 and thereafter. ARRA authorized direct purchases of goods and services by the federal government, transfers to states and local governments (for spending on infrastructure and other purposes), payments to individuals, and temporary tax reductions for individuals and businesses. CBO has estimated that the legislation raised real GDP by 1.3 percent to 3.5 percent during the second half of 2009 (relative to what it would have been without the stimulus). CBO projects that ARRA will increase real GDP by 1.5 percent to 4.5 percent during the first half of 2010, 1.2 percent to 3.8 percent in the second half of 2010, 0.6 percent to 2.0 percent in 2011, and by lesser amounts in subsequent years.[18] Consequently, although it will still add to the level of GDP, ARRA's contribution to growth will turn negative during the latter part of 2010.

The fiscal policy response to recessions includes not only discretionary actions such as ARRA, but also the federal budget's automatic tendency to moderate recessions as a result of the structure of federal tax and spending programs. The federal tax system and social safety-net programs automatically dampen swings in economic activity by decreasing tax payments to the government and increasing benefit payments to households when economic activity slows (and by having the opposite effect when economic activity quickens).[19] That automatic stabilizing effect is quite timely because it does not require legislative action. The automatic stabilizers increased the federal deficit by about one-third percent of GDP in fiscal year 2008 and 2 percent in 2009, and they will add roughly 2½ percent in both 2010 and 2011, in CBO's estimation. As the economic recovery strengthens and output moves closer to its potential level, support from the automatic stabilizers will wane.

Despite the budgetary impacts of ARRA and the automatic stabilizers, both of which increase the deficit in 2010 relative to 2009, CBO estimates that the federal deficit will drop from 9.9 percent of GDP in fiscal year 2009 to 9.2 percent this year. Rather than stemming from fiscal restraint in the usual sense, however, the reduction results from reduced outlays for the Troubled Asset Relief Program, Fannie Mae, and Freddie Mac (see Chapter 3). Without the large swings in estimated outlays for those activities, whose effects on output and employment are quite difficult to measure, the federal deficit would increase rather than decrease in fiscal year 2010.

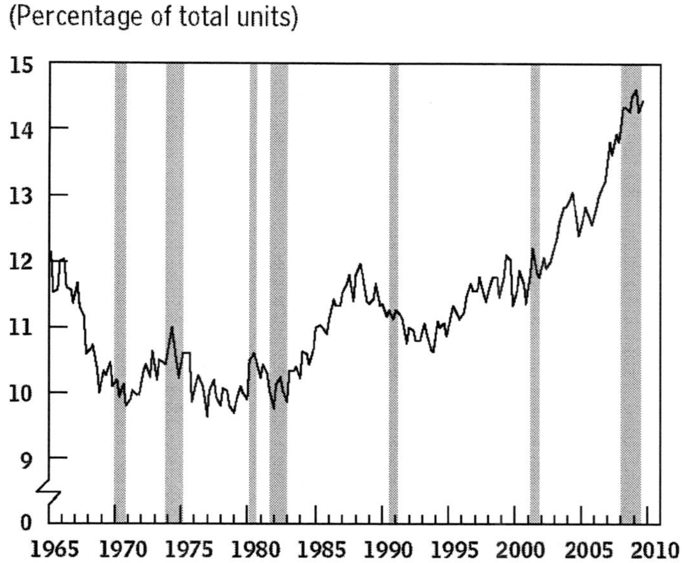

Sources: Congressional Budget Office; Department of Commerce, Bureau of the Census.
Notes: Housing units comprise both rental and owner-occupied dwellings.
Data are quarterly and are plotted through the fourth quarter of 2009

Figure 2-5. Vacant Housing Units.

Under current law, fiscal policy will be less stimulative in 2011. Growth in 2011 will be reduced by the expiration of the tax cuts provided in the Economic Growth and Tax Relief Reconciliation Act of 2001 and the Jobs and Growth Tax Relief Reconciliation Act of 2003 and by the expiration of the temporary relief from the alternative minimum tax. Because AMT relief ceased at the end of 2009, tax rates and liabilities will be higher in 2010. However, CBO anticipates that the impact of higher taxes under the AMT on economic behavior and growth will largely be delayed until 2011, when most of the added taxes will be paid if no further relief is enacted.[20] CBO estimates that, taken together, those tax changes will reduce growth only slightly between the fourth quarters of 2009 and 2010, reduce growth by 1.4 percentage points in 2011, and increase growth by 0.6 percent in 2012.

Investment

Both business and residential investment fell to extraordinarily low levels during the recession in response to the previous overbuilding of the housing stock and the falloff in demand for goods and services. Problems in the financial sector also contributed to the weakness in investment by raising the cost and reducing the availability of credit to firms and households. Private investment—comprising residential construction; businesses' purchases of equipment, software, and structures; and the change in businesses' inventories—declined by an estimated 24 percent during 2009, matching the largest drop previously recorded during the post–World War II period. In CBO's view, investment will begin to rebound this year as the demand for goods and services picks up and the excess stock of residential housing is whittled down. Nevertheless, the magnitude of that excess stock and the ongoing problems in financial markets, especially in the market for mortgages on commercial real estate, are likely to retard the pace of the recovery in the near term.

Housing. Home builders began construction on 550,000 residential housing units during 2009, well below the estimated 1.5 million units that would be necessary to keep up with the growth of the population and the replacement of obsolete units. That unusually low rate of housing starts primarily reflects the unusually high rate of vacancies among housing units (see Figure 2-5). CBO estimates that there were roughly 2.5 million excess vacant housing units, on average, during the second half of 2009.[21] That number has been fairly steady during the past two years despite very low levels of construction because the recession and a sharp rise in mortgage foreclosures have reduced the number of people and families able to maintain independent households.

Because it will take time to absorb the stock of excess vacant units and because of the continuing problems in mortgage markets, CBO expects that the recovery in residential investment will be tepid during 2010 and will contribute less to overall growth thereafter than it has during recoveries following past deep recessions. The difficulty of obtaining credit for commercial real estate is expected to inhibit the recovery of multifamily housing.

Business Fixed Investment. The rate of net business fixed investment—measured as total investment minus depreciation—dropped below 1 percent of GDP during the second half of 2009 (see Figure 2-6). At that rate, businesses' spending on plant and equipment was barely sufficient to cover their replacement needs. For that reason, any future growth in demand will probably generate stronger investment within a few quarters. CBO expects that real business fixed investment will begin to grow modestly during 2010, but net investment will remain quite low by historical standards. Investment in producers' durable equipment and software will lead the recovery; such spending began growing (in real terms) during the second half of 2009, and CBO anticipates that it will rise more rapidly than overall business fixed investment through 2012. Investment in nonresidential structures is expected to lag behind investment in equipment and software because spending for construction requires longer lead times to plan and execute. In addition, problems in the financial sector have hit commercial real estate especially hard, and leading indicators of commercial construction suggest further weakness in that sector during 2010. Nevertheless, CBO expects that overall investment in nonresidential structures will begin to recover during 2011 and then grow more vigorously thereafter.

Inventory Investment. The drop in sales during the recession caused businesses' inventories to rise sharply relative to their sales, and businesses responded by cutting production (see Figure 2-7). Typically, it takes about a year for firms to fully adjust their inventories to a large change in demand, so the sharp drop in demand in late 2008 and early 2009 caused businesses to trim real inventories at a record pace during the first three quarters of 2009. By late 2009, the inventory-to-sales ratio had nearly returned to its prerecession level, and the pace of the inventory drawdown slowed considerably—so it appears that the adjustment process is nearly complete. With inventories back in line, firms could increase their production to more closely match their sales. That increase in production probably added more than 2 percentage points to the annual growth of real GDP in the fourth quarter of 2009. CBO estimates that investment in inventories will turn positive in 2010, further contributing to GDP growth, but by less than it did in the fourth quarter of 2009. The need for businesses to maintain inventories consistent with growing sales will most likely lead to modest growth in inventories during the second half of 2010 and beyond.

Consumer Spending

Real consumer spending grew modestly last year, and CBO expects that its growth will remain subdued this year and next. Such spending declined steeply during the first part of the recession, bottomed out in mid-2009, and began a tepid recovery in the second half of last year, when it rose at an average annual rate of about 2½ percent. Federal fiscal policy, including the effects of ARRA and the temporary "Cash for Clunkers" program, contributed to that recovery. Over the next few years, the growth in consumer spending is likely to be restrained by slow growth in wages and salaries, the declining impact of ARRA, tax increases in 2011, weak gains in households' wealth, and continuing credit restraint. In CBO's forecast, real consumer spending rises at well below its historical average pace through 2011.

Real wage and salary income, the largest component of consumer income, declined during the recession at the fastest rate since the recession of 1973–1975. It is likely to recover only slowly, further restraining consumer spending. CBO expects that the continued high rate of unemployment will limit the growth of wage rates for the next few years, and the slow recovery will hold down the growth of employment.

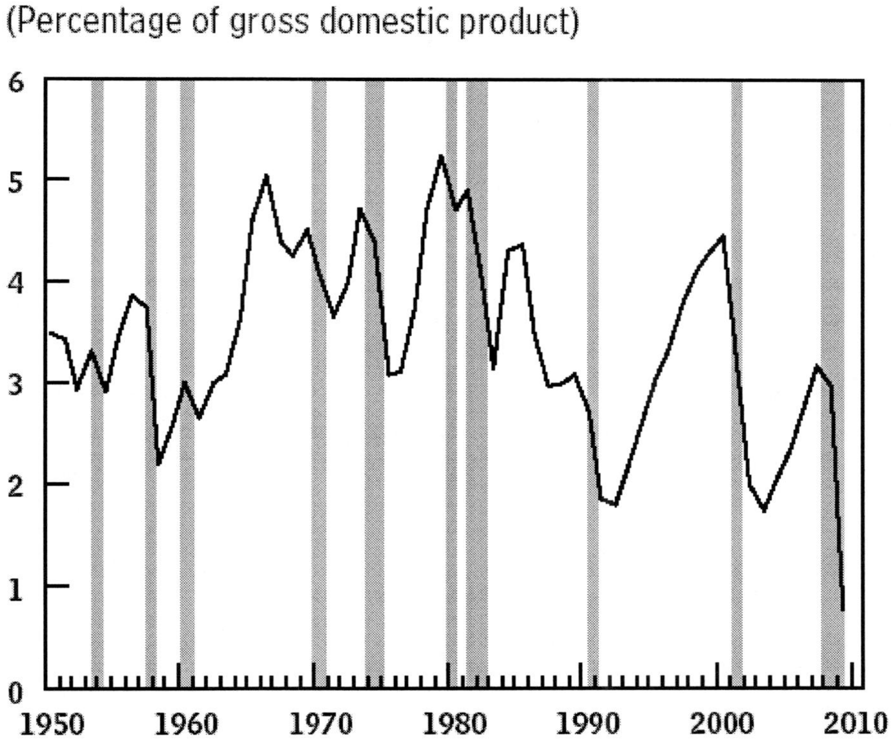

Sources: Congressional Budget Office; Department of Commerce, Bureau of Economic Analysis.

Notes: Business fixed investment (nonresidential structures and producers' durable equipment and software) is shown net of depreciation.

Data are annual and are plotted through 2009. The value for 2009 is estimated.

Figure 2-6. Net Business Fixed Investment.

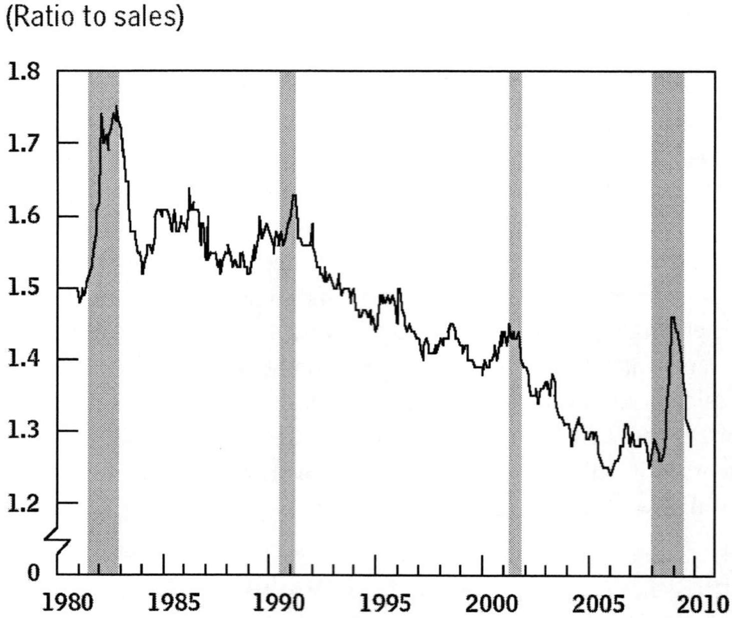

Sources: Congressional Budget Office; Department of Commerce, Bureau of the Census.

Notes: Data are for the summed inventories and sales of manufacturers, retailers, and merchant wholesalers.

Data are monthly and are plotted through November 2009.

Figure 2-7. Inventories.

In addition, fiscal stimulus will provide less support to consumer spending in the second half of this year, and the tax increases scheduled for 2011 will dampen spending. Although CBO expects that ARRA will continue to boost consumer spending (and other sources of aggregate demand) during 2010 and 2011, the magnitude of the boost will diminish. Moreover, under current law, federal personal income tax payments will increase sharply in 2011, primarily from the expiration of the tax cuts enacted in EGTRRA and JGTRRA and the expiration of the temporary relief from the alternative minimum tax. CBO expects personal income taxes to increase from $946 billion in fiscal year 2010 to nearly $1.3 trillion in 2011. As a consequence, after-tax income, which is likely to grow only slowly this year, will decline as taxes rise in 2011.

Small gains in households' wealth are also likely to limit consumer spending in the next few years. During the housing boom, when house prices were rising rapidly, many homeowners borrowed against their rising home equity to fund their spending. Housing equity has dropped with the fall in house prices, and CBO anticipates that weakness in house prices will persist through early 2012. Furthermore, the higher credit standards that have been required to obtain home mortgages in the past few years are likely to restrain borrowing by those homeowners with equity in their homes. Recently, rising stock prices have boosted consumers' wealth, but stock prices remain about 28 percent below what they were at the stock market peak in October 2007.

Higher standards for borrowing also are likely to rein in consumer spending in the near term. Banks began raising their standards on consumer loans in late 2007, after delinquencies on those loans had begun to move up, and they have continued to tighten them ever since.

Given the prospect of continued losses on their consumer loans and other loans, banks are likely to keep their standards for loans to consumers relatively high in the near term.

International Trade

International trade reduced the severity of the recession and will slightly dampen the speed of the recovery this year. Real net exports (exports minus imports) improved during the recession, increasing from about -$560 billion at the beginning of the recession to about -$350 billion by mid-2009, extending an improvement that began in 2006. Because imports fell by more than exports, total demand for domestic production fell less than did demand by U.S. consumers and businesses. The improvement in net exports resulted in part from relatively faster growth among the United States' trading partners than in the United States for several years before the recession. It also resulted from the long-standing decline in the exchange value of the U.S. dollar, which improved the competitiveness of U.S. goods and services in world markets. The real value of the dollar fell by more than 20 percent in terms of the currencies of U.S. trading partners between 2002 and 2008, lowering the prices of U.S. goods in international markets (see Figure 2-8).[22]

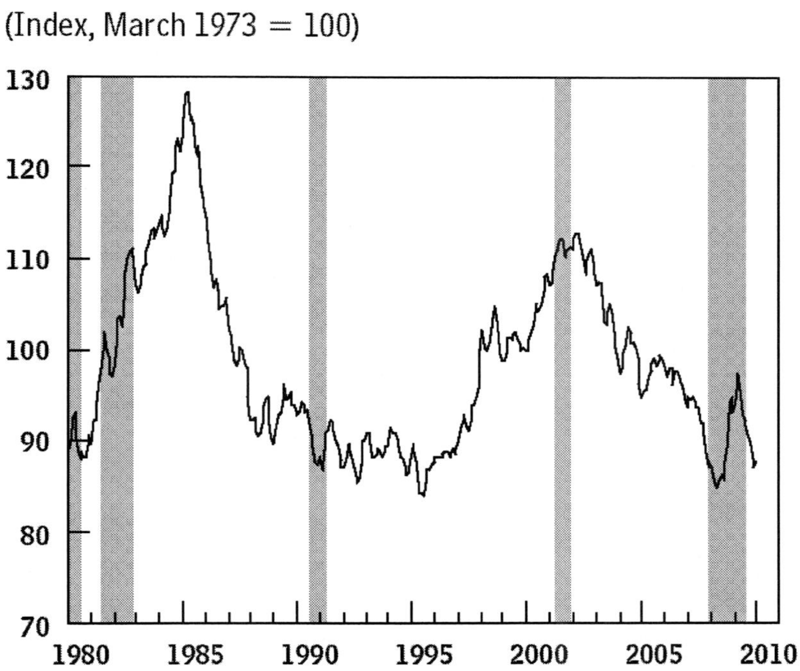

Sources: Congressional Budget Office; Federal Reserve.

Notes: The index is a weighted average of the foreign exchange values of the U.S. dollar against the currencies of a large group of major U.S. trading partners, adjusted for inflation. The index weights, which change over time, are derived from U.S. export shares and from U.S. and foreign import shares.

Data are monthly and are plotted through December 2009.

Figure 2-8. Trade-Weighted Exchange Value of the U.S. Dollar.

CBO expects net exports to fall slightly this year. The main reason is that the recession in the United States was less severe and the subsequent recovery will be stronger than in many other countries to which the United States exports goods and services. Specifically, real GDP in the Euro zone, the United Kingdom, Japan, and some emerging economies fell much more sharply than it did in the United States, and recoveries in many advanced foreign economies are expected to be more sluggish than the recovery in the United States this year.[23] Another reason that net exports are likely to fall slightly in 2010 is the effects of the temporary rise in the value of the dollar in late 2008 and early 2009, when international investors increased their purchases of U.S. assets during the most turbulent period of the financial crisis. CBO expects that net exports will increase next year as growth in foreign economies begins to outpace that in the United States and as the value of the dollar continues its long-term downward trend.

Factors Affecting Labor Markets through 2014

The recent recession was marked by extremely weak demand for labor. Payroll employment fell by 6.4 million between December 2007, when the recession started, and June 2009—the date at which most forecasters believe the recession ended—and by an additional 0.8 million during the second half of 2009.[24] That cumulative decline of 5.2 percent is the largest drop in employment in percentage terms since the period between September 1948 and October 1949. It also pushed the unemployment rate to more than 10 percent (nearly matching its peak since World War II), despite a considerable falloff in labor force participation (see Figure 2-9). Although employment has usually rebounded briskly following deep recessions, in this instance CBO envisions a slow recovery in employment and other measures of labor market performance. In particular, under current law, the unemployment rate is expected to remain at or above 10 percent throughout 2010 and above 9 percent through 2011.

Several factors are important to that outlook.[25] First and most important, output is expected to grow fairly slowly in this recovery. Following the two previous severe recessions in the postwar period, output rebounded particularly rapidly, as did employment. Real GDP grew by 6.2 percent in the four quarters following the 1973–1975 recession and by 7.7 percent in the same period following the 1981–1982 recession. In both instances, all of the jobs lost during the recession were regained within four quarters. In contrast, GDP rose modestly and employment remained much weaker following the two most recent recessions. Employment changed little during the four quarters following the 1990–1991 recession, when real GDP rose by 2.6 percent. And employment fell by more than 1 million in the six quarters following the 2001 recession, when real GDP grew at an average annual rate of 2.1 percent.

Second, average weekly hours worked in private industries fell sharply during the recession to a level well below their long-term downward trend (see Figure 2-10). Restoring existing employees' hours is one way that employers can increase labor input without having to bear the fixed costs of hiring new workers. Although average weekly hours increased in late 2009, they remain below the long-term trend, suggesting that many firms will increase workers' hours before hiring on a large scale.

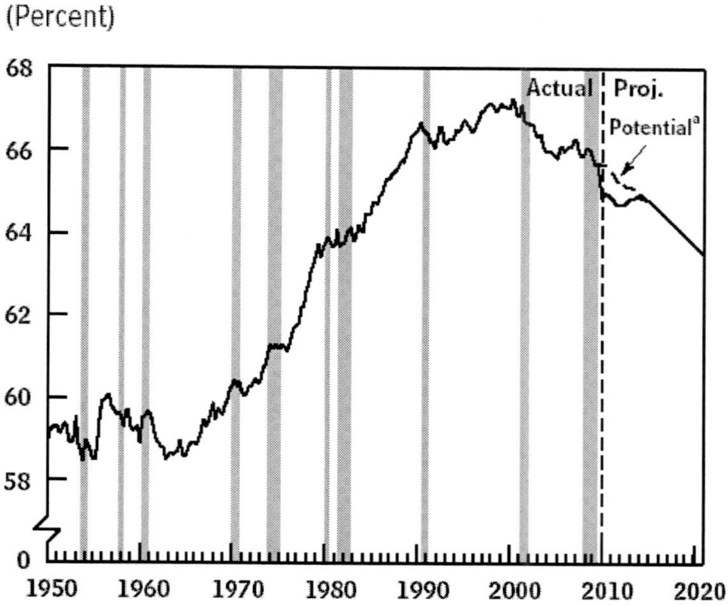

Sources: Congressional Budget Office; Department of Labor, Bureau of Labor Statistics.
Note: Data are quarterly and are plotted through the fourth quarter of 2020.
a. The potential rate is CBO's estimate of the labor force participation rate that would prevail if the economy was at full employment.

Figure 2-9. Labor Force Participation Rate.

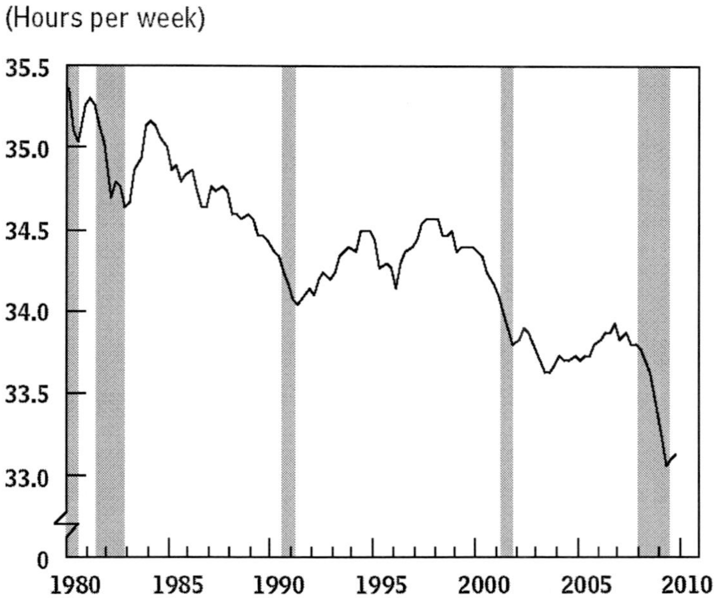

Sources: Congressional Budget Office; Department of Labor, Bureau of Labor Statistics.
Note: Data are quarterly and are plotted through the fourth quarter of 2009.

Figure 2-10. Average Weekly Hours Worked in the Nonfarm Business Sector.

Third, the movement of unemployed workers into new jobs will probably be more difficult in this recovery than in past recoveries. Recessions often accelerate the demise or shrinkage of less efficient and less profitable firms, especially those in declining industries and sectors. Thus, the share of unemployed workers whose previous job was permanently lost (or whose temporary job ended) tends to rise during recessions; the rise has been especially pronounced during the past two years (see Figure 2-11). At the same time, workers on temporary layoff represented a smaller percentage of the unemployed in this past recession than they did in earlier ones.

As a result of the surge in losses of permanent jobs (or completion of temporary jobs) during the recession, subsequent gains in employment will probably rely more than usual on the creation of new jobs, possibly in new firms that are located in different places and require workers with different skills than those needed in the jobs that have disappeared. For workers who have lost jobs because of a permanent layoff, the process of acquiring new skills can take time. (In contrast, it is easier for workers who have been laid off temporarily to return to their jobs because the employers already know the workers and the workers already have the right skills and are familiar with the work practices at the job.) For workers who own their homes and need to move to different geographic regions to find new jobs, the sharp declines in house prices during this recession, combined with the high loan-to-value ratios on many mortgages before the downturn, will hinder relocation: With a significant share of homeowners now owing more on their mortgages than their houses are worth, many people may not be able to sell their houses for enough money to enable them to relocate to new areas.

Although those factors suggest that the pace of job recovery is likely to be slow overall, two indicators have hinted that hiring conditions may improve to some extent in the near future. Employment in the category of temporary help services, a leading indicator for the labor market, experienced large gains in late 2009. In addition, during the second half of 2009, businesses achieved greater output by boosting productivity rather than by adding workers. Such surges in productivity are typical during the late stages of a recession or early months of a recovery, but in the past they have not lasted more than a few quarters.

Consequently, the pace of productivity growth will probably slow significantly in 2010, and if economic activity grows in line with CBO's forecast, some new hiring can be anticipated.

Factors Affecting Inflation through 2014

CBO estimates that the core rate of consumer price inflation, which excludes prices for food and energy, will edge lower over the next few quarters and remain very low—at close to 1 percent—for a few years, gradually increasing as the economy approaches full employment (see Figure 2-12). The principal factor behind that forecast is the large amount of excess productive capacity in the economy, including unemployed workers, vacant houses, and unused business equipment and structures. Excess capacity inhibits firms from raising prices, employees from bargaining for higher wages, and landlords from raising rents. As excess capacity diminishes, the inflation rate will inch up slowly, CBO projects.

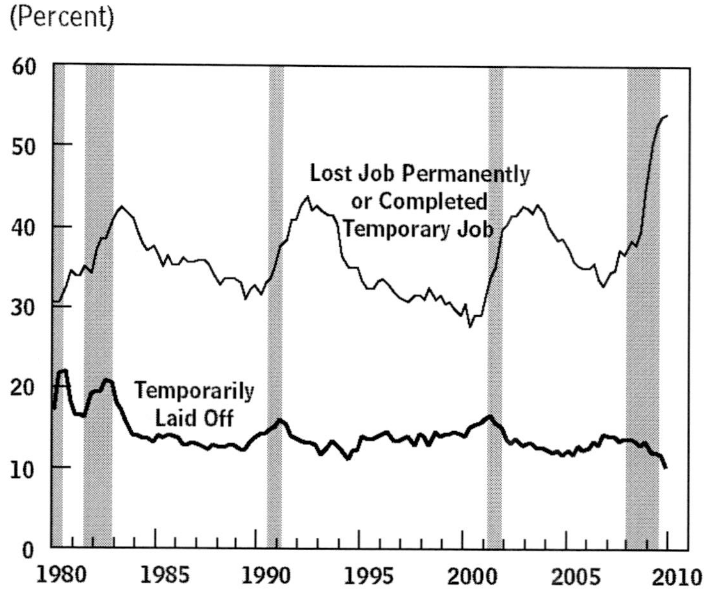

Sources: Congressional Budget Office; Department of Labor, Bureau of Labor Statistics.

Notes: The category of "All Unemployed Persons" includes people who have lost jobs as well as individuals who have quit their job, who are seeking a first job, or who are aiming to return to the labor force after some period of absence.

Data are quarterly and are plotted through the fourth quarter few of 2009.

Figure 2-11. People Who Have Lost Jobs as a Percentage of All Unemployed Persons.

Historically, inflation has slowed during periods in which the economy has excess capacity—that is, during recessions and early in recoveries. The short-term relationship between excess capacity and changes in inflation has varied over the years, but an extremely high level of excess capacity (including a high unemployment rate) has always been associated with a slowing in the core rate of inflation.[26] In keeping with that historical pattern, the annual rate of increase in the core PCE price index, which was running at about 2½ percent before the recent recession, has since fallen to about 1¼ percent. A major contributor to the slowdown in core inflation has been the rapid decline in rent inflation, which appears to be related to high vacancy rates, a sign of excess housing capacity (see Figure 2-13). CBO's inflation forecast incorporates a smaller effect of excess capacity on inflation than has been true, on average, in the past: Given the already low rate of inflation, further declines in inflation would mean that more wage earners and firms would have to accept nominal declines in wages and prices, and resistance to such cuts may be strong.

CBO expects that prices of imports, commodities, and food will tend to push up inflation slightly in the next few years, but not by enough to fully counteract the downward pressure from unused resources. Import prices for nonpetroleum goods and services fell by about 6 percent during the year ending in the third quarter of 2009, which probably lowered consumer price inflation. Such prices are likely to increase in the next two years as foreign economies recover and as the value of the dollar weakens further. However, evidence suggests that changes in nonpetroleum import prices have a limited effect on consumer price inflation in the United States.

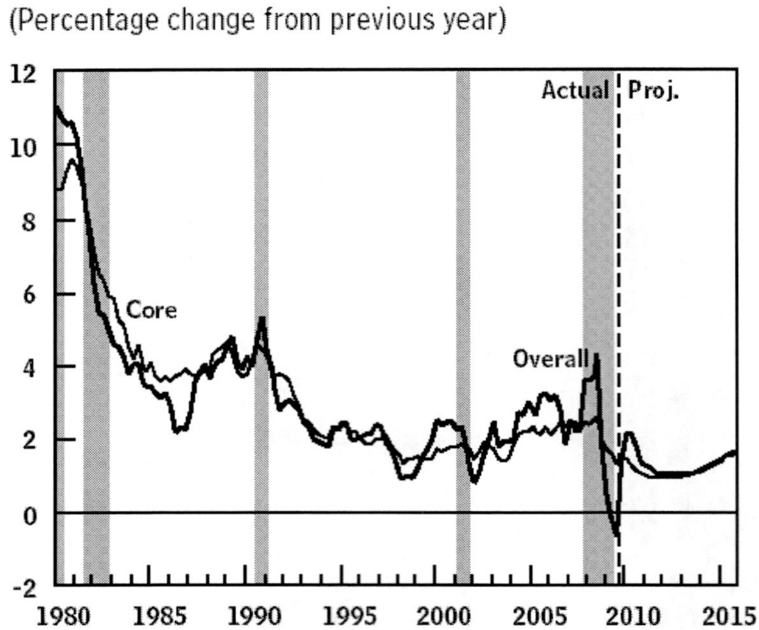

Sources: Congressional Budget Office; Department of Commerce, Bureau of Economic Analysis.

Notes: The overall inflation measure is the price index for personal consumption expenditures. The core rate excludes prices for food and energy.

Data are quarterly and are plotted through the fourth quarter of 2015.

Figure 2-12. Inflation.

Prices for many commodities (especially petroleum, metals, and some agricultural goods) have bounced back from their lows early in 2009, so overall inflation is likely to be slightly higher than core inflation this year. Petroleum prices rose from $39 per barrel in February 2009 to near $80 per barrel in mid-January (for West Texas intermediate crude oil), and energy analysts expect that prices will continue to rise this year. Natural gas prices did not increase during 2009, but analysts anticipate that those prices, too, will climb this year.

Prices for food to be consumed at home fell by almost 3 percent over the 12 months ending in December 2009, the greatest 12-month rate of decline since 1959, but food prices are expected to resume a more normal rate of increase this year. Prices for food commodities (such as corn, soybeans, wheat, and rice), which had increased sharply between 2006 and mid-2008, subsequently fell. The extraordinary drop in consumer food prices in 2009 largely reflects that decline in commodity prices. Prices of foodstuffs have stopped falling in recent months, however, and CBO expects that consumer food prices will average 1.5 percent growth over the next few years.

Forecasting inflation is always difficult, but the unprecedented amount of excess capacity in the economy and the extraordinary nature of the Federal Reserve's monetary policy actions during the financial crisis have made it even more difficult than usual. Some analysts maintain that even nominal wage and price levels are susceptible to the downward pressures of excess capacity. Those analysts expect that inflation will be lower than in CBO's forecast for the next few years; indeed, some analysts even anticipate a period of deflation. In contrast, many other analysts are concerned that it will be difficult for the Federal Reserve to avoid higher inflation, particularly two or three years from now. They fear that the Federal Reserve may be unable to trim its holdings of mortgage-backed securities and other long-term securities sufficiently rapidly.

The Outlook for 2015 to 2020

CBO does not try to project business-cycle fluctuations in the economy beyond the short term (in this case, beyond 2014) but instead identifies and projects trends in the factors that underlie potential output, including growth in the labor force, the rate of capital accumulation, and the growth of productivity. During the first half of the 10-year projection period, real GDP is expected to grow rapidly enough to close the substantial gap that existed in 2009 between it and potential GDP. Then, during the remainder of the projection period, real GDP is projected to grow at about the same rate as potential GDP. That approach does not preclude the possibility of recession in the latter years of the projection period; instead, it assumes that the likelihood of booms or recessions in the future is about the same as it was in the past.

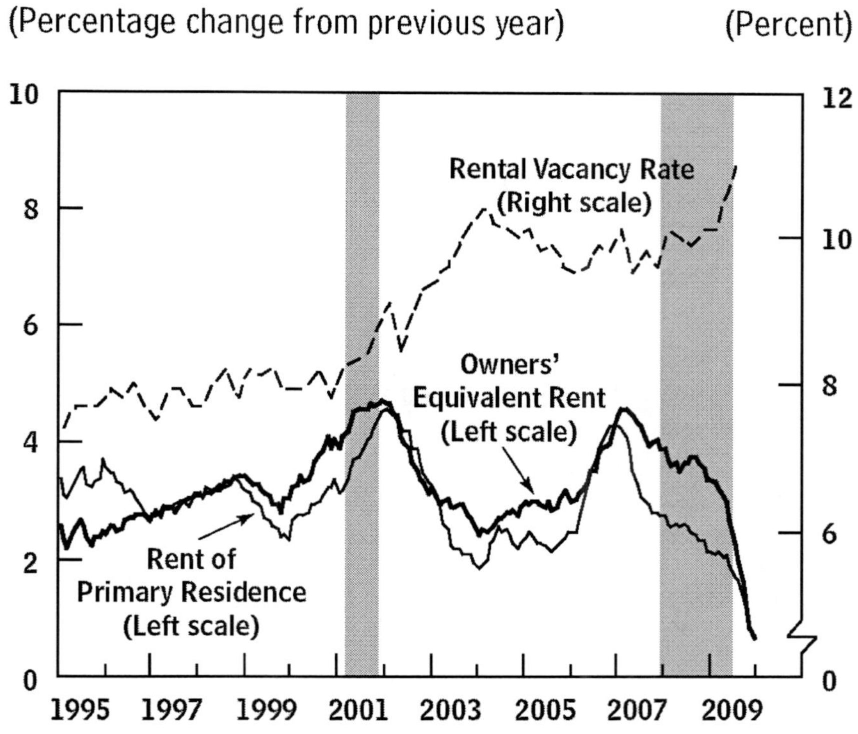

Sources: Congressional Budget Office; Department of Commerce, Bureau of the Census; Department of Labor, Bureau of Labor Statistics.

Note: The rental vacancy rate (right scale) is a quarterly measure and is plotted through the fourth quarter of 2009. The rental rates from the consumer price index for all urban consumers (left scale) are monthly measures and are plotted through December 2009.

Figure 2-13. Rental Vacancy Rate and Growth of Price Indexes for Rents.

On that basis, CBO projects that real GDP will grow at an average annual rate of 2.4 percent during the 2015–2020 period, which matches the growth rate that is projected for potential output during those years. The unemployment rate will average 5 percent between 2015 and 2020, which is equal to CBO's estimate of the natural rate of unemployment.

Inflation as measured by the PCE price index will average 1.7 percent annually during the latter years of the decade; core PCE prices are also projected to grow at an average annual rate of 1.7 percent. The interest rate on three-month Treasury bills will average 4.6 percent between 2015 and 2020, and the rate on 10-year Treasury notes will average 5.5 percent.

Potential Output

CBO expects output to converge to the economy's potential output by the end of 2014. Between now and 2014, potential output will grow at an average annual rate of 2.1 percent, CBO projects, well below the average growth rate of 3.4 percent during the past 60 years (see Table 2-2). During the 2015–2020 period, the average annual growth rate of potential output will pick up to 2.4 percent, still well below the historical average. In CBO's judgment, potential growth during the coming decade will be held down relative to historical experience by slower growth in three key components: potential hours worked, capital services, and total factor productivity (TFP). During the first five years of the projection period, potential growth is further depressed by a very slow pace of capital accumulation resulting from the plunge of business investment during the recession and its expected gradual recovery. In the second half of the 10-year period, the pace of capital accumulation picks up in response to the recovery in business investment, but it remains below the pace of previous decades.

Potential hours worked in the nonfarm business sector, which accounts for about three-fourths of the economy, are projected to grow at an average annual rate of 0.5 percent from 2015 through 2020, significantly below the long-term historical average of 1.4 percent. That slower growth in hours worked reflects a correspondingly slower growth in the potential labor force, which averages 0.6 percent annually—considerably lower than its historical annual average, which CBO estimates at 1.6 percent from 1950 through 2009. Population growth is expected to be slower during the next 10 years than it was during the previous 60 years, and the labor force participation rate—the percentage of people ages 16 and over who are employed or seeking work—is expected to decline during the next decade (see Figure 2-9 on page 35). That rate has been falling since 2000, but it had been increasing during most of the prior 50 years, boosting the growth of the labor force relative to the population.

Growth in capital services (the services provided by the capital stock) will average 2.1 percent during the 2010–2014 period and 3.5 percent between 2015 and 2020, in CBO's estimation. Those rates of growth are considerably lower than the average rate of 4 percent witnessed from 1950 through 2009. In the near term, growth in capital services is expected to be held back by very low rates of capital accumulation caused by the falloff in business investment related to the recession. During the second half of the projection period, the pace of capital accumulation is faster, but it is still below average because some private investment will be displaced by increased federal debt and because the slower projected growth in the labor force means that smaller increases in the stock of plant and equipment will be required to outfit the workforce with the same amount of capital per person.

The growth of potential total factor productivity—a measure of the combined productivity of labor and capital—will average 1.3 percent annually from 2015 to 2020, CBO projects. That projected rate is slightly below its average during the past 60 years but slightly above its average rate of growth since the major slowdown in productivity growth that occurred in the early 1970s.

Table 2-2. Key Assumptions in CBO's Projection of Potential Output

(By calendar year, in percent)									
	Average Annual Growth						Projected Average Annual Growth		
	1950-1973	1974-1981	1982-1990	1991-2001	2002-2009	Total, 1950-2009	2010-2014	2015-2020	Total, 2010-2020
	Overall Economy								
Potential Output	3.9	3.2	3.1	3.1	2.7	3.4	2.1	2.4	2.2
Potential Labor Force	1.6	2.5	1.6	1.2	1.0	1.6	0.7	0.6	0.7
Potential Labor Force Productivity[a]	2.3	0.7	1.5	1.9	1.7	1.8	1.3	1.8	1.6
	Nonfarm Business Sector								
Potential Output	4.0	3.5	3.3	3.5	3.0	3.6	2.3	2.8	2.5
Potential Hours Worked	1.4	2.2	1.7	1.2	0.7	1.4	0.5	0.5	0.5
Capital Input	3.8	4.3	4.1	4.7	2.9	4.0	2.1	3.5	2.9
Potential TFP	1.9	0.7	0.9	1.3	1.7	1.4	1.3	1.3	1.3
Potential TFP excluding adjustments	1.9	0.7	0.9	1.2	1.3	1.4	1.3	1.3	1.3
TFP adjustments	0	0	0	0.1	0.3	0.1	-0.1	*	0
Recession effect[b]	0	0	0	0	0	0	-0.1	*	0
Temporary adjustment[c]	0	0	0	0.1	0.3	0.1	0	0	0
Contributions to the Growth of Potential Output (Percentage points)									
Potential hours worked	0.9	1.6	1.2	0.8	0.5	1.0	0.4	0.4	0.4
Capital input	1.2	1.3	1.2	1.4	0.9	1.2	0.6	1.1	0.9
Potential TFP	1.9	0.7	0.9	1.3	1.7	1.4	1.3	1.3	1.3
Total Contributions	**4.0**	**3.5**	**3.3**	**3.5**	**3.0**	**3.6**	**2.3**	**2.7**	**2.5**
Potential Labor Productivity in the Nonfarm Business Sector[d]	2.6	1.3	1.6	2.3	2.3	2.2	1.7	2.2	2.0

Source: Congressional Budget Office.

Note: TFP = total factor productivity; GDP = gross domestic product; * = between -0.05 percent and zero.

a. The ratio of potential output to the potential labor force.

b. An adjustment to reflect the effects of the recession on potential output, beyond its impact on capital accumulation.

c. An adjustment for the unusually rapid growth of TFP between 2001 and 2003.

d. The estimated trend in the ratio of output to hours worked in the nonfarm business sector.

Recessions typically have little effect on potential output beyond the direct effect of lower investment on capital accumulation, and that effect tends to diminish in the long run when investment recovers to normal levels. (The resulting time pattern of growth in capital services is reflected in CBO's projection.) Other effects of recessions on potential output are possible, including those associated with declines in spending for research and development caused by falloffs in business revenues, but for most recessions they have been small.

Some analysts have raised concerns about persistent negative effects of the recent recession because of its unique characteristics, including the degree of disruption to financial markets and the labor market. The movement of workers across regions and industries may be more difficult in the wake of this recession than in the past because more workers appear to have been laid off permanently rather than temporarily and therefore may need to acquire new skills and move into new industries to find jobs. Moreover, the real estate slump may hinder workers' ability to relocate to new jobs because they cannot sell their houses at prices sufficient to allow them to move. And finally, empirical studies have found that business-cycle recoveries from recessions induced by financial crises are generally slower than recoveries from recessions caused by other factors. For example, if financial intermediation is hobbled for several years because of the crisis, then the process of allocating resources will be hampered as well, which could slow the growth of potential output. To reflect the possibility that such mechanisms will be operating in coming years, CBO has trimmed the growth rate of potential TFP by 0.1 percentage point for the next five years. Consequently, the level of potential TFP in 2015 and beyond is 0.5 percent lower than it otherwise would be.

Inflation, Unemployment, and Interest Rates

As measured by the PCE price index, inflation in CBO's forecast averages 1.7 percent per year between 2015 and 2020. CBO expects that monetary policy will determine the path of inflation during that period and that the Federal Reserve will choose to maintain the rate of PCE inflation near the top of its apparent target range. As measured by the change in the consumer price index, inflation is projected to average 1.9 percent between 2015 and 2020 (reflecting the different methods used to calculate that index).

CBO projects that unemployment will average 5 percent from 2015 to 2020, equal to CBO's estimate of the natural rate of unemployment. That estimate has been revised upward from 4.8 percent since last August, on the basis of both econometric evidence and an analysis of the recent trends in labor markets.

CBO's outlook for interest rates in the latter years of the decade reflects its projections for inflation and for inflation-adjusted interest rates. The rate on 3-month Treasury bills is projected to average 4.6 percent, and the rate on 10-year Treasury notes, 5.5 percent.

The Outlook for Income through 2020

Projections of federal tax revenues are based on projections of various categories of income—primarily wages and salaries, domestic corporate profits, proprietors' income, and interest and dividend income—as measured in the national income and product accounts compiled by the Bureau of Economic Analysis. Because the sum of all domestic income is approximately equal to nominal GDP, future levels of income in those categories can be decomposed into future levels and shares of nominal GDP.

The growth of nominal GDP reflects both the growth of real GDP and the rise in prices of goods and services produced in the United States (measured by the GDP price index). In 2010, in CBO's forecast, the GDP price index rises more slowly than the PCE price index because the rebound in energy prices that is under way affects the PCE price index much more than it does the GDP price index. After 2012, the two measures follow a similar track. Reflecting the growth of real GDP, nominal GDP rises relatively modestly in 2010 and 2011, averaging just over 3 percent. Nominal GDP averages about 6 percent growth over the following two years before converging to a trend growth rate of about 4 percent in the last years of the projection period.

Labor's share of GDP, which fell during the recession to its lowest value since World War II, will increase over the next 10 years to its average over the past 30 years, CBO projects.[27] In CBO's forecast, the elevated level of unemployment depresses labor income in 2010. Beyond 2010, CBO expects labor income to grow more rapidly than GDP (as conditions in labor markets improve) and, by 2020, to approach its average share of GDP between 1979 and 2008.

In previous forecasts, CBO had assumed that the labor share of income would return to its average for the entire post–World War II period; that longer-term average is about ½ percentage point above the average since 1979. The change in CBO's view reflects the fact that labor income as a share of GDP has stayed relatively low during most of the past three decades. Accordingly, a return to the longer-term historical average during the next 10 years would require a very rapid change from recent experience, and the weakness in labor market data suggest that such a rebound has become increasingly less likely.

Domestic corporate economic profits, another important category of income for revenue projections, have rebounded since the beginning of 2009 after a precipitous fall, and they are likely to continue to grow robustly in the near term. Domestic profits fell to 6 percent of GDP early in 2009, but CBO's forecast shows them rising to nearly 9 percent of GDP by mid-2010. (Economic profits differ from book profits—those reported by corporations—because they remove the effects of tax law on the timing of depreciation and inventory valuation.) Domestic profits are those that arise from corporate operations in the United States. CBO projects that domestic corporate economic profits as a share of GDP will start to fall during 2013, as higher interest rates and the recovery in borrowing by businesses increases interest payments by businesses.

Comparison with CBO's August 2009 Forecast

CBO's economic outlook has not changed substantially since the agency prepared its previous forecast in August 2009. However, two of the changes—faster growth in nominal GDP and lower interest rates—contribute to an improved budget outlook. The forecasts for wages and salaries and for corporate profits (categories of income that are important for projecting revenues) were revised upward for much of the next decade.

The faster projected growth in nominal GDP stems from faster growth in the GDP price index rather than faster growth in real GDP, which is about the same as that projected in the

August forecast for the 2010–2019 period as a whole (see Table 2-3). The average rate of increase in the GDP price index for the 2010–2019 period is about 0.2 percentage points faster in this projection than in the August 2009 projection, largely because of upward revisions to the projected increases in the prices of investment and consumption goods.

The projection of inflation (measured by growth in the PCE price index) was revised upward by between 0.3 percent and 0.4 percent over the next three years, in part because import prices are expected to increase more rapidly than CBO last projected, and also because excess capacity seems to be having a somewhat more modest impact on inflation than was previously thought. Inflation remains slightly higher (about 0.1 percentage point after 2015) in the remainder of the projection period than CBO projected in August. The CPI projection was generally revised less than the PCE price index, and it was virtually unchanged after 2015 (because it weights the components of consumption differently).

As a result of projecting a slightly lower growth rate of real GDP and a higher unemployment rate during the early stage of the recovery, CBO now expects interest rates to remain low for longer than it did last August. In CBO's forecast, short-term rates are lower than previously forecast by 0.3 percentage points in 2010 and 1 percentage point between 2011 and 2014. Long-term rates are also lower in the same period, though by a smaller margin. Participants in financial markets have also lowered their forecasts of short-term interest rates through 2010. For the latter years of the projection period, interest rates are similar to the rates in CBO's previous forecast.

The share of wages and salaries in GDP is lower throughout the projection period in this forecast than in the previous one, and the domestic corporate profit share is higher in the near term but lower in the latter years. Those changes are partly driven by revisions to historical data and partly by changes in methodology prompted by recent experience.

In July 2009, the Bureau of Economic Analysis published revisions to the national income and product accounts; those revisions indicated that wages and salaries were lower relative to GDP during the past 10 years than previously thought. The lower share in the recent data, combined with the likelihood of a more protracted period of high unemployment and low growth in wage rates, led CBO to forecast a lower share for wage and salary income in the near term. In addition, the downward revision for the past 10 years added to the evidence that the wage and salary share will not quickly return to its average since 1950. Therefore, in the latter years of the projection period, the wage and salary share is also somewhat lower than CBO forecast last August.

In contrast to the wage and salary revisions, the revisions to the corporate profit share of GDP in recent history were upward, and the current forecast indicates that profits will grow more quickly this year than was previously estimated. Therefore, the domestic corporate profit share of GDP is higher, on average, for the next five years in this forecast than in the forecast from last August. In the latter years of the projection period, however, the profit share falls below the amount forecast in August in response to an upward revision to projected interest payments by businesses.[28]

CBO estimates that the unemployment rate will be higher between 2010 and 2014 than it estimated last August, in part because of the forecast for slower growth of real GDP and slightly higher growth in productivity in the near term, but also because the dislocations in labor markets caused by the recession now appear to be more pervasive than previously estimated. CBO has also revised upward its estimate of the natural rate of unemployment for the 2015–2020 period, from 4.8 percent to 5.0 percent. That revision was based partly on econometric evidence and partly on an analysis of the recent trends in labor markets, especially the increase in the number of displaced workers and the growth in the number of workers unemployed for more than 27 weeks. Other factors, including shifts of employment between industries and regions generated by the recession and the difficulty that some workers may face in relocating because they cannot sell their houses, have probably boosted the unemployment rate recently and are likely to slow the rate of recovery in the labor market, but they are not expected to play a major role in the medium term.

The changes between the two forecasts have lowered projected deficits for every year of the 10-year period (see Appendix B, Table B-1). The lower interest rates reduced projected interest payments on the debt, and the faster growth in nominal GDP raised the projections of the incomes that underlie the revenue projections. Those effects were partly offset by higher projections of noninterest outlays—an increase that stemmed from higher inflation rates in the near term and higher unemployment rates throughout the projection period. On balance, changes in the economic outlook since August have caused the annual deficit projections to average about $45 billion lower for 2010 to 2014, and about $80 billion lower from 2015 to 2019.

Table 2-3. CBO's Current and Previous Economic Projections for Calendar Years 2009 to 2019

	Estimated	Forecast		Projected Annual Average	
	2009	2010	2011	2012–2014	2015–2019
Nominal GDP (Billions of dollars)					
January 2010	14,253	14,706	15,116	17,816 [a]	21,882 [b]
August 2009	14,163	14,570	15,146	17,488 [a]	21,320 [b]
Nominal GDP (Percentage change)					
January 2010	-1.3	3.2	2.8	5.6	4.2
August 2009	-0.7	2.9	4.0	4.9	4.0
Real GDP (Percentage change)					
January 2010	-2.5	2.2	1.9	4.4	2.4
August 2009	-2.5	1.7	3.5	4.2	2.4
GDP Price Index (Percentage change)					
January 2010	1.2	0.9	0.9	1.1	1.7
August 2009	1.8	1.1	0.4	0.7	1.6
PCE Price Index[c] (Percentage change)					
January 2010	0.2	1.9	1.1	1.2	1.7
August 2009	0.4	1.5	0.8	0.9	1.6
Consumer Price Index[d] (Percentage change)					
January 2010	-0.2	2.4	1.3	1.2	1.9
August 2009	-0.5	1.7	1.3	1.2	2.0
Unemployment Rate (Percent)					
January 2010	9.3	10.1	9.5	6.5	5.0
August 2009	9.3	10.2	9.1	5.9	4.8
Three-Month Treasury Bill Rate (Percent)					
January 2010	0.1	0.2	0.7	2.9	4.6
August 2009	0.2	0.6	1.7	3.9	4.7

	Estimated 2009	Forecast 2010	Forecast 2011	Projected Annual Average 2012–2014	Projected Annual Average 2015–2019
Ten-Year Treasury Note Rate (Percent)					
January 2010	3.2	3.6	3.9	4.5	5.5
August 2009	3.3	4.1	4.4	5.0	5.6
Tax Bases (Billions of dollars)					
Domestic economic profits					
January 2010	990	1,263	1,307	1,487 [a]	1,542 [b]
August 2009	943	1,022	1,133	1,393 [a]	1,689 [b]
Wages and salaries					
January 2010	6,329	6,517	6,671	8,061 [a]	9,938 [b]
August 2009	6,465	6,614	6,792	8,008 [a]	9,773 [b]
Tax Bases (Percentage of GDP)					
Domestic economic profits					
January 2010	6.9	8.6	8.6	8.6	7.4
August 2009	6.7	7.0	7.5	7.9	7.9
Wages and salaries					
January 2010	44.4	44.3	44.1	45.0	45.4
August 2009	45.6	45.4	44.8	45.6	45.9
Memorandum:					
Real Potential GDP (Percentage change)					
September 2008	2.2	1.7	1.6	2.3	2.4
March 2008	2.2	1.7	1.7	2.4	2.4

Sources: Congressional Budget Office; Department of Commerce, Bureau of Economic Analysis; Department of Labor, Bureau of Labor Statistics; Federal Reserve.

Notes: Percentage changes are measured from one year to the next.

GDP = gross domestic product.

a. Level in 2014.

b. Level in 2019.

c. The personal consumption expenditure price index.

d. The consumer price index for all urban consumers.

Comparison with Other Forecasts

CBO's forecast envisions a weaker recovery from the recession over the next two years than the current *Blue Chip* consensus of private forecasters or the central tendency of the forecasts from last November's meeting of the members of the Federal Reserve's Federal Open Market Committee (see Tables 2-4 and 2-5). CBO's forecast for inflation, while lower than that of the *Blue Chip* consensus, is similar to that of the Federal Reserve. Consistent with its outlook for slower real growth and lower inflation, CBO expects a slightly higher rate of unemployment than the other forecasters and lower interest rates than does the *Blue Chip* consensus. (The Federal Reserve does not publish a forecast of interest rates.)

The difference in the forecasts probably stems, at least in part, from differences in assumptions about fiscal policy. Although it is uncertain what private forecasters are assuming for fiscal policy during this year or next, most probably assume that the Congress will not allow all of the tax cuts enacted in 2001 and 2003 to expire as scheduled. Furthermore, they probably assume that lawmakers will extend some or all of the AMT relief enacted in previous years in 2010 and beyond, and some forecasters may expect that additional fiscal stimulus will occur this year. In contrast, CBO is required in its baseline projections to assume that current laws and policies remain unchanged. CBO estimates that the scheduled changes to tax law will dampen growth in 2011. If CBO assumed that all of the expiring tax provisions were extended beyond 2011 but no other stimulative fiscal measures were passed, the agency's forecast of the level of real GDP at the end of 2011 would be in line with the forecast of the *Blue Chip* consensus and near the lower end of the central tendency of the Federal Reserve's forecasts.

Table 2-4. Comparison of CBO and *Blue Chip* Consensus Economic Forecasts for Calendar Years 2009 to 2011

	Estimated 2009	**Forecast**	
		2010	**2011**
	Fourth Quarter to Fourth Quarter (Percentage Change)		
Nominal GDP (Percentage change)			
CBO	0.5	3.1	3.3
Blue Chip	0.6	4.4	4.9
Real GDP (Percentage change)			
CBO	-0.4	2.1	2.4
Blue Chip	-0.3	2.9	3.1
GDP Price Index (Percentage change)			
CBO	0.9	1.0	0.9
Blue Chip	0.9	1.4	1.7
Consumer Price Index[a] (Percentage change)			
CBO	1.7	1.6	1.1
Blue Chip	1.4	1.7	2.0
	Calendar Year Average (Percent)		
Unemployment Rate (Percent)			
CBO	9.3	10.1	9.5
Blue Chip	9.3	10.0	9.3
Three-Month Treasury Bill Rate (Percent)			
CBO	0.1	0.2	0.7
Blue Chip	0.2	0.5	1.8
Ten-Year Treasury Note Rate (Percent)			
CBO	3.2	3.6	3.9
Blue Chip	3.3	4.0	4.6

Sources: Congressional Budget Office; Aspen Publishers, *Blue Chip Economic Indicators* (January 10, 2010).

Notes: The *Blue Chip* consensus is the average of about 50 forecasts by private-sector economists.

GDP = gross domestic product.

[a] The consumer price index for all urban consumers.

Table 2-5. Comparison of Federal Reserve and CBO Forecasts for Calendar Years 2009 to 2012

	Federal Reserve		
	Range	**Central Tendency**	**CBO**
	2010 *Fourth Quarter to Fourth Quarter (Percentage change)*		
Real GDP	2.0 to 4.0	2.5 to 3.5	2.1
PCE Price Index	1.1 to 2.0	1.3 to 1.6	1.4
Core PCE Price Index[a]	0.9 to 2.0	1.0 to 1.5	1.0
	Average Level, Fourth Quarter (Percent)		
Civilian Unemployment Rate	8.6 to 10.2	9.3 to 9.7	10.0
	2011 *Fourth Quarter to Fourth Quarter (Percentage change)*		
Real GDP	2.5 to 4.6	3.4 to 4.5	2.4
PCE Price Index	0.6 to 2.4	1.0 to 1.9	1.1
Core PCE Price Index[a]	0.5 to 2.4	1.0 to 1.6	0.9
	Average Level, Fourth Quarter (Percent)		
Civilian Unemployment Rate	7.2 to 8.7	8.2 to 8.6	9.1
	2012 *Fourth Quarter to Fourth Quarter (Percentage change)*		
Real GDP	2.8 to 5.0	3.5 to 4.8	5.1
PCE Price Index	0.2 to 2.3	1.2 to 1.9	1.1
Core PCE Price Index[a]	0.2 to 2.3	1.0 to 1.7	1.0
	Average Level, Fourth Quarter (Percent)		
Civilian Unemployment Rate	6.1 to 7.6	6.8 to 7.5	7.2

Sources: Congressional Budget Office; Federal Reserve System.

Notes: The range of estimates from the Federal Reserve reflects all views of the members of the Federal Open Market Committee. The central tendency reflects the most common views of the committee's members.

GDP = gross domestic product.

[a] The personal consumption expenditure price index excluding prices for food and energy.

CBO anticipates a much lower average rate of inflation (based on the CPI-U) for 2010 and 2011 than the *Blue Chip* consensus, but CBO's forecast is near the lower end of the central tendency of the forecasts reported by the Federal Reserve. CBO's projection for CPI-U inflation beyond 2011 also appears to be lower than that of most private forecasters. The recent *Blue Chip* consensus forecast extends only through 2011, but other information (from surveys of forecasters and the implied inflation rates that can be derived from comparing yields on inflation-protected Treasury securities and yields on traditional securities) indicates expectations of an average CPI-U inflation rate of 2 percent to 2½ percent for 2010 to 2014 and approximately 3 percent for the following five years. In CBO's forecast, by contrast, the CPI-U grows at an average rate of 1.5 percent through 2014 and 1.9 percent, on average, for 2015 to 2020.

Interest rates in CBO's forecast are below those of the *Blue Chip* consensus for 2010 and substantially lower in 2011. The difference is probably attributable to the weaker growth and lower inflation in CBO's outlook. Weak growth and low inflation would encourage the

Federal Reserve to keep short-term interest rates lower than it would otherwise, which would also affect long-term interest rates.

3. THE SPENDING OUTLOOK

In the absence of changes to current laws and policies, federal spending will total $3.5 trillion in 2010, the Congressional Budget Office estimates, about the same amount the government spent in 2009. At 24.1 percent of gross domestic product, total outlays are expected to be slightly lower than they were last year but still considerably higher than the 20.7 percent they have averaged over the past 40 years. According to CBO's baseline projections, federal spending in the next decade will average almost 23 percent of GDP.

Total mandatory spending is projected to decline to $1.9 trillion this year from the $2.1 trillion recorded in 2009 (see Table 3-1). That dip is primarily a result of lower-than-expected costs for the Troubled Asset Relief Program and lower estimated costs for the government-sponsored enterprises (GSEs) Fannie Mae and Freddie Mac. Spending for most other mandatory programs will be higher in 2010 than was the case last year. Discretionary spending is projected to jump nearly 11percent in 2010, to $1.4 trillion. A sharp increase in nondefense spending accounts for much of that upsurge, which is chiefly a result of the funding provided in 2009 by the American Recovery and Reinvestment Act. (The upsurge is consistent with CBO's original estimate that such funding would not be spent until after 2009.) Payments for net interest, which fell in 2009, will rise in 2010 as the federal debt continues its steep climb. (See Box3-1 for descriptions of the three major types of federal spending.)

In developing its baseline projections, CBO follows the rules established in the Balanced Budget and Emergency Deficit Control Act of 1985 (although that act has now expired). Therefore, when projecting spending for mandatory programs, CBO assumes that existing law will remain unchanged and that future outlays will depend on the evolution of caseloads, benefit costs, and other factors. When projecting spending for discretionary programs, CBO assumes that the appropriations most recently enacted by the Congress will grow at the anticipated rate of inflation.

Under current law, CBO projects, mandatory spending will rise in coming years, although not as rapidly as it has over the past decade. CBO projects that mandatory outlays will increase by 5.1 percent in 2011 and by an average of 4.4 percent annually between 2012 and 2020, compared with an average growth rate of 6.4 percent between 1999 and 2008. The rate of growth in spending for those programs is projected to slow largely because, under current law, payments to doctors in the Medicare program are expected to decline and provisions that temporarily boost spending for Medicaid, unemployment compensation, and refundable tax credits are set to expire. Projected discretionary outlays are flat in 2011 and increase only slightly in the 2011–2020 period, rising by an average of 1.1 percent per year. In contrast, discretionary spending grew by an average of 7.5 percent annually over the past 10 years, well above the rate of inflation that guides CBO's baseline projection of such spending (see Table 3-2). Because of mounting debt and rising interest rates, outlays for net interest will increase dramatically during the next decade, averaging double-digit growth.

Table 3-1. CBO's Baseline Projections of Outlays

	Actual 2009	2010	2011	2012	2013	2014	2015	2016	2017	2018	2019	2020	Total, 2011-2015	Total, 2011-2020
	In Billions of Dollars													
Mandatory Outlays														
Social Security	678	700	726	759	797	836	878	927	982	1,041	1,103	1,170	3,996	9,220
Medicare	499	528	574	581	638	710	735	794	830	867	962	1,038	3,238	7,729
Medicaid	251	280	268	270	283	302	323	346	371	398	427	458	1,446	3,445
Other spending	861	621	675	581	570	564	568	591	601	604	631	643	2,959	6,028
Offsetting receipts	-195	-183	-198	-203	-211	-223	-232	-244	-259	-271	-285	-302	-1,067	-2,428
Subtotal	2,094	1,946	2,045	1,989	2,077	2,188	2,272	2,414	2,524	2,638	2,838	3,008	10,572	23,994
Discretionary Outlays														
Defense	656	690	701	696	705	716	730	749	761	773	795	813	3,548	7,440
Nondefense	581	682	670	649	641	640	644	653	665	677	691	705	3,244	6,634
Subtotal	1,237	1,371	1,371	1,344	1,346	1,357	1,373	1,402	1,426	1,450	1,486	1,518	6,792	14,074
Net Interest	187	207	233	280	333	396	459	519	572	624	676	723	1,701	4,816
Total	**3,518**	**3,524**	**3,650**	**3,613**	**3,756**	**3,940**	**4,105**	**4,335**	**4,521**	**4,712**	**5,000**	**5,250**	**19,065**	**42,883**
On-budget	3,001	2,968	3,073	3,010	3,122	3,276	3,409	3,602	3,747	3,894	4,134	4,332	15,889	35,598
Off-budget	517	556	577	603	634	665	697	733	774	818	866	917	3,176	7,285
	As a Percentage of Gross Domestic Product													
Mandatory Outlays														
Social Security	4.8	4.8	4.8	4.8	4.8	4.7	4.8	4.8	4.9	5.0	5.1	5.2	4.8	4.9
Medicare	3.5	3.6	3.8	3.7	3.8	4.0	4.0	4.1	4.1	4.2	4.4	4.6	3.9	4.1
Medicaid	1.8	1.9	1.8	1.7	1.7	1.7	1.8	1.8	1.8	1.9	2.0	2.0	1.7	1.8
Other spending	6.0	4.3	4.5	3.7	3.4	3.2	3.1	3.1	3.0	2.9	2.9	2.9	3.5	3.2

Table 3-1. (Continued)

	Actual 2009	2010	2011	2012	2013	2014	2015	2016	2017	2018	2019	2020	Total, 2011-2015	Total, 2011-2020
Offsetting receipts	-1.4	-1.3	-1.3	-1.3	-1.3	-1.3	-1.3	-1.3	-1.3	-1.3	-1.3	-1.3	-1.3	-1.3
Subtotal	14.7	13.3	13.6	12.6	12.5	12.4	12.3	12.6	12.6	12.7	13.1	13.3	12.7	12.8
Discretionary Outlays														
Defense	4.6	4.7	4.7	4.4	4.2	4.1	4.0	3.9	3.8	3.7	3.7	3.6	4.3	4.0
Nondefense	4.1	4.7	4.5	4.1	3.8	3.6	3.5	3.4	3.3	3.3	3.2	3.1	3.9	3.5
Subtotal	8.7	9.4	9.1	8.5	8.1	7.7	7.5	7.3	7.1	7.0	6.9	6.7	8.1	7.5
Net Interest	1.3	1.4	1.6	1.8	2.0	2.2	2.5	2.7	2.9	3.0	3.1	3.2	2.0	2.6
Total	**24.7**	**24.1**	**24.3**	**23.0**	**22.5**	**22.4**	**22.3**	**22.6**	**22.6**	**22.6**	**23.1**	**23.3**	**22.9**	**22.8**
On-budget	21.1	20.3	20.5	19.1	18.7	18.6	18.5	18.7	18.7	18.7	19.1	19.2	19.0	19.0
Off-budget	3.6	3.8	3.8	3.8	3.8	3.8	3.8	3.8	3.9	3.9	4.0	4.1	3.8	3.9
Memorandum:														
Gross Domestic Product														
(Billions of dollars)	14,236	14,595	14,992	15,730	16,676	17,606	18,421	19,223	20,036	20,82 3	21,66 7	22,544	83,425	187,719

Source: Congressional Budget Office.

BOX 3-1. CATEGORIES OF FEDERAL SPENDING

On the basis of its treatment in the budget process, federal spending can be divided into three broad categories:

Mandatory spending consists primarily of benefit programs, such as Social Security, Medicare, and Medicaid. The Congress generally determines spending for those programs by setting rules for eligibility, benefit formulas, and other parameters rather than by appropriating specific amounts each year. In making baseline projections, the Congressional Budget Office (CBO) assumes that existing laws and policies for those programs will remain unchanged and that most programs that are scheduled to expire will be extended instead. Mandatory spending also includes offsetting receipts—fees and other charges that are recorded as negative budget authority and outlays. Offsetting receipts differ from revenues in that revenues are collected in the exercise of the government's sovereign powers (for example, in the form of income taxes) whereas offsetting receipts generally are collected from other government accounts or from members of the public for businesslike transactions (for example, as premiums for Medicare or as rental payments and royalties for the drilling of oil or gas on public lands).

Discretionary spending is controlled by annual appropriation acts; policymakers decide each year how much money to provide for given activities. Appropriations fund a broad array of government activities, including those involved with defense, law enforcement, and transportation, for example. They also fund the national park system, disaster relief, and foreign aid. Some fees and other charges that are triggered by appropriation action are classified as offsetting collections, which are credited against gross discretionary spending.

CBO's baseline depicts the path of discretionary spending as directed by the provisions of the Balanced Budget and Emergency Deficit Control Act of 1985.[1] That act stated that current appropriations should be assumed to grow with inflation in the future. Although those provisions (contained in section 257 of the act) expired at the end of September 2006, CBO continues to follow their requirements in preparing its baseline for discretionary spending. Appropriations to date have provided a total of $1,228 billion in budget authority for fiscal year 2010—$684 billion for defense and $543 billion for nondefense activities.

In addition to spending from those appropriations, the baseline includes discretionary spending for highway infrastructure, highway and motor carrier safety, public transit, and airport infrastructure programs that receive mandatory budget authority from authorizing legislation. Each year, however, the annual appropriation acts control spending for those programs by limiting how much of the budget authority the Department of Transportation can obligate. For that reason, such obligation limitations are treated as a measure of discretionary resources, and the resulting outlays are considered discretionary spending. Transportation obligation limitations for 2010 total $54 billion.

Net interest includes interest paid on Treasury securities and other interest the government pays (for example, on late refunds issued by the Internal Revenue Service) minus interest that the government collects from various sources (such as from commercial banks that maintain Treasury tax and loan accounts). Net interest is determined by the size and composition of the government's debt, annual budget deficits or surpluses, and market interest rates.

[1] The inflation rates used in CBO's baseline, as specified by the Deficit Control Act, are the employment cost index for wages and salaries (applied to expenditures related to federal personnel) and the gross domestic product price index (for other expenditures).

Table 3-2. Average Annual Rates of Growth in Outlays since 1999 and as Projected in CBO's Baseline

(Percent)	Actual		Projected		
	1999–2008	2009	2010	2011[a]	2012–2020[a]
Mandatory	6.4	31.3	-7.1	5.1	4.4
Social Security	5.0	10.7	3.3	3.7	5.4
Medicare	8.0	9.4	5.9	8.6	6.8
Medicaid	7.1	24.6	11.4	-4.1	6.1
Other[b]	6.7	104.7	-34.3	9.0	-3.7
Discretionary	7.5	9.0	10.9	*	1.1
Defense	8.5	7.1	5.2	1.6	1.7
Nondefense	6.4	11.3	17.3	-1.7	0.6
Net Interest	0.5	-25.9	10.3	13.0	13.4
Total Outlays	**6.1**	**18.0**	**0.2**	**3.6**	**4.1**
Total Outlays Excluding Net Interest	**6.8**	**22.0**	**-0.4**	**3.0**	**3.2**
Memorandum:					
Consumer Price Index	2.8	-0.3	2.4	1.4	1.7
Nominal Gross Domestic Product	5.2	-1.4	2.5	2.7	4.6
Discretionary Budget Authority	8.3	26.9	-18.0	1.4	2.0
Defense	9.7	1.2	-1.5	1.3	2.0
Nondefense	6.7	62.6	-32.3	1.5	2.0

Source: Congressional Budget Office.

Note: * = between -0.05 percent and zero.

a. When constructing its baseline, CBO uses the employment cost index for wages and salaries to inflate discretionary spending related to federal personnel and the gross domestic product price index to adjust other discretionary spending.

b. Includes offsetting receipts (funds collected by government agencies from other government accounts or from the public in businesslike or market-oriented transactions that are recorded as offsets to outlays).

Federal spending reached 24.7 percent of GDP last year, which is well above the share it represented in 1970—19.3 percent. Much of the increase in spending between 1970 and 2009 can be traced to growth in mandatory spending, which rose sharply during that period, from 6.0 percent of GDP to 14.7 percent (see Figure 3-1). (On average, mandatory spending measured 9.7 percent of GDP over that period.) Meanwhile, discretionary spending dropped from 11.9 percent of GDP in 1970 to 8.7percent last year, averaging 8.8 percent over that period. Spending for net interest averaged 2.2 percent of GDP and ranged between 1.3 percent and 3.3 percent. In CBO's baseline projections for the next decade, total federal spending will slip to 22.3 percent of GDP in 2015 before resuming its upward trend and reaching 23.3 percent in 2020. Mandatory spending will also fall back as a share of the economy during the next several years and then turn back up; in 2020, mandatory spending is projected to equal 13.3 percent of GDP. Under the assumptions governing CBO's baseline, discretionary spending will decline relative to GDP after 2010; at 6.7 percent of GDP in 2020, it would be nearly as low as the share recorded in the late 1990s, which was also the lowest share seen during the past 40 years. Outlays for net interest will rise sharply relative to the economy and equal 3.2percent of GDP in 2020.

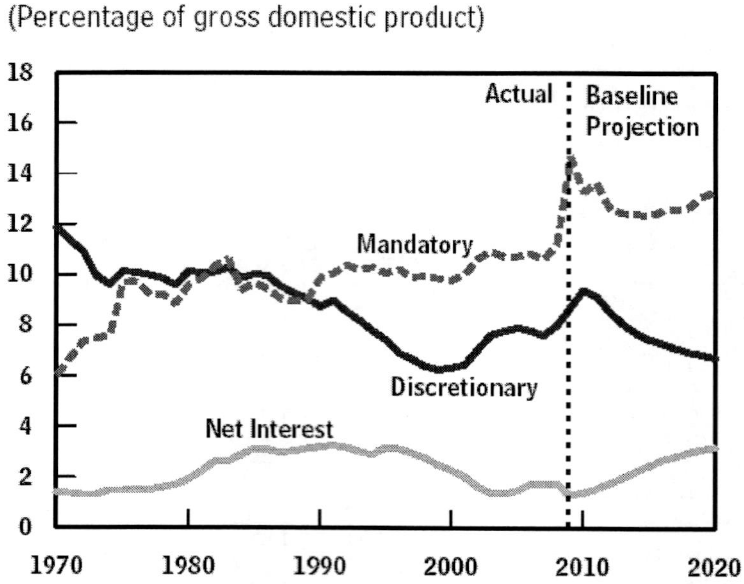

Sources: Congressional Budget Office; Office of Management and Budget.

Figure 3-1. Outlays, by Category, 1970 to 2020

Additional legislation could drive spending above the amounts currently projected or reduce spending below those amounts. For example, policymakers could increase the funding provided for discretionary programs beyond the amounts needed to maintain their real (inflation-adjusted) value; alternatively, they could reduce funding below those amounts. Also, emergency benefits for the unemployed were recently extended to those who will exhaust their regular benefits before the end of February. Extending those benefits further would result in additional costs. Likewise, under provisions of current law, payment rates for physicians' services under Medicare are slated to plummet beginning in March 2010; legislative action could alter that path and add to outlays for Medicare. Further, additional appropriations may be made for operations in Afghanistan later in the year. The costs of those possible actions are not included in CBO's baseline projections.

Mandatory Spending

Mandatory—or direct—spending programs account for more than half of federal outlays. The category includes spending for entitlement programs and certain other payments to people, businesses, nonprofit institutions, and state and local governments. In general, those payments are governed by statutory criteria and are not normally constrained by the annual appropriation process. Offsetting receipts (certain types of payments that federal agencies receive from the public and other government agencies) are classified as offsets to mandatory spending (that is, as credits against gross direct spending).

In 2009, mandatory outlays surged to $2.1 trillion from $1.6 trillion in 2008. CBO projects that mandatory spending will range between $1.9 trillion and $2.1 trillion through 2013 and then steadily increase in ensuing years, reaching $3.0 trillion in 2020 (see Table 3-3).

Relative to the size of the economy, mandatory spending is projected to fall from its peak of 14.7 percent of GDP in 2009. If no changes to mandatory programs are enacted this year, mandatory spending will total 13.3 percent of GDP in 2010 by CBO's estimate. After rising slightly in 2011 relative to the economy—mostly because of a calendar-related shift in the timing of some payments—mandatory spending will decline a bit and average 12.8 percent of GDP for the remainder of the projection period, well above the 11.0 percent average for such spending over the past 10 years. Despite the decline in the short term, the underlying long-term trend of increases in mandatory spending will be apparent during this decade: That spending is projected to rise steadily as a share of the economy from 2015 through 2020, growing from 12.3 percent to 13.3 percent of GDP over that period.

Over the next 10 years, nominal outlays for mandatory spending are projected to increase by 50 percent under current law, an average of 4.5 percent per year. Many mandatory programs—such as Social Security, Medicare, civilian and military retirement, and veterans' benefits—will grow steadily. In contrast, spending for counter-cyclical programs (programs like unemployment compensation that are designed to spend more during economic downturns) and costs recorded for the TARP and for housing GSEs (Fannie Mae and Freddie Mac) are expected to moderate in coming years after large increases in outlays related to the recession and the turmoil in the financial system.

CBO estimates that Social Security, Medicare, and Medicaid will account for about 70 percent of mandatory spending (excluding offsetting receipts) in 2010. On average, those programs tend to grow more rapidly than other types of mandatory spending. By 2020, the proportion of outlays for those "big three" programs will climb to 80 percent of mandatory spending under current law. Other programs that provide income security—such as unemployment compensation, the Supplemental Nutrition Assistance Program (SNAP, formerly called the Food Stamp program), and certain refundable tax credits—will account for nearly 20 percent of mandatory spending in 2010. By 2020, though, outlays for those income security programs will make up less than 10 percent of mandatory spending, as the economic expansion allows spending for many of those programs to recede to more normal levels and as certain changes to tax provisions that affect outlays take place as scheduled under current law. The remaining portion of mandatory spending includes benefits for civilian and military retirement, benefits for veterans, subsidies for the housing GSEs, outlays for the TARP, support for agriculture, student loans, and deposit insurance.

Table 3-3. CBO's Baseline Projections of Mandatory Spending

(Outlays, in billions of dollars)													
	Actual 2009	2010	2011	2012	2013	2014	2015	2016	2017	2018	2019	2020	Total, 2011-2015	Total, 2011-2020
Social Security	678	700	726	759	797	836	878	927	982	1,041	1,103	1,170	3,996	9,220
Medicare[a]	499	528	574	581	638	710	735	794	830	867	962	1,038	3,238	7,729
Medicaid	251	280	268	270	283	302	323	346	371	398	427	458	1,446	3,445
Income Security														
SNAP	56	70	75	75	74	71	69	67	65	62	62	61	365	681
Unemployment compensation	119	133	83	66	53	47	48	50	52	53	55	56	298	564
Supplemental Security Income	45	48	54	47	53	54	54	61	57	53	60	61	262	554
Earned income and child tax credits	67	72	69	42	43	44	45	44	44	45	45	45	244	467
Family support[b]	26	28	26	25	25	25	25	25	25	25	25	25	124	249
Child nutrition	16	17	18	19	20	20	21	22	23	24	24	25	98	216
Foster care	7	7	7	7	8	8	8	8	8	9	9	9	38	82
Making Work Pay and other tax credits[c]	13	24	19	*	*	*	*	*	*	*	*	*	20	22
Subtotal	348	400	352	282	275	270	270	277	274	271	281	283	1,449	2,834
Civilian and Military Retirement														
Federal civilian[d]	80	83	85	87	90	93	95	99	102	106	109	113	450	979
Military	50	51	51	52	53	54	55	57	58	60	61	63	266	565
Other	8	8	7	7	8	9	10	11	11	11	12	12	41	98
Subtotal	138	141	143	147	151	156	160	166	171	177	182	188	757	1,642
Veterans[e]														
Income security	46	49	56	50	56	57	58	64	60	56	62	63	276	581
Other	4	8	10	11	11	12	12	13	14	14	15	16	57	128
Subtotal	50	57	66	61	67	68	70	77	74	70	77	79	333	710
Other Programs														
Fannie Mae and Freddie Mac[f]	91	21	13	10	8	6	6	5	4	3	3	3	45	64
TARP	152	-67	4	4	3	3	*	*	*	*	*	*	15	16
Agriculture	17	19	18	12	17	16	16	16	16	16	17	17	80	161
MERHCF	8	8	9	9	10	11	12	13	14	15	16	17	50	124

Table 3-3. (Continued)

	Actual 2009	2010	2011	2012	2013	2014	2015	2016	2017	2018	2019	2020	Total, 2011-2015	Total, 2011-2020
Higher education	-18	-10	-2	-1	-1	-1	5	6	8	9	9	10	0	43
Universal Service Fund	8	8	9	9	9	9	9	9	9	9	9	9	44	90
CHIP	8	9	10	11	12	10	6	6	6	6	6	6	50	79
Social services	5	5	5	5	5	5	5	5	5	5	6	6	26	53
Deposit insurance	23	-4	12	-3	-18	-18	-17	-14	-9	-7	-4	-5	-44	-83
Other	32	33	36	33	31	28	26	25	29	29	29	30	154	295
Subtotal	325	22	113	91	77	70	68	71	82	86	91	92	420	843
Offsetting Receipts														
Medicare[g]	-74	-78	-86	-87	-93	-102	-107	-113	-120	-128	-139	-150	-475	-1,126
Employers' share of employees' retirement	-56	-60	-62	-63	-64	-66	-69	-71	-74	-77	-80	-83	-324	-711
Other	-65	-45	-50	-52	-54	-55	-57	-59	-65	-66	-66	-68	-268	-591
Subtotal	-195	-183	-198	-203	-211	-223	-232	-244	-259	-271	-285	-302	-1,067	-2,428
Total Mandatory														
Spending	**2,094**	**1,946**	**2,045**	**1,989**	**2,077**	**2,188**	**2,272**	**2,414**	**2,524**	**2,638**	**2,838**	**3,008**	**10,572**	**23,994**
Memorandum:														
Mandatory Spending Excluding Offsetting Receipts	2,289	2,129	2,243	2,192	2,288	2,411	2,504	2,658	2,783	2,909	3,124	3,310	11,639	26,422
Medicare Spending Net of Offsetting Receipts	425	450	487	494	545	608	628	680	709	739	824	888	2,763	6,603

Source: Congressional Budget Office.

Notes: Spending for the benefit programs shown above generally excludes administrative costs, which are discretionary.

SNAP = Supplemental Nutrition Assistance Program; TARP = Troubled Asset Relief Program; MERHCF = Department of Defense Medicare-Eligible Retiree Health Care Fund (including TRICARE for Life); CHIP = Children's Health Insurance Program; * = between zero and $500 million.

a. Excludes offsetting receipts (funds collected by government agencies from other government accounts or from the public in businesslike or market-oriented transactions that are recorded as offsets to outlays).

b. Includes Temporary Assistance for Needy Families and various programs that involve payments to states for child support enforcement and family support, child care entitlements, and research to benefit children.

c. This category also includes outlays for the following: the First-Time Homebuyer Credit; the American Opportunity Tax Credit; acceleration of Research and Experimentation Tax Credits in lieu of bonus depreciation; payments made when the credit for the alternative minimum tax exceeds a taxpayer's liability; and income tax rebates that result from the Economic Stimulus Act of 2008 (Public Law 110-185) and the American Recovery and Reinvestment Act of 2009 (P.L. 111-5).

d. Includes Civil Service, Foreign Service, Coast Guard, and other, smaller retirement programs as well as annuitants' health benefits.

e. Income security includes veterans' compensation, pensions, and life insurance programs. Other benefits are primarily education subsidies.

f. The amount recorded for 2009 reflects cash transfers from the Treasury to Fannie Mae and Freddie Mac. The amounts shown for 2010 through 2020 reflect CBO's estimate of the subsidy cost of new loans and guarantees made by those two entities in each year, adjusted for market risk.

g. Includes Medicare premiums and amounts paid by states from savings on Medicaid prescription drug costs.

Medicare and Medicaid

At $750 billion, gross outlays for the two major health programs, Medicare and Medicaid, accounted for just over 20 percent of federal spending (not including offsetting receipts) in 2009. Spending for those programs will grow by 7.7 percent in 2010, CBO estimates, which is roughly in line with growth rates seen over the past 10 years. Beyond 2010, CBO's baseline projections show that growth in federal spending for those two health programs will be somewhat slower than the average rate seen over the past 10 years. That slower projected growth is largely attributable to provisions of current law that reduce payments to doctors under Medicare and return federal matching rates for Medicaid payments to states to their prerecession levels.[29]

Medicare. The larger of the two programs, Medicare, provides subsidized medical insurance for the elderly and for some people with disabilities. Medicare has three programs: Part A (Hospital Insurance), Part B (Supplementary Medical Insurance), and Part D (the subsidy for outpatient prescription drugs).[30] People generally become eligible for Medicare at age 65 or two years after they become eligible for Social Security disability benefits. In 2009, Medicare had about 46 million beneficiaries; by 2020, that number is expected to climb to 61 million.

Gross spending for Medicare is expected to total $528 billion in 2010, an increase of almost 6 percent over the amount recorded last year. The figure for gross spending excludes receipts from premiums and some payments from states, which are discussed in the section on offsetting receipts.

Under current law, Medicare outlays will be constrained starting in March 2010 by the rate-setting system—the "sustainable growth rate" or SGR—that controls the fees paid for physicians' services. Under that system, CBO projects, those fees will be reduced by about 21 percent in March 2010 and by additional amounts in subsequent years. The Department of Defense Appropriations Act, 2010 (Public Law 111-118), extended the 2009 payment rates through February 2010. If future legislation overrides the scheduled reductions (as has happened in every year since 2003), spending on Medicare may be significantly greater than is projected in CBO's baseline. For example, if the scheduled reductions in physicians' fees were delayed by one year, so that payment rates remained at the 2009 level for the remainder of 2010 (before dropping by roughly 26 percent in 2011), outlays would increase by $6 billion in 2010 and by a total of $11 billion over the 2010–2020 period. Maintaining the nominal 2009 payment rates through 2020 would increase Medicare outlays over that period by about $300 billion.

Even with the constraining effect of the SGR, CBO anticipates that future spending for Medicare will grow by 7 percent per year, on average, in the coming decade. During that period, federal spending per beneficiary for Parts A and B will grow in nominal terms by close to 50percent, and per capita benefits for Part D will more than double. As a result, Medicare spending under CBO's projections will rise as a percentage of GDP, from 3.5 percent in 2009 to 4.6 percent by 2020. By that time, gross Medicare outlays will exceed $1 trillion, a figure that does not include receipts of premiums and some payments from states, which are discussed in the section on offsetting receipts.

Medicaid. Medicaid is a joint federal and state program that funds medical care for many of the nation's poor, elderly, and disabled. The federal government shares costs with states for approved services; that share varies from state to state but typically averages about 57 percent. Provisions in ARRA increased the federal portion of costs to about 68 percent, on average, through December 2010. Federal outlays for Medicaid totaled $251 billion in 2009—up nearly 25 percent from the previous year, principally as a result of those higher matching rates and higher enrollment caused by the elevated unemployment rate.

CBO estimates that Medicaid outlays will increase by another 11 percent in 2010, mostly because persistently high unemployment will continue to spur enrollment. Federal spending for Medicaid is expected to drop by about 4 percent in 2011 as the enhanced federal matching rates expire and as employment increases. For the balance of the projection period, spending for Medicaid will grow at an average annual rate of 6 percent, CBO estimates. About 66 million people were enrolled in Medicaid in 2009. Even though caseloads will fall somewhat in the short term as the economy improves, they will rise in the long run as the population increases and ages. In 2020, CBO estimates, 76 million people will be enrolled in Medicaid, and federal outlays for that program will total $458 billion, or about 2 percent of GDP.

Social Security

Social Security, which is the largest federal spending program, provides cash benefits to the elderly, people with disabilities, and their dependents. Social Security comprises two main parts: Old-Age and Survivors Insurance (OASI) and Disability Insurance (DI). Social Security outlays rose by nearly 11 percent in 2009, primarily as a result of a 5.8 percent cost-of-living adjustment (COLA) that went into effect in January 2009. In addition, onetime payments of $250 per person (totaling $13 billion) were provided last year under ARRA. Both OASI and DI also experienced higher-than-average increases in caseloads in 2009, with more than 51 million people receiving Social Security benefits.

CBO estimates that outlays for Social Security will reach $700 billion in 2010, or 4.8 percent of GDP. Over the next decade, spending for Social Security benefits will rise steadily as the nation's elderly population increases. In 2020, CBO estimates, Social Security outlays will total $1.2 trillion, about 5.2 percent of GDP. In that year, almost 69 million people will collect Social Security benefits.

Old-Age and Survivors Insurance. OASI, the larger of Social Security's two components, pays full benefits to workers who start collecting those benefits at age 66 or 67, depending on the year the worker was born; workers can choose to start collecting reduced benefits as early as age 62. The program also makes payments to eligible spouses and children and to some survivors (primarily elderly widows and young children) of deceased workers. OASI benefits totaled $545 billion in 2009.

About 42 million people received OASI in 2009. Over the 2010–2020 period, as more baby boomers become eligible for benefits under the program, the number of people collecting OASI will increase, CBO estimates, reaching 57 million by 2020. After receiving a steep cost-of-living adjustment in 2009, OASI beneficiaries did not get a COLA in 2010 because of a decline in the consumer price index during the previous year.[31] (Beneficiaries of Social Security and most other programs that provide COLAs are protected from a drop in benefit payments when prices fall. Thus, despite the drop in the consumer price index, individuals' benefits remain at last year's amounts.) Still, average benefits for OASI will experience a slight increase in 2010 because initial benefits for new beneficiaries, which are based on a retiree's lifetime wages, are expected to continue to rise.

Disability Insurance. Social Security's disability benefits are paid to workers who suffer debilitating health conditions before they are old enough to enroll in OASI. (Payments also are made to the eligible spouses and children of those recipients.) In 2009, the federal government paid $115 billion in disability benefits under DI.

The number of DI claimants jumped by 4 percent in 2009, to 9.3 million. Higher-than-average increases in caseloads are expected to continue through 2012, largely because high unemployment rates indicate meager job prospects for many of the disabled. However, after 2013, the annual rate of growth in caseloads is projected to average 1 percent as a strengthening economy leads fewer people to seek disability benefits and as a greater portion of the population qualifies for benefits under OASI. As is the case with OASI beneficiaries, those receiving benefits under DI did not receive a COLA this year.

Other Income Security Programs

The federal government also provides payments to people and other government entities to assist certain individuals or segments of the population: the disabled, the poor, the unemployed, needy families with children, and children who have been abused and neglected. Federal spending for SNAP, unemployment compensation, Supplemental Security Income (SSI), the refundable portions of the earned income tax credit (EITC) and the child tax credit, family support, foster care, and other services totaled $348 billion in 2009, or 2.4 percent of GDP—a significant increase over the $260 billion spent for those programs in 2008.[32] Many income security programs are countercyclical; therefore, outlays for benefits tend to rise automatically when the economy falters. In addition to those automatic increases, temporary measures enacted to augment payments to needy populations contributed to the rapid growth in spending in 2009 and will affect spending patterns in future years.

Assuming there are no changes in current law, CBO expects that spending on other income security programs will rise by nearly 15 percent in 2010. Under CBO's baseline projections, overall spending for those programs begins to drop in 2011 as the economy improves further and certain provisions of law expire. By 2020, spending on other income security programs will amount to 1.3 percent of GDP, CBO estimates.

Supplemental Nutrition Assistance Program. Outlays for SNAP shot up 41 percent in 2009, to $56 billion, as enrollment increased by 20 percent, to nearly 34 million. CBO estimates that the program's spending will climb by another 27 percent this year, to $70 billion. In past recessions, participation in the Food Stamp program (as SNAP was formerly known) continued to swell even after the unemployment rate has begun to recede; accordingly, CBO expects that the number of people collecting SNAP benefits will rise to almost 41 million this year and to nearly 44 million by 2012. Eventually, as the economic situation continues to improve, average monthly SNAP caseloads will decline, falling to 32 million by 2020, CBO projects.

According to CBO's estimates, the average benefit provided under SNAP will not change in 2010, partly because of provisions in ARRA. That law raised the maximum monthly benefit for a household of four from $588 to $668 in 2009. ARRA stipulates that that benefit will remain at $668 until the routine inflation adjustment that otherwise would be applied to the original benefit amount exceeds the increase provided in ARRA. Under CBO's current projections for inflation, the maximum SNAP benefit would not change until 2019.

Unemployment Compensation. Outlays for unemployment compensation soared from $43 billion in 2008 to $119 billion in 2009, spurred both by the recession and by legislation that enhanced benefits available to jobless individuals. CBO estimates that outlays will continue to increase in 2010, rising to $133 billion (0.9 percent of GDP) under current law. In subsequent years, outlays for unemployment compensation will fall as the economic recovery gradually results in a diminished unemployment rate and as temporary provisions that extended the availability of benefits to the long-term unemployed expire. In 2020, unemployment compensation will amount to about $56 billion, CBO estimates, or 0.2 percent of GDP, about the same share of the economy that it was in 2007.

Spending for unemployment compensation in the past few years has been affected by changes in law that temporarily provide additional benefits to people who lose their jobs. Those provisions currently allow individuals who exhaust their regular benefits to collect emergency unemployment compensation (EUC) for as many as 53 weeks. In addition, individuals currently receiving unemployment compensation receive a weekly supplement of $25. Under current law, payments for the supplement and for EUC start to phase out in March 2010. Still, according to CBO estimates, that additional compensation will amount to $43 billion in 2010.

Supplemental Security Income. SSI provides cash benefits to people of low income who are elderly or disabled. According to CBO's estimates, benefit payments for SSI—which totaled $45 billion in 2009—will jump by 7 percent in 2010, primarily because of higher caseloads. Benefits in 2011 are projected to rise by another 13 percent, although most of that growth is attributable to a shift in the timing of benefit payments that will occur because October 1, 2011 (the first day of fiscal year 2012), falls on a weekend. Consequently, 13 SSI benefit payments will be made in 2011 instead of the usual 12; without the timing shift, outlays for SSI would grow by about 4 percent next year.

Earned Income and Child Tax Credits. The EITC is a fully refundable credit available primarily to people with earnings and income that fall below an established maximum. The child tax credit is a partially refundable tax credit available to qualifying families with dependent children. Either credit reduces a filer's overall tax liability; if the credit exceeds the liability, the excess may be refunded, depending on the filer's earnings. The refundable portions (which are categorized as outlays) totaled $67 billion in 2009 and are projected to rise to $72 billion in 2010. Starting in 2012—the first full fiscal year in which tax receipts will reflect the expiration of provisions initially enacted in the Economic Growth and Tax Relief Reconciliation Act of 2001—the refundability of the child tax credit will be sharply limited, so its future effect on outlays will be greatly reduced. As a result, under current law, outlays for those credits will fall to $45 billion in 2020, CBO projects.

Family Support. Spending for family support programs—grants to states that help fund welfare programs, child support enforcement, and child care entitlements—is projected to rise from $26 billion last year to $28 billion in 2010. Over the next 10 years, such spending will drop back to about $25 billion per year. Two factors contribute to that decrease: First, the Emergency Fund provision that ARRA added to the Temporary Assistance for Needy Families (TANF) program expires at the end of 2010. Second, the regular TANF program is capped at roughly $17 billion annually (although some additional funding may be made available, depending on states' unemployment rates or their SNAP caseloads). Since the inception of TANF, states have spent less than they had available from the program, although many states have drawn on those reserves to support greater needs for family support in recent years. As those balances continue to be drawn down, and as the economy improves, spending for TANF will soon equal its annual funding level, in CBO's estimation.

Child Nutrition and Foster Care. CBO projects that spending for child nutrition, which provides cash and commodities for meals and snacks in schools, day care settings, and summer programs, is projected to rise by more than 5 percent in 2010, to $17 billion, and by another 6 percent in 2011, to $18 billion. That strong growth in spending is spurred by higher-than-average growth in reimbursement rates for meals and participation in the free-lunch program. Because those factors are not expected to persist, growth in spending for child nutrition will average roughly 4 percent annually from 2012 to 2020 in CBO's projections.

Federal grants to states for foster care and adoption assistance are expected to rise by nearly 8 percent in 2010 to $7 billion. Such spending is affected by the higher matching rates that are temporarily being used for Medicaid. After those provisions expire in December 2010, growth will average about 3 percent per year, CBO estimates.

Making Work Pay and Other Tax Credits. The American Recovery and Reinvestment Act of 2009 created a number of refundable tax credits. The largest is the Making Work Pay tax credit, which provides a credit of 6.2 percent of an eligible individual's earned income for tax years 2009 and 2010, up to a maximum of $400 for individuals ($800 for joint filers). The credit is fully refundable; the portion of the credit that exceeds a taxpayer's liability is categorized as outlays and those amounts are expected to total about $17 billion each in 2010 and 2011.

Another credit with significant temporary effects is the First-Time Homebuyer Credit, which provides a fully refundable credit of up to $8,000. (That credit was recently extended to apply to home purchases through April 2010 and expanded to make certain non-first-time buyers eligible for a credit of up to $6,500.) In addition, the American Opportunity Credit expands eligibility (including to those who owe no tax) and modifies the criteria for taxpayers to claim a credit for college expenses.

Other Federal Retirement and Disability Programs

Benefits for federal civilian and military retirees and payments for veterans' pensions and disability benefits totaled $188 billion in 2009, about 1.3 percent of GDP. CBO projects that spending for those benefits will grow at an average rate of roughly 3 percent annually. In 2020, such spending will amount to $267 billion according to CBO's baseline projections.

Civilian and Military Retirement. Retirement and survivors' benefits paid through the federal civilian retirement program (along with several smaller retirement programs for employees of various government agencies and for retired railroad workers) amounted to $88 billion in 2009. CBO projects that such outlays will grow by just over 3 percent annually in the next 10 years and that they will total $125 billion in 2020. Growth in federal retirement benefits is attributable primarily to cost-of-living adjustments and to rising federal salaries, which boost future benefits. (As with benefits for Social Security, civilian and military retirement benefits did not receive a COLA this year.)

One factor that restrains growth in retirement programs is the gradual replacement of the Civil Service Retirement System (CSRS) with the Federal Employees Retirement System (FERS). FERS covers employees hired after 1983 and provides a smaller defined benefit than that provided by CSRS. FERS recipients, however, are eligible to receive Social Security benefits through their federal employment (CSRS employees are not), and their contributions to the federal Thrift Savings Plan are matched in part by their employing agencies.

The federal government also provides retirement and disability benefits to personnel who retire from the uniformed services. Military annuities totaled $50 billion in 2009, and they are projected to grow by an average of just over 2 percent per year. Most of the growth in military retirement programs results from COLAs and other benefit increases.

Veterans' Benefits. Mandatory spending for veterans—including compensation, pensions, and burial and insurance benefits—grew from $41 billion in 2008 to $46 billion in 2009, an increase of about 12 percent. CBO expects that new claims for benefits will continue to rise rapidly this year; as a result, outlays will grow by 7 percent in 2010, to $49 billion. Outlays are anticipated to climb by another 14 percent in 2011, but much of that growth is because of a calendar-related shift in the timing of benefit payments: 13 payments will be made in that year, rather than the usual 12. CBO projects a declining rate of growth between 2012 and 2020—averaging about 3 percent—that results in outlays of about $63 billion in 2020.

Other Mandatory Spending

Spending for other mandatory programs increased dramatically in 2009 as the federal government undertook costly efforts to calm turbulent financial markets and to address the mortgage crisis. Last year, other mandatory spending totaled $325 billion. That category of mandatory spending is expected to drop significantly in 2010, to $22 billion, before leveling out at a range of between $70 billion and $90 billion per year during most of the coming decade.

Fannie Mae and Freddie Mac. In 2009, the Treasury recorded $91 billion in net outlays for the housing GSEs Fannie Mae and Freddie Mac. Because the Administration considers Fannie Mae and Freddie Mac to be nongovernmental entities for federal budgeting purposes, the net outlays recorded in the budget for 2009 reflect the Treasury's cash infusions to the two entities. (CBO expects that net cash infusions to those entities will total $35 billion in 2010.)

In contrast to the Administration's practices, CBO, when making its projections, accounts for the costs of the two entities' operations as if they were being conducted by a federal agency—because of the extraordinary degree of management and financial control that the government exercises over them.[33] Therefore, CBO calculates outlays for those entities as the estimated lifetime cost of new loans or guarantees on a fair value basis, as of the year of disbursement. The subsidy costs for new loans and guarantees provided in 2010 are expected to be $21 billion. As housing markets continue to stabilize, subsidy costs for new loans and guarantees will decline, CBO estimates, falling to just $3billion in 2018. Over the 2011–2020 period, net subsidy costs are expected to total $64 billion.

Troubled Asset Relief Program. The TARP was created by the Emergency Economic Stabilization Act of 2008 (EESA) in October of that year to enable the Secretary of the

Treasury to purchase or insure troubled assets. Authority for the program was initially set at $700 billion in assets and guarantees outstanding at any one time (the limit now stands at nearly $699 billion) and is in effect until October 3, 2010.

For 2009, the Treasury recorded a cost of $151 billion for activities undertaken by the program (and $90 million for administrative costs). Among those activities were purchases of preferred stock from financial institutions, a guarantee of a pool of assets held by Citigroup, and assistance to American International Group and two major automakers. Such costs are recorded in the budget using procedures similar to those specified in the Federal Credit Reform Act but are adjusted for the riskiness of the transactions.[34]

Market conditions have continued to improve, so it is not likely that the Treasury will use the full authority provided by EESA. Also, in the past few months, many institutions—including several large banks, such as JP Morgan Chase, Bank of America, and Wells Fargo—have repurchased the preferred stock that they sold to the government. As a result, CBO's estimate of the cost of the program over its lifetime has dropped from the $356 billion estimate the agency calculated last March to $99 billion. Because $151 billion in subsidy costs was already recorded in the budget in 2009, CBO estimates that a *negative* outlay will be recorded for fiscal year 2010 to reflect the changed circumstances.[35] The baseline projection therefore shows negative outlays of $67 billion in 2010. Outlays of $14 billion are projected over the 2011–2014 period, reflecting the cost of providing assistance to homeowners.

Support of Agriculture. Mandatory spending for agricultural support totaled $17 billion in 2009 and is projected to average about $16 billion per year over the 2010–2020 period. Spending will rise modestly in 2010 because of the projected disbursement of crop loss payments under the Supplemental Revenue Assistance (SURE) program authorized by the Food, Conservation, and Energy Act of 2008 (the farm bill). Mandatory spending for agriculture will dip sharply in 2012, to about $12 billion, largely because of changes in the timing of payments for crop insurance and commodity programs that were mandated in the 2008 farm bill. In subsequent years, spending for the crop insurance program is expected to rise as a result of projected increases in crop prices and the value of insured crops. The higher spending for crop insurance will be offset by the scheduled termination of authority for the Tobacco Trust Fund and the SURE program.

Remaining Mandatory Programs. Outlays for the remaining mandatory programs account for less than 3 percent of gross mandatory spending. Outlays for those programs, including the Department of Defense's Medicare-Eligible Retiree Health Care Fund (MERHCF), higher education, the Children's Health Insurance Program (CHIP), and deposit insurance totaled $65 billion in 2009. In 2020, CBO anticipates, overall spending on those programs will be $72 billion.

The MERHCF, which includes TRICARE for Life, provides health care benefits to retirees of the uniformed services (and to their dependents and surviving spouses) who are eligible for Medicare. Outlays for those benefits will total $8 billion in 2010, CBO estimates, about the same amount that was recorded in 2009, largely because of recent legislative changes that will lower the prices paid by the MERHCF for prescription drugs. Over the coming decade, spending from the MERHCF will rise at about the same rate as spending for other federal health care programs—by an average of roughly 8 percent each year—reaching $17 billion in 2020.

Outlays for mandatory higher education programs are projected to be negative in 2010 primarily because of a temporary program under which the Department of Education buys federally guaranteed student loans from the private sector. That program is set to expire on July 1, 2010. Federally guaranteed loans have higher costs or lower savings than comparable direct loans made by the government.[36] Thus, converting guaranteed loans to direct loans is estimated to yield budgetary savings in 2010. Over the 2011–2020 period, CBO projects, interest rates will rise, driving up the cost of the student loan programs and resulting in positive net outlays for student loan activity in future years. Over that period, mandatory outlays for higher education will total $43 billion, CBO estimates.

Net outlays for deposit insurance have increased in recent years because of the cost of resolving failed banks and credit unions. Cumulative losses for the Federal Deposit Insurance Corporation (FDIC) have been about $43 billion between 2008 and 2009. CBO expects that additional failures of banks and credit unions will occur, resulting in further losses at the FDIC of about $57 billion between 2010 and 2014. CBO expects that those costs will be offset in the future by proceeds from insurance premiums. The net costs of deposit insurance are recorded in the budget on a cash basis: When the government makes payments to cover losses for failing banks or credit unions, those payments are considered outlays; and when insurance premiums and sales of assets bring in new income in future years, those collections are negative outlays. Premiums also are projected to rise, keeping pace with the growth in insured deposits. As a result of those cost-recovery measures, CBO expects that receipts will exceed expenditures by about $83 billion over the 2011–2020 period.

What Causes Growth in Mandatory Spending?

Gross mandatory spending (which excludes offsetting receipts) will total $2.1 trillion in 2010, CBO estimates. In 2020, gross mandatory spending will be $3.3 trillion. The $1.2 trillion increase is attributable to cost-of-living and other automatic adjustments, other benefit increases, rising caseloads, and other factors (see Table 3-4).

COLAs and Other Automatic Adjustments. Annual changes in benefits that are pegged to inflation and other automatic adjustments account for about one-third of the growth that is projected for mandatory spending over the next 10 years. All major retirement programs grant automatic COLAs. There was no adjustment for 2010 because the change in the consumer price index for urban wage earners and clerical workers (the measure of inflation to which most COLAs are tied) was negative in the preceding year. CBO estimates that COLAs will be 0.1 percent in 2011, 1.2 percent in 2012 and 2013, and will average 1.8 percent annually from 2014 through 2020. The EITC and SNAP are indexed to other measures of inflation.[37]

Payment rates for Medicare services also are adjusted annually to reflect changes in the costs of goods and services used by providers and changes in economic factors such as GDP and productivity. The effect of those automatic increases on Medicare spending is suppressed by the sustainable growth rate formula, which sets a fee schedule for physicians' services. That mechanism sets a cumulative spending target for payments to physicians and for services related to medical visits, such as laboratory tests.

Left unaltered, the SGR formula would ultimately recoup spending in excess of the cumulative target by reducing payment rates for physicians' services or by holding increases below inflation (as measured by the Medicare economic index).[38] Assuming that current law remains in effect, CBO anticipates, the SGR formula will reduce payment rates for physicians' services by about 21 percent beginning in March 2010 and by 1 percent to 6 percent annually for the rest of the 2011–2020 period. At the end of that period, in 2020, cumulative Medicare spending for physicians' services as measured under the SGR will be nearly back in line with the formula's targets, but payment rates for physicians will be about two-thirds of what they were in 2009.

Table 3-4. Sources of Growth in Mandatory Outlays

(Billions of dollars)										
	2011	**2012**	**2013**	**2014**	**2015**	**2016**	**2017**	**2018**	**2019**	**2020**
Estimated Spending in 2010	2,129	2,129	2,129	2,129	2,129	2,129	2,129	2,129	2,129	2,129
Sources of Growth										
Cost-of-living and other automatic adjustments										
Medicare	6	15	28	45	65	89	113	139	171	205
Social Security	1	7	16	25	36	50	67	85	104	123
Other programs[a]	1	5	9	13	18	24	30	37	47	55
Subtotal	8	27	53	83	119	163	210	260	322	384
Other changes in benefits										
Medicare and Medicaid	5	32	66	123	134	148	185	226	252	284
Social Security	6	14	22	32	43	56	70	88	108	130
Other programs[a]	-37	-68	-67	-65	-64	-62	-59	-56	-53	-49
Subtotal	-26	-21	21	89	112	142	197	258	307	365
Increases in caseloads										
Medicare and Medicaid	8	14	21	37	52	72	93	119	159	201
Social Security	19	38	58	79	100	122	144	168	192	217
Other programs[a]	6	-3	-14	-20	-21	-21	-24	-23	-25	-27
Subtotal	33	49	65	96	131	173	214	264	325	391
Shifts in payment dates[b]	25	-25	0	0	0	33	3	-37	0	0
Other	74	33	20	14	13	18	29	34	40	41
Total	**114**	**63**	**159**	**282**	**375**	**529**	**654**	**780**	**995**	**1,180**
Projected Spending	2,243	2,192	2,288	2,411	2,504	2,658	2,783	2,909	3,124	3,310

Source: Congressional Budget Office.

Note: Amounts do not include the effects of offsetting receipts.

a. This category includes unemployment compensation, earned income and child tax credits, military and civilian retirement, veterans' benefits, child nutrition, the Supplemental Nutrition Assistance Program (formerly known as the Food Stamp program), and foster care.

b. Represents differences attributable to assumptions about the number of benefit checks that will be issued in a fiscal year. Benefit payments normally are made once a month, but in 2011 and 2016 there will be 13 monthly payments for Medicare, Supplemental Security Income, and veterans' compensation; in 2012 and 2018, those programs will issue 11 monthly payments.

When combined, the indexing and the SGR adjustments to Medicare payment rates result in increases in that program's spending of $6 billion in 2011 and $205 billion in 2020 and make up about 17 percent of projected growth in mandatory spending.[39]

Other Changes in Benefits. Other factors that contribute to rising benefits account for another one-third of the increase in mandatory spending through 2020. More than three-quarters of that figure is attributable to growth in spending for Medicare and Medicaid that cannot be tied to statutory adjustments in payments or to rising caseloads. Increased use of services—such as more frequent visits to doctors—contributes to higher spending, as does increased use of costly medical technology. Also, CBO projects that federal Medicaid costs will rise as states expand the services they cover—for example, by raising the limits on the number of home health visits the program covers.

Benefits for other programs also experience growth beyond automatic adjustments. Growth in wages, for example, affects Social Security payments, federal retirement benefits, and unemployment compensation. Rising wages also affect outlays for refundable tax credits by reducing eligibility and increasing the proportion of credits that will offset tax payments rather than be refunded.

Certain provisions of law will reduce mandatory spending in future years. Under current law, additional benefits for unemployment compensation, first enacted in 2008 (and subsequently expanded and extended), will phase out starting in March 2010. In January 2011, enhanced matching rates for Medicaid, temporarily provided under ARRA, will expire. Beginning in 2012, expiring provisions first enacted in EGTRRA will affect outlays for the EITC and the child tax credit by reducing the refundable portion of those credits. In addition, expiration of the Making Work Pay credit enacted in ARRA will reduce outlays for refundable credits starting in 2012. All of those factors will reduce mandatory spending by $49 billion in 2020, compared with spending in 2010.

Increases in Caseloads. CBO projects that an increase in the number of people who will be eligible for and claim benefits under certain mandatory programs will add $391 billion to mandatory spending in 2020, CBO estimates. The three largest programs (Medicare, Medicaid, and Social Security) will be responsible for increases of $418 billion over that time. On net, other mandatory benefit programs will serve fewer people in 2020 than in 2010, pushing down mandatory spending by $27 billion in 2020, CBO estimates. In particular, SNAP and unemployment compensation will see fewer beneficiaries by 2020 after experiencing record increases in 2010.

Other Factors. The timing of outlays for some mandatory programs over the projection period will depend on whether October 1, the first day of the fiscal year, falls on a weekday or on a weekend. If it falls on a Saturday or a Sunday, some benefits will be paid at the end of September, increasing spending for the preceding year but decreasing outlays for the forthcoming year. SSI, veterans' compensation and pension programs, and some Medicare payments will be affected by such calendar shifts. Those programs can make 11, 12, or 13 monthly payments in a fiscal year, and irregular numbers of benefit payments will affect mandatory spending in 2011, 2012, 2016, 2017, and 2018.

Spending for other mandatory programs is projected to be higher over the 2011–2020 period than in 2010. In 2020, such spending is projected to be $41 billion higher than it is estimated to be in 2010. Much of that increase results from negative outlays in 2010 for the TARP and student loans. For the reasons discussed earlier, those two programs are projected to record negative outlays of $77 billion in 2010. In 2020, the cost of student loans will amount to $10 billion, and outlays for TARP will be minimal. Taken together, outlays for those programs will be $87 billion higher in 2020 than in 2010. In CBO's estimation, that increase will be offset by reduced outlays for programs that are projected to spend less in 2020 than in 2010. In particular, outlays for the Making Work Pay tax credit are projected to be $23 billion lower than this year, and subsidy costs for commitments of Fannie Mae and Freddie Mac in 2020 are projected to be $17 billion lower than the costs of this year's commitments.

Offsetting Receipts

Offsetting receipts—which are recorded as negative outlays (that is, credits against direct spending)—are certain payments made to the federal government by citizens or businesses, and certain payments made by federal agencies to other federal agencies. They include beneficiaries' premiums for Medicare, federal agencies' retirement contributions for their employees, and payments for harvesting timber or extracting minerals from federal lands. In 2009, offsetting receipts totaled $195 billion (see Table 3-5).

Offsetting receipts for Medicare totaled $74 billion in 2009—more than one-third of all offsetting receipts. Over the coming years, those receipts will rise at about the same rate as spending for Medicare, totaling $150 billion in 2020 under CBO's baseline projections. The bulk of those receipts are premiums paid by Medicare beneficiaries, but the amount also includes payments made by states to cover a portion of low-income seniors' drug costs and recoveries of overpayments made to providers.

Other offsets to mandatory spending include the following: payments made by federal agencies for their employees' retirement benefits; proprietary receipts from royalties and other charges for production of oil and natural gas on federal lands; sales arising from harvested timber and minerals extracted from federal land; and various fees paid by users of public property and services.

In 2009, $56 billion in offsetting receipts consisted of intragovernmental transfers from federal agencies to the federal funds that are the source of employees' retirement benefits (mostly trust funds for Social Security and for military and civilian retirement). Those intragovernmental payments from agencies' operating accounts to the trust funds (or similar funds) have no net effect on outlays in the budget. Such payments will grow by about 3 percent per year, CBO estimates, reaching $83 billion in 2020.

Intragovernmental transfers also are made to the Department of Defense Medicare-Eligible Retiree Health Care Fund under the TRICARE for Life program; those payments totaled $11 billion in 2009. CBO projects that rising health care costs will cause those payments to rise by nearly 6 percent per year, to $19 billion in 2020. Those accrual payments are tied to the current number of military personnel and are intended to pay for the health care costs of future retirees.

Receipts stemming from the extraction of federally owned natural resources, particularly oil, natural gas, and minerals, totaled $11 billion in 2009. In 2020, CBO estimates, those receipts will total $20 billion.

Table 3-5. CBO's Baseline Projections of Offsetting Receipts

(Billions of dollars)													
	Actual 2009	**2010**	**2011**	**2012**	**2013**	**2014**	**2015**	**2016**	**2017**	**2018**	**2019**	**2020**	**Total, 2011-2015**	**Total, 2011-2020**
Medicare[a]	-74	-78	-86	-87	-93	-102	-107	-113	-120	-128	-139	-150	-475	-1,126
Employers' Share of Employees'														
Retirement														
Social Security	-14	-15	-16	-16	-17	-18	-19	-20	-20	-21	-22	-23	-85	-192
Military retirement	-18	-20	-21	-21	-21	-21	-21	-22	-22	-23	-24	-24	-104	-219
Civil service retirement and other	-24	-25	-25	-26	-27	-28	-29	-30	-31	-33	-34	-35	-135	-299
Subtotal	-56	-60	-62	-63	-64	-66	-69	-71	-74	-77	-80	-83	-324	-711
MERHCF	-11	-11	-11	-12	-13	-14	-14	-15	-16	-17	-18	-19	-64	-151
Natural-Resources-Related Receipts[b]	-11	-10	-14	-14	-16	-16	-17	-18	-19	-19	-19	-20	-77	-172
Electromagnetic Spectrum Auctions	-17	*	-1	-1	-1	*	0	0	0	0	0	0	-3	-3
Other	-26	-24	-24	-25	-25	-25	-25	-25	-29	-29	-28	-29	-124	-265
Total	**-195**	**-183**	**-198**	**-203**	**-211**	**-223**	**-232**	**-244**	**-259**	**-271**	**-285**	**-302**	**-1,067**	**-2,428**

Source: Congressional Budget Office.

Note: MERHCF = Department of Defense Medicare-Eligible Retiree Health Care Fund (including TRICARE for Life);

* = between -$500 million and zero.

a. Includes Medicare premiums and amounts paid by states from savings on Medicaid prescription drug costs.

b. Includes timber, mineral, and Outer Continental Shelf receipts and proceeds from sales of public land.

Table 3-6. Costs for Mandatory Programs That CBO's Baseline Assumes Will Continue Beyond Their Current Expiration Dates

(Billions of dollars)													
	2010	**2011**	**2012**	**2013**	**2014**	**2015**	**2016**	**2017**	**2018**	**2019**	**2020**	**Total, 2011-2015**	**Total, 2011-2020**
Supplemental Nutrition Assistance													
Program													
Budget authority	n.a.	n.a.	n.a.	73.9	71.4	69.0	66.7	64.4	62.1	61.9	60.9	214.3	530.3
Outlays	n.a.	n.a.	n.a.	70.9	71.5	69.1	66.8	64.5	62.2	61.9	60.9	211.4	527.8
Temporary Assistance													
for Needy Families													
Budget authority	n.a.	17.3	17.3	17.3	17.3	17.3	17.3	17.3	17.3	17.3	17.3	86.5	173.1
Outlays	n.a.	13.1	17.4	17.3	17.3	17.3	17.3	17.3	17.3	17.3	17.3	82.4	168.9
Commodity Credit													
Corporation[a]													
Budget authority	n.a.	n.a.	n.a.	2.5	10.6	11.2	11.5	11.8	12.0	12.2	12.6	24.2	84.3
Outlays	n.a.	n.a.	n.a.	0.9	9.5	10.4	11.0	11.5	11.8	12.2	12.6	20.7	79.8
Children's Health													
Insurance Program													
Budget authority	n.a.	n.a.	n.a.	n.a.	5.7	5.7	5.7	5.7	5.7	5.7	5.7	11.4	40.0
Outlays	n.a.	n.a.	n.a.	n.a.	9.6	6.2	5.9	5.9	5.9	5.9	6.0	15.7	45.3
Veterans' Compensation													
COLAs													
Budget authority	n.a.	0.1	0.6	1.3	1.8	2.5	3.7	4.5	5.1	6.7	7.8	6.3	34.1
Outlays	n.a.	0.1	0.6	1.2	1.8	2.5	3.7	4.4	5.1	6.6	7.7	6.1	33.5
Rehabilitation Services and Disability Research													
Budget authority	n.a.	3.1	3.2	3.2	3.2	3.3	3.3	3.4	3.4	3.5	3.6	15.9	33.1

	2010	2011	2012	2013	2014	2015	2016	2017	2018	2019	2020	Total, 2011-2015	Total, 2011-2020
Outlays	n.a.	1.9	2.9	3.1	3.2	3.2	3.3	3.3	3.4	3.5	3.5	14.4	31.4
Child Care Entitlements to States													
Budget authority	n.a.	2.9	2.9	2.9	2.9	2.9	2.9	2.9	2.9	2.9	2.9	14.6	29.2
Outlays	n.a.	2.4	2.9	2.9	2.9	2.9	2.9	2.9	2.9	2.9	2.9	14.0	28.6
Trade Adjustment													
Assistance for Workers													
Budget authority	n.a.	n.a.	0.7	1.0	1.0	1.0	1.0	1.1	1.1	1.1	1.1	3.7	9.1
Outlays	n.a.	n.a.	0.4	0.7	1.0	1.0	1.0	1.1	1.1	1.1	1.1	3.1	8.5
Child Nutrition[b]													
Budget authority	n.a.	0.6	0.6	0.6	0.6	0.7	0.7	0.7	0.7	0.8	0.8	3.1	6.8
Outlays	n.a.	0.5	0.6	0.6	0.6	0.7	0.7	0.7	0.7	0.7	0.8	3.0	6.7
Ground Transportation Programs Not Subject to Annual Obligation													
Limitations													
Budget authority	0.6	0.6	0.6	0.6	0.6	0.6	0.6	0.6	0.6	0.6	0.6	3.2	6.4
Outlays	0.2	0.4	0.6	0.6	0.6	0.6	0.6	0.6	0.6	0.6	0.6	2.8	6.0
Family Preservation and Support													
Budget authority	n.a.	n.a.	0.3	0.3	0.3	0.3	0.3	0.3	0.3	0.3	0.3	1.4	3.1
Outlays	n.a.	n.a.	0.1	0.3	0.3	0.3	0.3	0.3	0.3	0.3	0.3	1.1	2.8
Student Financial													
Assistance													
Budget authority	n.a.	n.a.	n.a.	n.a.	n.a.	n.a.	n.a.	n.a.	4.9	4.9	4.9	n.a.	14.7
Outlays	n.a.	n.a.	n.a.	n.a.	n.a.	n.a.	n.a.	n.a.	1.3	4.9	4.9	n.a.	11.1

Table 3-6. (Continued)

(Billions of dollars)	2010	2011	2012	2013	2014	2015	2016	2017	2018	2019	2020	Total, 2011-2015	Total, 2011-2020
Ground Transportation Programs Controlled by Obligation Limitations[c]													
Budget authority	40.0	40.0	40.0	40.0	40.0	40.0	40.0	40.0	40.0	40.0	40.0	200.0	399.9
Outlays	0	0	0	0	0	0	0	0	0	0	0	0	0
Air Transportation Programs Controlled by Obligation Limitations[c]													
Budget authority	2.0	3.6	3.6	3.6	3.6	3.6	3.6	3.6	3.6	3.6	3.6	18.0	36.1
Outlays	0	0	0	0	0	0	0	0	0	0	0	0	0
Natural Resources													
Budget authority	*	*	*	*	*	*	*	*	*	*	*	*	*
Outlays	*	*	*	*	*	-0.2	-0.1	*	*	*	*	-0.2	-0.3
Total													
Budget authority	**42.6**	**68.2**	**69.9**	**147.2**	**159.1**	**158.2**	**157.6**	**156.4**	**159.9**	**161.6**	**162.1**	**602.7**	**1,400.2**
Outlays	**0.2**	**18.4**	**25.3**	**98.5**	**118.3**	**114.1**	**113.6**	**112.6**	**112.7**	**118.0**	**118.7**	**374.7**	**950.2**

Source: Congressional Budget Office.

Note: n.a. = not applicable; COLAs = cost-of-living adjustments; * = between -$50 million and $50 million.

[a.] Agricultural commodity price and income supports under the Farm Security and Rural Investment Act of 2002 (FSRIA) generally expire after 2012. Although permanent price support authority under the Agricultural Adjustment Act of 1939 and the Agricultural Act of 1949 would then become effective, CBO continues to adhere to the rule in section 257(b)(2)(iii) of the Deficit Control Act (now expired) that indicates that the baseline should assume that FSRIA's provisions remain in effect.

[b.] Includes the Summer Food Service program and states' administrative expenses.

[c.] Authorizing legislation provides contract authority, which is counted as mandatory budget authority. However, because spending is subject to obligation limitations specified in annual appropriation acts, outlays are considered discretionary.

Legislation Assumed in the Baseline

In keeping with precedents established by the Deficit Control Act, CBO's baseline projections assume that some mandatory programs will be extended when their authorization expires, although the assumptions apply differently to programs created before and after the Balanced Budget Act of 1997. All direct spending programs that predate that act and have current-year outlays greater than $50 million are assumed to continue in CBO's baseline projections. For programs established after 1997, continuation is assessed program by program, in consultation with the House and Senate Budget Committees. CBO's baseline projections therefore assume continuance of a number of programs whose authorization expires within the current projection period.

In particular, CBO's baseline assumes continuance of a number of programs, including SNAP, TANF, CHIP, rehabilitation services, child care entitlement grants to states, trade adjustment assistance for workers, child nutrition, and family preservation and support programs. Most farm subsidies are assumed to continue as well. In addition, the Deficit Control Act directed CBO to assume that a cost-of-living adjustment for veterans' compensation would be granted each year. In CBO's projections, the assumption that expiring programs will continue does not have much effect on mandatory spending totals in 2010; however, that assumption leads to mandatory outlays totaling total $950 billion between 2011 and 2020 (see Table 3-6).

Discretionary Spending

Nearly 40 percent of federal outlays stem from budget authority provided in annual appropriation acts. That funding—referred to as discretionary—translates into outlays when the money is actually spent. Although some appropriations (for example, those designated for employees' salaries) are spent quickly, others (such as those intended for major construction projects) are disbursed over several years. In any given year, discretionary outlays include spending from new budget authority and from previous appropriations.

Total discretionary outlays are projected to increase from $1.24 trillion in 2009 to $1.37 trillion in 2010, representing growth of 11 percent. That growth is concentrated in nondefense programs and is bolstered by spending from ARRA, which helped boost budget authority for discretionary programs from $1.2 trillion in 2008 to $1.5 trillion in 2009. Based on the appropriations enacted for fiscal year 2010, that authority has dropped substantially this year, to $1.2 trillion (see Table 3-7). In particular, ARRA's discretionary funding of $281 billion has not been repeated in 2010, and funding for the military and diplomatic operations in Afghanistan and Iraq is $24 billion lower so far this year. (For detail on funding of those operations, see Box 1-1 in Chapter 1.) Excluding those two factors, budget authority provided thus far in 2010 is 3.3 percent higher than the amount provided last year.

Following the specifications of the Deficit Control Act, CBO assumes that funding for discretionary programs will keep pace with inflation; under that assumption, CBO projects that discretionary outlays will total $1.4 trillion in 2011—roughly the same amount projected for 2010. Outlays are expected to remain at about the same level for the next few years as spending from ARRA wanes. In 2020, discretionary outlays are projected to reach $1.5 trillion; as a percentage of GDP, they will fall from 9.1 percent in 2011 to 6.7 percent in 2020.

Trends in Discretionary Spending

In the mid-1980s, discretionary outlays equaled 10.0 percent of GDP; by 1999, such outlays had fallen to 6.2 percent (see Table 3-8). In 2002, spending for discretionary programs began to move upward again as a share of the economy. The terrorist attacks of September 11, 2001, and subsequent military operations in Afghanistan and Iraq accelerated that trend. Discretionary outlays rose to 7.0 percent of GDP in 2002 and reached 7.8 percent in 2005. As a percentage of GDP, such outlays dipped slightly in 2006 and 2007 but rose to 7.9 percent in 2008 and then jumped to 8.7 percent in 2009. CBO projects that total discretionary outlays as a share of GDP will show another substantial increase in 2010—rising to 9.4 percent of GDP—mostly as a result of spending related to ARRA. Excluding the effects of ARRA, discretionary outlays would represent 8.5 percent of GDP in 2009 and 8.7 percent in 2010.

Historically, trends in overall discretionary spending have been heavily influenced by spending on defense. During the late 1980s and the 1990s, defense outlays declined sharply as a share of the economy, sliding from 6.2 percent in 1986 to a low of 3.0 percent between 1999 and 2001. In 2002, defense outlays rose by 14 percent, to 3.3percent of GDP, not only because of operations in Afghanistan and other war-related activities, but also because of initiatives that were planned or funded before September 11, 2001. Defense outlays continued to climb as military operations began in Iraq, with increases of 16percent and 12.1 percent recorded in 2003 and 2004, respectively. Growth in defense spending generally slowed from 2005 to 2009, averaging increases of 8 percent. CBO projects that, under current law, outlays will rise from $656 billion in 2009 to $690 billion in 2010, an increase of 5.2 percent.

Nondefense discretionary programs encompass such activities as transportation, education grants, housing assistance, health-related research, most homeland security activities, the federal justice system, foreign aid, and maintenance of national parks. Spending for such programs has ranged between 3.2 percent and 4.0 percent of GDP since the mid-1980s; strong growth for most of the past decade has pushed such outlays from the lower to the higher end of that range. Excluding spending that stems from authority provided under ARRA, nondefense discretionary outlays are projected to increase by 7 percent from 2009 to 2010. However, with spending under ARRA included, such outlays will grow by 17 percent—a boost of about $100 billion this year—reaching 4.7 percent of GDP. Of the $268 billion in discretionary funding provided by ARRA, approximately $32 billion was disbursed in 2009; remaining amounts will be spent over several years, with about $99 billion expected to be spent in 2010.

Defense Discretionary Funding in 2010

Budget authority provided for defense discretionary programs is 1.5 percent lower thus far in 2010 than it was in 2009—a drop from $694 billion to $684 billion (see Table 3-7). That change primarily results from a decrease in funding for military operations in Iraq and Afghanistan from $146billion in 2009 to $130 billion in 2010. However, additional funding might be provided this year for operations in Afghanistan. Also, funding has declined because ARRA provided $13 billion for defense programs in 2009 but none for 2010. Partly offsetting the reduction (to date) is a $19 billion increase in funding not directly tied to operations in Iraq and Afghanistan—mainly for costs relating to military personnel and operations and maintenance. The Navy (including the Marine Corps) has received an increase of $9 billion for 2010; the Air Force and various defense agencies that support all the military services received an increase of about $10 billion for the year. The current funding for the Army—aside from appropriations designated to cover war-related costs—is slightly lower than it was last year.

Three major categories of funding within the Department of Defense account for about 80 percent of the defense appropriation: Funding for operations and maintenance ($272 billion) represents the largest portion of total budget authority for defense, with funding for military personnel and procurement adding another $150 billion and $130 billion, respectively. Appropriations for research and development ($80 billion) account for about 12 percent of total funding. And, accounting for the rest of the appropriation (about 8 percent), are funding for military construction and family housing ($25 billion), funding for the atomic energy activities within the Department of Energy ($17 billion), and funding for various defense-related programs in other departments and agencies ($7 billion).

Table 3-7. Growth in Discretionary Budget Authority, 2009 to 2010

(Billions of dollars)			
	Actual 2009	**Estimated 2010**	**Percentage Change**
Discretionary Budget Authority			
Defense			
War-related	146	130	-11.2
Other	548	554	1.1
Subtotal	694	684	-1.5
Nondefense	803	543	-32.3
Total	**1,498**	**1,228**	**-18.0**
Memorandum:			
Discretionary Budget Authority Excluding Funding for ARRA			
Defense			
War-related	146	130	-11.2
Other	535	554	3.5
Subtotal	682	684	0.3
Nondefense	535	544	1.6
Total	**1,217**	**1,228**	**0.9**

Source: Congressional Budget Office.

Notes: Does not include obligation limitations for certain transportation programs.

ARRA = American Recovery and Reinvestment Act of 2009.

Table 3-8. Defense and Nondefense Discretionary Outlays, 1985 to 2010

	Defense Outlays			Nondefense Outlays			Total Discretionary Outlays		
	In Billions of Dollars	As a Percentage of GDP	Percentage Change from Previous Year	In Billions of Dollars	As a Percentage of GDP	Percentage Change from Previous Year	In Billions of Dollars	As a Percentage of GDP	Percentage Change from Previous Year
1985	253	6.1	11.0	163	3.9	7.4	416	10.0	9.6
1986	274	6.2	8.2	165	3.7	1.2	439	10.0	5.5
1987	283	6.1	3.2	162	3.5	-1.8	444	9.5	1.3
1988	291	5.8	3.0	174	3.5	7.3	464	9.3	4.6
1989	304	5.6	4.5	185	3.4	6.6	489	9.1	5.3
1990	300	5.2	-1.3	200	3.5	8.4	501	8.7	2.4
1991	319	5.4	6.4	215	3.6	7.0	534	9.0	6.7
1992	303	4.8	-5.3	232	3.7	7.9	534	8.6	*
1993	292	4.4	-3.4	247	3.8	6.7	539	8.2	1.0
1994	282	4.0	-3.5	259	3.7	4.9	541	7.8	0.4
1995	274	3.7	-3.1	271	3.7	4.7	545	7.4	0.6
1996	266	3.4	-2.8	267	3.5	-1.7	533	6.9	-2.2
1997	272	3.3	2.1	276	3.4	3.3	547	6.7	2.7
1998	270	3.1	-0.5	282	3.3	2.3	552	6.4	0.9
1999	275	3.0	1.9	297	3.2	5.2	572	6.2	3.6
2000	295	3.0	7.1	320	3.3	7.9	615	6.3	7.5
2001	306	3.0	3.7	343	3.4	7.3	649	6.3	5.6
2002	349	3.3	14.0	385	3.7	12.2	734	7.0	13.1
2003	405	3.7	16.0	420	3.8	9.1	825	7.5	12.4
2004	454	3.9	12.1	441	3.8	4.9	895	7.7	8.4
2005	494	4.0	8.7	474	3.8	7.6	968	7.8	8.2
2006	520	3.9	5.3	496	3.8	4.6	1,016	7.7	5.0

	Defense Outlays			Nondefense Outlays			Total Discretionary Outlays		
	In Billions of Dollars	As a Percentage of GDP	Percentage Change from Previous Year	In Billions of Dollars	As a Percentage of GDP	Percentage Change from Previous Year	In Billions of Dollars	As a Percentage of GDP	Percentage Change from Previous Year
2007	548	3.9	5.4	493	3.5	-0.6	1,041	7.5	2.4
2008	612	4.2	11.8	522	3.6	6.0	1,135	7.9	9.0
2009	656	4.6	7.1	581	4.1	11.3	1,237	8.7	9.0
2010	690	4.7	5.2	682	4.7	17.3	1,371	9.4	10.9
Memorandum (Without funding from ARRA):									
2009	655	4.6	7.0	550	3.9	5.3	1,205	8.5	6.2
2010	685	4.7	4.6	587	4.0	6.7	1,272	8.7	5.6

Source: Congressional Budget Office.

Notes: The growth rates projected in the table include the effects of shifts in the timing of some defense payments.

GDP = gross domestic product; ARRA = American Recovery and Reinvestment Act of 2009; * = between zero and 0.05 percent.

Table 3-9. Nondefense Discretionary Funding, 2009 to 2010

(Billions of dollars)						
	2009			2010	Difference	
	ARRA[a]	Other	Total	Total	Other	Total
Transportation	50	86	136	90	4	-46
Education, Training, Employment, and Social Services	105	84	189	89	5	-100
Income Security	13	61	74	66	6	-8
Health	17	66	83	58	-8	-25
Veterans' Benefits and Services	1	48	49	53	5	4
International Affairs	*	58	58	53	-5	-5
Administration of Justice	5	49	54	52	2	-3
Natural Resources and Environment	17	39	56	36	-2	-19
General Science, Space, and Technology	5	29	35	31	2	-4
General Government	6	18	25	19	1	-6
Community and Regional Development	8	15	23	16	1	-7
Commerce and Housing Credit	8	5	13	10	4	-3
Agriculture	*	6	6	7	1	*
Medicare	0	5	5	6	1	1
Social Security	1	5	6	6	1	-1
Energy	30	13	43	5	-8	-38
Total	**268**	**589**	**857**	**598**	**9**	**-259**

Source: Congressional Budget Office.

Notes: Includes budgetary resources provided by obligation limitations for certain ground and air transportation programs.

ARRA = American Recovery and Reinvestment Act of 2009; * = between zero and $500 million.

[a.] ARRA also provided $13 billion in funding for defense.

Nondefense Discretionary Funding in 2010

Five categories account for more than 75 percent of the $598 billion in resources provided thus far in 2010 for nondefense discretionary activities (see Table 3-9). Transportation programs will receive $90 billion (15 percent) of the total, which includes $54 billion in obligation limitations for several surface and air transportation programs. Although those programs receive mandatory budget authority through authorizing legislation, the annual appropriation acts limit how much of that authority the Department of Transportation can obligate and thereby govern annual spending. Those limitations are treated as a measure of discretionary budgetary resources, and the resulting outlays are classified as discretionary.

Education, training, employment, and social services together will add another $89 billion, claiming another 15 percent of total nondefense discretionary funding.[40] Income security programs (mostly for housing and nutrition assistance) make up another $66 billion, representing 11 percent of the total.[41] Appropriations for health research and public health total $58 billion and make up 10 percent of the total. Finally, veterans' benefits and services, international affairs, and administration of justice each account for 9 percent of total discretionary funding for nondefense activities.

Excluding the discretionary funding provided in ARRA, funding for nondefense discretionary activities has increased by $9 billion, or by about 2 percent, from $589 billion in 2009 to $598 billion in 2010. Funding in each of the following areas—income security; education, training, employment, and social services; veterans' affairs; transportation; and commerce and housing credit—will increase by $4billion to $6 billion in 2010. Partially offsetting such growth is a decrease in budget authority because of funding that was provided in 2009 but not repeated in 2010, including an $8 billion appropriation to cover the subsidy costs of loans to automobile manufacturers for advanced technology vehicles and funding of $8 billion related to the flu pandemic.

Alternative Paths for Discretionary Spending

CBO estimates that discretionary budget authority in 2010 will total about $1.2 trillion and that obligation limitations related to transportation will total $54 billion. In the agency's baseline projections, such funding is assumed to grow each year with inflation. But unlike funding for many mandatory programs, discretionary funding is set each year, and the policy decisions made from year to year may differ greatly from an inflation-based projection. To illustrate how future funding might differ under other assumptions, CBO presents several alternative paths for discretionary spending and shows their budgetary consequences (see Table 3-10).

The first alternative path assumes that, after 2010, most funding will grow at the average annual rate of growth of nominal GDP (an average of 4.4 percent a year). Under that scenario, total discretionary outlays would exceed figures in CBO's baseline by $1.8 trillion over the projection period. Added debt-service costs would bring the cumulative increase in outlays to $2.1 trillion.

Two alternative paths address spending for operations in Iraq and Afghanistan and for other war-related activities. Outlays projected in the baseline derive from the following: funding provided in 2009 and prior years; funding ($130 billion) already provided for 2010; and the budget authority ($1.4 trillion) that CBO projects will be provided for those purposes over the 2011–2020 period (assuming that funding each year is set at $130 billion plus adjustments for inflation). Additional funding may be provided in 2010 as a result of the decision to increase U.S. forces in Afghanistan.

In subsequent years, the annual funding required for such activities may eventually be less than the amounts projected in the baseline if the number of deployed troops and the pace of operations diminish over time. Because of considerable uncertainty about those future operations, CBO has formulated two budget scenarios involving the deployment of U.S. forces to Iraq, Afghanistan, or theaters of operation elsewhere in the world. CBO estimates that the number of active-duty, reserve, and National Guard personnel deployed for those purposes in 2009 averaged about 220,000. Under both scenarios, reductions in personnel deployed to Iraq in 2010 would offset to varying degrees the increase in personnel deployed to Afghanistan. After 2010, force levels under the two scenarios are assumed to decline at different rates and to different sustained levels. (The force levels projected under either scenario could represent various allocations of forces between Iraq, Afghanistan, and other regions. Many other outcomes—some costing more and some less—are also possible. See Chapter 1 for more details.)

Table 3-10. CBO's Projections of Discretionary Spending Under Selected Policy Alternatives

(Billions of dollars)													
	Actual 2009	**2010**	**2011**	**2012**	**2013**	**2014**	**2015**	**2016**	**2017**	**2018**	**2019**	**2020**	**Total, 2011-2015**	**Total, 2011-2020**
Baseline: Discretionary Resources Grow at the Rate of Inflation After 2010[a]														
Budget Authority														
Defense	694	684	693	703	714	726	741	757	774	792	809	828	3,577	7,538
Nondefense	803	543	552	559	567	576	588	601	615	628	642	657	2,841	5,984
Total	**1,498**	**1,228**	**1,245**	**1,261**	**1,281**	**1,302**	**1,329**	**1,358**	**1,389**	**1,420**	**1,452**	**1,485**	**6,418**	**13,522**
Outlays														
Defense	656	690	701	696	705	716	730	749	761	773	795	813	3,548	7,440
Nondefense	581	682	670	649	641	640	644	653	665	677	691	705	3,244	6,634
Total	1,237	1,371	1,371	1,344	1,346	1,357	1,373	1,402	1,426	1,450	1,486	1,518	6,792	14,074
Most Discretionary Resources Grow at the Rate of Nominal Gross Domestic Product After 2010[b]														
Budget Authority														
Defense	694	684	701	730	768	804	836	869	903	937	972	1,009	3,839	8,530
Nondefense	803	543	559	588	625	661	691	723	755	788	821	855	3,124	7,066
Total	**1,498**	**1,228**	**1,260**	**1,318**	**1,393**	**1,464**	**1,527**	**1,593**	**1,659**	**1,725**	**1,793**	**1,864**	**6,962**	**15,596**
Outlays														
Defense	656	690	706	714	746	780	812	850	879	908	947	983	3,758	8,325
Nondefense	581	682	674	667	682	706	731	759	791	822	854	887	3,460	7,572
Total	1,237	1,371	1,380	1,381	1,428	1,486	1,543	1,609	1,670	1,729	1,801	1,870	7,218	15,897
Troops Deployed for Military Operations in Iraq and Afghanistan and Other War-Related Activities Decrease to 30,000 by 2013														
Budget Authority														
Defense	694	684	683	639	620	618	626	639	653	668	683	699	3,186	6,528
Nondefense	803	543	552	559	567	576	588	601	615	628	642	657	2,841	5,984
Total	**1,498**	**1,228**	**1,234**	**1,198**	**1,186**	**1,194**	**1,214**	**1,240**	**1,267**	**1,297**	**1,326**	**1,356**	**6,026**	**12,513**
Outlays														
Defense	656	690	699	664	638	624	624	636	643	652	671	687	3,249	6,538

	Actual 2009	2010	2011	2012	2013	2014	2015	2016	2017	2018	2019	2020	Total, 2011-2015	Total, 2011-2020
Nondefense	581	682	670	649	641	640	644	653	665	677	691	705	3,244	6,634
Total	**1,237**	**1,371**	**1,369**	**1,312**	**1,279**	**1,265**	**1,268**	**1,288**	**1,308**	**1,329**	**1,362**	**1,392**	**6,493**	**13,172**
Troops Deployed for Military Operations in Iraq and Afghanistan and Other War-Related Activities Decrease to 60,000 by 2015														
Budget Authority														
Defense	694	720	720	713	687	661	654	661	672	688	703	720	3,435	6,879
Nondefense	803	543	552	559	567	576	588	601	615	628	642	657	2,841	5,984
Total	1,498	1,264	1,272	1,272	1,254	1,238	1,241	1,262	1,287	1,316	1,346	1,377	6,276	12,864
Outlays														
Defense	656	698	721	717	703	680	664	665	666	673	692	707	3,485	6,888
Nondefense	581	682	670	649	641	640	644	653	665	677	691	705	3,244	6,634
Total	**1,237**	**1,379**	**1,391**	**1,365**	**1,344**	**1,321**	**1,308**	**1,317**	**1,331**	**1,350**	**1,383**	**1,412**	**6,729**	**13,522**
Most Discretionary Resources Are Frozen at the 2010 Level														
Budget Authority														
Defense	694	684	684	685	686	687	687	688	689	690	691	692	3,429	6,880
Nondefense	803	543	545	545	544	543	543	543	543	542	542	542	2,720	5,432
Total	**1,498**	**1,228**	**1,230**	**1,230**	**1,230**	**1,230**	**1,230**	**1,231**	**1,232**	**1,232**	**1,233**	**1,234**	**6,150**	**12,312**
Outlays														
Defense	656	690	695	682	682	682	683	688	684	681	686	688	3,424	6,852
Nondefense	581	682	666	638	622	611	603	599	597	594	593	592	3,140	6,114
Total	**1,237**	**1,371**	**1,361**	**1,320**	**1,304**	**1,293**	**1,286**	**1,286**	**1,281**	**1,276**	**1,279**	**1,279**	**6,564**	**12,966**

Source: Congressional Budget Office.

Note: Nondefense discretionary outlays are usually higher than budget authority because of spending from the Highway Trust Fund and the Airport and Airway Trust Fund that is subject to obligation limitations set in appropriation acts. The budget authority for such programs is provided in authorizing legislation and is not considered discretionary.

[a] Inflation in CBO's baseline is projected using the inflators specified in the Balanced Budget and Emergency Deficit Control Act of 1985: the gross domestic product price index and the employment cost index for wages and salaries.

[b] This alternative assumes that appropriations for operations in Iraq and Afghanistan enacted for 2010 are projected at baseline levels (that is, increased at the rate of inflation).

Table 3-11. CBO's Baseline Projections of Federal Interest Outlays

(Billions of dollars)													
	Actual 2009	**2010**	**2011**	**2012**	**2013**	**2014**	**2015**	**2016**	**2017**	**2018**	**2019**	**2020**	**Total, 2011-2015**	**Total, 2011-2020**
Interest on Treasury														
Debt Securities														
(Gross interest)[a]	383	428	451	508	573	652	730	804	873	942	1,008	1,070	2,913	7,609
Interest Received by Trust Funds														
Social Security	-118	-120	-119	-119	-122	-126	-133	-141	-151	-161	-171	-180	-619	-1,422
Other trust funds[b]	-64	-71	-64	-69	-74	-78	-81	-83	-84	-86	-89	-89	-366	-797
Subtotal	-182	-191	-183	-188	-195	-205	-214	-224	-235	-246	-260	-269	-985	-2,219
Other Interest[c]	-15	-29	-34	-39	-44	-51	-55	-60	-66	-71	-72	-77	-224	-570
Other Investment Income[d]	*	-1	*	*	-1	-1	-1	-1	-1	-1	*	*	-2	-5
Total Net Interest														
Outlays	**187**	**207**	**233**	**280**	**333**	**396**	**459**	**519**	**572**	**624**	**676**	**723**	**1,701**	**4,816**

Source: Congressional Budget Office.

Note: * = between -$500 million and $500 million.

a. Excludes interest costs on debt issued by agencies other than the Treasury (primarily the Tennessee Valley Authority).

b. Mainly the Civil Service Retirement, Military Retirement, Medicare, and Unemployment Insurance Trust Funds.

c. Primarily interest on loans to the public.

d. Earnings on private investments by the National Railroad Retirement Investment Trust.

The final scenario assumes that most discretionary budget authority and obligation limitations would be frozen at the nominal 2010 levels for the entire projection period.[42] Total discretionary outlays for the 10-year period would be $1.1 trillion lower than those projected in the baseline. Debt-service adjustments would reduce spending by another $180 billion, for a total of $1.3 trillion. Under that scenario, total discretionary spending would fall to about 5 percent of GDP by 2020, the lowest share in more than 50 years.

Net Interest

Net interest payments accounted for about 5 percent of overall federal spending in 2009. Under CBO's baseline projections, that figure is expected to rise to 6 percent in 2010 and then climb to nearly 14 percent in 2020. Net interest is primarily determined by the amount that the Treasury pays on the debt that it issues to the public. The Treasury also issues debt to other government accounts, but such transactions are basically for bookkeeping purposes and have no effect on the total deficit. In addition, the Treasury both pays and collects interest in a variety of other areas, but the amounts are significantly smaller than the interest paid on Treasury borrowing.

The federal government's interest payments depend primarily on market interest rates and the amount of debt held by the public. The Congress and the President influence the latter through legislation that governs spending and taxes and, thus, the extent of government borrowing. Interest rates are determined largely by market forces and by policies set by the Federal Reserve System.

Baseline Projections of Net Interest

From 2003 to 2008, net interest costs increased, on average, by 11 percent annually. The rise in costs during that time period is attributable mostly to rising short-term interest rates and increases in debt held by the public. However, substantial decreases in both short- and long-term interest rates in 2009 helped push net interest costs down from $253 billion in 2008 to $187 billion—a drop of 26 percent—even though debt held by the public increased by $1.7 trillion. Net interest fell to 1.3 percent of GDP in 2009, compared with 1.8 percent in 2008.

CBO projects that interest costs in 2010 will increase by 10 percent to $207 billion (or 1.4 percent of GDP). Much of that increase will result from continued heavy borrowing. Debt held by the public is projected to increase from $7.5 trillion at the end of 2009 to $8.8 trillion at the end of 2010. In addition, interest rates on most Treasury notes (securities ranging from a 2- to 10-year maturity) are expected to rise by about 30 basis points.

Under current baseline assumptions, net interest costs are expected to increase dramatically through the rest of the projection period. Rapidly rising debt and interest rates will drive net interest costs from just over $200 billion in 2010 to over $700 billion in 2020—more than a threefold increase (see Table 3-11). Debt held by the public is projected to nearly double over the next 10 years, reaching $15.0 trillion by the end of 2020.[43] In addition, CBO estimates that the interest rate paid on 91-day Treasury bills will rise from less than 0.25 percent in 2010 to 4.8 percent in 2020 and that the rate on 10-year Treasury notes will increase from 3.5 percent in 2010 to 5.6 percent in 2020. As a result, net interest as a percentage of GDP is projected to reach 3.2 percent in 2020, more than double the percentage in 2010.

Interest on Governmental Holdings

The Treasury has issued about $4.3 trillion in securities to federal trust funds and other government accounts. Similar in composition to debt held by the public, those securities consist of bills, notes, bonds, inflation-protected securities, and zero-coupon bonds. However, the interest paid on those securities has no impact on net federal spending because it is credited to accounts elsewhere in the budget. In 2010, trust funds will be credited with $191 billion of such intragovernmental interest, CBO estimates, mostly for the Social Security and Civil Service Retirement and Disability trust funds. Over the 10-year baseline period, interest credited to trust funds will total more than $2 trillion, CBO projects.

Other Interest

The $29 billion in other interest that CBO anticipates the government will receive in 2010 represents the net result of many transactions, including interest payments and interest collections. Among the interest outflows from the government are payments for interest on tax refunds that are issued more than 45 days after the date on which they were filed and interest payments made for bonds issued after the savings and loan crisis of the 1980s. Together, those payments are expected to total $5billion in 2010 and to average about $7 billion per year thereafter.

The largest interest collections come from the credit financing accounts, which have been established to record the cash transactions related to federal loan and loan guarantee programs. For those programs, net subsidy costs are recorded in the budget, but the cash flows that move through the credit financing accounts are not. Credit financing accounts both pay interest to and receive interest from on-budget Treasury accounts; but, on net, more interest is paid to the Treasury than is received from it. CBO estimates that such receipts will total $22 billion in 2010, steadily increasing to as much as $37 billion in 2020. In the near term, interest payments from the TARP, from the program to purchase mortgage-backed securities, and from the student loan program dominate the annual totals.

CBO also projects interest earnings of $6 billion for the current year on balances credited to the TRICARE for Life program. (Because those are intragovernmental payments between the Treasury and the Department of Defense, they have no net effect on the budget.) The roughly $7 billion in remaining interest collections that CBO estimates for 2010 is spread among a large number of accounts, including payments from the Federal Financing Bank, as well as earnings on the Nuclear Waste Fund, the U.S. Postal Service Retiree Health Benefits Fund, and the National Railroad Retirement Investment Trust, among others.

4. The Revenue Outlook

The Congressional Budget Office projects that total federal revenues will be about $2.2 trillion in 2010, a 3.3 percent increase from 2009, under the assumption that current laws and policies will remain in effect. As a share of gross domestic product, revenues will edge up slightly, from a nearly 60-year low of 14.8 percent in 2009 to 14.9 percent in 2010 (see Figure

4-1). CBO expects that about 60 percent of the increase in federal revenues will come from increased remittances from the Federal Reserve System to the Treasury; those payments will rise markedly because of the Federal Reserve's recent actions to stabilize financial markets to support the economy. According to CBO's projections, revenues other than those remittances will increase by only 1.3 percent in 2010, about a percentage point less than the anticipated increase in GDP.

Several tax provisions enacted over the past decade are set to expire in December 2010. Because of those expirations and a strengthening economic recovery, CBO projects that revenues will increase substantially after 2010, rising by about 23 percent in 2011 and by another 11 percent in 2012, to reach 18.8 percent of GDP in 2012 (see Figure 4-2). The expiration of tax provisions accounts for about two-thirds of the increase in CBO's baseline projection of revenues relative to GDP between 2010 and 2012.[44] Most of the provisions originally enacted in the Economic Growth and Tax Relief Reconciliation Act of 2001 and the Jobs and Growth Tax Relief Reconciliation Act of 2003 are set to expire, as are the Making Work Pay tax credit (enacted in the American Recovery and Reinvestment Act of 2009) and many other provisions. In addition, temporary relief from the individual alternative minimum tax expired at the end of 2009; the step-up in AMT liability will have its largest effect on revenues starting in 2011.

Revenues are projected to grow faster than GDP in 2011 and 2012 for three additional reasons. First, the experience of previous downturns indicates that, as economic activity picks up and prices of financial assets rise, wage and salary income, corporate profits, and other types of taxable incomes are likely to grow more rapidly than is GDP. Second, the recession led to a temporary acceleration of tax payments because taxpayers were slow to adjust withholding as tax liabilities fell; CBO estimates that this factor raised receipts in 2008 but should reduce them in 2010. Payments in 2011 and 2012 should return to a more normal relationship with tax liabilities. Third, CBO anticipates that the unexplained recent weakness in individual and corporate income taxes—beyond that attributable to available economic data—will gradually fade.

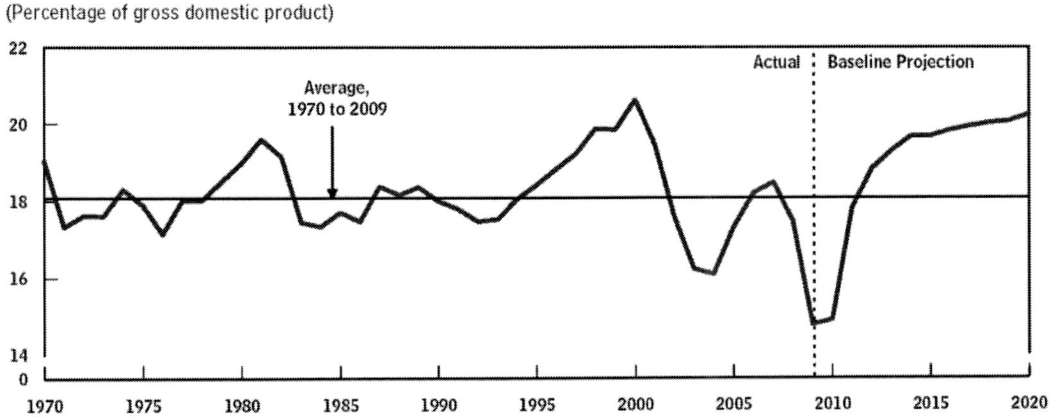

Source: Congressional Budget Office.

Figure 4-1. Total Revenues, 1970 to 2020.

According to CBO's baseline projections, revenues will continue rising from 2013 through 2020 (the end of the projection period) to reach 20.2 percent of GDP. Growth in individual income tax receipts accounts for almost all of the increase, mostly because real (inflation-adjusted) growth in income will push more income into higher tax brackets and because inflation will increase revenues from the AMT (see Figure 4-3 on page 78).

However, if the expiring provisions of EGTRRA, JGTRRA, and other tax legislation were extended and if the AMT was indexed for inflation, revenues would be substantially lower than those shown in CBO's baseline projections. Instead, revenues would rise more slowly relative to GDP in 2011 and 2012 and would reach roughly 17.5 percent of GDP in 2020.

CBO's projections for revenues from 2010 to 2013 are a little lower than those that it published in August 2009: by about $90 billion in 2010, by about $45 billion in 2011 and 2012, and by just a slight amount in 2013.[45] The downward revisions, amounting to about 2 percent of revenues projected over that period, primarily reflect smaller-than-anticipated collections for corporate and individual income taxes since August; whatever factors generated this weakness are assumed to dissipate slowly during the next five years, and tax receipts are expected to return to their historical relationships to taxable incomes. Revenue over the period from 2014 to 2019 has been revised upward by about $75 billion per year (about 2percent), on average, relative to CBO's projections in August 2009. Higher projected corporate profits are responsible for much of the revision in 2014 and 2015, and higher projected wages and salaries are the dominant factor for 2016 and beyond. Legislation enacted last fall also contributed to those changes, causing CBO to reduce its revenue projections by $44 billion for 2010 but to raise them by the same amount for the rest of the projection period. (For a more detailed discussion of the changes to the revenue projections, see AppendixB.)

Sources of Revenues

Federal revenues come from individual income taxes, social insurance (payroll) taxes, corporate income taxes, excise taxes, estate and gift taxes, remittances from the Federal Reserve, customs duties, and miscellaneous fees and fines. Individual income tax receipts are the largest source of federal revenue, averaging about 45 percent of the total during the past 40 years. Those receipts and receipts from corporate income taxes (which are the third-largest source of revenue) have accounted for most of the historical variation in total revenues, and they account for most of the projected changes in revenues between 2010 and 2020.

Since 1970, total revenues have averaged just above 18 percent of GDP; they reached a high of 20.6 percent in 2000 and fell to a low of 14.8 percent in 2009. Receipts from individual and corporate income taxes have been especially volatile during the past 15 years or so. Between 1992 and 2000, individual income tax receipts grew at an average annual rate of nearly 10 percent, reaching a peak of 10.2 percent of GDP in 2000 (see Figure 4-3). For the four years after 2000, individual receipts declined as a share of GDP, falling to 6.9 percent of GDP by 2004. The downturn in revenues began as a result of the stock market decline and the 2001 recession, and it was reinforced by tax legislation enacted between 2001 and 2004. Income growth picked up substantially in 2004, and individual income tax receipts increased by an average of nearly 13 percent annually from 2005 to 2007; the 2007 mark of 8.4 percent of GDP roughly matches the average since 1970. Since 2007, the recession and financial crisis, as well as the legislative responses to those problems, caused individual tax receipts to fall markedly. In 2009, individual receipts totaled just 6.4 percent of GDP, the lowest share since 1950.

Receipts from corporate income taxes averaged slightly more than 2 percent of GDP from 1995 to 2000, but then fell to 1.2 percent of GDP in 2003. Corporate income tax receipts rose sharply after 2003, reaching 2.7 percent of GDP in 2006 and 2007 and accounting for more than half of the increase in total receipts relative to GDP between 2003 and 2007. Just two years later, in 2009, corporate tax receipts dropped to 1.0 percent of GDP, the lowest percentage since the 1930s. That variability over the past decade and the 55 percent decline in corporate receipts in 2009 have several sources: changes in corporate profits from current production relative to GDP; fluctuations in the effective tax rate on profits arising from changes in capital gains realizations, deductions for bad debts, the mix of profitable and unprofitable firms, and other factors; and changes in tax law, particularly the rules for depreciation of equipment that businesses purchase.

Receipts from social insurance taxes (the second-largest source of federal revenue) have been more stable relative to the size of the economy than have receipts from income taxes, fluctuating between 6.2 percent and 6.8percent of GDP since the mid-1980s. During the preceding quarter century, social insurance taxes had claimed a steadily growing share of GDP, largely because of legislated increases in tax rates and bases. Revenues from the remaining sources (other taxes, duties, remittances, fees, and fines) have declined relative to GDP during the past 40 years, primarily because of the steady decline in excise taxes relative to GDP. Revenue from those sources totaled 1.1 percent of GDP in 2009.

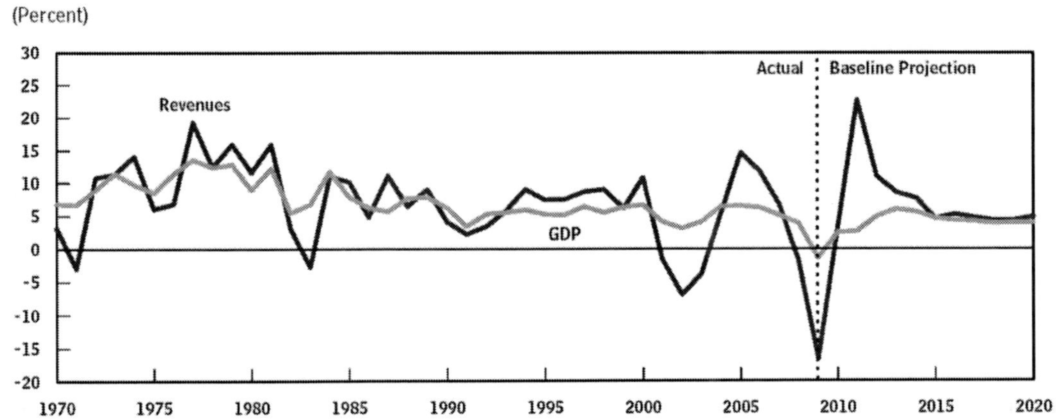

Source: Congressional Budget Office.

Figure 4-2. Annual Growth of Federal Revenues and Gross Domestic Product, 1970 to 2020.

Current Projections

CBO projects that total federal revenues will rebound sharply from the current historically low amounts relative to GDP starting in 2011. Much of that increase stems from individual income tax revenues, which—in CBO's projections under current law—will remain low relative to GDP at 6.5 percent this year but climb sharply to reach 9.1 percent of GDP in 2012 and 10.9 percent of GDP by 2020 (see Table 4-1). Social insurance receipts are projected to edge down in 2010 relative to GDP but to rebound in 2011 to average 6.3 percent of GDP through 2020, the same share seen during the past five years. Corporate income tax receipts also are projected to remain low relative to GDP in 2010, at 1.0 percent, but then to rise to 2.2 percent of GDP in 2014 before declining to 1.8 percent of GDP in 2020. Revenues from the remaining sources are projected to measure 1.4 percent of GDP in 2010, because of temporary increases in Federal Reserve remittances, and to slip to 1.3 percent of GDP from 2013 to 2020.

Individual Income Taxes

Individual income tax receipts account for four-fifths of the projected increase in total revenues relative to GDP over the next 10 years. Almost half of the increase in those receipts relative to the size of the economy results from the currently scheduled expiration of a host of tax provisions. The rest results from such factors as the recovery from the recession in the near term and structural features of the individual income tax system over the longer term.

Projected Receipts from 2010 Through 2012. Individual income tax receipts will grow by 3.3 percent in 2010, after declining in 2008 and 2009, according to CBO's baseline projection (see Table 4-2). That growth stems largely from the effects of the Economic Stimulus Act of 2008 (ESA) and ARRA, both of which lowered receipts in 2009 relative to 2010. ESA provided rebates to taxpayers, reducing revenues largely in 2008 but also in 2009; and the partial expensing provisions of ARRA will reduce individual income tax receipts (by cutting the taxable incomes of noncorporate businesses) by a smaller amount in 2010 than in 2009. Taxable personal income, as measured in the national income and product accounts (NIPAs), a broad indicator of the tax base for individual income taxes, is projected to grow by just 0.3 percent in 2010, well below the 2.5 percent expected growth of GDP. Taxable personal income includes wages and salaries, dividends, interest, rental income, and proprietors' income. Wages and salaries, the largest source of personal income, will grow by 0.9 percent in 2010, CBO projects, and withholding for income and payroll taxes is likely to follow a similar path.

Individual income tax receipts are projected to surge by 33 percent in 2011 and by 14 percent in 2012. The increases are generated partly by faster growth in taxable personal income (2.9 percent in 2011 and 5.4 percent in 2012) as the recovery strengthens. The more important causes, however, are the scheduled changes to tax rules, including the expiration of higher exemption amounts for the individual AMT and the expiration after 2010 of provisions originally enacted in 2001 in EGTRRA, in 2003 in JGTRRA, and in 2009 in ARRA.

Table 4-1. CBO's Projections of Revenues

	Actual 2009	2010	2011	2012	2013	2014	2015	2016	2017	2018	2019	2020	Total, 2011-2015	Total, 2011-2020
	In Billions of Dollars													
Individual Income Taxes	915	946	1,258	1,434	1,595	1,729	1,854	1,969	2,091	2,199	2,316	2,448	7,870	18,894
Social Insurance Taxes	891	878	934	993	1,056	1,115	1,165	1,212	1,260	1,310	1,361	1,416	5,263	11,822
Corporate Income Taxes	138	147	266	318	350	394	365	387	393	401	403	416	1,693	3,693
Excise Taxes	62	70	77	80	82	83	85	86	87	87	88	89	406	843
Estate and Gift Taxes	23	16	15	38	43	48	53	56	59	63	66	70	197	511
Federal Reserve	34	77	74	52	41	42	48	47	48	50	53	55	257	511
Customs Duties	22	24	28	32	35	37	38	39	41	43	47	51	170	392
Other	17	17	16	17	17	17	17	17	17	17	17	17	85	171
Total	**2,105**	**2,175**	**2,670**	**2,964**	**3,218**	**3,465**	**3,625**	**3,814**	**3,996**	**4,170**	**4,352**	**4,563**	**15,941**	**36,836**
On-budget	1,451	1,533	1,997	2,253	2,463	2,668	2,789	2,943	3,088	3,225	3,369	3,539	12,170	28,335
Off-budget[a]	654	642	673	711	754	797	836	871	908	945	982	1,024	3,771	8,501
Memorandum:														
Gross Domestic Product	14,236	14,595	14,992	15,730	16,676	17,606	18,421	19,223	20,036	20,823	21,667	22,544	83,425	187,719
	As a Percentage of Gross Domestic Product													
Individual Income Taxes	6.4	6.5	8.4	9.1	9.6	9.8	10.1	10.2	10.4	10.6	10.7	10.9	9.4	10.1
Social Insurance Taxes	6.3	6.0	6.2	6.3	6.3	6.3	6.3	6.3	6.3	6.3	6.3	6.3	6.3	6.3
Corporate Income Taxes	1.0	1.0	1.8	2.0	2.1	2.2	2.0	2.0	2.0	1.9	1.9	1.8	2.0	2.0
Excise Taxes	0.4	0.5	0.5	0.5	0.5	0.5	0.5	0.4	0.4	0.4	0.4	0.4	0.5	0.4
Estate and Gift Taxes	0.2	0.1	0.1	0.2	0.3	0.3	0.3	0.3	0.3	0.3	0.3	0.3	0.2	0.3
Federal Reserve	0.2	0.5	0.5	0.3	0.2	0.2	0.3	0.2	0.2	0.2	0.2	0.2	0.3	0.3
Customs Duties	0.2	0.2	0.2	0.2	0.2	0.2	0.2	0.2	0.2	0.2	0.2	0.2	0.2	0.2
Other	0.1	0.1	0.1	0.1	0.1	0.1	0.1	0.1	0.1	0.1	0.1	0.1	0.1	0.1
Total	**14.8**	**14.9**	**17.8**	**18.8**	**19.3**	**19.7**	**19.7**	**19.8**	**19.9**	**20.0**	**20.1**	**20.2**	**19.1**	**19.6**
On-budget	10.2	10.5	13.3	14.3	14.8	15.2	15.1	15.3	15.4	15.5	15.6	15.7	14.6	15.1
Off-budget[a]	4.6	4.4	4.5	4.5	4.5	4.5	4.5	4.5	4.5	4.5	4.5	4.5	4.5	4.5

Source: Congressional Budget Office.

Note: Receipts from the Federal Reserve and other receipts, consisting of fees and fines, are combined in a category called "miscellaneous receipts" in the federal budget.

[a] Revenues generated for the two Social Security trust funds (the Old-Age and Survivors Insurance Trust Fund and the Disability Insurance Trust Fund) are off-budget.

Table 4-2. CBO's Projections of Individual Income Tax Receipts and the NIPAs Tax Base

	Actual 2009	2010	2011	2012	2013	2014	2015	2016	2017	2018	2019	2020	Total, 2011-2015[a]	Total, 2011-2020[a]
Individual Income Tax Receipts														
In billions of dollars	915	946	1,258	1,434	1,595	1,729	1,854	1,969	2,091	2,199	2,316	2,448	7,870	18,894
As a percentage of GDP	6.4	6.5	8.4	9.1	9.6	9.8	10.1	10.2	10.4	10.6	10.7	10.9	9.4	10.1
Annual growth rate	-20.1	3.3	33.0	14.0	11.2	8.4	7.2	6.2	6.2	5.2	5.3	5.7	14.4	10.0
Taxable Personal Income														
In billions of dollars	9,510	9,537	9,818	10,350	11,054	11,802	12,447	13,047	13,639	14,198	14,792	15,422	55,471	126,569
As a percentage of GDP	66.8	65.3	65.5	65.8	66.3	67.0	67.6	67.9	68.1	68.2	68.3	68.4	66.5	67.4
Annual growth rate	-3.6	0.3	2.9	5.4	6.8	6.8	5.5	4.8	4.5	4.1	4.2	4.3	5.5	4.9
Individual Receipts as a ercentage of Taxable														
Personal Income	9.6	9.9	12.8	13.9	14.4	14.7	14.9	15.1	15.3	15.5	15.7	15.9	14.2	14.9

Source: Congressional Budget Office.

Notes: The tax base in this table (taxable personal income) reflects income as measured by the national income and product accounts rather than as reported on tax returns. An important difference, therefore, is that it excludes capital gains realizations.

NIPAs = national income and product accounts; GDP = gross domestic product.

[a] Measures expressed in billions of dollars are the cumulative amounts over the period. Measures expressed as a percentage of GDP or taxable personal income are averages over the period. Measures expressed as annual growth rates are the average rates compounded annually over the period, including growth in 2011.

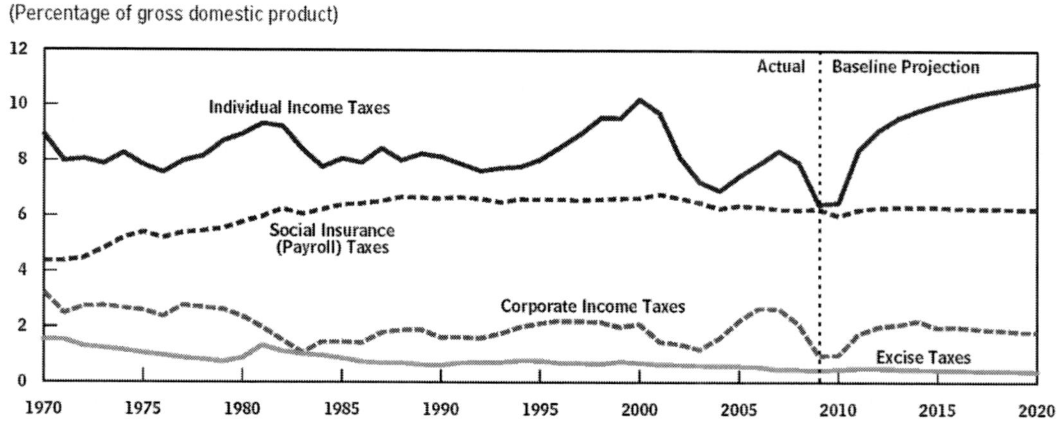

Source: Congressional Budget Office.

Figure 4-3. Revenues, by Source, 1970 to 2020.

Scheduled Changes in Tax Law. Expiration of higher exemption amounts for the AMT in 2010, and the expiration of provisions in EGTRRA, JGTRRA, and ARRA in 2011, will increase individual income tax receipts, especially in 2011 and 2012. CBO projects that those changes account for about 2.0 of the 2.6 percentage point increase in individual income tax revenues relative to GDP from 2010 through 2012 (see Box4-1).

Under current law, the expiration of the higher exemption amounts for the AMT after 2009 will boost revenues sharply in 2011, increasing revenues as a share of GDP by about 0.4 percentage points. In February 2009, the Congress increased the AMT exemption amounts for 2009 to keep the number of taxpayers affected at about 4 million, roughly the same as in 2008. The tax relief expired at the end of December 2009, and although relief from the AMT has been renewed in the form of an annual "patch" since 2001, the baseline reflects tax law as it currently exists. As a result, CBO projects that the number of taxpayers affected by the AMT will jump to about 27 million in 2010 and that tax liabilities from the Congress increased the AMT exemption amounts for 2009 to keep the number of taxpayers affected at about 4 million, roughly the same as in 2008. The tax relief expired at the end of December 2009, and although relief from the AMT has been renewed in the form of an annual "patch" since 2001, the baseline reflects tax law as it currently exists. As a result, CBO projects that the number of taxpayers affected by the AMT will jump to about 27 million in 2010 and that tax liabilities from the AMT will rise sharply (see Figure 4-4).[46] Therefore, CBO projects that receipts from the AMT will jump from $40billion in 2010 to $103 billion in 2011.[47] CBO expects that the additional AMT liability from 2010 will be paid almost entirely in 2011 because many taxpayers will be unaware of the change or might expect lawmakers once again to raise the AMT's exemption amounts temporarily. Even those taxpayers who anticipate and plan for the expiration might use the safe-harbor provisions in the tax code to delay payments without penalty until 2011.[48]

The expiration of provisions in EGTRRA, JGTRRA, and ARRA will increase receipts in both 2011 and 2012. Most of the effect stems from the impending increases in statutory tax rates on ordinary income, capital gains, and dividends, as well as a contraction of the tax brackets and standard deductions for joint filers to less than twice those for single taxpayers. The rest results from a smaller child tax credit, an end to the Making Work Pay tax credit, and other scheduled changes.

The increase in the tax rate for capital gains realizations, which is scheduled to take effect in 2011 after the lower rates enacted in JGTRRA expire, will reduce capital gains realizations but increase overall income tax revenues from capital gains, CBO projects.[49] Because taxpayers tend to realize fewer gains at higher tax rates, those higher rates reduce the long-run average amount of gains relative to the size of the economy. However, higher tax rates also increase the amount of revenue collected on a given amount of realizations. The former effect only partially offsets the latter, so the net effect of the increase in capital gains tax rates will be to increase revenues from that source despite somewhat lower realizations.[50]

Other Factors. CBO projects an increase of 0.6 percentage points in individual income tax receipts as a share of GDP between 2010 and 2012 from other factors, the largest of which is an acceleration of the payment of taxesduring the recession. Many taxpayers might not have adjusted their withholding in response to declining liabilities for tax years 2008 and 2009. Because those taxpayers had more withheld from their wages than they needed to pay in taxes—that is, their "overwithholding" was more than normal or their "underwithholding" was less than normal—they received abnormally large refunds (or made smaller payments) upon filing their taxes.[51] CBO projects that receipts will be lower in fiscal year 2010 both because of the large refunds paid to such taxpayers for their 2009 taxes and because many taxpayers will adjust their withholding and estimated tax payments to more closely match their actual liabilities for 2010. CBO projects that taxpayers will receive smaller refunds in fiscal year 2011 because they will not be overwithheld more than normal for the previous year, thus boosting receipts relative to 2010.

Another factor is that the unexplained weakness in recent receipts, which is beyond what can be accounted for in current economic data, is assumed under CBO's baseline to gradually dissipate over the next several years. That assumption causes projected tax revenues to grow relative to the size of the economy by 0.2 percentage points between 2010 and 2012. In addition, growth of personal income (especially wages and salaries) relative to GDP, rising real income (which will cause more income to be taxed in higher tax brackets), and an expected increase in taxable pension distributions as the population ages, are projected to cause receipts to rise relative to GDP between 2010 and 2012.

Increases in capital gains realizations, in the absence of the effects of the impending changes in tax rates, will also boost revenues relative to GDP over the next two years, CBO projects. Capital gains realizations declined by an estimated 46 percent in calendar year 2008 and by an additional 16percent in 2009, reflecting recent economic turmoil and steep declines in the stock and housing markets (see Table 4-3). However, strong growth initially in corporate profits and then in business and residential fixed investment is projected to drive a rebound in realizations of capital gains between 2009 and 2012. By that time, realizations are projected to be near their long-term historical average ratio of realizations to GDP, adjusted for the tax rate on gains. In CBO's projections, that ratio stays roughly the same through 2020.

Projected Receipts Beyond 2012. In CBO's baseline projections, revenues from personal income taxes rise as a share of GDP (and as a share of taxable personal income) in each year of the projection period after 2010, reaching 10.9 percent of GDP by 2020—or 4.4 percentage points higher than is projected for 2010 and 1.8 percentage points higher than is projected for 2012. Several factors contribute to that increase.

Table 4-3. Actual and Projected Capital Gains Realizations and Tax Receipts

	Capital Gains Realizations[a]		Capital Gains Tax Receipts[b]	
	In Billions of Dollars	As a Percentage of GDP	In Billions of Dollars	As a Percentage of Individual Income Tax Receipts
1995	180	2.4	40	6.8
1996	261	3.3	54	8.3
1997	365	4.4	72	9.8
1998	455	5.2	84	10.1
1999	553	5.9	99	11.3
2000	644	6.5	119	11.8
2001	349	3.4	100	10.0
2002	269	2.5	58	6.8
2003	323	2.9	50	6.3
2004	499	4.2	61	7.6
2005	690	5.5	86	9.3
2006	798	6.0	109	10.5
2007	924	6.6	126	10.8
2008	496	3.4	105	9.2
2009	418	2.9	60	6.5
2010	540	3.7	56	6.0
2011	447	3.0	77	6.1
2012	622	3.9	84	5.9
2013	661	3.9	111	6.9
2014	698	3.9	119	6.9
2015	731	3.9	127	6.8
2016	764	3.9	133	6.7
2017	797	3.9	139	6.6
2018	830	3.9	145	6.6
2019	864	3.9	151	6.5
2020	902	4.0	158	6.4

Source: Congressional Budget Office.

Notes: Capital gains realizations are the sum of net capital gains from tax returns reporting a net gain.

Data for gains realized after 2007 and data for tax receipts in all years are estimated or projected by CBO.

Data for gains realized before 2008 are estimated by the Treasury Department.

a. Calendar year basis.

b. Fiscal year basis. This measure is CBO's estimate of when tax liabilities resulting from capital gains realizations are paid to the Treasury.

Characteristics that are inherent in the individual income tax system will cause average tax rates (taxes as a percentage of income) to rise after 2012, thereby increasing the receipts generated by a given amount of economic activity. Real bracket creep, in which the growth of inflation-adjusted income causes more income to be taxed in higher tax brackets, will cause a projected 0.9 percentage point increase relative to GDP from 2013 through 2020 (in addition to an increase of about 0.1 percentage point between 2010 and 2012). Real bracket creep occurs because the income tax brackets are indexed for price inflation but not for income growth in excess of inflation. Also, the individual AMT is projected to claim a growing share of rising nominal income because it is not indexed for inflation. That trend would hold even without the scheduled expiration of the higher AMT exemption in 2010, which itself is expected to boost receipts sharply in 2011. The rising share of income subject to the AMT, excluding the effects of the scheduled changes in law, will cause revenues relative to GDP in CBO's baseline projections to increase by 0.2 percentage points from 2013 to 2020.

Taxable income growth also raises receipts from individual income taxes relative to GDP after 2012. Taxable distributions from certain tax-deferred retirement accounts, such as traditional individual retirement accounts and 401(k) plans, are expected to increase as the population ages, raising individual income tax receipts relative to GDP by 0.3 percentage points in CBO's projections. Contributions to those accounts were exempt from taxation when they were made initially, thus reducing the amount of taxable income reported to the Internal Revenue Service (IRS) in earlier years. As retirees take distributions from those accounts, the money becomes taxable. In addition, revenues are projected to increase by another 0.2 percentage points relative to GDP as a result of rising interest income, dividends, and income from wages and salaries.

Box 4-1. Effect of Expiring Tax Provisions on CBO's Revenue Baseline

In preparing its revenue baseline, the Congressional Budget Office (CBO) assumes that current law remains in effect. Thus, CBO assumes that most cur rent tax provisions expire as scheduled and that no additional legislation is enacted.[1] Under that framework, the baseline serves as a neutral benchmark that legislators and others can apply as they assess the potential effects of changes in policy.

The scheduled expiration of tax provisions has substantial consequences for CBO's baseline projections, especially after 2010, when most provisions originally enacted in the Economic Growth and Tax Relief Rec onciliation Act of 2001 (EGTRRA) and the Jobs and Growth Tax Relief Reconciliation Act of 2003 are scheduled to expire. Altogether, CBO projects that expiring tax provisions will increase revenues by about 2.7 percentage points of gross domestic product (GDP) between 2010 and 2012 (see the table to the right) and that the revenue share of GDP will stay approximately at that higher level until the end of the projection period in 2020.[2] The scheduled expiration of lower tax rates on individual income, initially enacted in 2001, will lead to the largest increase in revenues relative to GDP—about 1.3 percent of GDP between 2010 and 2012. The expiring tax rovisions include the establishment of the 10 percent tax rate bracket, which under current law will revert to 15 percent in 2011; lower statutory tax rates of 25, 28, 33, and 35 percent, which will revert to rates of 28, 31, 36, and 39.6 percent; the expanded 15 percent tax bracket and the standard deduction for married couples, which after 2010 will contract to less than twice those for single taxpayers; the reduced top tax rates of 15 percent on long-term capital gains realizations and dividends, which will return to the pre 2003 rates of 20 percent for capital gains and 39.6 percent for dividends; and the end of the phase out of itemized deductions and personal exemptions for higher-income taxpayers, with the phaseout returning after 2010. In addition, the temporary "AMT patch," enacted in 2001 to hold down the number of taxpayers affected and then extended annually, expired at the end of 2009. The largest revenue-increasing effect of that change will be seen in 2011 because of the lag between the year in which AMT liabilities increase (2010) and the year in which taxpayers are likely to pay those taxes (2011).

CBO's baseline also projects an increase in individual income tax revenues after 2010 as the child credit reverts from $1,000 to $500, the amount in effect before EGTRRA was enacted. The expiration of that provision contributes to increases in revenues of about 0.1 percent of GDP. The Making Work Pay tax credit (up to $400 for single taxpayers and $800 for married couples), which was enacted in the American Recovery and Reinvestment Act of 2009 (Public Law 111-5), also expires after 2010, increasing projected revenues by about 0.3 percent of GDP.

The Worker, Homeownership, and Business Assistance Act of 2009 temporarily expanded the ability of businesses to use recent losses to obtain refunds of taxes paid in the past. That provision reduces CBO's baseline projection of corporate income tax revenues by about 0.2 percent of GDP in 2010 but produces a small increase in revenues in 2011 and 2012, when fewer losses are available to be carried forward, yielding an increase in revenues of about 0.3 percent of GDP from 2010 to 2012.

Contributions to the Increase in BaselineRevenues from 2010 to2012
(Percentage of gross domestic product)

Expiring Provision	Legislation	Revenue Increase
Income Tax Rates[a]	EGTRRA, JGTRRA	1.3
Making Work Pay Credit	ARRA	0.3
Expanded Carrybacks	WHBAA	0.3
Child Tax Credit	EGTRRA	0.1
Estate and Gift Tax	EGTRRA	0.1
Other Individual	Various	0.3
Other Corporate and Excise	Various	0.3
Total		**2.7**
Memorandum:		
Individual Income Tax Provisions		2.0

Source: Congressional Budget Office.

Notes: Estimates do not include effects on outlays for refundable credits.

EGTRRA = Economic Growth and Tax Relief Reconciliation Act of 2001; JGTRRA = Jobs and Growth Tax Relief Reconciliation Act of 2003; ARRA = American Recovery and Reinvestment Act of 2009; WHBAA = Worker, Homeownership, and Business Assistance Act of 2009.

[a] Includes the alternative minimum tax.

As a result of legislation enacted in 2001, estate tax rates have steadily declined and the effective exemption amount has increased, culminating in the repeal of the estate tax and a reduction in gift tax rates in 2010. However, those changes are themselves slated to expire at the end of the year, when estate and gift tax provisions revert to the rates and exemption amounts scheduled for 2011 before the 2001 legislation was enacted. As a result, CBO projects, estate and gift tax revenue will increase by more than 0.1 percent of GDP between 2010 and 2012 and by almost 0.2 percent of GDP over the 10-year projection period.

Numerous other provisions of law set to expire in 2010 or 2011 result in baseline projections of increased revenues for the next decade; the expiration of those provisions adds revenues equal to 0.6 percent of GDP from 2010 to 2012. Among the expiring provisions are the tax credit for first-time home-buyers, the partial expensing of investment in equipment, the deferral of business income arising from debt reacquisition, income and excise tax credits forethanol-blended motor fuels, preferential rules for recognizing active financing income from international sources, the tax credit for research and experimentation, the exclusion from taxation of a portion of unemployment benefits, subsidies for unemployed workers who pay premiums to continue their health insurance, and the additional standard deduction for property taxes. Some of those provisions, such as the research and experimentation credit, have existed for many years and have been extended routinely. Others, such as the health insurance subsidies, have only recently been enacted.

[1] An exception is made for expiring excise taxes dedicated to trust funds, which CBO assumes are extended at current rates.

[2] The estimates do not include budgetary effects that would result from the influence of those provisions on the broader economy. The estimates also do not include the effects on outlays for refundable tax credits.

Finally, CBO's projection assumes that the gradual tapering off of the unexplained weakness in recent receipts, relative to available economic data, will increase revenues relative to the size of the economy by 0.2 percentage points between 2012 and 2016 (in addition to the increase of 0.2 percentage points between 2010 and 2012).

Social Insurance Taxes

After temporarily dipping slightly in 2010 and 2011, social insurance taxes are projected to remain steady at 6.3 percent of GDP in 2012 and thereafter, the same as the percentage recorded in 2009 (see Table 4-4). Relative to wages and salaries, the appropriate tax base for those payroll taxes, social insurance taxes are projected to decline to 13.7 percent in 2010 but then to rebound to 14.1 percent in 2011 before declining gradually to 13.8 percent by 2020.

Sources of Social Insurance Revenues. The largest sources of social insurance tax revenues are payroll taxes for the Social Security program (specifically, the Old-Age, Survivors, and Disability Insurance, or OASDI) and Medicare's Hospital Insurance program (also called Part A). A small share of such revenues comes from unemployment insurance payroll taxes and from contributions to federal retirement programs (see Table 4-5). The premiums for Medicare Part B (the Supplementary Medical Insurance program) and Part D

Table 4-4. CBO's Projections of Social Insurance Tax Receipts and the Social Insurance Tax Base

	Actual 2009	2010	2011	2012	2013	2014	2015	2016	2017	2018	2019	2020	Total, 2011-2015[a]	Total, 2011-2020[a]
Social Insurance Tax Receipts														
In billions of dollars	891	878	934	993	1,056	1,115	1,165	1,212	1,260	1,310	1,361	1,416	5,263	11,822
As a percentage of GDP	6.3	6.0	6.2	6.3	6.3	6.3	6.3	6.3	6.3	6.3	6.3	6.3	6.3	6.3
Annual growth rate	-1.0	-1.4	6.4	6.3	6.3	5.6	4.5	4.0	4.0	4.0	3.9	4.1	5.8	4.9
Wages and Salaries														
In billions of dollars	6,374	6,432	6,638	7,027	7,504	7,961	8,349	8,726	9,099	9,459	9,841	10,254	37,479	84,859
As a percentage of GDP	44.8	44.1	44.3	44.7	45.0	45.2	45.3	45.4	45.4	45.4	45.4	45.5	44.9	45.2
Annual growth rate	-2.5	0.9	3.2	5.9	6.8	6.1	4.9	4.5	4.3	4.0	4.0	4.2	5.4	4.8
Social Insurance Tax														
Receipts as a Percentage of Wages and Salaries	14.0	13.7	14.1	14.1	14.1	14.0	14.0	13.9	13.8	13.8	13.8	13.8	14.0	13.9

Source: Congressional Budget Office.

Notes: The tax base in this table (wages and salaries) reflects income as measured by the national income and product accounts rather than as reported on tax returns.

GDP = gross domestic product.

[a] Measures expressed in billions of dollars are the cumulative amounts over the period. Measures expressed as a percentage of GDP or wages and salaries are averages over the period. Measures expressed as annual growth rates are the average rates compounded annually over the period, including growth in 2011.

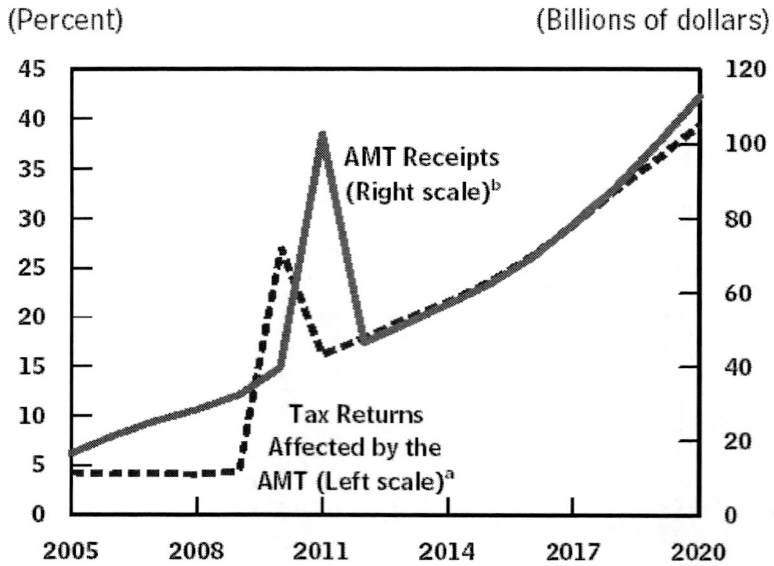

Source: Congressional Budget Office.

Note: The alternative minimum tax (AMT) requires some taxpayers to calculate the tax they owe using a more limited set of exemptions, deductions, and credits than is applicable under the regular individual income tax. See Congressional Budget Office *The Alternative Minimum Tax,* Issue Brief (January 15, 2010).

[a] Based on the calendar year.

[b] Based on the fiscal year.

Figure 4-4. Effects of the Individual Alternative Minimum Tax in CBO's Baseline.

(the prescription drug program) are considered offsets to spending because participation in those programs is voluntary; therefore, those funds are considered offsetting receipts on the spending side of the budget and do not appear on the revenue side of the budget.

Sources of Social Insurance Revenues. The largest sources of social insurance tax revenues are payroll taxes for the Social Security program (specifically, the Old-Age, Survivors, and Disability Insurance, or OASDI) and Medicare's Hospital Insurance program (also called Part A). A small share of such revenues comes from unemployment insurance payroll taxes and from contributions to federal retirement programs (see Table 4-5). The premiums for Medicare Part B (the Supplementary Medical Insurance program) and Part D (the prescription drug program) are considered offsets to spending because participation in those programs is voluntary; therefore, those funds are considered offsetting receipts on the spending side of the budget and do not appear on the revenue side of the budget.

Social Security and Medicare payroll taxes are calculated as a percentage of earnings—15.3 percent for the two taxes combined. The Medicare tax (1.45 percent of earnings paid by the employer and by the employee) applies to all earnings, whereas the Social Security tax (6.2 percent of earnings paid by the employer and by the employee) applies only up to a taxable maximum that is indexed to the growth of average earnings over time. Receipts from OASDI taxes will remain fairly stable relative to the size of the economy, as long as earnings remain a stable percentage of GDP and the distribution of earnings remains relatively unchanged.

Table 4-5. CBO's Projections of Social Insurance Tax Receipts, by Source

(Billions of dollars)													
	Actual 2009	2010	2011	2012	2013	2014	2015	2016	2017	2018	2019	2020	Total, 2011-2015	Total, 2011-2020
Social Security	654	642	673	711	754	797	836	871	908	945	982	1,024	3,771	8,501
Medicare	191	183	193	205	219	232	244	255	266	277	288	300	1,093	2,479
Unemployment Insurance	38	46	61	70	75	78	78	78	78	80	83	84	361	763
Railroad Retirement	4	4	4	4	5	5	5	5	5	5	5	6	23	49
Other Retirement	4	4	3	__3	3	3	3	3	3	3	3	3	15	29
Total	**891**	**878**	**934**	**993**	**1,056**	**1,115**	**1,165**	**1,212**	**1,260**	**1,310**	**1,361**	**1,416**	**5,263**	**11,822**

Source: Congressional Budget Office.

Payments for social insurance and individual income taxes are combined when employers make payments throughout the year. Employers are later required to report to the Treasury Department the breakdown for the two sources. The distribution of receipts for the individual income and payroll taxes is estimated initially by the Treasury Department and corrected later. CBO's baseline projection anticipates an adjustment to the allocation of receipts in 2010 to correct an overstatement of social insurance receipts in prior years, which will cause a dip in social insurance receipts as a percentage of wages and salaries and as a percentage of GDP in 2010. That adjustment by the Treasury Department is expected to reallocate about $18 billion of social insurance receipts in 2010 to individual income taxes; the adjustment has no effect on total revenues.

Projected Receipts. Social insurance receipts are projected in CBO's baseline to decline slightly as a percentage of GDP, from 6.3 percent in 2009 to 6.0 percent in 2010. About half of that change is the result of the allocation adjustment just discussed. The other half is attributable to a decrease in wages and salaries as a percentage of GDP. Social insurance receipts also will decline as a percentage of earnings between 2009 and 2010, almost entirely because of the allocation adjustment.

Social insurance tax receipts are projected to increase to 6.2 percent of GDP in 2011 and to 6.3 percent from 2012 to 2020. The stable revenue share reflects the offsetting effects of increases in wages and salaries relative to GDP and decreases in social insurance receipts as a share of wages and salaries throughout that period. Receipts fall as a share of wages in part because the share of earnings above the OASDI taxable maximum will continue to drift higher and thus the share of earnings subject to the OASDI tax will fall over time.[52] CBO also projects slower growth in unemployment insurance receipts because states will only gradually replenish unemployment insurance trust funds that have been depleted by the recession.

Corporate Income Taxes

Receipts from corporate income taxes account for about one-sixth of the projected increase in total revenues relative to GDP over the next 10 years. Between 2009 and 2014, corporate tax receipts are projected to rise from 1.0 percent of GDP to 2.2 percent of GDP, spurred by a rebound in profits during the expected economic recovery and by an end to legislative and other factors that have reduced corporate receipts during the past few years. During the remainder of the 10-year projection period, declines in profits relative to the size of the economy are expected to reduce corporate receipts to 1.8 percent of GDP by 2020.

Projected Receipts from 2010 Through 2012. Corporate tax receipts in CBO's projections generally follow the pattern projected for taxable corporate profits. CBO makes several adjustments to profits from current production (economic profits) as measured in the NIPAs to estimate taxable corporate profits, which more closely approximate the tax base. Those adjustments include the following: substituting CBO's estimates of past and future tax depreciation for the depreciation used in measuring economic profits that more closely matches the loss in value of capital in the production process; subtracting profits of S corporations, which generally are smaller businesses that satisfy certain criteria and elect to have their profits taxed immediately to the owners under the individual income tax, rather than first at the corporate level and again at the individual level when disbursed as dividends;

subtracting profits earned by U.S. corporations abroad and adding earnings by foreign corporations on their U.S. operations; and adding realizations of capital gains.

CBO projects that corporate income tax receipts will rise in dollar terms in 2010, increasing by 6.1 percent to $147 billion (see Table 4-6) but remaining near 1.0 percent of GDP. CBO expects that profits will increase sharply in 2010, stemming from the effects of economic recovery and the expiration at the end of 2009 of provisions that allowed businesses to partially expense (immediately deduct from taxable income) 50 percent of investments in equipment. (Those provisions were enacted for 2008 in ESA and renewed through 2009 in ARRA.) However, corporate income tax receipts will rise much more slowly in 2010 than will profits, in part because the Worker, Homeownership, and Business Assistance Act of 2009 (WHBAA) expanded the "carryback" period for net operating losses.[53] Based on estimates by the staff of the Joint Committee on Taxation at the time of enactment, CBO projects that the expanded carryback window will reduce 2010 receipts by about $33 billion. Provisions in ARRA that relate to the deferral of income from the cancellation of indebtedness also are projected to reduce corporate tax receipts in 2010 relative to 2009.[54] In addition, because corporate income tax payments through December 2009 have remained below those observed in 2008, despite taxable profits that CBO estimates rose above the prior years' amounts by the end of 2009, growth of corporate receipts is expected to remain sluggish in 2010.

Corporate receipts are projected to jump to 2.0 percent of GDP by 2012 as a result of the expiration of the carry-back provisions, the waning effects of the cancellation-of-indebtedness provision, and an increase in profits relative to GDP through 2011. In addition, CBO projects that the recent weakness in collections that is not explained by available data on corporate profits and other measures used in forecasting receipts will gradually wane between 2010 and 2014.

Projected Receipts Beyond 2012. Corporate income tax receipts will remain near 2.1 percent of GDP in most years between 2012 and 2017 in CBO's baseline projection. Receipts are projected to increase more than usual in 2014, to 2.2 percent of GDP, and to decline in 2015 to 2.0 percent of GDP, partly because of a provision in WHBAA that shifts about $18 billion in corporate tax payments into 2014 that otherwise would have been made in 2015. Without the timing shifts, receipts would be 2.1 percent of GDP between 2013 and 2015.

Corporate tax receipts are projected to decline to 2.0 percent of GDP between 2016 and 2017 and then to slip further, to 1.8 percent of GDP by 2020, in line with the share recorded in the early 1990s. That pattern largely reflects a slight decline in corporate taxable profits relative to GDP as interest payments of corporations rise because of higher interest rates.

Excise Taxes

Receipts from federal excise taxes are projected to continue their long-term decline as a share of GDP, edging down from 0.5 percent in 2010 to 0.4 percent during the latter part of the 10-year projection period. Most excise taxes—those that generate more than 80 percent of total federal excise tax revenues—are levied either on each unit of good or on the transaction rather than as a percentage of value. Thus, excise tax receipts grow with increases in real output, but they do not grow as quickly as nominal GDP because they do not rise as prices increase.

Table 4-6. CBO's Projections of Corporate Income Tax Receipts and Tax Bases

	Actual 2009	2010	2011	2012	2013	2014	2015	2016	2017	2018	2019	2020	Total, 2011-2015[a]	Total, 2011-2020[a]
Corporate Income Tax														
Receipts														
In billions of dollars	138	147	266	318	350	394	365	387	393	401	403	416	1,693	3,693
As a percentage of GDP	1.0	1.0	1.8	2.0	2.1	2.2	2.0	2.0	2.0	1.9	1.9	1.8	2.0	2.0
Annual growth rate	-54.6	6.1	81.6	19.4	10.0	12.6	-7.2	6.0	1.5	1.9	0.7	3.1	20.0	11.0
Corporate Economic Profits														
In billions of dollars	1,222	1,545	1,640	1,730	1,838	1,901	1,911	1,921	1,960	2,000	2,063	2,136	9,021	19,101
As a percentage of GDP	8.6	10.6	10.9	11.0	11.0	10.8	10.4	10.0	9.8	9.6	9.5	9.5	10.8	10.2
Annual growth rate	-16.0	26.4	6.2	5.5	6.2	3.5	0.5	0.5	2.0	2.1	3.1	3.5	4.3	3.3
Taxable Corporate Profits[b]														
In billions of dollars	692	1,153	1,222	1,258	1,326	1,372	1,375	1,380	1,406	1,430	1,471	1,523	6,554	13,766
As a percentage of GDP	4.9	7.9	8.2	8.0	8.0	7.8	7.5	7.2	7.0	6.9	6.8	6.8	7.9	7.3
Annual growth rate	-28.3	66.6	6.0	2.9	5.4	3.5	0.2	0.4	1.9	1.7	2.9	3.5	3.6	2.8
Corporate Receipts as a Percentage of Taxable Profits	20.0	12.7	21.8	25.3	26.4	28.7	26.6	28.1	28.0	28.0	27.4	27.3	25.8	26.8

Source: Congressional Budget Office.

Notes: The tax bases in this table (corporate economic profits and taxable corporate profits) reflect income as measured in the national income and product accounts rather than as reported on tax returns.

GDP = gross domestic product.

a. Measures expressed in billions of dollars are the cumulative amounts over the period. Measures expressed as a percentage of GDP or taxable profits are averages over the period. Measures expressed as annual growth rates are the average rates compounded annually over the period, including growth in 2011.

b. Taxable corporate profits are defined as economic profits plus economic depreciation minus book depreciation; minus profits earned by the Federal Reserve System, transnational corporations, and S corporations; and minus deductible payments of state and local corporate taxes. They include capital gains realized by corporations and profits from inventory revaluation.

Table 4-7. CBO's Projections of Excise Tax Receipts, by Category

(Billions of dollars)	Actual 2009	2010	2011	2012	2013	2014	2015	2016	2017	2018	2019	2020	Total, 2011-2015	Total, 2011-2020
Highway Taxes	30.4	30.1	34.3	36.6	37.9	38.9	39.6	39.9	40.2	40.4	40.7	41.1	187.3	389.6
Tobacco Taxes	13.3	17.9	17.6	17.4	17.2	16.9	16.7	16.5	16.2	16.0	15.7	15.4	85.9	165.7
Airport Taxes	10.5	10.3	10.6	11.3	12.1	12.9	13.6	14.3	15.0	15.7	16.5	17.3	60.6	139.5
Alcohol Taxes	9.1	9.3	9.5	9.7	9.8	10.0	10.2	10.3	10.5	10.7	10.9	11.0	49.1	102.6
Other Excise Taxes	-0.9	2.8	4.6	4.6	4.6	4.6	4.6	4.5	4.6	4.6	4.3	4.4	22.8	45.2
Total	**62.5**	**70.4**	**76.6**	**79.5**	**81.6**	**83.4**	**84.7**	**85.6**	**86.5**	**87.3**	**88.0**	**89.2**	**405.8**	**842.5**

Source: Congressional Budget Office.

Table 4-8. CBO's Projections of Other Sources of Revenue

(Billions of dollars)	Actual 2009	2010	2011	2012	2013	2014	2015	2016	2017	2018	2019	2020	Total, 2011-2015	Total, 2011-2020
Estate and Gift Taxes	23	16	15	38	43	48	53	56	59	63	66	70	197	511
Federal Reserve System														
Earnings	34	77	74	52	41	42	48	47	48	50	53	55	257	511
Customs Duties	22	24	28	32	35	37	38	39	41	43	47	51	170	392
Fees and Fines														
Universal Service Fund[a]	8	8	8	8	9	9	9	9	9	9	9	9	43	88
Other	9	9	8	8	8	9	9	9	9	8	8	8	42	84
Subtotal	17	17	16	17	17	17	17	17	17	17	17	17	85	171
Total	**98**	**134**	**134**	**139**	**136**	**144**	**156**	**160**	**166**	**173**	**183**	**193**	**709**	**1,585**

Source: Congressional Budget Office.

[a] Fees on certain telecommunications services finance the Universal Service Fund.

Most excise taxes fall into one of four major categories: those associated with highway use, tobacco purchases, airport and airway use, or alcohol purchases (see Table 4-7). Almost half of all excise receipts come from taxes dedicated to the Highway Trust Fund—primarily taxes on gasoline and diesel fuel, including blends of those fuels with ethanol. Receipts from highway taxes are expected to decrease by 1 percent in 2010, which would mark the fifth consecutive year of declining revenues from that source. CBO projects that aggregate consumption of motor fuel—gasoline, ethanol, and diesel—will hold nearly steady in 2010, but that highway tax receipts will be depressed by an increase in the consumption of ethanol-blended fuels, which are taxed at a lower effective tax rate than gasoline. Highway tax receipts are then projected to increase at an average annual rate of more than 10 percent in 2011 and 2012 before settling into an average growth rate of about 1.5 percent for the remainder of the projection period. Only a small portion of the large increase in 2011 and 2012 can be attributed to increased fuel usage, as aggregate fuel consumption is projected to rise by an average of 1 percent in those years. Instead, the jump in receipts is driven mostly by changes in the taxation of ethanol-blended fuels. The expiration of lower effective tax rates on those fuels during fiscal year 2011 is projected to generate about $5 billion in additional revenue per year.

The economic downturn caused a significant decline in air travel in 2009, leading to a drop of more than 10 percent in aviation tax receipts. CBO expects that those receipts will decline again in 2010, by a little more than 2 percent, a rate consistent with air traffic data through the early part of the year. CBO projects that aviation revenues will increase in subsequent years, at an average annual growth rate of more than 5 percent from 2011 to 2020. That growth rate exceeds the growth rate for real GDP in the same period because the main components of aviation excise taxes are levied as a percentage of dollar value, so receipts increase with inflation. Most of those taxes are scheduled to expire on March 31, 2010, but as specified in the Balanced Budget and Emergency Deficit Control Act of 1985, CBO assumes in its baseline that expiring excise taxes dedicated to trust funds will be extended.[55]

Tobacco tax receipts are projected to increase by just under $5 billion (or 34 percent) in 2010, the first full year after the Children's Health Insurance Program Reauthorization Act of 2009 increased tax rates on tobacco products. Those tax increases, which became effective in April 2009, included a 62 cent per pack increase in the excise tax on cigarettes. Tobacco tax revenues are projected to fall by a little more than 1 percent per year in 2011 and beyond, which is consistent with the long-term historical decline in tobacco consumption.

CBO projects that receipts from alcohol taxes will rise by about 2 percent per year through 2020. That growth is roughly in line with the rate of growth of real GDP over that period.

CBO's baseline projections also reflect changes in other excise taxes. In March 2009, an IRS ruling stated that a chemical known as black liquor was an eligible fuel under the alternative-fuel mixture credit, and producers could receive a refundable excise tax credit worth 50 cents per gallon of fuel produced. Black liquor is a by-product of the paper-milling process, and the ruling allowed firms that produce the chemical to claim the credit. The IRS paid more than $4 billion in such claims for the credit in 2009, and CBO estimates that another $1billion to $2billion in refunds was made after the endof the fiscal year and before the credit expired on December 31, 2009. Along with the increase in tobacco tax revenues, the expiration of the alternative-fuel mixture credit explains much of the growth of nearly 13 percent projected for excise tax receipts in 2010.

Estate and Gift Taxes

Receipts from estate and gift taxes under current law will fall from 0.2 percent of GDP in 2009 to 0.1 percent of GDP in 2010 and 2011 and then increase to 0.2 percent in 2012 and 0.3 percent of GDP thereafter, according to CBO's baseline projections. That projection reflects major changes in those taxes under current law: The estate and generation-skipping transfer taxes were eliminated for 2010 but will be reinstated (at rates higher and exemption amounts lower than those of recent years) in 2011, when EGTRRA's provisions related to estate and gift taxes expire. The gift tax remains in place in 2010, with a tax rate of 35 percent on gifts that exceed the $1million lifetime exemption. Under current law, starting in 2011, the estate, generation-skipping transfer, and gift taxes will have a top marginal tax rate of 55 percent and an effective exemption amount of $1 million.[56]

CBO's projections of estate and gift tax receipts take into account the incentives provided by the repeal and then the reinstatement of the estate and generation-skipping transfer taxes. EGTRRA gave taxpayers an incentive to make taxable gifts in 2010, when the gift tax rate is 35 percent, instead of making them in earlier or later years, when the tax rates are higher. Because gift tax liabilities are typically paid in April of the year after the gift is made, CBO projects that gift tax receipts will be much higher than usual in 2011, reflecting the large number of taxable gifts made in 2010. CBO projects that estate tax receipts in 2011 will be about $1.2 billion and will result primarily from late tax payments from the estates of those who died in 2009, because the estate tax will not be in effect in 2010 under current law.[57] After 2011, estate and gift tax receipts will return to roughly the same share of GDP as that seen in the early 1970s, according to CBO's baseline projection.

Receipts from the Federal Reserve System

The earnings of the Federal Reserve System are counted as revenues when they are remitted to the Treasury. The amount of those remittances reflects the income generated by the various activities of the Federal Reserve less the cost of generating that income. Federal Reserve income has a variety of sources: interest on Treasury and other securities the Federal Reserve holds, interest on loans to banks, fees on services rendered to banks, and gains (or losses) on holdings of foreign-denominated assets. The Federal Reserve pays interest—currently at a rate close to the federal funds rate—on reserves held at the Federal Reserve by depository institutions. Because it pays no interest on currency (Federal Reserve notes) in circulation, which normally is the Federal Reserve's largest liability, income typically well exceeds costs. (The Federal Reserve's actions also clearly influence revenues from all sources by affecting the economy overall.)

In the face of the most severe financial crisis since the Great Depression, the Federal Reserve has taken extraordinary measures to stabilize financial markets. Starting in 2007, it began to provide additional liquidity to depository institutions by extending existing mechanisms; one example is the provision of longer-term loans through the "discount window."[58] The size of the Federal Reserve's asset portfolio did not increase immediately because it simultaneously reduced its holdings of Treasury securities. By September 2008, however, deteriorating conditions in credit markets led the Federal Reserve to provide additional liquidity to financial markets through several new programs without offsetting the impact on its balance sheet by significantly reducing its holdings of Treasury securities. As a result, the Federal Reserve's portfolio grew rapidly, more than doubling to about $2.3 trillion by the end of December 2008, and it remained above $2trillion throughout most of 2009. Despite the expanded portfolio, remittances from the Federal Reserve to the Treasury did not increase immediately—largely because the initial methods of providing liquidity did not earn returns substantially above the rate paid by the Federal Reserve to obtain the funds. Therefore, remittances in 2009, which totaled $34 billion, remained at about 0.2percent of GDP, the same as in the seven years prior.

CBO's baseline projection shows remittances more than doubling in 2010 and 2011—to more than $70 billion annually or 0.5 percent of GDP (see Table 4-8). That increase is attributable to the Federal Reserve's purchase of longer-term and riskier securities—in support of the housing market and the broader economy—that have a significantly higher expected return than the rate on the reserves used to finance them. Beginning in January 2009, the Federal Reserve significantly ramped up its purchases of agency debt: It purchased securities from Fannie Mae, Freddie Mac, and the Federal Home Loan Banks and mortgage-backed securities guaranteed by Fannie Mae, Freddie Mac, and Ginnie Mae. Its holdings of such securities reached roughly $900 billion by the end of 2009. The Federal Reserve also purchased additional long-term Treasury securities; those holdings rose by about 80 percent in 2009 to reach about $350 billion by the end of December, and they yield higher returns than shorter-term Treasury securities.

On the basis of announcements by the Federal Reserve, CBO anticipates that the size of the Federal Reserve's portfolio will peak in 2010 and gradually decline thereafter. As a result, remittances to the Treasury will fall to 0.3 percent of GDP in 2012 and will remain at about 0.2percent through the rest of the 10-year projection period, according to CBO's baseline projections.

Other Sources of Receipts

Customs duties and other miscellaneous receipts yielded only about 2 percent of total revenues, or about 0.3 percent of GDP, in 2009. CBO projects that receipts from those sources will remain fairly steady as a share of GDP throughout the 10-year projection period.

Effects of Expiring Tax Provisions

CBO's baseline revenue projections are based on the assumption that current tax laws will remain unaltered and thus that the provisions currently scheduled to expire will do so. The one exception involves the expiration of excise taxes dedicated to trust funds; under the rules that CBO follows in its baseline projections, those taxes are assumed to continue regardless of whether they are scheduled to expire.

CBO's baseline projections reflect the expiration under current law of roughly 150 tax provisions, almost all of which would reduce revenues if they were extended. CBO and the staff of the Joint Committee on Taxation estimate that if all of the tax provisions that are assumed to expire in the baseline were extended, projected deficits would be higher than in the baseline by about $56 billion in 2010, by $341 billion in 2011, by $492 billion in 2012, and by increasing amounts throughout the 10-year projection period, reaching $675 billion in 2020.[59] For the entire period from 2011 to 2020, deficits would increase by about $5.6 trillion.[60] Those estimates do not include the effects on debt service or on the economy of extending the provisions. Most of the budgetary effects would be on federal revenues, but extending the provisions also would affect outlays for refundable taxcredits.[61]

From a budgetary perspective, the most significant expiring provisions are those originally enacted in EGTRRA and JGTRRA and amended by several other laws. Several provisions that combine to produce significant budgetary effects are set to expire at the end of the current calendar year: They involve reduced tax rates on dividends, capitalgains, and ordinary income; a higher child credit; the elimination of the estate tax; and an expanded standard deduction and an increase in the size of the 15 percent tax bracket for married couples. If the expiring provisions originally enacted in EGTRRA and JGTRRA were extended, CBO and the staff of the Joint Committee on Taxation estimate that budget deficits would increase by about $2.6 trillion from 2011 through 2020 (excluding the effects on debt service). That amount includes about $2.3 trillion in lower revenues and more than $200 billion in higher outlays.[62]

Another expiring provision with a significant budgetary effect is the current AMT patch. The estimated effects described above include about $530 billion for extending the exemption at the 2009 levels and another $530 billion for an interaction between extending those exemption amounts and the provisions of EGTRRA and JGTRRA that affect individual income taxes (with both figures excluding the effect on debt service). The interaction results because the number of taxpayers subject to the AMT is higher if the EGTRRA tax provisions are extended. Because the exemption amounts for the AMT would not increase with inflation, the number of taxpayers subject to the AMT would increase over time—albeit by many fewer than if the temporarily higher AMT exemption amounts were allowed to expire.[63]

The remaining provisions consist of a broad range of tax legislation that, if extended, would reduce baseline revenue projections by a total of almost $2 trillion over the period from 2011 to 2020 (excluding the effect on debt service). The largest effects stem from extending the Making Work Pay tax credit ($571 billion), the partial expensing of investment property ($301 billion), and the first-time homebuyer credit ($178 billion).

APPENDIX A. THE AMERICAN RECOVERY AND REINVESTMENT ACT OF 2009

In February 2009, lawmakers enacted the American Recovery and Reinvestment Act (ARRA) in response to significant weakness in the economy.[64] The legislation contained numerous spending and revenue provisions that can be grouped in several categories:

- Providing funds to states and localities—for example, by raising federal matching rates under Medicaid, providing aid for higher education, and increasing financial support for some transportation projects;
- Supporting people in need—such as by extending and expanding unemployment benefits and increasing benefits under the Supplemental Nutrition Assistance Program (formerly the Food Stamp program);
- Purchasing goods and services—for instance, by funding construction or investment activities that could take several years to complete; and

- Providing temporary tax relief for individuals and businesses—such as by raising exemption amounts for the alternative minimum tax, adding a new Making Work Pay tax credit, and creating enhanced deductions for depreciation of business equipment.

When ARRA was being considered, the Congressional Budget Office (CBO) and the staff of the Joint Committee on Taxation (JCT) estimated that it would increase budget deficits by a total of $787 billion between fiscal years 2009 and 2019.[65] Of that amount, about $575 billion was projected to stem from increased outlays and $212 billion from reduced revenues. (A $24 billion provision to subsidize health insurance costs for unemployed people that CBO originally classified as outlays for the 2009–2019 period was later categorized by the Administration as a reduction in revenues.) About half of ARRA's total budgetary impact through 2019, a deficit increase of about $399 billion, was estimated to occur in 2010.

Table A-1. Estimated Direct Effects of the American Recovery and Reinvestment Act of 2009

(Billions of dollars)	Actual 2009	2010	2011–2019	Total, 2009–2019
Outlays[a]				
Department of Health and Human Services programs				
Medicaid	32	42	19	93
Other	1	12	27	41
Refundable tax credits	2	33	36	71
Unemployment compensation	27	31	2	60
Supplemental Nutrition Assistance Program	5	11	39	54
Department of Education programs				
State Fiscal Stabilization Fund	12	31	10	54
Other (Including Pell grants)	9	19	17	44
Department of Transportation programs	4	15	28	47
Department of Energy programs	1	5	36	42
Build America Bonds	0	2	28	30
Social Security	13	*	1	14
Other	7	23	46	76
Total Outlays	112	224	289	626
Revenues	-88 [b]	-180	31	-236
Total Direct Effect on the Deficit[a]	**-200**	**-404**	**-258**	**-862**

Sources: Congressional Budget Office and the Department of the Treasury.

Note: * = between zero and $500 million.

a. The numbers shown here for outlays include only spending directly resulting from ARRA; the effect on spending from regular appropriations or other authorizations (which may have been supplanted in any given year by funding from ARRA) is not included in this table. CBO estimates that the effect on the deficit in 2009 and 2010 is less than the amounts shown here because additional spending from ARRA was partly offset by reduced spending from regular appropriations. (The opposite could be true from 2011 to 2019.)

b. CBO's estimate of the extent to which ARRA reduced revenues in 2009.

Through last September (the end of fiscal year 2009), ARRA's effects on spending and revenues appear to have been close to what CBO and JCT had anticipated. The law's budgetary impact for 2010 is also expected to be near the original estimate. Looking ahead, it appears that ARRA will have larger effects in later years than originally estimated. All told, CBO now anticipates that the law will increase deficits by $862 billion between 2009 and 2019 (see Table A-1).

Budgetary Impact of ARRA in 2009

In its original cost estimate for ARRA, CBO projected that federal agencies would spend an additional $120 billion, on net, in the remaining months of 2009, including spending from the new ARRA authority and related reductions in spending from some regular appropriations. That outlay figure included nearly $14 billion in payments for the health insurance premiums of unemployed workers, which were ultimately recorded as a reduction to federal revenues (because the payments were conveyed by reducing the amount of withholding taxes that businesses remit and requiring them to pass the savings on to their employees by charging lower premiums). With those payments excluded, CBO's estimate of about $106 billion in outlays from ARRA in 2009 proved to be quite accurate: Preliminary data from the Treasury showed spending of $112 billion. In a few cases, agencies that received ARRA funding for certain programs spent less from their regular funding for those programs than they would have otherwise (perhaps between $5 billion and $10 billion less), so the net change in outlays attributable to ARRA was probably a bit smaller than CBO initially estimated.

Five programs accounted for more than 80 percent of the outlays from ARRA in 2009: Medicaid, unemployment compensation, Social Security, the State Fiscal Stabilization Fund (which makes grants to state and local governments, mostly to maintain funding levels for education), and student financial aid. Higher federal matching rates for Medicaid accounted for $32 billion; additional payments for unemployment benefits cost $27 billion; Social Security beneficiaries received payments of $13 billion; spending through the State Fiscal Stabilization Fund added $12 billion; and direct assistance to college students (mostly for Pell grants) added $7 billion.

Although total spending from ARRA in 2009 was roughly in line with CBO's estimate, the cost of some individual components varied from the amounts initially anticipated. Most significantly, outlays for additional unemployment compensation were about $10 billion higher than CBO originally estimated, because the unemployment rate was higher than anticipated and people continued to collect benefits for a longer period of time.[66] In addition, ARRA spending by the Department of Education for Pell grants was about $6 billion greater than CBO's original estimate—but those higher-than-expected outlays were partly offset by lower-than-expected spending from funds provided through the annual appropriation process. In the opposite direction, spending for Medicaid was about $2 billion lower in 2009 than CBO had expected, and outlays for other programs of the Department of Health and Human Services (HHS), such as health research, were several billion dollars lower. Infrastructure-related spending from ARRA also fell short of CBO's initial estimates. For example, such spending by the Departments of Transportation, Energy, and Commerce totaled just over $5 billion in 2009, compared with CBO's original estimate of about $8 billion.

ARRA also included provisions that reduced taxes, which JCT estimated would lower revenues by about $65 billion in 2009 (or by $79 billion adjusted for the reclassification of payments for health insurance premiums). The provision in ARRA that had the greatest impact on revenues last year was the Making Work Pay tax credit, which offset the tax payments of people below certain income thresholds by as much as $400 per single filer or $800 per couple filing jointly. CBO estimates that the credit reduced revenues by $29 billion in 2009—about $9 billion more than anticipated—because it was implemented more quickly than expected. As a result, the revenue loss from the credit in 2010 is now expected to be smaller.

In addition, corporate taxes were reduced by provisions in ARRA that affect how businesses calculate depreciation. JCT estimated that such provisions would lower revenues by $24 billion in 2009. It is not possible, however, to determine how close the actual effects of those and other revenue provisions in ARRA were to initial estimates. A major reason is that estimates of the effects of revenue provisions in pending legislation often assume that taxpayers will adjust their behavior in some way in response to the provisions; such adjustments cannot be easily tracked. Consequently, although some information may become available in coming years that gives a general indication of the accuracy of past revenue estimates, it is usually not possible to fully assess the accuracy of such estimates—except in some instances when they involve new taxes, credits, or deductions.

Estimated Budgetary Impact of ARRA in 2010

CBO currently estimates that ARRA's direct effect on the deficit (excluding some offsetting effects on other spending) will peak in 2010 at $404 billion. Outlays stemming from ARRA are expected to total $224 billion this year, and the law's tax provisions are anticipated to reduce revenues by about $180 billion.

Nearly half of the outlays resulting from ARRA in 2010 will be for programs administered by HHS or the Department of Education. Most of the HHS outlays ($42 billion) will come from the enhanced matching rates for Medicaid. Various other HHS programs are expected to spend $12 billion. The majority of the Department of Education's ARRA spending in 2010 ($31 billion) is projected to go for the State Fiscal Stabilization Fund, with another $19 billion expected to be spent on Pell grants and other education programs.

Other large sums resulting from ARRA this year will be disbursed by the Department of the Treasury for refundable tax credits[67] and by the Department of Labor for unemployment compensation.[68] In addition, highway programs and the Supplemental Nutrition Assistance Program (SNAP) are each expected to spend more than $10 billion this year as a result of ARRA.

The law's largest effect on revenues in 2010 will come from the provision offering temporary relief from the individual alternative minimum tax. That provision reduced tax liabilities in calendar year 2009, and JCT estimates that it will reduce revenues in fiscal year 2010 by about $80 billion. Other provisions that are expected to decrease revenues this year include various tax credits for individuals and families (including the Making Work Pay credit) and tax incentives for businesses.

Estimated Budgetary Impact of ARRA between 2011 and 2019

Spending from ARRA will begin to slow later this year, CBO estimates, but will remain significant for the next few years. In CBO's baseline projections, outlays resulting from ARRA total $135 billion in 2011, $56 billion in 2012, and $100 billion over the 2013–2019 period.

ARRA's net effect on revenues after 2011 will generally be to increase tax receipts, CBO and JCT project. Provisions affecting individual income tax payments will expire over time, and some tax savings incurred by businesses last year and this year will lead to additional tax payments in the future.

Changes from CBO's Initial Cost Estimate for ARRA

CBO's current projection of ARRA's budgetary impact over the 2009–2019 period—a total increase in deficits of $862 billion—is about $75 billion greater than the agency originally estimated. Most of that difference is on the outlay side of the budget (adjusted for the reclassifica tion of the health insurance subsidy). Revenue estimates, in total, have not changed.

Almost two-thirds of the increase in CBO's 2009–2019 projection involves income security programs. Outlays for unemployment compensation in 2009 and 2010 are now estimated to be $21 billion higher than initially expected. In addition, CBO has raised its estimate of the effect of ARRA on SNAP benefits by a total of $34 billion to reflect the lower projections of inflation in its current economic outlook. Normally, SNAP benefits are adjusted annually according to increases in the cost of a market basket of food served at home. Provisions in ARRA, however, set the maximum benefit for a family of four at $668 a month, 13.6 percent higher than the maximum benefit at the time the law was enacted. Under ARRA, the maximum benefit will remain at that higher amount until inflation causes the unadjusted benefit to exceed the ARRA-mandated one. CBO now estimates that the maximum SNAP benefit will stay at the amount stipulated by ARRA until 2019—whereas when the law was enacted, CBO's inflation projections were higher, and CBO expected that the ARRA-stipulated benefit would be in effect only through 2013.

Most of the rest of the increase in projected outlays involves the Build America Bond program, which pays state and local governments for 35 percent of their interest costs on taxable government bonds issued in 2009 and 2010 to finance capital spending. Participation in the program has already risen to a level significantly higher than CBO's and JCT's original estimates—over $60 billion in new bonds have been issued since the program began in April. That higher-than-expected issuance prompted CBO to add $26 billion to its projection of outlays for the program between 2010 and 2019.

Some current projections of spending from ARRA are lower than CBO's original estimates. For example, CBO now believes that outlays stemming from the enhanced matching rates for Medicaid, which expire at the end of 2010, will be a total of $3 billion lower than the agency estimated last year.

In terms of revenues, the only provisions in ARRA for which CBO has updated its estimates are the Making Work Pay credit and the subsidies for health insurance costs of unemployed workers. Because the tax credit was put in place sooner than anticipated, CBO reduced its estimate of revenue losses from the credit in 2010 by about $9 billion. (That change offset an increase of the same size in the credit's estimated revenue effect in 2009.) Other than the reclassification of the $24 billion in health insurance subsidies, CBO does not have enough information on which to base updated estimates of ARRA's remaining revenue provisions at this time.

Appendix B. Changes in CBO's Baseline since August 2009

The Congressional Budget Office (CBO) projects that—absent further legislation affecting spending and revenues—the deficit for fiscal year 2010 will be $1.35 trillion, $32 billion lower than the deficit CBO projected last August, when it completed its previous baseline projections (see Table B-1).[69] CBO's baseline updates have also decreased projected deficits over the 2010–2019 period, by $427 billion. In August, CBO projected a cumulative deficit of $7.1 trillion from 2010 through 2019; the agency's current projection shows a 10-year total of $6.7 trillion for that period. Those revisions reflect changes to CBO's economic forecast, the effects of legislation enacted since August, and technical changes (those not directly related to changes in law or in CBO's economic outlook) in response to new information about the operations of certain programs.

CBO constructs its baseline in accordance with the provisions of the Balanced Budget and Emergency Deficit Control Act of 1985 and the Congressional Budget and Impoundment Control Act of 1974. Although the provisions of the Deficit Control Act pertaining to the baseline expired at the end of September 2006, the agency generally continues to follow that law's specifications in preparing its baseline. When estimating revenues and mandatory spending, CBO assumes that current laws will remain in place throughout the 10-year projection period, with only a few exceptions.[70] To project discretionary spending, CBO adjusts current-year appropriations to reflect the effects of inflation and certain other factors, as specified in the Deficit Control Act. The resulting baseline projections are not intended to predict future budgetary outcomes; rather, they serve as a benchmark that lawmakers can use to measure the effects of spending or revenue proposals.

Relative to its previous estimates for 2010, CBO has reduced projected revenues by $89 billion (or 4 percent) and projected outlays by $121 billion (or 3 percent). A large drop in the estimated cost of the Troubled Asset Relief Program (TARP)—$147 billion—dominates the reduction in outlays projected for 2010. Other changes in estimates of outlays for the fiscal year are modest. CBO's new estimate of revenues for 2010 reflects reductions resulting from recent legislation and technical factors, including the fact that tax receipts since August have been weaker than expected, offset in part by increases stemming from a somewhat more favorable outlook for corporate profits.

The decrease of $427 billion in projected deficits over the 2010–2019 period stems mostly from changes to CBO's economic forecast. Those changes, particularly a reduction in projected interest rates and an increase in inflation for certain years, lower the cumulative deficit by $626 billion. Changes from enacted legislation further lower the 10-year deficit total, by $16 billion. Technical changes to spending projections also reduce projected deficits (by $113 billion over 10 years), but technical changes to revenues increase projected deficits by a larger amount ($327 billion over 10 years).

Changes to Projections of Outlays

The $121 billion decrease in estimated outlays for 2010 is the net effect of a drop in outlays of $152 billion because of economic and technical changes (mostly the latter), partially offset by a $31 billion increase in outlays resulting from legislative changes. The technical changes stem largely from a reduction in the projected cost of the TARP.

For the 2011–2019 period, projected outlays are down by $35 billion (or 0.1 percent). Decreases in projected outlays for net interest ($465 billion) and other reductions in projected outlays are mostly offset by increases in a variety of programs.

Legislative Changes

Legislation enacted since CBO prepared its August baseline has had little effect on the agency's updated projections. New legislation has resulted in additional projected outlays totaling $31 billion in 2010 that are nearly evenly split between mandatory and discretionary programs. However, over the entire 10-year baseline period, legislative changes produce only a modest decrease in projected outlays ($15 billion).

Mandatory Spending. Recently enacted legislation will add $14 billion to mandatory outlays for unemployment compensation this year, CBO estimates. The Worker, Homeownership, and Business Assistance Act of 2009 (WHBAA, Public Law 111-92) lengthened the duration of the temporary program for emergency unemployment compensation (EUC) by 20 weeks, adding two tiers of benefits. People who exhaust regular benefits now can receive as many as 53 weeks of additional benefits under EUC. Amendments to the Department of Defense Appropriations Act (P.L. 111-118) extended the program for two months, through February 2010. Without that extension, individuals who had exhausted their regular benefits after January 1, 2010, would not have been able to receive EUC.

Discretionary Defense Spending. Legislation enacted since August has caused CBO to lower projected outlays for defense by $87 billion over the 2010–2019 period. That reduction is the net result of two partially offsetting changes. First, the Congress has provided the Department of Defense (DoD) with $130 billion for military operations in Iraq and Afghanistan thus far for 2010—$16 billion less than was appropriated for that purpose in 2009 (although additional funding may be provided later this year for operations in Afghanistan). The extrapolation of that lower amount decreases projected outlays by $168 billion from 2010 through 2019. The Congress also increased funding for defense programs not directly related to operations in Iraq and Afghanistan. For 2009, the Congress provided $535 billion for such purposes (an amount that when adjusted for inflation would equal $546 billion in 2010). For 2010, the Congress has provided $554 billion in defense funding not directly related to operations in Iraq and Afghanistan. Extrapolating that change through 2019 increases projected outlays by $81 billion over the 10-year period.

Table B-1. Changes in CBO's Baseline Projections of the Deficit since August 2009

(Billions of dollars)												
	2010	**2011**	**2012**	**2013**	**2014**	**2015**	**2016**	**2017**	**2018**	**2019**	**Total, 2010-2014**	**Total, 2010-2019**
Total Deficit as Projected in August 2009	-1,381	-921	-590	-538	-558	-558	-620	-626	-622	-722	-3,988	-7,137
Changes to Revenue Projections												
Legislative	-44	4	7	8	26	-14	5	5	3	1	1	*
Economic	51	46	25	30	62	76	79	81	75	74	214	598
Technical	-96	-97	-79	-41	-25	-15	-7	3	12	17	-338	-327
Total Changes to Revenues	**-89**	**-47**	**-46**	**-3**	**63**	**48**	**77**	**88**	**90**	**92**	**-123**	**271**
Changes to Outlay Projections												
Legislative changes												
Mandatory outlays												
Unemployment compensation	14	0	0	0	0	0	0	0	0	0	14	14
Other	4	1	*	1	-1	*	*	*	-1	*	5	5
Subtotal, mandatory	18	1	*	1	-1	*	*	*	-1	*	19	19
Discretionary outlays												
Defense	*	-3	-8	-10	-10	-11	-11	-11	-11	-11	-32	-87
Nondefense	13	11	8	5	3	1	*	*	1	1	40	44
Subtotal, discretionary	13	8	*	-5	-7	-9	-11	-11	-10	-10	8	-43
Net interest outlays (Debt service)	*	1	2	2	1	1	1	*	*	-1	6	8
Subtotal, legislative changes	**31**	**10**	**2**	**-2**	**-7**	**-8**	**-9**	**-10**	**-11**	**-10**	**34**	**-15**
Economic changes												
Mandatory outlays												
Medicare	4	13	10	9	18	16	16	18	20	28	54	153
Medicaid	*	2	2	2	2	4	5	7	8	10	8	41
Social Security	*	*	5	7	6	3	2	2	2	2	17	28

	2010	2011	2012	2013	2014	2015	2016	2017	2018	2019	Total, 2010-2014	Total, 2010-2019
Unemployment compensation	-1	3	5	5	4	4	2	2	2	2	15	28
Student loans	-4	-5	-5	-4	-4	-3	-2	-1	-1	-1	-22	-29
Other	2	2	5	6	5	4	5	4	4	5	20	43
Subtotal, mandatory	1	14	21	25	31	29	28	32	36	47	92	264
Discretionary outlays	*	4	7	10	13	15	17	18	19	20	35	124
Net interest outlays												
Debt service	*	-1	-2	-4	-7	-11	-16	-20	-25	-29	-15	-116
Rate effect and inflation	-6	-17	-21	-36	-49	-44	-38	-32	-28	-27	-130	-299
Subtotal, net interest	-7	-19	-24	-40	-56	-55	-54	-52	-52	-56	-145	-415
Subtotal, economic changes	**-5**	**-1**	**5**	**-5**	**-12**	**-11**	**-9**	**-2**	**2**	**10**	**-18**	**-28**
Technical changes												
Mandatory outlays												
TARP	-147	-11	-6	*	3	*	*	*	*	*	-160	-160
Veterans' benefits and services	2	7	7	9	10	10	11	9	8	8	36	82
SNAP	4	6	5	6	8	9	10	10	9	9	30	77
Medicaid	-4	-2	-4	-3	-3	-6	-7	-7	-9	-10	-17	-55
Social Security	3	4	4	4	4	5	5	6	6	6	20	47
Build America Bonds	2	3	3	3	3	3	3	3	3	3	13	26
Student loans	-4	-3	-3	-2	-2	-2	-1	-1	-1	-1	-14	-21
Fannie Mae and Freddie Mac	-5	-8	-5	-6	1	2	2	1	*	*	-23	-17
Unemployment compensation	11	2	*	*	*	*	*	*	*	*	12	13
Deposit insurance	-18	7	1	-8	-2	1	2	4	5	2	-20	-6
Other	14	-1	5	8	9	2	-4	-2	1	-1	36	32

Table B-1. (Continued)

	2010	2011	2012	2013	2014	2015	2016	2017	2018	2019	Total, 2010-2014	Total, 2010-2019
Subtotal, mandatory	-143	3	7	13	31	24	21	22	23	15	-88	17
Discretionary outlays	-20	-11	-6	-6	-7	-7	-6	-6	-7	-7	-50	-83
Net interest outlays												
Debt service	*	1	4	9	14	16	19	22	29	35	28	148
Other	16	10	2	-12	-39	-45	-38	-38	-27	-24	-23	-196
Subtotal, net interest	16	10	6	-3	-25	-28	-19	-17	2	10	4	-47
Subtotal, technical changes	**-147**	**3**	**7**	**4**	**-2**	**-11**	**-4**	*	**18**	**18**	**-134**	**-113**
Total Changes to Outlays	**-121**	**12**	**13**	**-3**	**-20**	**-30**	**-22**	**-13**	**9**	**18**	**-119**	**-156**
Total Impact on the Deficit[a]	**32**	**-59**	**-60**	*	**83**	**78**	**99**	**100**	**80**	**74**	**-4**	**427**
Total Deficit as Projected in Janaury 2010	-1,349	-980	-650	-539	-475	-480	-521	-525	-542	-649	-3,992	-6,709
Memorandum:[a]												
Total Legislative Changes	-75	-6	5	10	33	-5	14	15	14	11	-33	16
Total Economic Changes	56	47	21	35	74	87	88	83	73	63	233	626
Total Technical Changes	51	-100	-86	-45	-23	-3	-3	3	-6	-1	-204	-214

Source: Congressional Budget Office.

Note: * = between -$500 million and $500 million; TARP = Troubled Asset Relief Program; SNAP = Supplemental Nutrition Assistance Program.

[a] Negative numbers represent an increase in the deficit; positive numbers represent a decrease in the deficit.

Discretionary Nondefense Spending. CBO now projects an increase in outlays for discretionary nondefense programs totaling $13 billion for 2010 and $44 billion from 2010 to 2019. Those totals are the result of several offsetting changes. In CBO's previous baseline, projections for discretionary programs were based on the funding provided in 2009; for the new estimates, CBO used the appropriations provided for 2010 to create updated projections for future years. On net, updating the projections to account for the more recent appropriations resulted in higher outlays over the 10-year period than CBO projected in its previous baseline. Programs with the most significant increases include veterans' health (up by $77 billion over 10 years); the periodic census (up by $43 billion); and income security programs (up by $36 billion). A number of other programs account for smaller increases in projected outlays totaling $74 billion over the 10-year period. The following agencies and programs received funding for 2010 that resulted in lower projected outlays over the 2010–2019 period: the Department of Health and Human Services (down by $57 billion over 10 years); U.S. participation in the International Monetary Fund (down by $60billion); a Department of Energy auto loan program for the development of advanced technology vehicles (down by $49 billion); and other programs with smaller reductions totaling $20 billion through 2019.

Net Interest. Because of legislative changes, CBO's projections of the cumulative deficit in 2010 and 2011 increased by $79 billion (excluding interest) and decreased by $103 billion over the 2012–2019 period. Although net legislative changes reduced CBO's projections of the cumulative deficit for the 10-year period by $24 billion, those changes added to overall debt-service costs (by $8 billion) because the years in which deficits were projected to increase as a result of enacted legislation occur early in the period.

Economic Changes

In updating its economic forecast, CBO modified its projections of certain economic variables that affect outlays, including inflation, the unemployment rate, and interest rates. Such revisions caused the agency to decrease its estimate of outlays by $5 billion for 2010 and by $28 billion over the 2010–2019 period. Projected interest costs declined substantially, offset by increases in estimated outlays for Medicare, Medicaid, Social Security, and unemployment compensation.

Medicare. Payment rates for most Medicare services are adjusted each year on the basis of actual rates of inflation for a recent period or to account for projected rates of inflation. Because inflation is expected to be higher in the near term than CBO forecast in August, payment rates for most Medicare services are now projected to be higher over the 2011–2019 period. (Payment rates for 2010 have already been set and also turned out to be a little higher than CBO expected in August.) By 2019, payment rates will be almost 4 percent higher than previously anticipated, according to CBO's updated estimates. As a result, CBO has increased projected spending for Medicare over the 10-year period by $153 billion, or 2.5 percent.

Medicaid. As with the Medicare program, a higher projected rate of inflation leads to higher projected payment rates to providers serving Medicaid patients. Those increased payment rates boost estimated Medicaid spending by $41 billion over the 2010–2019 period relative to the August baseline.

Social Security. As a result of economic changes, projected spending for Social Security has increased by $28 billion over the 2010–2019 period. As CBO had expected, Social Security beneficiaries did not receive a cost-of-living adjustment (COLA) in January 2010. However, CBO now anticipates that there will be a 0.1 percent COLA in January 2011, rather than no COLA (as CBO previously projected). The updated projections for COLAs over the 10-year period are expected to increase benefit payments beginning in 2011 and to raise outlays for Social Security over the 2011–2019 period by $50 billion. However, revisions to CBO's projections of the growth of wages and salaries reduce estimated benefit payments between 2010 and 2019, offsetting the increase by about $22 billion.

Unemployment Compensation. In contrast with its August economic forecast, CBO now estimates that the rate of unemployment will remain high for a longer period of time, staying near 10 percent through 2011 and then dropping to 8.4 percent in 2012 (for the 2010–2019 period, CBO's January estimates are 0.3 percentage points higher per year, on average). As a result, CBO has raised its estimate of outlays for unemployment compensation by $28 billion over the 2010–2019 period.

Student Loans. In CBO's updated economic forecast, projections of lower interest rates reduce expected outlays in the federal student loan program by $29 billion between 2010 and 2019. As required by the Federal Credit Reform Act of 1990, CBO estimates most of the costs of the federal student loan programs on a net-present-value basis. In particular, the present value of all loan-related cash flows is calculated by discounting those expected cash flows to the year of disbursement, using the rates for comparable maturities on U.S. Treasury borrowing. When Treasury rates decline, the estimated present value of future cash flows associated with student loans increases (that is, such cash flows are discounted less) and payments to lenders decrease. Thus, relative to the August baseline, the projected costs of the federal student loan programs have declined.

Discretionary Spending. CBO projects spending for discretionary programs using the gross domestic product (GDP) price index and the employment cost index (ECI) for wages and salaries. For all years of the forecast after 2010, CBO has increased its estimate of the GDP price index relative to its previous forecast. The estimate of the ECI for 2011 is also higher, though the updates for that index for 2012 and 2013 are slightly negative. Those changes generate higher projections of discretionary outlays for 2011 through 2019, totaling $124 billion over that 10-year period.

Net Interest. Economic revisions to CBO's projections of spending on net interest have two components: the effects of changes in the agency's economic outlook related to interest rates and inflation and the effects of changes in borrowing resulting from the impact of economic changes on other outlays and on revenues. The former effect was more than double the latter effect in CBO's updated projections, resulting in a decrease of $415 billion in net outlays for interest over the 2010–2019 period.

Specifically, CBO's current economic forecast projects lower interest rates for all Treasury securities than did the August forecast. Such changes mainly occur from 2011 to 2016, when the decrease in projected rates for 3-month Treasury bills ranges from 6 basis points to 79 basis points (a basis point is one one-hundredth of a percentage point). During that same period, the decrease in projected rates on 10-year notes ranges from 15 basis points to 55 basis points. The reduction in rates brings down projected outlays for net interest over the 2010–2019 period by nearly $300 billion. In addition, changes in the economic outlook have decreased the government's projected borrowing needs (primarily through higher estimates of revenues) by an amount that lowers outlays for net interest between 2010 and 2019 by $116 billion.

Technical Changes

For 2010, technical revisions to CBO's estimates account for a net decrease in outlays of $147 billion. By far the largest change for this year results from an adjustment to the projected cost of activities funded through the TARP; CBO has lowered its estimate of outlays for that program by $147 billion in 2010. Changes in other areas of the budget for 2010 roughly offset one another. For the remainder of the period, technical changes result in projected increases in outlays of $33 billion.

TARP. CBO has reduced projected outlays for the TARP by a total of $160 billion over the 2010–2019 period. Those changes mostly reflect an updated evaluation of the riskiness of the activities undertaken by the program. In the past few months, many institutions—including several large banks such as JP Morgan Chase, Bank of America, and Wells Fargo—have repurchased the preferred stock that they sold to the government, thereby reducing the net budget impact of the program. In addition, market conditions have continued to improve, it appears that the Treasury will not use the full authority it was provided originally, and CBO now estimates that the TARP will disburse $27 billion less for assistance to homeowners than was previously projected. Altogether, the estimated cost of the program has dropped sharply, with CBO now estimating total net costs of $99 billion for the TARP over its lifetime, compared with the $241 billion estimated last August. Since $151 billion in outlays was already recorded for last year (excluding administrative costs), CBO's baseline shows *negative* net TARP outlays for the 2010–2019 period of $53 billion. That sum consists of negative outlays of $67 billion in 2010 and cumulative positive outlays of $14 billion in future years.[71]

Veterans' Benefits and Services. New claims for veterans' disability benefits have increased substantially in recent years (up from about 800,000 in 2005 to more than 1 million in 2009). To keep up with such growth, the Department of Veterans Affairs has made significant additions to its staff to process the additional claims in a timely fashion. The combination of additional benefit payments and increases in staff pushed up spending for veterans' disability compensation from $40 billion in 2008 to $44 billion in 2009. CBO expects that the number of claims and the need to process them promptly will remain high; it has therefore increased projected outlays for veterans' benefits and services by $2 billion for 2010 and by $82 billion over the 2010–2019 period.

Supplemental Nutrition Assistance Program (SNAP). Projected outlays for SNAP between 2010 and 2019 have grown by $77 billion since August because CBO has raised its estimate of participation in the program. In fiscal year 2009, participation in SNAP increased significantly and more than 6 million people were added to the program. CBO had anticipated growth in participation for 2009, but the actual rate of increase exceeded the agency's expectations. During past recessions, participation in SNAP continued to grow for almost two years after the rate of unemployment began to decline; therefore, CBO now expects participation to continue to grow in fiscal years 2010 and 2011. However, although there has not been a large change in CBO's forecast of employment since August, the increase in program participation in response to poor economic and labor market conditions has been much greater than CBO previously expected.

Medicaid. Because of technical changes, CBO now projects that spending for Medicaid will be $55 billion lower over the 2010–2019 period than was projected in August. Because actual Medicaid spending was lower than anticipated in 2009, CBO reduced its projection of Medicaid spending for the 2010–2019 period by about $68 billion. In addition, lower projected increases in payment rates to physicians and lower projected spending by the Children's Health Insurance Program (CHIP) reduced CBO's estimates for Medicaid spending by a total of about $10 billion.[72] Those reductions are partially offset by several factors: greater spending for Medicare premiums on behalf of Medicaid enrollees who are also enrolled in Medicare; higher growth in the number of low-income people who are uninsured (some of whom will ultimately be covered by Medicaid); and a number of other small adjustments.

Social Security. CBO has made modest revisions to projections of spending for Social Security because of updated information about the Old-Age and Survivors Insurance program and the Disability Insurance program. The agency now estimates that the number of people receiving benefits under the Old-Age and Survivors Insurance program will increase relative to the August baseline, as will the average monthly benefit payment. In addition, CBO expects that retroactive benefits provided in the Disability Insurance program will be higher. Such changes increase projected outlays for 2010 and 2011. However, lower projections of average awards for new beneficiaries of the Disability Insurance program, coupled with smaller anticipated increases in certain caseloads, reduce estimated outlays from 2012 through 2019. On net, those changes boost Social Security outlays each year through 2019, for a total increase over the projection period of $47 billion (0.5 percent).

Build America Bonds. In February 2009, the American Recovery and Reinvestment Act of 2009 created the Build America Bonds program, which provides a subsidy payment to state and local governments for 35 percent of their interest costs on taxable government bonds issued in 2009 and 2010 to finance capital expenditures. Participation in the program has already risen to a level significantly beyond estimates supplied by the Joint Committee on Taxation—over $60 billion in new bonds have been issued since the program began in April. Adjusting for the higher-than-expected demand leads to an estimated $2billion in additional outlays for 2010 and an estimated $26 billion in additional outlays over the 2010–2019 period.

Student Loans. CBO lowered its estimate of outlays for the federal student loan programs by $21 billion over the 2010–2019 period for several technical reasons. First, under a temporary program begun late in 2008 and in effect through July 2010, private lenders can sell to the government federally guaranteed loans they have issued; those loans then become direct loans, which have lower costs than guaranteed loans. Sales of those loans have been much higher than CBO had anticipated in August. Second, many schools have switched from the guaranteed loan program to the direct loan program. And third, loan volume increased significantly, which lowers costs in the early years because the subsidy calculations under credit reform indicate budgetary savings from new direct and guaranteed loans in those years.[73] Those changes all result in lower estimated program costs for new student loans.

Fannie Mae and Freddie Mac. CBO has decreased its estimate of the cost to the government of the activities of Fannie Mae and Freddie Mac by $5 billion for 2010 and by $17 billion for the 2010–2019 period. CBO now projects that the cumulative cost of the government's backing for those two housing enterprises over the 10-year period will be $81 billion, as compared with the $99 billion the agency estimated this past August.[74] Such subsidies represent the expected cost, on the basis of fair-value accounting, of new mortgages guaranteed by Fannie Mae and Freddie Mac as well as their other activities. CBO uses the jumbo-conforming spread (the difference between interest rates on mortgages above and below the conforming loan limit, or $417,000 for a single-family home in 2009 in much of the United States) as a proxy for estimating the discount rate for cash flows related to mortgage guarantees; that spread has continued to decrease over the past several months, leading to a drop in the subsidy rates applied to mortgage guarantees relative to CBO's previous baseline.

Unemployment Compensation. For the 2010–2019 period, CBO has increased its estimate for unemployment compensation by about $13 billion, for technical reasons. Most of that change is expected to occur in 2010 and results from the expectation that many people will remain on the unemployment rolls for a longer period of time. Higher projections for the average duration of unemployment (based on data from 2009) lead not only to estimates of higher outlays for regular benefits, but also to the expectation that more claims for emergency benefits (which are available to individuals who exhaust regular benefits) will be filed.

Deposit Insurance. CBO has lowered its estimates of net outlays for deposit insurance by $18 billion in 2010, primarily because of action taken by the Federal Deposit Insurance Corporation (FDIC) that accelerated the collection of insurance premiums paid by banks. In December 2009, institutions insured by the FDIC paid $46 billion to the government that otherwise would have been due over the 2010–2012 period, increasing receipts in fiscal year 2010 by about $30 billion relative to the projections in CBO's August baseline. However, CBO anticipates that outlays in 2010 for failed institutions will also be higher, offsetting roughly half of that increase in premiums. On balance, CBO has lowered its estimate of net outlays over the 2010–2019 period by about $6 billion, reflecting amounts that will be collected in the future to cover the higher-than-projected losses in fiscal year 2009.

Discretionary Spending. Upward and downward adjustments in several areas of the budget have resulted in a net decrease of $20 billion in estimated discretionary outlays for 2010 and a net decrease of $83 billion for the 2010–2019 period. In particular, CBO has lowered its estimate of defense outlays by $6 billion for 2010 and by $15 billion from 2010 through 2019 to reflect slower-than-anticipated spending, primarily for operations and maintenance and military construction. The most significant revisions in the 10-year baseline for nondefense programs include lower expected outlays for the Pell Grant program ($40 billion), as a result of a change in CBO's methodology for estimating outlays from future appropriations, and lower expected outlays for highways ($13 billion), reflecting updates to the program's projected rate of spending as well as the current financial conditions in individual states.

Net Interest. As result of technical updates, CBO's estimate of net interest outlays is $16 billion higher for 2010 but $47 billion lower for the 2010–2019 period.

The change for 2010 is mostly attributable to a reduced estimate of interest received from the nonbudgetary credit financing accounts that record cash flows for the TARP. (Those nonbudgetary accounts borrow from the Treasury to finance TARP investments and pay interest to the Treasury on that borrowing.) As a result of lower-than-anticipated borrowing to finance the program and accelerated repurchases of preferred stock, the financing accounts have maintained lower balances and, therefore, will pay less interest this year.

Over the 10-year period, CBO has reduced projected interest costs by $196 billion as a result of changes to the projected mix of Treasury borrowing and increased receipts from nonbudgetary credit-financing accounts apart from the TARP. CBO has altered its projected mix of Treasury borrowing by shifting borrowing in later years away from 10-year notes to shorter-term notes (2- 3-, 5-, and 7-year notes), thus lowering projected interest costs during the baseline period. In addition, two programs—the direct student loan program and an incentive program for the manufacturing of advanced technology vehicles—are now projected to issue more loans than anticipated in CBO's previous baseline. Direct loan programs require up-front funds from the Treasury to issue the loans, and the nonbudgetary credit-financing accounts then pay interest on those borrowed funds. Accordingly, higher volumes of direct loans lead to higher interest payments to the Treasury.

Changes to Projections of Revenues

Relative to its August 2009 baseline, CBO has lowered its projections of revenues by $89 billion in 2010 but increased them by $271 billion (or 0.8 percent) over the 2010–2019 period. CBO estimates that revenues will be lower than projected in the August baseline through 2013; the revenue changes turn positive in 2014, in general, grow annually from 2015 through 2019. Those increases stem largely from revisions to CBO's economic forecast, which add about $600 billion to projected revenues over the 10-year period. Weaker tax receipts since August and other technical factors have resulted in lower projected receipts in the first few years of the projection period, and recently enacted legislation has resulted in lower projected revenues for 2010 but higher amounts in ensuing years.

Economic Changes

Because of the revisions CBO has made to its economic outlook since August, the agency has raised projected revenues by $51 billion in 2010 and by an average of about $60 billion per year over the 2011–2019 period. The most significant effects stem from the following: increases in the profit share of GDP through 2013, which bring about higher projections for corporate profits and corporate income tax receipts; and higher nominal GDP after 2012, which boosts personal incomes and corporate profits and thus revenues from the major sources of tax revenue (individual and corporate income taxes and payroll taxes).[75] Increases in the GDP price index, rather than in real GDP, cause nominal GDP to rise steadily after 2012 relative to CBO's August projection.

CBO's expectation of stronger growth in corporate profits at the beginning of the projection period, relative to the August baseline, is the main driver of the higher revenue projections. As a result, CBO has raised its projections for corporate income tax receipts for 2010 through 2013 by an average of about $40 billion annually.

Beyond 2013, in CBO's estimation, overall taxable income is projected to be higher because of the higher nominal GDP. The profit share of GDP is expected to gradually return to the share projected in August, and the wage and salary share is projected to be lower. The profit share begins to fall back to the previously projected level, largely because business interest payments, some of which accrue to individuals in taxable form, are expected to be higher. The lower wage and salary share of GDP offsets only a portion of the higher nominal GDP, yielding higher wages and salaries than projected in August; the higher amount of GDP boosts profits slightly above the August projection, and the projection of interest earnings of individuals is also higher. As a result of the changes to the economic projections, revenues from all the major tax sources are expected to be higher.

Technical Changes

As a result of technical factors, CBO lowered it projections for receipts between 2010 and 2016 by a total of $360 billion and raised them by $32 billion for the 2017 through 2019 period. Receipts are projected to be $96 billion lower in 2010 and $97 billion lower in 2011 because of those technical changes. The downward revisions mainly reflect lower-than-anticipated receipts for corporate and individual income taxes since August, offset partially by higher anticipated remittances by the Federal Reserve as a result of changes to its portfolio of assets.

Corporate and individual income tax collections since August have been weaker than CBO anticipated, despite expectations for higher growth in corporate profits as measured in the national income and product accounts. That development is most responsible for the weaker outlook for revenues at the beginning of the projection period. Corporate profits in the second half of calendar year 2009 grew more rapidly than CBO previously projected, but corporate receipts fell short of expected amounts. As a result, the agency has lowered its estimate of corporate receipts in fiscal year 2010, which accounts for about half of the total reduction attributable to technical factors.

Recent collections of individual income tax receipts have also been weaker than CBO expected in the summer, resulting in a lower estimate of receipts for 2010. In addition, the agency has reduced its projection of receipts derived from individuals' making final payments to satisfy their income tax liability for tax year 2009, which will be collected when taxpayers file returns in 2010. CBO based that adjustment on its analysis of the effects on tax payments of last year's large increase in unemployment and of the gap between GDP and potential GDP.

CBO does not expect the disparity between recent income tax collections and taxable incomes as reported in the national income accounts to be permanent. As a result, the agency has phased out the initial downward changes to income tax receipts, with that phase-out beginning in 2011 and finishing in 2016.

Technical factors account for CBO's raising its projection of Federal Reserve earnings; the increase in those earnings, which are counted as revenues when they are remitted to the

Treasury, offsets a portion of the downward adjustments to income taxes that were made for technical reasons. To reflect changes in the Federal Reserve's portfolio, CBO has raised projected receipts from the Federal Reserve by almost $20 billion in both 2010 and 2011. In particular, the Federal Reserve has increased its purchases of mortgage-backed securities by amounts that exceed those expected last summer; those assets should yield a return for the Federal Reserve that is well above the interest it pays on the corresponding amount of reserves. The Federal Reserve also markedly shifted away from purchases of Treasury bills to purchases of higher-yielding, longer-term Treasury securities, which caused an additional upward revision to projected Federal Reserve receipts. Those two changes to the Federal Reserve's expected portfolio contribute to higher, albeit diminishing, receipts beyond 2011. Relative to its forecast in August, CBO now expects the Federal Reserve's earnings to be higher by about $48 billion from 2012 to 2019 because of technical changes. Over the longer term, CBO continues to expect the Federal Reserve's portfolio of assets to gradually return to the size and composition that existed before the financial crisis.

CBO made one additional change for technical reasons—to unemployment insurance receipts—that shifts projected receipts from 2010 through 2016 to later years. CBO revised its assumptions about the speed at which states will replenish their depleted unemployment trust funds, assuming that more states will delay measures to increase revenues collected by their unemployment tax systems because of the continuing weak economy. Those changes reduce CBO's projections of unemployment insurance receipts through 2016 and increase them thereafter.

Legislative Changes

CBO has lowered its baseline revenue projections by $44 billion in 2010 and raised them by $44 billion over the 2011–2019 period to incorporate the effects of legislation enacted since August. Five tax provisions account for most of the changes.

Most significantly, the Worker, Homeownership, and Business Assistance Act of 2009 increased the ability of corporations to use current losses to obtain refunds of previously paid taxes, lowering revenues from corporate income taxes by an estimated $33 billion in 2010. Because corporations using those losses to offset previous tax liability today will not have the losses available to offset future taxes, the provision causes an increase in projected revenues of $23 billion over the 2011–2019 period.

That legislation also expanded and extended the first-time homebuyer credit for several months into calendar year 2010. CBO expects those changes, which included expanding the credit to apply to certain existing homeowners, will lower individual income taxes by a total of $8 billion in 2010 and 2011 and raise them by $2 billion over the 2012–2019 period, when some recapture of the credit occurs for recipients who sell their homes within three years of purchase. WHBAA also delayed, until 2018, the implementation of certain tax rules that were scheduled to take effect in 2011. Those rules allow corporations with worldwide operations to reduce their U.S. income taxes by allocating more of their interest expenses to U.S. profits. CBO raised its projections of corporate income taxes by about $20 billion over the 2011–2020 period to reflect that change in law. In addition, WHBAA changed the timing for payment of corporate income taxes. The legislation results in an expected shift of $18 billion in payments from 2015 into 2014, with no effect on revenues over the full projection period.

The appropriation act for the Department of Defense extended and expanded the tax credit for continuation of health insurance coverage for workers who become unemployed. It expanded the amount of time that individuals can draw the subsidies and also extended the date by which the newly unemployed may qualify. As a result, CBO lowered its projected revenues from individual income taxes by $6 billion over the 2010–2011 period.

APPENDIX C. HOW CHANGES IN ECONOMIC PROJECTIONS CAN AFFECT BUDGET PROJECTIONS

The federal budget is highly sensitive to economic conditions. Revenues depend on the amount of taxable income, including wages and salaries, other (nonwage) income, and corporate profits. Those types of income generally rise or fall with overall economic activity. Spending for many mandatory programs is pegged to inflation, either directly (as with Social Security) or indirectly (as with Medicaid). In addition, the Treasury regu larly refinances portions of the government's outstanding debt—and issues more debt to finance any new deficit spending—at market interest rates. Thus, the amount that the federal government spends for interest on its debt is directly tied to those rates.

To show how projections for the economy can affect projections of the federal budget, the Congressional Budget Office (CBO) has constructed simplified "rules of thumb." The rules provide rough orders of magnitude for gauging how changes in individual economic variables, taken in isolation, would affect the budget totals. The rules of thumb are not intended to substitute for a full analysis of the implications of alternative economic forecasts.

The rules of thumb are applied to four areas of analysis:

- Real (inflation-adjusted) growth of the nation's gross domestic product (GDP),
- Interest rates,
- Inflation, and
- Wages and salaries as a share of GDP.

CBO's rule of thumb for real growth shows the effects of rates that are 0.1 percentage point lower each year, beginning in January 2010, than the growth rates that underlie the agency's baseline budget projections. (Projections for the budget are summarized in Chapter 1; economic projections are described in Chapter 2.) The rules of thumb for interest rates and the rate of inflation assume that those rates are 1 percentage point higher every year, also starting in January 2010, than the rates in the baseline. The final rule assumes that, beginning in January 2010, wages and salaries as a percentage of GDP are 1 percentage point more each year than in the baseline. Correspondingly, corporate profits are assumed to be 1percentage point smaller each year relative to GDP. (The scenario incorporates no changes in projected nominal or real GDP.)

Each rule of thumb is roughly symmetrical. Thus, if economic growth was higher or interest rates, inflation, or wages and salaries as a percentage of GDP were lower than CBO projects, the effects would be about the same as those shown here, but with the opposite sign.

CBO chose the variations of 0.1 percentage point or 1 percentage point solely for the sake of simplicity. Those changes do not necessarily indicate the extent to which actual economic performance might differ from CBO's assumptions. For example, although the rule of thumb for real GDP shows the effects of a 0.1 percentage point change in the average rate of growth over the next 10years, the standard deviation of growth rates of real GDP over 10-year periods is roughly six times larger, or about 0.6 percentage points.[76] However, the 1 percentage point change used in the rules of thumb for the other variables ends up much closer to historical deviations for those variables. The standard deviation for the 10-year average of real interest rates is about 1.5 percentage points for 10-year Treasury notes. Standard deviations for inflation and for wages and salaries as a percentage of GDP are about 1.9 and 2.1 percent, respectively.

Lower Real Growth

Stronger economic growth improves the budget's bottom line; weaker growth worsens it. The first rule of thumb illustrates the effect of slightly weaker-than-expected economic growth on federal revenues and outlays.[77]

CBO's baseline shows real GDP increasing by 2.2 percent in calendar year 2010, by 1.9 percent in 2011, by an average of 4.4 percent from 2012 to 2014 and by 2.4 percent from 2015 to 2020. Subtracting 0.1 percentage point from each of those rates implies that, by 2020, GDP would be roughly 1 percent smaller than in CBO's baseline.

Slower growth of GDP (other things being equal) would have several effects on the budget. For example, it would imply less growth in taxable income and thus lower tax revenues—$1 billion less in 2010 and $50 billion less in 2020 (see Table C-1). With a smaller amount of revenues, the federal government would need to borrow more and incur higher interest costs. Payments to service federal debt would be slightly larger during the first few years of the 10-year projection period and substantially larger in later years, with the increase reaching $13 billion by 2020. Mandatory spending, however, would be only minimally affected by slower economic growth: Medicare outlays would be slightly lower, but that decrease would be partially offset by higher outlays for the refundable portions of the earned income and child tax credits.[78]

All in all, if growth in real GDP each year was 0.1 percentage point lower than is assumed in CBO's baseline, annual deficits would be larger by amounts that would climb to $62 billion in 2020. The cumulative deficit for 2011 to 2020 would rise by $288 billion.

Higher Interest Rates

The second rule of thumb illustrates the sensitivity of the budget to changes in interest rates, which affect the flow of interest payments to and from the federal government. When the budget is in deficit, the Treasury must borrow additional funds from the public—by selling bonds and other securities—to cover any shortfall. (The Treasury currently issues 1-, 3-, 6-, and 12-month bills; 2-, 3-, 5-, 7-, and 10-year notes; 5-, 10-, and 20-year inflation-protected securities; and 30-year bonds.) If the budget were in surplus, the Treasury would use some of its income to reduce federal debt held by the public. In either case, the Treasury refinances a substantial portion of the nation's debt each year at market interest rates. Those rates also determine how much the Federal Reserve earns on its holdings of securities (which are counted in debt held by the public), which in turn affects federal revenues.

If interest rates on all types of Treasury securities were 1 percentage point higher each year through 2020, compared with the interest rates underlying the baseline, and all other economic variables were unchanged, the government's interest costs would be $17 billion greater in 2010 (see Table C-1). Most marketable government debt is in the form of coupon securities, which consist of notes, inflation-protected securities, and bonds. As Treasury securities mature, they are replaced with new issues. Therefore, the budgetary effects of higher interest rates would mount each year, climbing to an additional $135 billion in 2020 under this scenario.

As part of its conduct of monetary policy, the Federal Reserve buys and sells Treasury and other securities, including recently a large amount of mortgage-related securities. The Federal Reserve also pays interest on reserves held at the Federal Reserve by depository institutions. The interest that the Federal Reserve earns on its portfolio of securities and the amount that it pays on reserves helps determine its profits, which are counted as revenues when they are remitted to the Treasury. If all interest rates each year were 1 percentage point higher than CBO projects, the Federal Reserve's profits—and thus its remittances to the Treasury—would increase by amounts growing from $1 billion in 2010 to $12 billion in 2020.

The larger deficits generated by the increase in interest payments would require the Treasury to raise more cash than is assumed in the baseline. The extra borrowing results in further increases in the annual cost of servicing the debt that would grow to $61 billion in 2020.

All told, if interest rates were a full percentage point higher than the rates assumed in CBO's baseline, the budget's bottom line would worsen by increasing amounts over the projection period, from $16 billion in 2010 to $184 billion in 2020. The cumulative deficit over the 10-year period would grow by $1.1 trillion. That total is more than $700 billion larger than the effect CBO calculated just two years ago and is a direct result of the huge increase in debt that has accumulated recently and that is expected to continue to mount in CBO's baseline projections. In January 2008, CBO projected that debt held by the public would total about $5 trillion by 2018; the current baseline projects that debt held by the public will reach $15 trillion in the next decade.[79]

Higher Inflation

The third rule of thumb shows the budgetary effect of inflation that is 1 percentage point higher than it is in the baseline. Higher inflation increases both revenues and outlays, with a net effect relative to the current baseline of increasing budget deficits.

Higher inflation leads to increases in wages and other income, which translate directly into more income and payroll taxes being withheld from people's paychecks. The effect of inflation on revenues is dampened (with a lag) because the thresholds for various tax rate brackets are indexed to rise with inflation. The faster growth in prices also boosts corporate profits, leading to increased federal receipts from businesses' quarterly estimated tax payments.

Table C-1. How Selected Economic Changes Might Affect CBO's Baseline Budget Projections

(Billions of dollars)												
	2010	**2011**	**2012**	**2013**	**2014**	**2015**	**2016**	**2017**	**2018**	**2019**	**2020**	**Total, 2011-2015**	**Total, 2011-2020**
	Growth Rate of Real GDP Is 0.1 Percentage Point Lower per Year												
Change in Revenues	-1	-4	-7	-11	-16	-21	-26	-31	-37	-43	-50	-59	-247
Change in Outlays													
Mandatory spending	*	*	*	*	*	*	*	*	*	-1	-1	*	-2
Debt service	*	*	*	1	1	2	4	5	7	10	13	4	43
Total	*	*	*	1	1	2	3	5	7	9	12	4	41
Change in Deficit[a]	**-1**	**-4**	**-8**	**-12**	**-17**	**-23**	**-29**	**-36**	**-44**	**-53**	**-62**	**-63**	**-288**
	Interest Rates Are 1 Percentage Point Higher per Year												
Change in Revenues	1	4	6	8	9	10	10	11	11	11	12	38	94
Change in Outlays													
Higher rates	17	46	65	78	88	97	103	112	118	126	135	373	966
Debt service	*	1	3	6	12	17	24	32	41	51	61	39	248
Total	18	47	68	84	99	114	128	143	158	176	196	412	1,214
Change in Deficit[a]	**-16**	**-43**	**-62**	**-76**	**-90**	**-104**	**-117**	**-133**	**-147**	**-165**	**-184**	**-374**	**-1,120**
	Inflation Is 1 Percentage Point Higher per Year												
Change in Revenues	13	42	77	116	159	206	256	310	369	435	508	598	2,475
Change in Outlays													
Discretionary spending	0	7	18	30	44	58	74	90	107	124	143	157	695
Mandatory spending	2	14	31	50	71	94	123	153	186	219	267	260	1,209
Higher rates[b]	23	54	76	89	100	111	120	128	136	145	155	430	1,114
Debt service	*	1	2	5	9	13	18	23	28	34	40	30	173
Total	25	76	127	175	224	276	334	394	458	522	605	877	3,191

	2010	2011	2012	2013	2014	2015	2016	2017	2018	2019	2020	Total, 2011-2015	Total, 2011-2020
Change in Deficit[a]	**-12**	**-34**	**-50**	**-59**	**-65**	-70	-79	**-84**	-89	-88	-98	-279	-715
	Wages and Salaries' Share of GDP Is 1 Percentage Point Higher per Year												
Change in Revenues	11	8	8	11	13	13	13	14	15	16	17	53	127
Change in Outlays (Debt service)	*	*	*	-1	-2	-3	-3	-4	-5	-7	-8	-6	-33
Change in Deficit[a]	**11**	**9**	**9**	**12**	**15**	**15**	**16**	**18**	**20**	**22**	**24**	**59**	**160**
Memorandum:													
Deficit in CBO's													
January 2010 Baseline	-1,349	-980	-650	-539	-475	-480	-521	-525	-542	-649	-687	-3,124	-6,047

Source: Congressional Budget Office.

Note: GDP = gross domestic product; * = between -$500 million and $500 million.

[a] Negative amounts indicate an increase in the deficit or a decrease in the surplus.

[b] The change in outlays attributable to higher rates in this scenario is different from the estimate in the rule of thumb for interest rates because the principal on the Treasury's inflation-protected securities grows with inflation.

Higher inflation increases spending for many federal benefit programs and also results in projections of increased discretionary spending. Many mandatory programs adjust benefits automatically each year to reflect price increases. Social Security, federal employees' retirement programs, Supplemental Security Income, disability compensation for veterans, the Supplemental Nutrition Assistance Program (formerly known as Food Stamps), and child nutrition programs, among others, are adjusted (with a lag) for changes in the consumer price index or one of its components. Many Medicare payment rates also are adjusted annually for inflation. Other programs, such as Medicaid, are not formally indexed to price changes but grow with inflation nonetheless. In addition, to the extent that initial benefit payments to participants in retirement and disability programs are related to wages, changes in nominal wages as a result of inflation will be reflected in future outlays for those programs. Finally, future spending for discretionary programs is projected on the basis of assumed rates of growth in wages and prices. (The discretionary baseline holds funding levels constant in real terms by adjusting the most recent annual appropriation amounts for such anticipated inflation.)

Inflation also has an impact on federal net interest outlays because it affects nominal long-term interest rates. For example, if inflation rises, nominal interest rates will climb (under the assumption that all real variables are held unchanged), and new federal borrowing will incur higher interest costs. For this rule of thumb, CBO assumed that nominal interest rates would rise in step with inflation. Inflation-indexed securities also would incur higher projected costs with higher inflation.

If inflation each year was 1 percentage point higher than the rate in CBO's baseline, total revenues over the 10-year period would be 6.7 percent larger than in the baseline, and outlays would be 7.4 percent larger (see Table C-1). Over the period from 2011 to 2020, the deficit would increase by a total of $715 billion (of which $173 billion would be for debt service).

Wages and Salaries as a Larger Shareof GDP

Because different types of income are taxed at different rates, changes over time in the share of total income represented by each type have contributed to changes in federal tax receipts measured as a percentage of GDP. Considerable uncertainty surrounds projections of those income shares.

Two important income categories for federal revenues are wages and salaries and corporate profits. Wages and salaries are the most highly taxed form of income; they are subject to the individual income tax and to payroll taxes for Social Security (up to a maximum annual amount) and Medicare. Thus, an additional dollar of wages and salaries will produce more revenues than will an additional dollar of corporate profits, CBO assumes. Higher wages and salaries and correspondingly smaller profits will thus result in larger federal revenues.

In CBO's baseline projections, wages and salaries equal about 45 percent of GDP, on average, between 2010 and 2020, and taxable corporate profits equal 7 percent (see Chapter 4). If, instead, wages and salaries each year were 1 percentage point larger relative to GDP and corporate profits were 1 percentage point smaller, annual revenues would be $11 billion greater in 2010 and $17 billion greater by 2020 (see Table C-1).

One year stands out in the pattern of increasing revenues under this scenario. In 2011, revenues would increase by $8 billion, which is less than the $11 billion increase in 2010. That modest decline in the annual increase occurs because corporations generally pay taxes more slowly on what they owe for profits than individual taxpayers will pay for wages (and wages are subject to automatic withholding). Those slower payments delay the drop in corporate receipts—from 2010 to 2011. In addition, businesses can carry forward any losses they incur in earlier years to help reduce their tax liability in subsequent years—specifically, in 2011 and beyond; those effects make the decline in corporate receipts larger in 2011 than in 2010.

The larger amount of revenues that would result from an increase in wages and salaries as a share of GDP would further improve the budget's bottom line by reducing the borrowing costs assumed in the baseline in each year of the projection period. The decrease in interest payments would gradually reach $8 billion by 2020. Overall, under this scenario, the cumulative 10-year deficit would be $160 billion smaller than in CBO's baseline.

APPENDIX D. TRUST FUNDS AND MEASURES OF FEDERAL DEBT

The federal government uses several accounting mechanisms for linking earmarked receipts (money designated for a specific purpose) with corresponding expenditures; some of those mechanisms are trust funds (such as the Social Security trust funds), others are special funds (such as the fund the Department of Defense uses to finance its health care program for military retirees) or revolving funds (such as the Federal Employees Group Life Insurance fund). Although trust funds are designated as such by law, there is no substantive difference between trust funds and the other types of funds.

When trust funds and other government funds have receipts in excess of amounts needed for current expenditures, they are credited with nonmarketable Treasury debt known as government account series securities. At the end of 2009, about $4.3 trillion in such securities was outstanding, mostly credited to the Social Security trust funds. (That amount can serve as a measure of how much receipts, including interest, have exceeded outlays over time for the programs financed through those funds.) The value of the outstanding securities (that is, the debt held by government accounts) is combined with the amount of debt held by the public (described in Chapter 1) in two measures of the government's debt: gross federal debt and debt subject to limit.

Trust Funds

In total, the federal budget has more than 200 trust funds, although most of the money is credited to fewer than a dozen of them. Among the largest trust funds are the two for Social Security (the Old-Age and Survivors Insurance Trust Fund and the Disability Insurance [DI] Trust Fund) and the funds dedicated to Medicare's Hospital Insurance (HI) program (also known as Part A), civil service retirement, and military retirement.

When a trust fund receives payroll taxes or other income that is not needed to pay benefits immediately, the Treasury credits the fund and uses the excess cash to reduce the amount of new federal borrowing that is needed to finance the governmentwide deficit. That is, if other tax and spending policies are unchanged, the government borrows less from the public than it would in the absence of those excess funds. The reverse is the case when revenues for a trust fund program fall short of expenses. Thus, the balances of trust funds are not a measure of resources available to pay future obligations for the respective programs; those resources will need to come from federal revenues or additional borrowing in the years those obligations are due.

Including the cash receipts and expenditures of trust funds in the budget totals along with receipts and expenditures of other federal programs is useful for assessing how all federal activities taken together affect the economy and financial markets. Therefore, the Congressional Budget Office (CBO), the Administration's Office of Management and Budget, and other fiscal analysts generally focus on the total deficit rather than on the deficit with or without particular trust funds. That comprehensive view of the government's fiscal activities is often called the "unified budget."

According to CBO's current baseline projection, trust funds as a group are expected to run a surplus of $119 billion in 2010 and $1.6 trillion from 2011 through 2020 (see Table D-1).That surplus is bolstered by interest and other sums transferred from elsewhere in the budget. Such intragovernmental transfers, which are projected to total $590 billion in 2010, reallocate costs from one category of the budget to another but do not directly change the total deficit or the government's borrowing needs. If intragovernmental transfers are excluded and only income from sources outside the government is counted, the trust funds as a whole are projected to run annual deficits that will increase from $471 billion in 2010 to $907 billion in 2020.

Total trust fund surpluses are dominated by those for the Old-Age and Survivors Insurance portion of the Social Security program. Including interest and other intragovernmental payments, CBO estimates a surplus of $110 billion for that fund this year and a cumulative surplus of nearly $1.5 trillion from 2011 through 2020. The DI program is projected to run annual deficits through the entire projection period. For Social Security as a whole, the estimated surpluses peak at $139 billion in 2015 and decline to $107 billion in 2020. Excluding interest (which accounts for the bulk of the intragovernmental transfer), surpluses for Social Security become deficits of $28 billion in 2010 and $202 billion over the period from 2011 to 2020 (see Figure D-1).

In the absence of legislative action, the Highway Trust Fund, the DI Trust Fund, and the HI Trust Fund will exhaust their balances during the baseline period, CBO projects. The Highway Trust Fund required an infusion from the Treasury's general fund of $7 billion in 2009. Depending on cash flows, the Highway Trust Fund could again be unable to meet obligations in a timely manner in 2010; CBO estimates that a transfer of several billion dollars could be needed to maintain the balance above the $4 billion that the Department of Transportation suggests as a minimum. Because the rate of unemployment is projected to remain high, CBO estimates that the Unemployment Trust Fund, which received $8 billion from the general fund last year, will require another $50 billion in 2010. That transfer was provided for in the Consolidated Appropriations Act of 2010.

Economic weakness and rising health care costs are projected to cause a continuing decline in the balances of the HI and DI Trust Funds during the baseline period. CBO projects that the HI fund will exhaust its balance in 2016 and the DI fund will be exhausted in 2018. Once balances are exhausted, the programs eventually would be unable to immediately cover their obligations.

Measures of Federal Debt

At the end of 2009, debt held by the public totaled approximately $7.5 trillion. In CBO's current baseline projections, that measure of debt will soar to $15 trillion in 2020. Debt held by the public (see Chapter 1) is the most meaningful measure for assessing the relationship between federal debt and the economy because it represents the amount that the government has borrowed in the financial markets to pay for its operations and activities; such borrowing competes with other participants in credit markets for financial resources. In contrast, debt held by trust funds and other government accounts represents *internal* transactions of the government and thus has no effect on credit markets. Combined, debt held by the public and debt held by government accounts form the basis of two other measures of debt: gross federal debt and debt subject to limit.

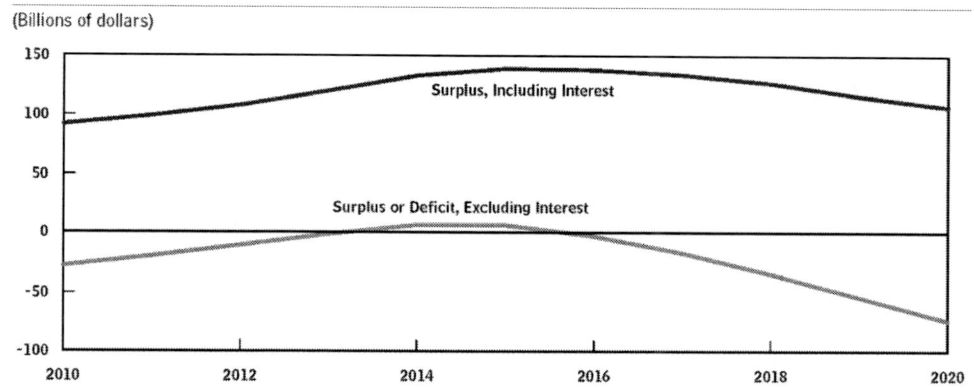

Source: Congressional Budget Office.

Figure D-1. Total Surplus or Deficit of the Social Security Trust Funds.

Gross Federal Debt

Gross federal debt consists of debt held by the public and debt issued to government accounts. CBO projects that, under current law, gross federal debt will increase in every year of the 2010–2020 period, reaching $21.4 trillion in 2020—roughly 80 percent more than its total of $11.9 trillion at the end of 2009 (see Table D-2). That increase stems from a near doubling of debt held by the public and an increase of 48 percent in debt held by government accounts; the latter mostly represents the impact of the cumulative trust fund surpluses projected over the next decade.

Debt Subject to Limit

The Treasury's authority to issue debt has a statutory ceiling. Although the limit applies to debt held by the public and by government accounts, it does not include debt issued by agencies other than the Treasury, which is included in debt held by the public and gross federal debt. That debt includes the $23 billion issued by the Tennessee Valley Authority and the $12 billion issued by the Federal Financing Bank.[80] The current debt ceiling, which was set in December 2009 in Public Law 111-123, is $12.394 trillion. By CBO's estimates, under current policies, that ceiling will be reached early in calendar year 2010 (see Figure D-2).

Table D-1. CBO's Baseline Projections of Trust Fund Surpluses or Deficits

	(Billions of dollars)											
	Actual 2009	**2010**	**2011**	**2012**	**2013**	**2014**	**2015**	**2016**	**2017**	**2018**	**2019**	**2020**
Social Security												
Old-Age and Survivors Insurance	146	110	120	130	143	155	162	163	160	155	146	136
Disability Insurance	-9	-18	-21	-23	-23	-23	-23	-25	-26	-28	-29	-30
Subtotal, Social Security	**137**	**92**	**99**	**108**	**120**	**133**	**139**	**138**	**134**	**127**	**116**	**107**
Medicare												
Hospital Insurance (Part A)	-9	-30	-42	-39	-48	-62	-62	-73	-79	-88	-115	-136
Supplementary Medical Insurance (Part B)	3	2	18	13	7	2	10	9	11	11	9	12
Subtotal, Medicare	**-7**	**-28**	**-25**	**-26**	**-41**	**-61**	**-53**	**-64**	**-69**	**-77**	**-107**	**-124**
Military Retirement	25	43	48	52	55	60	66	72	79	85	92	100
Civilian Retirement[a]	26	18	18	17	17	17	17	18	20	21	22	22
Unemployment Insurance	-54	4	5	8	8	8	18	19	20	26	29	31
Highway and Mass Transit	*	-8	-9	-14	-14	-15	-15	-14	-14	-14	-14	-15
Airport and Airway	*	*	*	*	1	2	2	3	3	4	5	5
Other[b]	4	1	1	2	2	2	3	2	3	3	4	4
Total Trust Fund Surplus	**131**	**119**	**137**	**146**	**148**	**147**	**179**	**174**	**176**	**175**	**147**	**130**
Intragovernmental Transfers to Trust Funds[c]	556	590	628	633	670	719	756	811	858	899	973	1,038
Net Budgetary Impact of Trust Fund Programs[d]	**-410**	**-471**	**-491**	**-487**	**-522**	**-572**	**-577**	**-636**	**-682**	**-724**	**-826**	**-907**

Source: Congressional Budget Office.

Note: * = between -$500 million and $500 million.

a. Includes Civil Service Retirement, Foreign Service Retirement, and several smaller retirement trust funds.

b. Primarily trust funds for railroad workers' retirement, federal employees' health and life insurance, Superfund, and various insurance programs for veterans.

c. Includes interest paid to trust funds, payments from the Treasury's general fund to the Supplementary Medical Insurance program, the employer's share of payments for employees' retirement, lump-sum payments to the Civil Service and Military Retirement Trust Funds, taxes on Social Security benefits, and smaller miscellaneous payments.

d. Negative numbers indicate that the trust fund transactions add to total budget deficits.

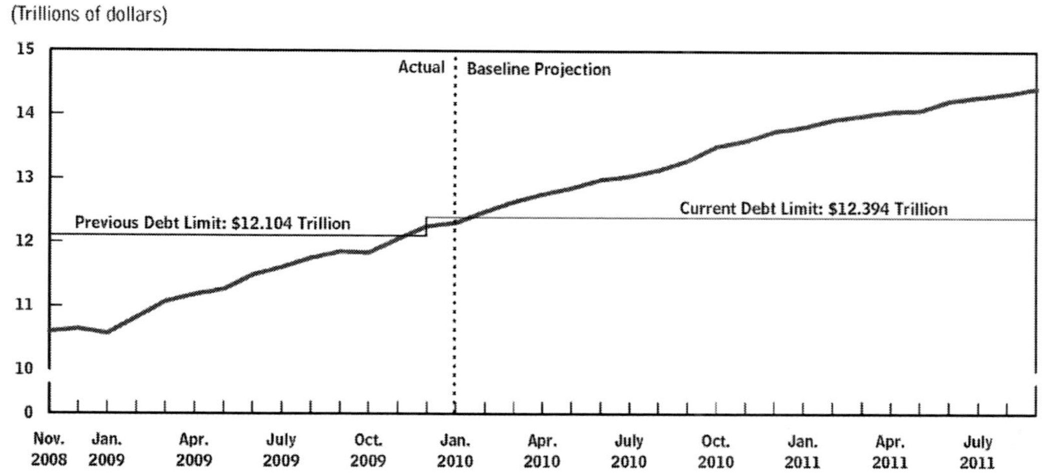

Source: Congressional Budget Office.

Figure D-2. Debt Subject to Limit, November 2008 to September 2011.

APPENDIX E. CBO'S ECONOMIC PROJECTIONS FOR 2009 TO 2020

The tables in this appendix expand on the information in Chapter 2 by showing the Congressional Budget Office's (CBO's) year-by-year economic projections for 2009 to 2020 (by calendar year in Table E-1 and by fiscal year in Table E-2). CBO does not forecast cyclical fluctuations in its projections for years after 2014.

Instead, the projected values shown in the tables for 2015 through 2020 reflect CBO's assessment of average values for that period. That assessment takes into account economic and demographic trends but does not attempt to forecast the frequency or size of fluctuations in the business cycle.

APPENDIX F. HISTORICAL BUDGET DATA

This appendix provides historical data for revenues, outlays, and the deficit or surplus—in forms consistent with the projections in Chapters 1, 3, and 4—for fiscal years 1970 to 2009. The data are shown both in nominal dollars and as a percentage of gross domestic product. Data come from the Congressional Budget Office and the Office of Management and Budget. Some of the numbers have been revised since January 2008, the last time these tables were published.

Federal revenues, outlays, the deficit or surplus, and debt held by the public are shown in Tables F-1 and F-2. Revenues, outlays, and the deficit or surplus have both on-budget and off-budget components. Social Security's receipts and outlays were placed off-budget by the Balanced Budget and Emergency Deficit Control Act of 1985. For the sake of consistency, the tables show the budgetary components of Social Security as off-budget before that year. The Postal Service was moved off-budget by the Omnibus Reconciliation Act of 1989.

Table D-2. CBO's Baseline Projections of Federal Debt

(Billions of dollars)												
	Actual 2009	**2010**	**2011**	**2012**	**2013**	**2014**	**2015**	**2016**	**2017**	**2018**	**2019**	**2020**
Debt Held by the Public	7,544	8,797	9,785	10,479	11,056	11,556	12,055	12,595	13,133	13,678	14,329	15,027
Debt Held by Government Accounts												
Social Security	2,504	2,595	2,695	2,802	2,922	3,055	3,194	3,332	3,466	3,592	3,709	3,815
Other government accounts [a]	1,826	1,868	1,915	1,978	2,051	2,112	2,200	2,284	2,368	2,459	2,531	2,599
Total	**4,330**	**4,463**	**4,610**	**4,780**	**4,974**	**5,167**	**5,394**	**5,616**	**5,834**	**6,051**	**6,240**	**6,415**
Gross Federal Debt	11,874	13,260	14,395	15,259	16,030	16,723	17,449	18,211	18,967	19,729	20,568	21,442
Debt Subject to Limit[b]	11,853	13,239	14,374	15,238	16,007	16,701	17,426	18,188	18,944	19,706	20,545	21,418

Source: Congressional Budget Office.

Note: Figures are as of the end of the year.

a. Mainly the Civil Service Retirement and Disability, Military Retirement, Medicare, and Unemployment Insurance Trust Funds.

b. Differs from the gross federal debt primarily because debt issued by agencies other than the Treasury, as well as debt issued by the Federal Financing Bank, is excluded from the debt limit. The current debt limit is $12.394 trillion.

Table E-1. CBO's Year-by-Year Forecast and Projections for Calendar Years 2009 to 2020

	Estimated	Forecast		Projected								
	2009	2010	2011	2012	2013	2014	2015	2016	2017	2018	2019	2020
Nominal GDP (Billions of dollars)	14,253	14,706	15,116	15,969	16,918	17,816	18,622	19,425	20,231	21,033	21,882	22,770
Nominal GDP (Percentage change)	-1.3	3.2	2.8	5.6	5.9	5.3	4.5	4.3	4.1	4.0	4.0	4.1
Real GDP (Percentage change)	-2.5	2.2	1.9	4.6	4.8	3.9	2.9	2.5	2.3	2.2	2.2	2.3
GDP Price Index (Percentage change)	1.2	0.9	0.9	1.0	1.1	1.3	1.6	1.7	1.8	1.8	1.8	1.8
PCE Price Index[a] (Percentage change)	0.2	1.9	1.1	1.1	1.1	1.3	1.6	1.7	1.8	1.8	1.8	1.8
Core PCE Price Index[b] (Percentage change)	1.5	1.2	1.0	1.0	1.0	1.3	1.5	1.7	1.7	1.8	1.8	1.8
Consumer Price Index[c] (Percentage change)	-0.2	2.4	1.3	1.2	1.1	1.3	1.7	1.9	2.0	2.0	2.0	2.0
Core Consumer Price Index[d] (Percentage change)	1.8	1.5	1.0	0.9	1.0	1.3	1.7	1.9	2.0	2.0	2.0	2.0
Employment Cost Index[e] (Percentage change)	1.5	1.6	1.4	2.1	2.5	2.9	3.0	3.0	3.0	3.0	3.0	3.0
Unemployment Rate (Percent)	9.3	10.1	9.5	8.0	6.3	5.3	5.1	5.0	5.0	5.0	5.0	5.0
Three-Month Treasury Bill Rate (Percent)	0.1	0.2	0.7	1.9	3.0	3.9	4.2	4.4	4.7	4.8	4.8	4.8
Ten-Year Treasury Note Rate (Percent)	3.2	3.6	3.9	4.2	4.5	4.9	5.2	5.4	5.6	5.6	5.6	5.6
Tax Bases (Billions of dollars)												
Domestic economic profits	990	1,263	1,307	1,387	1,462	1,487	1,471	1,468	1,484	1,506	1,542	1,588
Wages and salaries	6,329	6,517	6,671	7,149	7,624	8,061	8,445	8,818	9,189	9,554	9,938	10,365
Tax Bases (Percentage of GDP)												
Domestic economic profits	6.9	8.6	8.6	8.7	8.6	8.3	7.9	7.6	7.3	7.2	7.0	7.0
Wages and salaries	44.4	44.3	44.1	44.8	45.1	45.2	45.3	45.4	45.4	45.4	45.4	45.5

Sources: Congressional Budget Office; Department of Commerce, Bureau of Economic Analysis; Department of Labor, Bureau of Labor Statistics; Federal Reserve Board.

Notes: Percentage changes are measured from one year to the next.

GDP = gross domestic product; PCE = personal consumption expenditure.

a. The personal consumption expenditure price index.

b. The personal consumption expenditure price index excluding prices for food and energy.

c. The consumer price index for all urban consumers.

d. The consumer price index for all urban consumers excluding prices for food and energy.

e. The employment cost index for wages and salaries of workers in private industry.

Table E-2. CBO's Year-by-Year Forecast and Projections for Fiscal Years 2009 to 2020

	Actual	Forecast		Projected									
	2009	2010	2011	2012	2013	2014	2015	2016	2017	2018	2019	2020
Nominal GDP (Billions of dollars)	14,236	14,595	14,992	15,730	16,676	17,606	18,421	19,223	20,036	20,823	21,667	22,544
Nominal GDP (Percentage change)	-1.4	2.5	2.7	4.9	6.0	5.6	4.6	4.4	4.2	3.9	4.1	4.0
Real GDP (Percentage change)	-2.9	1.6	1.8	3.9	4.9	4.3	3.0	2.6	2.4	2.1	2.3	2.2
GDP Price Index (Percentage change)	1.5	0.9	0.9	1.0	1.1	1.2	1.5	1.7	1.8	1.8	1.8	1.8
PCE Price Index[a] (Percentage change)	0.3	1.9	1.2	1.1	1.1	1.2	1.5	1.7	1.8	1.8	1.8	1.8
Core PCE Price Index[b] (Percentage change)	1.7	1.3	1.0	0.9	1.0	1.2	1.5	1.7	1.7	1.8	1.8	1.8
Consumer Price Index[c] (Percentage change)	-0.3	2.4	1.4	1.2	1.1	1.3	1.6	1.9	2.0	2.0	2.0	2.0
Core Consumer Price Index[d] (Percentage change)	1.8	1.7	1.0	0.9	1.0	1.2	1.6	1.9	2.0	2.0	2.0	2.0
Employment Cost Index[e] (Percentage change)	1.9	1.5	1.4	1.9	2.4	2.8	3.0	3.0	3.0	3.0	3.0	3.0
Unemployment Rate (Percent)	8.5	10.2	9.8	8.4	6.7	5.4	5.1	5.0	5.0	5.0	5.0	5.0
Three-Month Treasury Bill Rate (Percent)	0.2	0.2	0.5	1.5	2.7	3.7	4.1	4.4	4.6	4.8	4.8	4.8
Ten-Year Treasury Note Rate (Percent)	3.2	3.5	3.8	4.2	4.5	4.8	5.1	5.3	5.6	5.6	5.6	5.6
Tax Bases (Billions of dollars)												
Domestic economic profits	905	1,226	1,298	1,362	1,445	1,487	1,476	1,466	1,482	1,497	1,532	1,576
Wages and salaries	6,374	6,432	6,638	7,027	7,504	7,961	8,349	8,726	9,099	9,459	9,841	10,254
Tax Bases (Percentage of GDP)												
Domestic economic profits	6.4	8.4	8.7	8.7	8.7	8.4	8.0	7.6	7.4	7.2	7.1	7.0
Wages and salaries	44.8	44.1	44.3	44.7	45.0	45.2	45.3	45.4	45.4	45.4	45.4	45.5

Sources: Congressional Budget Office; Department of Commerce, Bureau of Economic Analysis; Department of Labor, Bureau of Labor Statistics; Federal Reserve Board.

Notes: Percentage changes are measured from one year to the next.

GDP = gross domestic product; PCE = personal consumption expenditure.

a. The personal consumption expenditure price index.

b. The personal consumption expenditure price index excluding prices for food and energy.

c. The consumer price index for all urban consumers.

d. The consumer price index for all urban consumers excluding prices for food and energy.

e. The employment cost index for wages and salaries of workers in private industry.

The major sources of federal revenues (including off-budget revenues) are presented in Tables F-3 and F-4. Social insurance taxes include payments by employers and employees for Social Security, Medicare, Railroad Retirement, and unemployment insurance, as well as pension contributions by federal workers. Excise taxes are levied on certain products and services, such as gasoline, alcoholic beverages, and air travel. Estate and gift taxes are levied on assets when they are transferred. Miscellaneous receipts consist of earnings of the Federal Reserve System and income from numerous fees and charges.

Total outlays for major categories of spending appear in Tables F-5 and F-6. (Those totals include on- and off-budget outlays.) Spending controlled by the appropriation process is classified as discretionary. Spending governed by permanent laws, such as those that set eligibility requirements for certain programs, is considered mandatory. Offsetting receipts include the government's contributions to retirement programs for its employees, fees, charges (such as Medicare premiums), and receipts from the use of federally controlled land and offshore territory. Net interest (function 900 of the budget) comprises the interest paid by the government on federal debt offset by its interest income.

Tables F-7 and F-8 divide discretionary spending into its defense, international, and domestic components. Tables F-9 and F-10 classify mandatory spending by the three major entitlement programs—Social Security, Medicare, and Medicaid—and by other categories of mandatory spending. Income-security programs provide benefits to recipients with limited income and assets; those programs include unemployment compensation, Supplemental Security Income, and the Supplemental Nutrition Assistance Program (SNAP, formerly known as Food Stamps.) Other federal retirement and disability programs provide benefits to federal civilian employees, members of the military, and veterans. The category of other mandatory programs includes the activities of the Commodity Credit Corporation, the Medicare-Eligible Retiree Health Care Fund, the subsidy costs of federal student loan programs, the Universal Service Fund (which reduces the cost of telecommunications services for selected areas and individuals), the Children's Health Insurance Program, and the Social Services Block Grant program.

The remaining tables, F-11 through F-13, show estimates of the cyclically adjusted budget deficit or surplus and its outlay and revenue components. The cyclically adjusted budget deficit or surplus attempts to filter out the effects that fluctuations in output and unemployment related to the business cycle have on revenues and outlays; it also incorporates other adjustments. The change in that deficit or surplus is commonly used to measure the short-term impact of fiscal policy on total demand. Table F-11 also presents estimates of potential and actual gross domestic product.

Table F-1. Revenues, Outlays, Deficits, Surpluses, and Debt Held by the Public, 1970 to 2009, in Billions of Dollars

	Revenues	Outlays	Deficit (-) or Surplus				Debt Held by the Public[a]
			On-Budget	Social Security	Postal Service	Total	
1970	192.8	195.6	-8.7	5.9	n.a.	-2.8	283.2
1971	187.1	210.2	-26.1	3.0	n.a.	-23.0	303.0
1972	207.3	230.7	-26.1	3.1	-0.4	-23.4	322.4
1973	230.8	245.7	-15.2	0.5	-0.2	-14.9	340.9
1974	263.2	269.4	-7.2	1.8	-0.8	-6.1	343.7
1975	279.1	332.3	-54.1	2.0	-1.1	-53.2	394.7
1976	298.1	371.8	-69.4	-3.2	-1.1	-73.7	477.4
1977	355.6	409.2	-49.9	-3.9	0.2	-53.7	549.1
1978	399.6	458.7	-55.4	-4.3	0.5	-59.2	607.1
1979	463.3	504.0	-39.6	-2.0	0.9	-40.7	640.3
1980	517.1	590.9	-73.1	-1.1	0.4	-73.8	711.9
1981	599.3	678.2	-73.9	-5.0	-0.1	-79.0	789.4
1982	617.8	745.7	-120.6	-7.9	0.6	-128.0	924.6
1983	600.6	808.4	-207.7	0.2	-0.3	-207.8	1,137.3
1984	666.4	851.8	-185.3	0.3	-0.4	-185.4	1,307.0
1985	734.0	946.3	-221.5	9.4	-0.1	-212.3	1,507.3
1986	769.2	990.4	-237.9	16.7	*	-221.2	1,740.6
1987	854.3	1,004.0	-168.4	19.6	-0.9	-149.7	1,889.8
1988	909.2	1,064.4	-192.3	38.8	-1.7	-155.2	2,051.6
1989	991.1	1,143.7	-205.4	52.4	0.3	-152.6	2,190.7
1990	1,032.0	1,253.0	-277.6	58.2	-1.6	-221.0	2,411.6
1991	1,055.0	1,324.2	-321.4	53.5	-1.3	-269.2	2,689.0
1992	1,091.2	1,381.5	-340.4	50.7	-0.7	-290.3	2,999.7
1993	1,154.3	1,409.4	-300.4	46.8	-1.4	-255.1	3,248.4
1994	1,258.6	1,461.8	-258.8	56.8	-1.1	-203.2	3,433.1
1995	1,351.8	1,515.8	-226.4	60.4	2.0	-164.0	3,604.4
1996	1,453.1	1,560.5	-174.0	66.4	0.2	-107.4	3,734.1
1997	1,579.2	1,601.1	-103.2	81.3	*	-21.9	3,772.3
1998	1,721.7	1,652.5	-29.9	99.4	-0.2	69.3	3,721.1
1999	1,827.5	1,701.8	1.9	124.7	-1.0	125.6	3,632.4
2000	2,025.2	1,789.0	86.4	151.8	-2.0	236.2	3,409.8
2001	1,991.1	1,862.9	-32.4	163.0	-2.3	128.2	3,319.6
2002	1,853.1	2,010.9	-317.4	159.0	0.7	-157.8	3,540.4
2003	1,782.3	2,159.9	-538.4	155.6	5.2	-377.6	3,913.4
2004	1,880.1	2,292.9	-568.0	151.1	4.1	-412.7	4,295.5
2005	2,153.6	2,472.0	-493.6	173.5	1.8	-318.3	4,592.2
2006	2,406.9	2,655.1	-434.5	185.2	1.1	-248.2	4,829.0
2007	2,568.0	2,728.7	-342.2	186.5	-5.1	-160.7	5,035.1
2008	2,524.0	2,982.6	-641.9	186.4	-3.1	-458.6	5,803.1
2009	2,104.6	3,518.2	-1,550.6	137.3	-0.3	-1,413.6	7,544.0

Sources: Congressional Budget Office; Office of Management and Budget.

Note: n.a. = not applicable; * = between -$50 million and $50 million.

[a]. End of year.

Table F-2. Revenues, Outlays, Deficits, Surpluses, and Debt Held by the Public, 1970 to 2009, as a Percentage of Gross Domestic Product

	Revenues	Outlays	Deficit (-) or Surplus				Debt Held by the Public[a]
			On-Budget	Social Security	Postal Service	Total	
1970	19.0	19.3	-0.9	0.6	n.a.	-0.3	28.0
1971	17.3	19.5	-2.4	0.3	n.a.	-2.1	28.1
1972	17.6	19.6	-2.2	0.3	*	-2.0	27.4
1973	17.6	18.7	-1.2	*	*	-1.1	26.0
1974	18.3	18.7	-0.5	0.1	-0.1	-0.4	23.9
1975	17.9	21.3	-3.5	0.1	-0.1	-3.4	25.3
1976	17.1	21.4	-4.0	-0.2	-0.1	-4.2	27.5
1977	18.0	20.7	-2.5	-0.2	*	-2.7	27.8
1978	18.0	20.7	-2.5	-0.2	*	-2.7	27.4
1979	18.5	20.2	-1.6	-0.1	*	-1.6	25.6
1980	19.0	21.7	-2.7	*	*	-2.7	26.1
1981	19.6	22.2	-2.4	-0.2	*	-2.6	25.8
1982	19.2	23.1	-3.7	-0.2	*	-4.0	28.7
1983	17.5	23.5	-6.0	*	*	-6.0	33.1
1984	17.3	22.2	-4.8	*	*	-4.8	34.0
1985	17.7	22.8	-5.3	0.2	*	-5.1	36.4
1986	17.5	22.5	-5.4	0.4	*	-5.0	39.5
1987	18.4	21.6	-3.6	0.4	*	-3.2	40.6
1988	18.2	21.3	-3.8	0.8	*	-3.1	41.0
1989	18.4	21.2	-3.8	1.0	*	-2.8	40.6
1990	18.0	21.9	-4.8	1.0	*	-3.9	42.1
1991	17.8	22.3	-5.4	0.9	*	-4.5	45.3
1992	17.5	22.1	-5.5	0.8	*	-4.7	48.1
1993	17.5	21.4	-4.6	0.7	*	-3.9	49.3
1994	18.0	21.0	-3.7	0.8	*	-2.9	49.2
1995	18.4	20.6	-3.1	0.8	*	-2.2	49.1
1996	18.8	20.2	-2.3	0.9	*	-1.4	48.4
1997	19.2	19.5	-1.3	1.0	*	-0.3	45.9
1998	19.9	19.1	-0.3	1.1	*	0.8	43.0
1999	19.8	18.5	*	1.4	*	1.4	39.4
2000	20.6	18.2	0.9	1.5	*	2.4	34.7
2001	19.5	18.2	-0.3	1.6	*	1.3	32.5
2002	17.6	19.1	-3.0	1.5	*	-1.5	33.6
2003	16.2	19.7	-4.9	1.4	*	-3.4	35.6
2004	16.1	19.6	-4.9	1.3	*	-3.5	36.8
2005	17.3	19.9	-4.0	1.4	*	-2.6	36.9
2006	18.2	20.1	-3.3	1.4	*	-1.9	36.5
2007	18.5	19.6	-2.5	1.3	*	-1.2	36.2
2008	17.5	20.7	-4.4	1.3	*	-3.2	40.2
2009	14.8	24.7	-10.9	1.0	*	-9.9	53.0

Sources: Congressional Budget Office; Office of Management and Budget.

Note: n.a. = not applicable; * = between -0.05 percent and 0.05 percent.

[a] End of year.

Table F-3. Revenues by Major Source, 1970 to 2009, in Billions of Dollars

	Individual Income Taxes	Corporate Income Taxes	Social Insurance Taxes	Excise Taxes	Estate and Gift Taxes	Customs Duties	Miscellaneous Receipts	Total Revenues
1970	90.4	32.8	44.4	15.7	3.6	2.4	3.4	192.8
1971	86.2	26.8	47.3	16.6	3.7	2.6	3.9	187.1
1972	94.7	32.2	52.6	15.5	5.4	3.3	3.6	207.3
1973	103.2	36.2	63.1	16.3	4.9	3.2	3.9	230.8
1974	119.0	38.6	75.1	16.8	5.0	3.3	5.4	263.2
1975	122.4	40.6	84.5	16.6	4.6	3.7	6.7	279.1
1976	131.6	41.4	90.8	17.0	5.2	4.1	8.0	298.1
1977	157.6	54.9	106.5	17.5	7.3	5.2	6.5	355.6
1978	181.0	60.0	121.0	18.4	5.3	6.6	7.4	399.6
1979	217.8	65.7	138.9	18.7	5.4	7.4	9.3	463.3
1980	244.1	64.6	157.8	24.3	6.4	7.2	12.7	517.1
1981	285.9	61.1	182.7	40.8	6.8	8.1	13.8	599.3
1982	297.7	49.2	201.5	36.3	8.0	8.9	16.2	617.8
1983	288.9	37.0	209.0	35.3	6.1	8.7	15.6	600.6
1984	298.4	56.9	239.4	37.4	6.0	11.4	17.0	666.4
1985	334.5	61.3	265.2	36.0	6.4	12.1	18.5	734.0
1986	349.0	63.1	283.9	32.9	7.0	13.3	19.9	769.2
1987	392.6	83.9	303.3	32.5	7.5	15.1	19.5	854.3
1988	401.2	94.5	334.3	35.2	7.6	16.2	20.2	909.2
1989	445.7	103.3	359.4	34.4	8.7	16.3	23.2	991.1
1990	466.9	93.5	380.0	35.3	11.5	16.7	28.0	1,032.0
1991	467.8	98.1	396.0	42.4	11.1	15.9	23.6	1,055.0
1992	476.0	100.3	413.7	45.6	11.1	17.4	27.2	1,091.2
1993	509.7	117.5	428.3	48.1	12.6	18.8	19.4	1,154.3
1994	543.1	140.4	461.5	55.2	15.2	20.1	23.1	1,258.6
1995	590.2	157.0	484.5	57.5	14.8	19.3	28.5	1,351.8
1996	656.4	171.8	509.4	54.0	17.2	18.7	25.5	1,453.1
1997	737.5	182.3	539.4	56.9	19.8	17.9	25.4	1,579.2
1998	828.6	188.7	571.8	57.7	24.1	18.3	32.6	1,721.7
1999	879.5	184.7	611.8	70.4	27.8	18.3	34.9	1,827.5
2000	1,004.5	207.3	652.9	68.9	29.0	19.9	42.8	2,025.2
2001	994.3	151.1	694.0	66.2	28.4	19.4	37.8	1,991.1
2002	858.3	148.0	700.8	67.0	26.5	18.6	33.9	1,853.1
2003	793.7	131.8	713.0	67.5	22.0	19.9	34.5	1,782.3
2004	809.0	189.4	733.4	69.9	24.8	21.1	32.6	1,880.1
2005	927.2	278.3	794.1	73.1	24.8	23.4	32.8	2,153.6
2006	1,043.9	353.9	837.8	74.0	27.9	24.8	44.6	2,406.9
2007	1,163.5	370.2	869.6	65.1	26.0	26.0	47.6	2,568.0
2008	1,145.7	304.3	900.2	67.3	28.8	27.6	50.0	2,524.0
2009	915.3	138.2	890.9	62.5	23.5	22.5	51.7	2,104.6

Sources: Congressional Budget Office; Office of Management and Budget.

Table F-4. Revenues by Major Source, 1970 to 2009, as a Percentage of Gross Domestic Product

	Individual Income Taxes	Corporate Income Taxes	Social Insurance Taxes	Excise Taxes	Estate and Gift Taxes	Customs Duties	Miscellaneous Receipts	Total Revenues
1970	8.9	3.2	4.4	1.6	0.4	0.2	0.3	19.0
1971	8.0	2.5	4.4	1.5	0.3	0.2	0.4	17.3
1972	8.1	2.7	4.5	1.3	0.5	0.3	0.3	17.6
1973	7.9	2.8	4.8	1.2	0.4	0.2	0.3	17.6
1974	8.3	2.7	5.2	1.2	0.4	0.2	0.4	18.3
1975	7.8	2.6	5.4	1.1	0.3	0.2	0.4	17.9
1976	7.6	2.4	5.2	1.0	0.3	0.2	0.5	17.1
1977	8.0	2.8	5.4	0.9	0.4	0.3	0.3	18.0
1978	8.2	2.7	5.5	0.8	0.2	0.3	0.3	18.0
1979	8.7	2.6	5.6	0.7	0.2	0.3	0.4	18.5
1980	9.0	2.4	5.8	0.9	0.2	0.3	0.5	19.0
1981	9.4	2.0	6.0	1.3	0.2	0.3	0.5	19.6
1982	9.2	1.5	6.3	1.1	0.2	0.3	0.5	19.2
1983	8.4	1.1	6.1	1.0	0.2	0.3	0.5	17.5
1984	7.8	1.5	6.2	1.0	0.2	0.3	0.4	17.3
1985	8.1	1.5	6.4	0.9	0.2	0.3	0.4	17.7
1986	7.9	1.4	6.4	0.7	0.2	0.3	0.5	17.5
1987	8.4	1.8	6.5	0.7	0.2	0.3	0.4	18.4
1988	8.0	1.9	6.7	0.7	0.2	0.3	0.4	18.2
1989	8.3	1.9	6.7	0.6	0.2	0.3	0.4	18.4
1990	8.1	1.6	6.6	0.6	0.2	0.3	0.5	18.0
1991	7.9	1.7	6.7	0.7	0.2	0.3	0.4	17.8
1992	7.6	1.6	6.6	0.7	0.2	0.3	0.4	17.5
1993	7.7	1.8	6.5	0.7	0.2	0.3	0.3	17.5
1994	7.8	2.0	6.6	0.8	0.2	0.3	0.3	18.0
1995	8.0	2.1	6.6	0.8	0.2	0.3	0.4	18.4
1996	8.5	2.2	6.6	0.7	0.2	0.2	0.3	18.8
1997	9.0	2.2	6.6	0.7	0.2	0.2	0.3	19.2
1998	9.6	2.2	6.6	0.7	0.3	0.2	0.4	19.9
1999	9.6	2.0	6.6	0.8	0.3	0.2	0.4	19.8
2000	10.2	2.1	6.6	0.7	0.3	0.2	0.4	20.6
2001	9.7	1.5	6.8	0.6	0.3	0.2	0.4	19.5
2002	8.1	1.4	6.6	0.6	0.3	0.2	0.3	17.6
2003	7.2	1.2	6.5	0.6	0.2	0.2	0.3	16.2
2004	6.9	1.6	6.3	0.6	0.2	0.2	0.3	16.1
2005	7.5	2.2	6.4	0.6	0.2	0.2	0.3	17.3
2006	7.9	2.7	6.3	0.6	0.2	0.2	0.3	18.2
2007	8.4	2.7	6.3	0.5	0.2	0.2	0.3	18.5
2008	7.9	2.1	6.2	0.5	0.2	0.2	0.3	17.5
2009	6.4	1.0	6.3	0.4	0.2	0.2	0.4	14.8

Sources: Congressional Budget Office; Office of Management and Budget.

Table F-5. Outlays for Major Categories of Spending, 1970 to 2009, in Billions of Dollars

	Discretionary Spending	Mandatory Spending		Net Interest	Total Outlays
		Programmatic Spending[a]	Offsetting Receipts		
1970	120.3	72.4	-11.5	14.4	195.6
1971	122.5	86.9	-14.1	14.8	210.2
1972	128.5	100.8	-14.1	15.5	230.7
1973	130.4	116.0	-18.0	17.3	245.7
1974	138.2	130.9	-21.2	21.4	269.4
1975	158.0	169.5	-18.3	23.2	332.3
1976	175.6	189.1	-19.6	26.7	371.8
1977	197.1	203.7	-21.5	29.9	409.2
1978	218.7	227.4	-22.8	35.5	458.7
1979	240.0	247.0	-25.6	42.6	504.0
1980	276.3	291.3	-29.2	52.5	590.9
1981	307.9	339.4	-37.9	68.8	678.2
1982	326.0	370.8	-36.0	85.0	745.7
1983	353.3	410.6	-45.3	89.8	808.4
1984	379.4	405.6	-44.2	111.1	851.8
1985	415.8	448.2	-47.1	129.5	946.3
1986	438.5	461.8	-45.9	136.0	990.4
1987	444.2	474.2	-52.9	138.6	1,004.0
1988	464.4	505.1	-56.8	151.8	1,064.4
1989	488.8	545.8	-59.9	169.0	1,143.7
1990	500.6	625.1	-57.0	184.3	1,253.0
1991	533.3	701.5	-105.0	194.4	1,324.2
1992	533.8	716.9	-68.5	199.3	1,381.5
1993	539.4	736.1	-64.8	198.7	1,409.4
1994	541.4	785.7	-68.2	202.9	1,461.8
1995	544.9	816.8	-78.0	232.1	1,515.8
1996	532.7	857.1	-70.4	241.1	1,560.5
1997	547.2	895.2	-85.2	244.0	1,601.1
1998	552.1	942.5	-83.2	241.1	1,652.5
1999	572.0	979.2	-79.1	229.8	1,701.8
2000	614.8	1,031.8	-80.5	222.9	1,789.0
2001	649.3	1,096.1	-88.7	206.2	1,862.9
2002	734.3	1,195.6	-89.9	170.9	2,010.9
2003	825.4	1,282.0	-100.6	153.1	2,159.9
2004	895.5	1,346.2	-109.0	160.2	2,292.9
2005	968.5	1,447.3	-127.8	184.0	2,472.0
2006	1,016.7	1,552.2	-140.5	226.6	2,655.1
2007	1,040.9	1,628.3	-177.6	237.1	2,728.7
2008	1,134.8	1,788.1	-193.1	252.8	2,982.6
2009	1,237.0	2,288.7	-194.7	187.3	3,518.2

Sources: Congressional Budget Office; Office of Management and Budget.

[a] Excludes offsetting receipts.

Table F-6. Outlays for Major Categories of Spending, 1970 to 2009, as a Percentage of Gross Domestic Product

	Discretionary Spending	Mandatory Spending		Net Interest	Total Outlays
		Programmatic Spending[a]	Offsetting Receipts		
1970	11.9	7.2	-1.1	1.4	19.3
1971	11.3	8.1	-1.3	1.4	19.5
1972	10.9	8.6	-1.2	1.3	19.6
1973	9.9	8.9	-1.4	1.3	18.7
1974	9.6	9.1	-1.5	1.5	18.7
1975	10.1	10.9	-1.2	1.5	21.3
1976	10.1	10.9	-1.1	1.5	21.4
1977	10.0	10.3	-1.1	1.5	20.7
1978	9.9	10.3	-1.0	1.6	20.7
1979	9.6	9.9	-1.0	1.7	20.2
1980	10.1	10.7	-1.1	1.9	21.7
1981	10.1	11.1	-1.2	2.3	22.2
1982	10.1	11.5	-1.1	2.6	23.1
1983	10.3	11.9	-1.3	2.6	23.5
1984	9.9	10.5	-1.2	2.9	22.2
1985	10.0	10.8	-1.1	3.1	22.8
1986	10.0	10.5	-1.0	3.1	22.5
1987	9.5	10.2	-1.1	3.0	21.6
1988	9.3	10.1	-1.1	3.0	21.3
1989	9.1	10.1	-1.1	3.1	21.2
1990	8.7	10.9	-1.0	3.2	21.9
1991	9.0	11.8	-1.8	3.3	22.3
1992	8.6	11.5	-1.1	3.2	22.1
1993	8.2	11.2	-1.0	3.0	21.4
1994	7.8	11.3	-1.0	2.9	21.0
1995	7.4	11.1	-1.1	3.2	20.6
1996	6.9	11.1	-0.9	3.1	20.2
1997	6.7	10.9	-1.0	3.0	19.5
1998	6.4	10.9	-1.0	2.8	19.1
1999	6.2	10.6	-0.9	2.5	18.5
2000	6.3	10.5	-0.8	2.3	18.2
2001	6.3	10.7	-0.9	2.0	18.2
2002	7.0	11.3	-0.9	1.6	19.1
2003	7.5	11.7	-0.9	1.4	19.7
2004	7.7	11.5	-0.9	1.4	19.6
2005	7.8	11.6	-1.0	1.5	19.9
2006	7.7	11.7	-1.1	1.7	20.1
2007	7.5	11.7	-1.3	1.7	19.6
2008	7.9	12.4	-1.3	1.8	20.7
2009	8.7	16.1	-1.4	1.3	24.7

Sources: Congressional Budget Office; Office of Management and Budget.

a. Excludes offsetting receipts.

Table F-7. Discretionary Outlays, 1970 to 2009, in Billions of Dollars

	Defense	International	Domestic	Total
1970	81.9	4.0	34.4	120.3
1971	79.0	3.8	39.7	122.5
1972	79.3	4.6	44.6	128.5
1973	77.1	4.8	48.5	130.4
1974	80.7	6.2	51.3	138.2
1975	87.6	8.2	62.2	158.0
1976	89.9	3.3	82.4	175.6
1977	97.5	8.0	91.6	197.1
1978	104.6	8.5	105.6	218.7
1979	116.8	9.1	114.1	240.0
1980	134.6	12.8	128.9	276.3
1981	158.0	13.6	136.3	307.9
1982	185.9	12.9	127.2	326.0
1983	209.9	13.6	129.8	353.3
1984	228.0	16.3	135.1	379.4
1985	253.1	17.4	145.3	415.8
1986	273.8	17.7	147.0	438.5
1987	282.5	15.2	146.5	444.2
1988	290.9	15.7	157.8	464.4
1989	304.0	16.6	168.2	488.8
1990	300.1	19.1	181.4	500.6
1991	319.7	19.7	193.9	533.3
1992	302.6	19.2	212.0	533.8
1993	292.4	21.6	225.4	539.4
1994	282.3	20.8	238.3	541.4
1995	273.6	20.1	251.2	544.9
1996	266.0	18.3	248.4	532.7
1997	271.7	19.0	256.5	547.2
1998	270.2	18.1	263.8	552.1
1999	275.5	19.5	277.0	572.0
2000	295.0	21.3	298.5	614.8
2001	306.1	22.5	320.7	649.3
2002	349.0	26.2	359.1	734.3
2003	405.0	27.9	392.5	825.4
2004	454.1	33.8	407.6	895.5
2005	493.6	39.0	435.9	968.5
2006	520.0	36.1	460.6	1,016.7
2007	547.9	34.8	458.2	1,040.9
2008	612.4	37.5	484.9	1,134.8
2009	655.8	43.0	538.1	1,237.0

Sources: Congressional Budget Office; Office of Management and Budget.

Table F-8. Discretionary Outlays, 1970 to 2009, as a Percentage of Gross Domestic Product

	Defense	International	Domestic	Total
1970	8.1	0.4	3.4	11.9
1971	7.3	0.3	3.7	11.3
1972	6.7	0.4	3.8	10.9
1973	5.9	0.4	3.7	9.9
1974	5.6	0.4	3.6	9.6
1975	5.6	0.5	4.0	10.1
1976	5.2	0.2	4.7	10.1
1977	4.9	0.4	4.6	10.0
1978	4.7	0.4	4.8	9.9
1979	4.7	0.4	4.6	9.6
1980	4.9	0.5	4.7	10.1
1981	5.2	0.4	4.5	10.1
1982	5.8	0.4	3.9	10.1
1983	6.1	0.4	3.8	10.3
1984	5.9	0.4	3.5	9.9
1985	6.1	0.4	3.5	10.0
1986	6.2	0.4	3.3	10.0
1987	6.1	0.3	3.1	9.5
1988	5.8	0.3	3.1	9.3
1989	5.6	0.3	3.1	9.1
1990	5.2	0.3	3.2	8.7
1991	5.4	0.3	3.3	9.0
1992	4.8	0.3	3.4	8.6
1993	4.4	0.3	3.4	8.2
1994	4.0	0.3	3.4	7.8
1995	3.7	0.3	3.4	7.4
1996	3.4	0.2	3.2	6.9
1997	3.3	0.2	3.1	6.7
1998	3.1	0.2	3.0	6.4
1999	3.0	0.2	3.0	6.2
2000	3.0	0.2	3.0	6.3
2001	3.0	0.2	3.1	6.3
2002	3.3	0.2	3.4	7.0
2003	3.7	0.3	3.6	7.5
2004	3.9	0.3	3.5	7.7
2005	4.0	0.3	3.5	7.8
2006	3.9	0.3	3.5	7.7
2007	3.9	0.3	3.3	7.5
2008	4.2	0.3	3.4	7.9
2009	4.6	0.3	3.8	8.7

Sources: Congressional Budget Office; Office of Management and Budget.

Table F-9. Outlays for Mandatory Spending, 1970 to 2009, in Billions of Dollars

	Social Security	Medicare	Medicaid	Income Security[a]	Other Retirement and Disability	Other Programs	Offsetting Receipts	Total
1970	29.6	6.8	2.7	8.2	12.4	12.7	-11.5	60.9
1971	35.1	7.5	3.4	13.4	14.5	13.1	-14.1	72.9
1972	39.4	8.4	4.6	16.4	16.2	15.8	-14.1	86.7
1973	48.2	9.0	4.6	14.5	18.5	21.3	-18.0	98.0
1974	55.0	10.7	5.8	17.4	20.9	21.2	-21.2	109.8
1975	63.6	14.1	6.8	28.9	26.4	29.6	-18.3	151.1
1976	72.7	16.9	8.6	37.6	27.7	25.6	-19.6	169.5
1977	83.7	20.8	9.9	34.6	31.2	23.6	-21.5	182.2
1978	92.4	24.3	10.7	32.1	33.9	34.0	-22.8	204.5
1979	102.6	28.2	12.4	32.2	38.7	32.9	-25.6	221.4
1980	117.1	34.0	14.0	44.3	44.4	37.6	-29.2	262.1
1981	137.9	41.3	16.8	49.9	50.8	42.6	-37.9	301.5
1982	153.9	49.2	17.4	53.2	55.0	42.1	-36.0	334.7
1983	168.5	55.5	19.0	64.0	58.0	45.6	-45.3	365.3
1984	176.1	61.1	20.1	51.7	59.8	36.8	-44.2	361.3
1985	186.4	69.7	22.7	52.3	61.0	56.2	-47.1	401.0
1986	196.5	74.2	25.0	54.2	63.4	48.4	-45.9	415.9
1987	205.1	79.9	27.4	55.0	66.5	40.2	-52.9	421.2
1988	216.8	85.7	30.5	57.3	71.1	43.7	-56.8	448.2
1989	230.4	93.2	34.6	46.8	57.3	83.5	-59.9	485.9
1990	246.5	107.0	41.1	51.0	60.0	119.5	-57.0	568.1
1991	266.8	114.2	52.5	61.3	64.4	142.3	-105.0	596.5
1992	285.2	129.4	67.8	72.4	66.5	95.6	-68.5	648.4
1993	302.0	143.2	75.8	79.8	68.4	66.9	-64.8	671.3
1994	316.9	159.6	82.0	88.3	72.3	66.5	-68.2	717.5
1995	333.3	177.1	89.1	94.3	75.3	47.8	-78.0	738.8
1996	347.1	191.3	92.0	98.3	77.3	51.1	-70.4	786.7
1997	362.3	207.9	95.6	101.0	80.6	47.9	-85.2	809.9
1998	376.1	211.0	101.2	101.8	83.0	69.4	-83.2	859.3
1999	387.0	209.3	108.0	107.2	85.7	82.0	-79.1	900.0
2000	406.0	216.0	117.9	112.8	88.1	90.9	-80.5	951.3
2001	429.4	237.9	129.4	114.7	93.0	91.8	-88.7	1,007.4
2002	452.1	253.7	147.5	129.1	96.1	117.2	-89.9	1,105.7
2003	470.5	274.2	160.7	141.0	99.9	135.9	-100.6	1,181.4
2004	491.5	297.2	176.2	189.9	104.0	87.3	-109.0	1,237.2
2005	518.7	332.6	181.7	196.1	111.8	106.4	-127.8	1,319.5
2006	543.9	373.6	180.6	199.2	113.5	141.4	-140.5	1,411.8
2007	581.4	436.0	190.6	202.4	122.9	95.0	-177.6	1,450.7
2008	612.1	456.0	201.4	259.9	129.4	129.2	-193.1	1,595.0
2009	677.7	499.0	250.9	348.5	138.1	374.5	-194.7	2,093.9

Sources: Congressional Budget Office; Office of Management and Budget.

a. Includes unemployment compensation, Supplemental Security Income, the refundable portion of the earned income and child tax credits, the Supplemental Nutrition Assistance Program (formerly known as Food Stamps), family support, child nutrition, and foster care.

Table F-10. Outlays for Mandatory Spending, 1970 to 2009, as a Percentage of Gross Domestic Product

	Social Security	Medicare	Medicaid	Income Security[a]	Other Retirement and Disability	Other Programs	Offsetting Receipts	Total
1970	2.9	0.7	0.3	0.8	1.2	1.3	-1.1	6.0
1971	3.3	0.7	0.3	1.2	1.3	1.2	-1.3	6.7
1972	3.3	0.7	0.4	1.4	1.4	1.3	-1.2	7.4
1973	3.7	0.7	0.4	1.1	1.4	1.6	-1.4	7.5
1974	3.8	0.7	0.4	1.2	1.4	1.5	-1.5	7.6
1975	4.1	0.9	0.4	1.9	1.7	1.9	-1.2	9.7
1976	4.2	1.0	0.5	2.2	1.6	1.5	-1.1	9.8
1977	4.2	1.1	0.5	1.8	1.6	1.2	-1.1	9.2
1978	4.2	1.1	0.5	1.4	1.5	1.5	-1.0	9.2
1979	4.1	1.1	0.5	1.3	1.5	1.3	-1.0	8.9
1980	4.3	1.2	0.5	1.6	1.6	1.4	-1.1	9.6
1981	4.5	1.4	0.6	1.6	1.7	1.4	-1.2	9.9
1982	4.8	1.5	0.5	1.7	1.7	1.3	-1.1	10.4
1983	4.9	1.6	0.6	1.9	1.7	1.3	-1.3	10.6
1984	4.6	1.6	0.5	1.3	1.6	1.0	-1.2	9.4
1985	4.5	1.7	0.5	1.3	1.5	1.4	-1.1	9.7
1986	4.5	1.7	0.6	1.2	1.4	1.1	-1.0	9.4
1987	4.4	1.7	0.6	1.2	1.4	0.9	-1.1	9.1
1988	4.3	1.7	0.6	1.1	1.4	0.9	-1.1	8.9
1989	4.3	1.7	0.6	0.9	1.1	1.5	-1.1	9.0
1990	4.3	1.9	0.7	0.9	1.0	2.1	-1.0	9.9
1991	4.5	1.9	0.9	1.0	1.1	2.4	-1.8	10.1
1992	4.6	2.1	1.1	1.2	1.1	1.5	-1.1	10.4
1993	4.6	2.2	1.2	1.2	1.0	1.0	-1.0	10.2
1994	4.5	2.3	1.2	1.3	1.0	1.0	-1.0	10.3
1995	4.5	2.4	1.2	1.3	1.0	0.7	-1.1	10.1
1996	4.5	2.5	1.2	1.3	1.0	0.7	-0.9	10.2
1997	4.4	2.5	1.2	1.2	1.0	0.6	-1.0	9.9
1998	4.3	2.4	1.2	1.2	1.0	0.8	-1.0	9.9
1999	4.2	2.3	1.2	1.2	0.9	0.9	-0.9	9.8
2000	4.1	2.2	1.2	1.1	0.9	0.9	-0.8	9.7
2001	4.2	2.3	1.3	1.1	0.9	0.9	-0.9	9.9
2002	4.3	2.4	1.4	1.2	0.9	1.1	-0.9	10.5
2003	4.3	2.5	1.5	1.3	0.9	1.2	-0.9	10.8
2004	4.2	2.5	1.5	1.6	0.9	0.7	-0.9	10.6
2005	4.2	2.7	1.5	1.6	0.9	0.9	-1.0	10.6
2006	4.1	2.8	1.4	1.5	0.9	1.1	-1.1	10.7
2007	4.2	3.1	1.4	1.5	0.9	0.7	-1.3	10.4
2008	4.2	3.2	1.4	1.8	0.9	0.9	-1.3	11.0
2009	4.8	3.5	1.8	2.4	1.0	2.6	-1.4	14.7

Sources: Congressional Budget Office; Office of Management and Budget.

a. Includes unemployment compensation, Supplemental Security Income, the refundable portion of the earned income and child tax credits, the Supplemental Nutrition Assistance Program (formerly known as Food Stamps), family support, child nutrition, and foster care.

Table F-11. Deficits, Surpluses, Debt, and Related Series, 1970 to 2009

	Billions of Dollars			Percentage of Potential GDP			Gross Domestic Product (Billions of dollars)	
		Cyclically Adjusted			Cyclically Adjusted			
	Deficit (-) or Surplus	Deficit (-) or Surplus	Debt Held by the Public	Deficit (-) or Surplus	Deficit (-) or Surplus	Debt Held by the Public	Actual[a]	Potential
1970	-3	-6	283	-0.3	-0.6	28.1	1,013	1,009
1971	-23	-19	303	-2.1	-1.7	27.7	1,080	1,095
1972	-23	-22	322	-2.0	-1.9	27.3	1,177	1,181
1973	-15	-27	341	-1.2	-2.2	26.8	1,311	1,272
1974	-6	-16	344	-0.4	-1.2	24.4	1,438	1,411
1975	-53	-36	395	-3.3	-2.2	24.4	1,560	1,617
1976	-74	-51	477	-4.1	-2.9	26.7	1,738	1,791
1977	-54	-42	549	-2.7	-2.1	27.4	1,974	2,002
1978	-59	-61	607	-2.7	-2.8	27.5	2,217	2,211
1979	-41	-50	640	-1.6	-2.0	25.9	2,501	2,476
1980	-74	-59	712	-2.7	-2.1	25.7	2,724	2,771
1981	-79	-58	789	-2.5	-1.9	25.4	3,057	3,109
1982	-128	-68	925	-3.8	-2.0	27.1	3,224	3,412
1983	-208	-124	1,137	-5.7	-3.4	31.0	3,441	3,671
1984	-185	-159	1,307	-4.7	-4.1	33.3	3,844	3,921
1985	-212	-199	1,507	-5.1	-4.8	36.0	4,146	4,182
1986	-221	-212	1,741	-5.0	-4.8	39.3	4,404	4,424
1987	-150	-138	1,890	-3.2	-2.9	40.3	4,651	4,687
1988	-155	-163	2,052	-3.1	-3.3	41.1	5,008	4,988
1989	-153	-175	2,191	-2.9	-3.3	41.0	5,399	5,342
1990	-221	-234	2,412	-3.9	-4.1	42.3	5,734	5,707
1991	-269	-216	2,689	-4.4	-3.5	44.1	5,930	6,092
1992	-290	-214	3,000	-4.5	-3.3	46.8	6,242	6,414
1993	-255	-193	3,248	-3.8	-2.9	48.3	6,587	6,727
1994	-203	-163	3,433	-2.9	-2.3	48.6	6,977	7,059
1995	-164	-138	3,604	-2.2	-1.9	48.6	7,341	7,418
1996	-107	-78	3,734	-1.4	-1.0	47.9	7,718	7,790
1997	-22	-28	3,772	-0.3	-0.3	46.1	8,212	8,183
1998	69	29	3,721	0.8	0.3	43.5	8,663	8,563
1999	126	38	3,632	1.4	0.4	40.5	9,208	8,978
2000	236	102	3,410	2.5	1.1	36.0	9,821	9,484
2001	128	48	3,320	1.3	0.5	33.0	10,225	10,070
2002	-158	-133	3,540	-1.5	-1.3	33.4	10,544	10,601
2003	-378	-306	3,913	-3.4	-2.7	35.0	10,980	11,166
2004	-413	-372	4,296	-3.5	-3.2	36.5	11,686	11,767
2005	-318	-313	4,592	-2.6	-2.5	36.9	12,446	12,451
2006	-248	-264	4,829	-1.9	-2.0	36.6	13,225	13,193
2007	-161	-162	5,035	-1.2	-1.2	36.2	13,896	13,922
2008	-459	-408	5,803	-3.1	-2.8	39.7	14,439	14,608
2009	-1414	-1105	7,544	-9.3	-7.3	49.7	14,236	15,168

Sources: Congressional Budget Office; Department of Commerce, Bureau of Economic Analysis; Office of Management and Budget.

a. CBO calculated fiscal year numbers from seasonally adjusted quarterly national income and product account data from the Bureau of Economic Analysis.

Table F-12. Cyclically Adjusted Deficit or Surplus and Related Series, 1970 to 2009, in Billions of Dollars

	Budget Deficit (-) or Surplus	Cyclical Contributions	Cyclically Adjusted Deficit (-) or Surplus	Cyclically Adjusted Revenues	Cyclically Adjusted Outlays
1970	-3	4	-6	192	198
1971	-23	-4	-19	191	210
1972	-23	-1	-22	209	231
1973	-15	12	-27	220	248
1974	-6	10	-16	255	272
1975	-53	-18	-36	293	329
1976	-74	-23	-51	313	364
1977	-54	-12	-42	364	405
1978	-59	2	-61	398	459
1979	-41	10	-50	456	506
1980	-74	-15	-59	528	588
1981	-79	-21	-58	615	673
1982	-128	-60	-68	665	733
1983	-208	-84	-124	663	787
1984	-185	-27	-159	689	848
1985	-212	-14	-199	744	943
1986	-221	-9	-212	775	987
1987	-150	-12	-138	866	1,004
1988	-155	8	-163	905	1,068
1989	-153	22	-175	973	1,148
1990	-221	13	-234	1,020	1,255
1991	-269	-53	-216	1,100	1,315
1992	-290	-76	-214	1,150	1,364
1993	-255	-63	-193	1,203	1,396
1994	-203	-40	-163	1,293	1,456
1995	-164	-25	-138	1,378	1,517
1996	-107	-30	-78	1,481	1,559
1997	-22	6	-28	1,575	1,603
1998	69	40	29	1,688	1,659
1999	126	87	38	1,747	1,709
2000	236	135	102	1,901	1,799
2001	128	80	48	1,915	1,867
2002	-158	-25	-133	1,861	1,994
2003	-378	-72	-306	1,837	2,143
2004	-413	-41	-372	1,911	2,283
2005	-318	-5	-313	2,160	2,473
2006	-248	16	-264	2,398	2,662
2007	-161	1	-162	2,574	2,736
2008	-459	-50	-408	2,565	2,973
2009	-1,414	-308	-1,105	2,327	3,433

Sources: Congressional Budget Office; Office of Management and Budget.

Table F-13. Cyclically Adjusted Deficit or Surplus and Related Series, 1970 to 2009, as a Percentage of Gross Domestic Product

	Budget Deficit (-) or Surplus	Cyclical Contributions	Cyclically Adjusted Deficit (-) or Surplus	Cyclically Adjusted Revenues	Cyclically Adjusted Outlays
1970	-0.3	0.4	-0.6	19.0	19.7
1971	-2.1	-0.4	-1.7	17.5	19.2
1972	-2.0	-0.1	-1.9	17.7	19.5
1973	-1.2	1.0	-2.2	17.3	19.5
1974	-0.4	0.7	-1.2	18.1	19.3
1975	-3.3	-1.1	-2.2	18.1	20.3
1976	-4.1	-1.3	-2.9	17.5	20.3
1977	-2.7	-0.6	-2.1	18.2	20.2
1978	-2.7	0.1	-2.8	18.0	20.8
1979	-1.6	0.4	-2.0	18.4	20.4
1980	-2.7	-0.5	-2.1	19.1	21.2
1981	-2.5	-0.7	-1.9	19.8	21.7
1982	-3.8	-1.7	-2.0	19.5	21.5
1983	-5.7	-2.3	-3.4	18.1	21.4
1984	-4.7	-0.7	-4.1	17.6	21.6
1985	-5.1	-0.3	-4.8	17.8	22.5
1986	-5.0	-0.2	-4.8	17.5	22.3
1987	-3.2	-0.3	-2.9	18.5	21.4
1988	-3.1	0.2	-3.3	18.1	21.4
1989	-2.9	0.4	-3.3	18.2	21.5
1990	-3.9	0.2	-4.1	17.9	22.0
1991	-4.4	-0.9	-3.5	18.0	21.6
1992	-4.5	-1.2	-3.3	17.9	21.3
1993	-3.8	-0.9	-2.9	17.9	20.7
1994	-2.9	-0.6	-2.3	18.3	20.6
1995	-2.2	-0.3	-1.9	18.6	20.4
1996	-1.4	-0.4	-1.0	19.0	20.0
1997	-0.3	0.1	-0.3	19.2	19.6
1998	0.8	0.5	0.3	19.7	19.4
1999	1.4	1.0	0.4	19.5	19.0
2000	2.5	1.4	1.1	20.0	19.0
2001	1.3	0.8	0.5	19.0	18.5
2002	-1.5	-0.2	-1.3	17.6	18.8
2003	-3.4	-0.6	-2.7	16.5	19.2
2004	-3.5	-0.3	-3.2	16.2	19.4
2005	-2.6	*	-2.5	17.3	19.9
2006	-1.9	0.1	-2.0	18.2	20.2
2007	-1.2	*	-1.2	18.5	19.7
2008	-3.1	-0.3	-2.8	17.6	20.4
2009	-9.3	-2.0	-7.3	15.3	22.6

Sources: Congressional Budget Office; Office of Management and Budget.
Note: * = between -0.05 percent and 0.05 percent.

APPENDIX G. CONTRIBUTORS TO THE REVENUE AND SPENDING PROJECTIONS

The following Congressional Budget Office staff prepared the revenue and spending projections in this report:

Revenue Projections

David Weiner	Deputy Assistant Director
Mark Booth	Unit Chief
Janet Holtzblatt	Unit Chief
Paul Burnham	Retirement income
Grant Driessen	Excise taxes
Barbara Edwards	Social insurance taxes, Federal Reserve System earnings
Zachary Epstein	Customs duties, miscellaneous receipts
Jennifer Gravelle	Depreciation
Pamela Greene	Corporate income taxes, estate and gift taxes
Ed Harris	Individual income taxes
Athiphat Muthitacharoen	Estate tax modeling
Larry Ozanne	Capital gains realizations
Kevin Perese	Tax modeling
Kristy Piccinini	Capital gains realizations
Kurt Seibert	Refundable tax credits, depreciation
Joshua Shakin	Individual income taxes

Spending Projections

Defense, International Affairs, and Veterans' Affairs

Sarah Jennings	Unit Chief
John Chin	International development and security assistance, international financial institutions
Kent Christensen	Defense (projections, working capital funds, procurement, scorekeeping)
Sunita D'Monte	International affairs, veterans' health care
Raymond Hall	Defense (research and development, stockpile sales, atomic energy)
David Newman	Defense (military construction and family housing, military activities in Iraq and Afghanistan), veterans' housing
Dawn Sauter Regan	Defense (military personnel)
Matthew Schmit	Military retirement, military health care

Jason Wheelock	Defense (other programs, operations and maintenance, compensation for radiation exposure, compensation for energy employees' occupational illness)
Camille Woodland	Veterans' readjustment benefits, reservists' educational benefits, military retirement
Dwayne Wright	Veterans' compensation and pensions

Health Systems and Medicare

Thomas Bradey	Unit Chief
Stephanie Cameron	Medicare, Public Health Service
Mindy Cohen	Medicare
April Grady	Medicare
Jean Hearne	Medicare
Lori Housman	Medicare
Jamease Kowalczyk	Medicare, Public Health Service
Julie Lee	Medicare
Lara Robillard	Medicare

Income Security and Education

Sam Papenfuss	Unit Chief
Christina Hawley Anthony	Unemployment insurance, training programs, Administration on Aging, Smithsonian, arts and humanities, report coordinator
Chad Chirico	Housing assistance, Fannie Mae and Freddie Mac, Troubled Asset Relief Program
Sheila Dacey	Old-Age and Survivors Insurance, Social Security trust funds, Pension Benefit Guaranty Corporation
Kathleen FitzGerald	Supplemental Nutrition Assistance Program (formerly the Food Stamp program) and other nutrition programs
Emily Holcombe	Child nutrition
Justin Humphrey	Elementary and secondary education, Pell grants, student loans
Deborah Kalcevic	Student loans, higher education
Jonathan Morancy	Child Support Enforcement, Temporary Assistance for Needy Families, foster care, Social Services Block Grant program, child care programs, child and family services
David Rafferty	Disability Insurance, Supplemental Security Income

Income Security and Education (Continued)

Alan Stoffer	Low-Income Home Energy Assistance Program, refugee assistance, Pension Benefit Warranty Corporation

Low-Income Health Programs and Prescription Drugs

Kate Massey	Unit Chief
Julia Christensen	Food and Drug Administration, prescription drug issues
Sean Dunbar	Medicaid, Children's Health Insurance Program, Public Health Service
Kirstin Nelson	Medicaid, Federal Employees Health Benefits program, Public Health Service
Andrea Noda	Medicare Part D, Medicaid prescription drug policy, Public Health Service
Lisa Ramirez-Branum	Medicaid, Public Health Service
Robert Stewart	Medicaid, Children's Health Insurance Program, Indian Health Service
Ellen Werble	Food and Drug Administration, prescription drug issues, Public Health Service
Rebecca Yip	Medicare Part D, Medicaid prescription drug policy

Natural and Physical Resources

Kim Cawley	Unit Chief
Megan Carroll	Energy, air transportation
Mark Grabowicz	Justice, Postal Service
Kathleen Gramp	Deposit insurance, energy, Outer Continental Shelf receipts, spectrum auction receipts
Gregory Hitz	Agriculture
Daniel Hoople	Community and regional development, Federal Emergency Management Agency, deposit insurance
David Hull	Agriculture
Jeff LaFave	Science and space exploration, Bureau of Indian Affairs, conservation and land management, other natural resources
James Langley	Agriculture
Susanne Mehlman	Pollution control and abatement, Federal Housing Administration and other housing credit programs
Matthew Pickford	General government
Sarah Puro	Highways, Amtrak
Deborah Reis	Recreation, water transportation, legislative branch, conservation and land management
Aurora Swanson	Water resources, Fannie Mae and Freddie Mac
Susan Willie	Mass transit, commerce, Small Business Administration, Universal Service Fund

Other

Janet Airis	Unit Chief, Scorekeeping; legislative branch appropriation bill
Jeffrey Holland	Unit Chief, Projections
Shane Beaulieu	Computer support
Edward Blau	Authorization bills
Barry Blom	Federal pay, monthly Treasury data, report coordinator

Jared Brewster	Interest on the public debt, national income and product accounts, report coordinator
Joanna Capps	Appropriation bills (Interior and the environment, Labor–Health and Human Services)
Mary Froehlich	Computer support
Wendy Kiska	Troubled Asset Relief Program
Amber Marcellino	Federal civilian retirement, other interest, report coordinator
Joseph Mattey	Deposit insurance
Damien Moore	Fannie Mae and Freddie Mac
Virginia Myers	Appropriation bills (Commerce–Justice, financial services, general government)
Jennifer Reynolds	Appropriation bills (Agriculture, foreign relations)
Mark Sanford	Appropriation bills (Defense, Homeland Security)
Esther Steinbock	Appropriation bills (Transportation–Housing and Urban Development, military construction and veterans' affairs, energy and water)
Santiago Vallinas	Other retirement, Report coordinator
Patrice Watson	Database system administrator

GLOSSARY

This glossary defines economic and budgetary terms as they apply to *The Budget and Economic Outlook;* it also acts as a general reference for readers. In some cases, the entries sacrifice technical precision for the sake of brevity and clarity. Where appropriate, entries note the sources of data for economic variables as follows:

- (BEA) refers to the Bureau of Economic Analysis in the Department of Commerce,
- (BLS) refers to the Bureau of Labor Statistics in the Department of Labor,
- (CBO) refers to the Congressional Budget Office,
- (FRB) refers to the Federal Reserve Board, and
- (NBER) refers to the National Bureau of Economic Research (a private entity).

Accrual accounting: A system of accounting in which revenues are recorded when they are earned and outlays are recorded when goods are received or services are performed, even though the actual receipt of revenues and payment for goods or services may occur, in whole or in part, at a different time. Compare with cash accounting.

adjusted gross income (AGI): All income that is subject to taxation under the individual income tax after "above-the-line" deductions for such things as alimony payments and certain contributions to individual retirement accounts. Personal exemptions and the standard or itemized deductions are subtracted from AGI to determine taxable income.

advance appropriation: Budget authority provided in an appropriation act that is first available for obligation in a fiscal year after the year for which the appropriation was enacted. The amount of the advance appropriation is included in the budget totals for the year in which it will become available. See appropriation act, budget authority, fiscal year, and obligation; compare with forward funding, obligation delay, and unobligated balances.

aggregate demand: Total purchases of a country's output of goods and services by consumers, businesses, governments, and foreigners during a given period. (BEA) Compare with domestic demand.

AGI: See adjusted gross income.

alternative minimum tax (AMT): A tax intended to limit the extent to which higher-income people can reduce their tax liability (the amount they owe) through the use of preferences in the tax code. Taxpayers subject to the AMT are required to recalculate their tax liability on the basis of a more limited set of exemptions, deductions, and tax credits than would normally apply. The amount by which a taxpayer's AMT calculation exceeds his or her regular tax calculation is that person's AMT liability.

American Recovery and Reinvestment Act of 2009 (ARRA, Public Law 111-5): This act provided appropriations for several federal programs and increased or extended some benefits payable under Medicaid, unemployment compensation, and nutrition assistance, among others. ARRA also reduced individual and corporate income taxes and made other changes to tax laws.

AMT: See alternative minimum tax.

appropriation act: A law or legislation under the jurisdiction of the House and Senate Committees on Appropriations that provides authority for federal programs or agencies to incur obligations and make payments from the Treasury. Each year, the Congress considers regular appropriation acts, which fund the operations of the federal government for the upcoming fiscal year. The Congress may also consider supplemental, deficiency, or continuing appropriation acts (joint resolutions that provide budget authority for a fiscal year until the regular appropriation for that year is enacted). See budget authority, fiscal year, and obligation.

ARRA: See American Recovery and Reinvestment Act of 2009.

asset-backed security: Security backed by real estate or another type of asset; a claim on an income flow, such as expected interest payments on loans, payments on leases, royalty payments, or receivables; a claim on the principal of a loan; or a claim on the expected appreciation of an asset.

authorization act: A law or legislation under the jurisdiction of a committee *other than* the House and Senate Committees on Appropriations that establishes or continues the operation of a federal program or agency, either indefinitely or for a specified period. An authorization act may suggest the budget authority needed to fund the program or agency, which is then provided in a future appropriation act. However, for some programs, the authorization itself may provide the budget authority. See appropriation act and budget authority.

automatic stabilizers: Taxes that decrease and expenditures that increase when the economy goes into a recession (and vice-versa when the economy booms) without requiring any action on the part of the government. Stabilizers tend to reduce the depth of recessions and dampen booms.

Balanced Budget and Emergency Deficit Control Act of 1985 (Public Law 99-177): Referred to in CBO's reports as the Deficit Control Act, it also has been known as Gramm-Rudman-Hollings. Among other changes to the budget process, the law established rules that governed the calculation of CBO's baseline. In addition, it set specific deficit targets as well as procedures for sequestration to reduce spending if those targets were exceeded. The targets were changed to discretionary spending limits and pay-as-you-go (PAYGO) controls by the Budget Enforcement Act of 1990. However, the discretionary spending limits and the sequestration procedure to enforce them expired on September 30, 2002. PAYGO and its sequestration procedure were rendered ineffective on December 2, 2002, when P.L. 107-312 reduced all PAYGO balances to zero. The remaining provisions, including the rules that govern the calculation of the baseline, expired on September 30, 2006. CBO, however, continues to follow the methodology prescribed in the law for establishing baselines. See baseline, discretionary spending limits, pay-as-you-go, and sequestration.

baseline: A benchmark for measuring the budgetary effects of proposed changes in federal revenues or spending. As defined in the Deficit Control Act, the baseline is the projection of new budget authority, outlays, revenues, and the deficit or surplus into the budget year and out-years on the basis of current laws and policies, calculated following the rules set forth in section 257 of that law. Section 257 expired in September 2006, but CBO continues to prepare baselines following the methodology prescribed in the section. Estimates consistent with section 257 are used by the House and Senate Committees on the Budget in implementing the pay-as-you-go rules in each House. See Balanced Budget and Emergency Deficit Control Act of 1985, budget authority, deficit, fiscal year, outlays, pay-as-you-go, revenues, and surplus.

basis point: One one-hundredth of a percentage point. (For example, the difference between interest rates of 5.5percent and 5.0 percent is 50 basis points.)

***Blue Chip* consensus forecast:** The average of about 50private-sector economic forecasts compiled and published monthly by Aspen Publishers, Inc.

book depreciation: See depreciation.

book profits: Profits calculated using book (or tax) depreciation and standard accounting conventions for inventories. Different from economic profits, book profits are referred to as "profits before tax" in the national income and product accounts. See depreciation, economic profits, and national income and product accounts.

budget authority: Authority provided by law to incur financial obligations that will result in immediate or future outlays of federal government funds. Budget authority may be provided in an appropriation act or authorization act and may take the form of borrowing authority, contract authority, entitlement authority, or authority to obligate and expend offsetting collections or receipts. Offsetting collections and receipts are classified as negative budget authority. See appropriation act, authorization act, contract authority, offsetting collections, offsetting receipts, and outlays.

Budget Enforcement Act of 1990: Among other changes to the budget process, this law established discretionary spending limits and pay-as-you-go controls by amending the Balanced Budget and Emergency Deficit Control Act of 1985. See Balanced Budget and Emergency Deficit Control Act of 1985, discretionary spending limits, and pay-as-you-go.

budget function: One of 20 general-subject categories into which budgetary resources are grouped so that all budget authority and outlays can be presented according to the national interests being addressed. There are 17 broad budget functions, including national defense, international affairs, energy, agriculture, health, income security, and general government. Three other functions—net interest, allowances, and undistributed offsetting receipts—are included to complete the budget. See budget authority, net interest, offsetting receipts, and outlays.

budget resolution: A concurrent resolution, adopted by both Houses of Congress, that sets forth a Congressional budget plan for the budget year and at least four out-years. The plan consists of targets for spending and revenues; subsequent appropriation acts and authorization acts that affect revenues or direct spending are expected to comply with those targets. The targets are enforced in each House of Congress through procedural mechanisms set forth in law and in the rules of each House. See appropriation act, authorization act, direct spending, fiscal year, and revenues.

budget year: See fiscal year.

budgetary resources: All sources of authority provided to federal agencies that permit them to incur financial obligations, including new budget authority, unobligated balances, direct spending authority, and obligation limitations. See budget authority, direct spending, obligation limitation, and unobligated balances.

business cycle: Fluctuations in overall business activity accompanied by swings in the unemployment rate, interest rates, and corporate profits. Over a business cycle, real (inflation-adjusted) activity rises to a *peak* (its highest level during the cycle) and then falls until it reaches a *trough* (its lowest level following the peak), whereupon it starts to rise again, defining a new cycle. Business cycles are irregular, varying in frequency, magnitude, and duration. (NBER) See real and unemployment rate.

business fixed investment: Spending by businesses on structures, equipment, and software. Such investment is labeled "fixed" to distinguish it from investment in inventories. See inventories.

Capacity utilization rate: The seasonally adjusted output of the nation's factories, mines, and electric and gas utilities expressed as a percentage of their capacity to produce output. A facility's capacity is the greatest output it can maintain with a normal work pattern. (FRB)

capital: Tangible and intangible resources that can be used or invested to produce a stream of benefits over time. *Physical capital*—also known as *fixed capital* or the *capital stock*—consists of land and the stock of products set aside to support future production and consumption, including business inventories and *capital goods* (residential and nonresidential structures and producers' durable equipment). *Human capital* is the education, training, work experience, and other attributes that enhance the ability of the labor force to produce goods and services. The *capital* of a business is the sum advanced and put at risk by the business's owners: For example, *bank capital* is the sum put at risk by the owners of a bank. In an accounting sense, capital is a business's net worth or equity—the difference between its assets and liabilities. *Financial capital* is wealth held in the form of financial instruments (such as stocks, bonds, and mortgages) rather than held directly in the form of physical capital.

capital gains and losses: The increase or decrease in the value of an asset that comes from the increase or decrease in the asset's market price after its purchase. A capital gain or loss is "realized" when the asset is sold.

capital income: Income derived from wealth, such as stock dividends, realized capital gains, or the owner's profits from a business. See capital gains and losses.

capital services: A measure of how much the stock of physical capital contributes to the flow of production.

cash accounting: A system of accounting in which revenues are recorded when they are actually received and outlays are recorded when payment is made. Compare with accrual accounting.

central bank: A government-established agency responsible for conducting monetary policy and overseeing credit conditions. The Federal Reserve System fulfills those functions in the United States. See Federal Reserve System and monetary policy.

central tendency: The range of projections, truncated to exclude the three highest and the three lowest projections, in the Federal Open Market Committee's quarterly reports on the economic projections of the Federal Reserve's governors and Reserve Bank presidents. Those reports are published twice a year in the minutes of the Federal Open Market Committee meetings and twice a year in the Federal Reserve's *Monetary Policy Report.*

COLA: See cost-of-living adjustment.

commercial paper: A short-term money market security, generally sold by a large bank or corporation to raise funds to meet short term obligations (for example, payroll) that is sometimes backed by collateral but more typically is backed by the good faith of the borrower.

compensation: All of the income due to an employee for his or her work during a given period. In addition to wages, salaries, bonuses, and stock options, compensation includes fringe benefits and the employer's share of payroll taxes for social insurance programs, such as Social Security. (BEA)

Congressional Budget Act of 1974: The short title for Titles I–IX of the Congressional Budget and Impoundment Control Act of 1974, as amended (2 U.S.C. §§ 601–661). The act established a process through which the Congress could systematically consider the total spending policy of the United States and determine priorities for allocating budgetary resources. The process calls for procedures for coordinating Congressional revenue and spending decisions made in separate tax, appropriations, and legislative measures. It established the House and Senate Budget Committees, the Congressional Budget Office, and the requirements for adopting concurrent resolutions on the budget and the reconciliation process. See Balanced Budget and Emergency Deficit Control Act of 1985, credit reform, and UMRA.

conservatorship: The legal process by which an external entity (in the case of Fannie Mae and Freddie Mac, the federal government) establishes control and oversight of a company to put it in a sound and solvent condition.

constant dollar: A measure of spending or revenues in a given year that has been adjusted for differences in prices (such as inflation) between that year and a base year. See inflation and real; compare with current dollar and nominal.

consumer confidence: An index of consumer optimism that is based on surveys of consumers' attitudes about current and future economic conditions. One such measure, the index of consumer sentiment, is constructed by the University of Michigan's Survey Research Center. The Conference Board constructs a similar measure, the consumer confidence index.

consumer price index (CPI): An index of the cost of living commonly used to measure inflation. The Bureau of Labor Statistics publishes the CPI-U, an index of consumer prices based on the typical market basket of goods and services consumed by all urban consumers, and the CPI-W, an index of consumer prices based on the typical market basket of goods and services consumed by urban wage earners and clerical workers. (BLS) See inflation.

consumer sentiment index: See consumer confidence.

consumption: In principle, the value of goods and services purchased and used up during a given period by households and governments. In practice, the Bureau of Economic Analysis counts purchases of many long-lasting goods (such as cars and clothes) as consumption even though the goods are not used up. Consumption by households alone is also called consumer spending. See national income and product accounts.

contract authority: Authority provided by law to enter into contracts or incur other obligations in advance of, or in excess of, funds available for that purpose. Although it is a form of budget authority, contract authority does not provide the funds to make payments.

Those funds must be provided later, usually in a subsequent appropriation act (called a liquidating appropriation). Contract authority differs from a federal agency's inherent authority to enter into contracts, which may be exercised only within the limits of available appropriations. See appropriation act, budget authority, and obligation.

core inflation: A measure of the rate of inflation that excludes changes in the prices of food and energy. See consumer price index, inflation, and price index for personal consumption expenditures.

cost-of-living adjustment (COLA): An annual increase in payments to reflect price inflation.

CPI: See consumer price index.

credit reform: A system of budgeting and accounting for federal credit activities that focuses on the cost of subsidies conveyed in federal credit assistance. The system was established by the Federal Credit Reform Act of 1990 and took effect at the beginning of fiscal year 1992. See credit subsidy, Federal Credit Reform Act of 1990, financing account, liquidating account, and program account.

credit subsidy: The estimated long-term cost to the federal government of a direct loan or loan guarantee.

That cost is calculated on the basis of net present value, excluding federal administrative costs and any incidental effects on revenues or outlays. For direct loans, the subsidy cost is the net present value of loan disbursements minus repayments of interest and principal, adjusted for estimated defaults, prepayments, fees, penalties, and other recoveries. For loan guarantees, the subsidy cost is the net present value of estimated payments by the government to cover defaults and delinquencies, interest subsidies, or other payments, offset by any payments to the government, including origination and other fees, penalties, and recoveries. See outlays and present value.

current-account balance: A summary measure of a country's current transactions with the rest of the world, including net exports, net unilateral transfers, and net factor income (primarily the capital income from foreign property received by residents of a country offset by the capital income from property in that country flowing to residents of foreign countries). (BEA) See net exports and unilateral transfers.

current dollar: A measure of spending or revenues in a given year that has not been adjusted for differences in prices (such as inflation) between that year and a base year. See inflation and nominal; compare with constant dollar and real.

current year: The fiscal year in progress. See fiscal year.

cyclical deficit or surplus: The part of the federal budget deficit or surplus that results from the business cycle. The cyclical component reflects the way in which the deficit or surplus automatically increases or decreases during economic expansions or recessions.

(CBO) See business cycle, deficit, expansion, recession, and surplus; compare with cyclically adjusted budget deficit or surplus.

cyclically adjusted budget deficit or surplus: The federal budget deficit or surplus that would occur under current law if the influence of the business cycle was removed—that is, if the economy operated at potential gross domestic product. (CBO) See business cycle, deficit, potential gross domestic product, and surplus; compare with cyclical deficit or surplus.

Debt: In the case of the federal government, the total value of outstanding bills, notes, bonds, and other debt instruments issued by the Treasury and other federal agencies. That debt is referred to as *federal debt* or *gross debt.* It has two components: *debt held by the public* (federal debt held by nonfederal investors, including the Federal Reserve System) and *debt held by government accounts* (federal debt held by federal government trust funds, deposit insurance funds, and other federal accounts). *Debt subject to limit* is federal debt that is subject to a statutory limit on the total amount issued. The limit applies to gross federal debt except for a small portion of the debt issued by the Treasury and the small amount of debt issued by other federal agencies (primarily the Tennessee Valley Authority and the Postal Service).

debt service: Payment of scheduled interest obligations on outstanding debt. As used in *The Budget and Economic Outlook,* debt service refers to a change in interest payments resulting from a change in estimates of the deficit or surplus. See deficit, net interest, and surplus.

deficit: The amount by which the federal government's total outlays exceed its total revenues in a given period, typically a fiscal year. The *primary deficit* is that total deficit excluding net interest. See fiscal year, net interest, outlays, and revenues; compare with surplus.

Deficit Control Act: See Balanced Budget and Emergency Deficit Control Act of 1985.

deflation: A drop in prices that is so broadly based that general indexes of prices, such as the consumer price index, register continuing declines. Deflation is usually caused by a collapse in aggregate demand. See aggregate demand and consumer price index.

demand: See aggregate demand and domestic demand.

deposit insurance: The guarantee by a federal agency that an individual depositor at a participating depository institution will receive the full amount of the deposit (currently up to $250,000) if the institution becomes insolvent.

depreciation: A decline in the value of a currency, financial asset, or capital good. When applied to a capital good, depreciation usually refers to loss of value because of obsolescence, wear, or destruction (as by fire or flood) and is also called *consumption of fixed capital. Book depreciation* (also known as *tax depreciation*) is the depreciation that the tax code allows businesses to deduct when they calculate their taxable profits. It typically occurs more rapidly than *economic depreciation,* which is the actual decline in the value of an asset. Both measures of depreciation appear as part of the national income and product accounts. See book profits and national income and product accounts.

devaluation: The act of a government to lower the fixedexchange rate of its currency. The government implements a devaluation by announcing that it will no longer maintain the existing rate by buying and selling its currency at that rate. See exchange rate.

direct spending: Synonymous with *mandatory spending,* direct spending is the budget authority provided by laws other than appropriation acts and the outlays that result from that budget authority. (As used in *The Budget and Economic Outlook,* direct spending refers only to the outlays that result from budget authority provided in laws other than appropriation acts.) See appropriation act, budget authority, and outlays; compare with discretionary spending and entitlement.

discount rate: The interest rate that the Federal Reserve System charges on a loan it makes to a bank. Such loans, when allowed, enable a bank to meet its reserve requirements without reducing its lending. Alternatively, the discount rate is the interest rate used to compute the present value of future payments (such as for pension plans). See Federal Reserve System and present value.

discouraged workers: Jobless people who are available for work but not actively seeking it because they think they have poor prospects of finding a job. Discouraged workers are not included in measures of the labor force or the unemployment rate. (BLS) See labor force and unemployment rate.

discretionary spending: The budget authority that is provided and controlled by appropriation acts and the outlays that result from that budget authority. See appropriation act, budget authority, and outlays; compare with direct spending.

discretionary spending limits (or caps): Statutory ceilings imposed on the amount of budget authority provided in appropriation acts in a fiscal year and on the outlays that are made in that year. The limits originally were established in the Budget Enforcement Act of 1990. Under that law, if the estimated budget authority provided in all appropriation acts for a fiscal year (or the outlays resulting from that budget authority) exceeded the spending limit for that year, a sequestration—a cancellation of budget authority provided for programs funded by appropriation acts—would be triggered. All discretionary spending limits and the sequestration procedure to enforce them expired on September 30, 2002. See appropriation act, Balanced Budget and Emergency Deficit Control Act of 1985, budget authority, Budget Enforcement Act of 1990, discretionary spending, fiscal year, outlays, and sequestration.

disposable personal income: Personal income—the income that people receive, including transfer payments—minus the taxes and fees that people pay to governments. (BEA) See transfer payments.

domestic demand: Total purchases of goods and services, regardless of their origin, by U.S. consumers, businesses, and governments during a given period. Domestic demand equals gross domestic product minus net exports. (BEA) See gross domestic product and net exports; compare with aggregate demand.

ECI: See employment cost index.

Economic Growth and Tax Relief Reconciliation Act of 2001 (EGTRRA, Public Law 107-16): Legislation that significantly reduced tax liabilities (the amount of tax owed) between 2001 and 2010 by cutting individual income tax rates, increasing the child tax credit, repealing estate taxes, raising deductions for married couples who file joint returns, increasing tax benefits for pensions and individual retirement accounts, and creating additional tax benefits for education. EGTRRA phased in many of those changes, including some that just became fully effective in 2010. Although some of the law's provisions have been made permanent, most are scheduled to expire on or before December 31, 2010. For legislation that modified provisions of EGTRRA, see Jobs and Growth Tax Relief Reconciliation Act of 2003.

economic profits: Corporations' profits, adjusted to remove distortions in depreciation allowances caused by tax rules and to exclude the effect of inflation on the value of inventories. Economic profits are a better measure of profits from current production than are the book profits reported by corporations. Economic profits are referred to as "corporate profits with inventory valuation and capital consumption adjustments" in the national income and product accounts. (BEA) See book profits, depreciation, inflation, inventories, and national income and product accounts.

economic stimulus: Federal fiscal or monetary policies aimed at promoting economic activity, used primarily during recessions. Such policies include reductions in taxes, increases in federal spending, reductions in interest rates, and other support for financial markets and institutions.

effective tax rate: The ratio of taxes paid to a given tax base. For individual income taxes, the effective tax rate is typically expressed as the ratio of taxes paid to adjusted gross income. For corporate income taxes, it is the ratio of taxes paid to book profits. For some purposes—such as calculating an overall tax rate on all income—an effective tax rate is computed on a base that includes the untaxed portion of Social Security benefits, interest on tax-exempt bonds, and similar items. It can also be computed on a base of personal income as measured by the national income and product accounts. The effective tax rate is a useful measure because the tax code's various exemptions, credits, deductions, and tax rates make actual ratios of taxes paid to income different from statutory tax rates. See adjusted gross income and book profits; compare with marginal tax rate and statutory tax rate.

EGTRRA: See Economic Growth and Tax Relief Reconciliation Act of 2001.

Emergency Economic Stabilization Act of 2008 (Division A, Public Law 110-343): The law that created the Troubled Asset Relief Program to purchase and insure some types of assets thus promoting stability in financial markets. See Troubled Asset Relief Program.

emergency liquidity facilities: Programs the Federal Reserve established in response to the 2008–2009 financial crisis to provide short-term loans to financial institutions. Such lending helped avert the distressed sale of assets that could have caused some institutions to become insolvent or enter bankruptcy.

employment: Work performed or services rendered in exchange for compensation. Two estimates of employment are commonly used. One comes from the so-called establishment survey of employers (the Department of Labor's Current Employment Statistics Survey), which measures employment as the estimated number of nonfarm wage and salary jobs. (Thus, a person with more than one job may be counted more than once.) The other estimate comes from the so-called household survey (the Census Bureau's Current Population Survey), which measures employment as the estimated number of people employed. (Thus, someone with more than one job is counted only once.) The household survey is based on a smaller sample than the establishment survey and therefore yields a more volatile estimate of employment. See compensation and unemployment rate.

employment cost index (ECI): An index of the weighted-average cost of an hour of labor—comprising the cost to the employer of wage and salary payments, employee benefits, and payroll taxes for social insurance programs, such as Social Security. The ECI is structured so that it is not affected by changes in the mix of occupations in the labor force or the mix of employment by industry. (BLS)

entitlement: A legal obligation of the federal government to make payments to a person, group of people, business, unit of government, or similar entity that meets the eligibility criteria set in law and for which the budget authority is not provided in advance in an appropriation act. Spending for entitlement programs is controlled through those programs' eligibility criteria and benefit or payment rules. The best-known entitlements are the government's major benefit programs, such as Social Security and Medicare. See appropriation act and budget authority; compare with direct spending.

establishment survey: See employment.

estate and gift taxes: A linked set of federal taxes on estates, gifts, and generation-skipping transfers to tax the transfer of wealth from one generation to the next and to limit the extent to which wealth can be given away during life to avoid taxation at death.

exchange rate: The number of units of a foreign currency that can be bought with one unit of the domestic currency, or vice versa.

excise tax: A tax levied on the purchase of a specific type of good or service, such as tobacco products or air transportation services.

expansion: A phase of the business cycle that begins when gross domestic product exceeds its previous peak and extends until gross domestic product reaches its next peak. (NBER) See business cycle and gross domestic product; compare with recession and recovery.

expenditure account: An account established within federal funds and trust funds to record appropriations, obligations, and outlays (as well as offsetting collections) that are usually financed from an associated receipt account. See federal funds, obligation, outlays, and trust funds; compare with receipt account.

Fannie Mae (Federal National Mortgage Association): A government-sponsored enterprise founded during the Great Depression and federally chartered in 1968 as a shareholder-owned corporation that operates exclusively in the secondary mortgage market. Private lenders originate loans in the primary mortgage market. Fannie Mae provides liquidity to the mortgage market by purchasing qualifying mortgages from private lenders, pooling and securitizing the mortgages, then selling them as mortgage-backed securities (MBSs) in the secondary market. The company also holds MBSs and whole loans in its portfolio. Fannie Mae is now in conservatorship. See asset-backed security, conservatorship, government-sponsored enterprise, and mortgage-backed securities.

FCRA: See Federal Credit Reform Act of 1990.

Federal Credit Reform Act of 1990 (FCRA, Title V of the Congressional Budget Act of 1974): Legislation that changed the treatment of direct loans and loan guarantees in the federal budget. FCRA is intended to ensure that the full lifetime cost of credit programs is considered. It required that the federal budget record all costs and collections associated with a new loan or loan guarantees on a present-value basis in the year in which the loan is disbursed. Under credit reform, the federal cash flows associated with loans and loan guarantees are discounted to that time of disbursement using the rates on Treasury securities of comparable maturity. See credit reform.

federal funds: In the federal accounting structure, all accounts through which collections of money and expenditures are recorded, except those classified by law as trust funds. Federal funds include several types of funds, one of which is the general fund. See general fund; compare with trust funds.

federal funds rate: The interest rate that financial institutions charge each other for overnight loans of their monetary reserves. A rise in the federal funds rate (compared with other short-term interest rates) suggests a tightening of monetary policy, whereas a fall suggests an easing. (FRB) See monetary policy and short-term interest rate.

Federal Open Market Committee: The group within the Federal Reserve System that determines the stance of monetary policy. The open-market desk at the Federal Reserve Bank of New York implements that policy with open-market operations (the purchase or sale of government securities), which influence short-term interest rates—especially the federal funds rate—and the growth of the money supply. The committee is composed of 12members, including the 7 members of the Board of Governors of the Federal Reserve System, the president of the Federal Reserve Bank of New York, and a rotating group of 4 of the other 11 presidents of the regional Federal Reserve Banks. See federal funds rate, Federal Reserve System, monetary policy, and short-term interest rate.

Federal Reserve System: The central bank of the UnitedStates. The Federal Reserve is responsible for setting the nation's monetary policy and overseeing credit conditions. See central bank and monetary policy.

Freddie Mac (Federal Home Loan Mortgage Corporation): A government-sponsored enterprise founded in 1970 and federally chartered in 1989 as a shareholder-owned corporation that operates exclusively in the secondary mortgage market. Private lenders originate loans in the primary mortgage market. Freddie Mac provides liquidity to the mortgage market by purchasing qualifying mortgages from private lenders, pooling and securitizing the mortgages, then selling them as mortgage-backed securities (MBSs) in the secondary market. The company also holds MBSs and whole loans in its portfolio. Freddie Mac is now in conservatorship. See asset-backed security, conservatorship, government-sponsored enterprise, and mortgage-backed securities.

financing account: A nonbudgetary account required for a credit program (by the Federal Credit Reform Act of 1990) that holds balances, receives credit subsidy payments from the program account, and records all cash flows with the public that result from obligations or commitments made under the program since October 1, 1991. The cash flow in each financing account for a fiscal year is shown in the federal budget as an "other means of financing." See credit reform, credit subsidy, means of financing, and program account; compare with liquidating account.

fiscal policy: The government's tax and spending policies, which influence the amount and maturity of government debt as well as the level, composition, and distribution of national output and income. See debt.

fiscal year: A yearly accounting period. The federal government's fiscal year begins October 1 and ends September 30. Fiscal years are designated by the calendar years in which they end—for example, fiscal year 2011 will begin on October 1, 2010, and end on September 30, 2011. The *budget year* is the fiscal year for which the budget is being considered; in relation to a session of Congress, it isthe fiscal year that starts on October 1 of the calendar year in which that session of Congress began. See out-year.

foreign direct investment: Financial investment by which a person or an entity acquires a lasting interest in, and a degree of influence over the management of, a business enterprise in a foreign country. (BEA)

forward funding: The provision of budget authority that becomes available for obligation in the last quarter of a fiscal year and remains available during the following fiscal year. Forward funding typically finances ongoing education grant programs. See **budget** authority, fiscal year, and obligation; compare with advance appropriation, obligation delay, and unobligated balances.

GDI: See gross domestic income.

GDP: See gross domestic product.

GDP gap: The difference between potential and actual gross domestic product, expressed as a percentage of potential GDP. See gross domestic product and potential gross domestic product.

GDP price index: A summary measure of the prices of all goods and services that make up gross domestic product. The change in the GDP price index is used as a measure of inflation in the overall economy. See gross domestic product and inflation.

general fund: One category of federal funds in the government's accounting structure. The general fund records all revenues and offsetting receipts not earmarked by law for a specific purpose and all spending financed by those revenues and receipts. See federal funds, offsetting receipts, and revenues; compare with trust funds.

Ginnie Mae (Government National Mortgage Association): A government-owned corporation within the Department of Housing and Urban Development that guarantees mortgage-backed securities backed by federally insured or guaranteed loans. See mortgage-backed securities.

GNP: See **gross national product.**

government-sponsored enterprise (GSE): A financial institution created by federal law, generally though a federal charter, to carry out activities such as increasing credit availability for borrowers, reducing borrowing costs, or enhancing liquidity in particular sectors of the economy, notably agriculture and housing. Two housing GSEs (Fannie Mae and Freddie Mac) were taken into federal conservatorship in 2008. See conservatorship, Fannie Mae, and Freddie Mac.

grants: Transfer payments from the federal government to state and local governments or other recipients to help fund projects or activities that do not involve substantial federal participation. See transfer payments.

grants-in-aid: Grants from the federal government to state and local governments to help provide for programs of assistance or service to the public.

gross debt: See debt.

gross domestic income (GDI): The sum of all income earned in the domestic production of goods and services. In theory, GDI should equal gross domestic product, but measurement difficulties leave a statistical discrepancy between the two. (BEA) See gross domestic product.

gross domestic product (GDP): The total market value of goods and services produced domestically during a given period. That value is conceptually equal to gross domestic income, but measurement difficulties result in a statistical discrepancy between the two. The components of GDP are consumption (household and government), gross investment (private and government), and net exports. (BEA) See consumption, gross investment, and net exports.

gross investment: A measure of additions to the capital stock that does not subtract depreciation of existing capital. See capital and depreciation.

gross national product (GNP): The total market value of goods and services produced during a given period by labor and capital supplied by residents of a country, regardless of where the labor and capital are located. That value is conceptually equal to the total income accruing to residents of the country during that period (national income). GNP differs from gross domestic product primarily by including the capital income that residents earn from investments abroad and excluding the capital income that nonresidents earn from domestic investment. See gross domestic product and national income.

Home equity: The value that an owner has in a home, calculated by subtracting the value of any outstanding mortgage (or other loan) secured by the property for the home's current market value.

household survey: See **employment.**

Inflation: Growth in a general measure of prices, usually expressed as an annual rate of change. See consumer price index, core inflation, GDP price index, price index for personal consumption expenditures.

inventories: Stocks of goods held by businesses for further processing or for sale. (BEA)

investment: *Physical investment* is the current product set aside during a given period to be used for future production; an addition to the capital stock. As measured by the national income and product accounts, *private domestic investment* consists of investment in residential and nonresidential structures, producers' durable equipment, and the change in business inventories. *Financial investment* is the purchase of a financial security, such as a stock, bond, or mortgage. *Investment in human capital* is spending on education, training, health services, and other activities that increase the productivity of the workforce. Investment in human capital is not treated as investment by the national income and product accounts. See capital, inventories, national income and product accounts, and productivity.

JGTRRA: See Jobs and Growth Tax Relief Reconciliation Act of 2003.

Jobs and Growth Tax Relief Reconciliation Act of 2003 (JGTRRA, Public Law 108-27): Legislation that reduced taxes by advancing to 2003 the effective date of several tax reductions previously enacted in the Economic Growth and Tax Relief Reconciliation Act of 2001. JGTRRA also increased the exemption amount for the individual alternative minimum tax, reduced the tax rates for income from dividends and capital gains, and expanded the portion of capital purchases that businesses could immediately deduct through 2004. The tax provisions were set to expire on various dates. (The law also provided an estimated $20 billion for fiscal relief to states.) See alternative minimum tax and Economic Growth and Tax Relief Reconciliation Act of 2001.

Labor force: The number of people age 16 or older in the civilian noninstitutional population who have jobs or who are available for work and are actively seeking jobs. (The civilian noninstitutional population excludes members of the armed forces on active duty and people in penal or mental institutions or in homes for the elderly or infirm.) The *labor force participation rate* is the labor force as a percentage of the civilian noninstitutional population age 16 or older. (BLS) See potential labor force.

labor productivity: See productivity.

liquidating account: A budgetary account associated with a credit program that records all cash flows resulting from direct loan obligations and loan guarantee commitments made under that program before October 1, 1991. See credit reform; compare with financing account and program account.

liquidity: The ease with which an asset can be sold for cash. An asset is highly liquid if it comes in standard units that are traded daily in large amounts by many buyers and sellers. Among the most liquid of assets are U.S. Treasury securities.

loan-to-value ratio: The relationship between the amount of a loan (such as a mortgage) and the value of the underlying collateral, usually determined when the loan is made; one measure lenders use to assess a loan's riskiness.

long-term interest rate: The interest rate earned by a note or bond that matures in 10 or more years.

Mandatory spending: See direct spending.

marginal tax rate: The tax rate that would apply to an additional dollar of a taxpayer's income. Compare with effective tax rate and statutory tax rate.

MBSs: See mortgage-backed securities.

means of financing: Means by which a budget deficit is financed or a surplus is used. Means of financing are not included in the budget totals. The primary means of financing is borrowing from the public. In general, the cumulative amount borrowed from the public (debt held by the public) will increase if there is a deficit and decrease if there is a surplus, although other factors can affect the amount that the government must borrow. Those factors, known as *other means of financing,* include reductions (or increases) in the government's cash balances, seigniorage, changes in outstanding checks, changes in accrued interest costs included in the budget but not yet paid, and cash flows reflected in credit financing accounts. See debt, deficit, financing account, seigniorage, and surplus.

monetary policy: The strategy of influencing changes in the money supply and interest rates to affect output and inflation. An "easy" monetary policy suggests faster growth of the money supply and initially lower short-term interest rates intended to increase aggregate demand, but it may lead to higher inflation. A "tight" monetary policy suggests slower growth of the money supply and higher interest rates in the near term in an attempt to reduce inflationary pressure by lowering aggregate demand. The Federal Reserve System sets monetary policy in the United States. See aggregate demand, Federal Reserve System, inflation, and short-term interest rate.

mortgage-backed securities (MBSs): Securities issued by financial institutions to investors with the payments of interest and principal backed by the payments on a package of mortgages. MBSs are structured by their sponsors to create multiple classes of claims, or *tranches,* of different seniority, based on the cash flows from the underlying mortgages. Investors holding securities in the safest, or most senior, tranche stand first in line to receive payments from borrowers and require the lowest contractual interest rate of all the tranches. Investors holding the least senior securities stand last in line to receive payments, after all more senior claims have been paid. Hence, they are first in line to absorb losses on the underlying mortgages. In return for assuming that risk, holders of the least senior tranche require the highest contractual interest rate of all the tranches.

National income: Total income earned by U.S. residents from all sources, including employees' compensation (wages, salaries, benefits, and employers' share of payroll taxes for social insurance programs), corporate profits, net interest, rental income, and proprietors' income. See gross national product.

national income and product accounts (NIPAs): Official U.S. accounts that track the level and composition of gross domestic product, the prices of its components, and the way in which the costs of production are distributed as income. (BEA) See gross domestic product.

national saving: Total saving by all sectors of the economy: personal saving, business saving (corporate after-tax profits not paid as dividends), and government saving (budget surpluses). National saving represents all income not consumed, publicly or privately, during a given period. (BEA) See national income, net national saving, personal saving, and surplus.

natural rate of unemployment: The rate of unemployment arising from all sources except fluctuations in aggregate demand. Those sources include *frictional unemployment,* which is associated with normal turnover of jobs, and *structural unemployment,* which includes unemployment caused by mismatches between the skills of available workers and the skills necessary to fill vacant positions and unemployment caused when wages exceed their market-clearing levels because of institutional factors, such as legal minimum wages, the presence of unions, social conventions, or employer wage-setting practices intended to increase workers' morale and effort. See aggregate demand and unemployment rate.

net exports: The exports of goods and services produced in a country minus the country's imports of goods and services produced elsewhere; also referred to as the *trade balance.*

net federal government saving: A term used in the national income and product accounts to identify the difference between federal current receipts and federal current expenditures (including consumption of fixed capital). When receipts exceed expenditures, net federal government saving is positive (formerly identified in the national income and product accounts as a federal government surplus); when expenditures exceed receipts, net federal government saving is negative (formerly identified in the national income and product accounts as a federal government deficit). See capital and national income and product accounts.

net interest: In the federal budget, net interest comprises the government's interest payments on debt held by the public (as recorded in budget function 900), offset by interest income that the government receives on loans and cash balances and by earnings of the National Railroad Retirement Investment Trust. See budget function and debt.

net national saving: National saving minus depreciation of physical capital. See capital, depreciation, and national saving.

NIPAs: See **national income and product accounts**.

nominal: A measure based on current-dollar value. *Nominal* income and spending are measured in current dollars. The *nominal interest rate* on debt selling at par is the ratio of the current-dollar interest paid in any year to the current-dollar value of the debt when it was issued. The nominal interest rate on debt initially issued or now selling at a discount includes as a payment the estimated yearly equivalent of the difference between the redemption price and the discounted price. The *nominal exchange rate* is the rate at which a unit of one currency trades for a unit of another currency. See current dollar; compare with real.

Obligation: A legally binding commitment by the federal government that will result in outlays, immediately or in the future. See outlays.

obligation delay: Legislation that precludes the obligation of an amount of budget authority provided in an appropriation act or in some other law until some time after the first day on which that budget authority would normally be available. For example, language in an appropriation act for fiscal year 2010 that precludes obligation of an amount until March 1 is an obligation delay; without that language, the amount would have been available for obligation on October 1, 2009 (the first day of fiscal year 2010). See appropriation act, budget authority, fiscal year, and obligation; compare with advance appropriation, forward funding, and unobligated balances.

obligation limitation: A provision of a law or legislation that restricts or reduces the availability of budget authority that would have become available under another law. Typically, an obligation limitation is included in an appropriation act. The limitation may affect budget authority provided in that act, but more often, it affects direct spending that has been provided in an authorization act. Generally, when an appropriation act routinely places an obligation limitation on direct spending, the limitation is treated as a discretionary resource and the associated outlays are treated as discretionary spending. See appropriation act, authorization act, budget authority, direct spending, discretionary spending, and outlays.

off-budget: Spending or revenues sometimes excluded from the budget totals by law. The revenues and outlays of the two Social Security trust funds (the Old-Age and Survivors Insurance Trust Fund and the Disability Insurance Trust Fund) and the transactions of the Postal Service are off-budget. See outlays, revenues, and trust funds.

offsetting collections: Funds collected by government agencies from other government accounts or from the public in business-like or market-oriented transactions that are required by law to be credited directly to an expenditure account. Offsetting collections, which are treated as negative budget authority and outlays, are credits against the budget authority and outlays (either direct or discretionary spending) of the account to which they are credited. Collections that result from the government's exercise of its sovereign or governmental powers are ordinarily classified as revenues, although they are classified as offsetting collections when the law requires it. See budget authority, direct spending, discretionary spending, expenditure account, and outlays; compare with offsetting receipts and revenues.

offsetting receipts: Funds collected by government agencies from other government accounts or from the public in business-like or market-oriented transactions that are credited to a receipt account. Offsetting receipts, which are treated as negative budget authority and outlays, offset gross budget authority and outlays in calculations of total direct spending. Collections that result from the government's exercise of its sovereign or governmental powers are ordinarily classified as revenues, although they are classified as offsetting receipts when the law requires it. See budget authority, direct spending, outlays, and receipt account; compare with offsetting collections and revenues.

other means of financing: See **means of financing**.

outlays: Spending to pay a federal obligation. Outlays may pay for obligations incurred in a prior fiscal year or in the current year; hence, they flow partly from unexpended balances of prior-year budget authority and partly from budget authority provided for the current year. For most categories of spending, outlays are recorded on a cash accounting basis. However, outlays for interest ondebt held by the public are recorded on an accrual accounting basis, and outlays for direct loans and loan guarantees (since credit reform) reflect estimated subsidy costs instead of cash transactions. See accrual accounting, budget authority, cash accounting, credit reform, debt, fiscal year, and obligation.

output gap: See GDP gap.
out-year: A fiscal year following the budget year. See fiscal year.

Pay-as-you-go (PAYGO): Procedures established in House and Senate rules that are intended to ensure that laws that affect direct spending or revenues are budget neutral. The Senate and the House have had such rules in place since 1993 and 2007, respectively. The

Senate rule was adopted in its current form in the budget resolution for 2008 (H. Con. Res. 21, 110th Congress). The House rule was adopted in its current form in the resolution adopting rules of the House (H. Res. 5, 111th Congress). The House and Senate rules focus on net deficit effects over two time spans: a 6-year period consisting of the current year, the upcoming budget year, and the following 4 years; and an 11-year period consisting of the current year, the upcoming budget year, and the subsequent 9 years. The net effect that a piece of legislation would have on the deficit is determined on the basis of estimates made relative to the baseline that underlies the current Congressional budget resolution. The PAYGO rules in the House and Senate are each enforced by a point of order. A supermajority of 60 votes is required to waive a point of order in the Senate; in the House, a point of order may be waived by a majority vote. PAYGO also refers to the procedures established in the Budget Enforcement Act of 1990 that required the cancellation of budgetary resources available for direct spending programs if, in any budget year, the deficit increased as a result of the total budgetary effects of applicable laws. Those procedures were rendered ineffective on December 2, 2002, by Public Law 107-312. See Balanced Budget and Emergency Deficit Control Act of 1985, deficit, direct spending, fiscal year, point of order, revenues, sequestration, and surplus.

PCE price index: See price index for personal consumption expenditures.

personal income: See disposable personal income.

personal saving: Saving by households. Personal saving equals disposable personal income minus spending for consumption and interest payments. The *personal saving rate* is personal saving as a percentage of disposable personal income. (BEA) See consumption and disposable personal income; compare with private saving.

Phillips curve: A hypothesized inverse relationship between changes in wage rates and the unemployment rate (the *wage Phillips curve*) or between inflation and the unemployment rate (the *price Phillips curve*). Generally, wages and prices rise faster when the unemployment rate is low, but the relationship is not fixed over time, and in some circumstances, such as during the oil price shocks of the 1970s, the relationship breaks down. Named after A.W.H. Phillips, who noted the relationship in 1957.

point of order: The procedure by which a member of a legislature (or similar body) questions an action that is being taken, or that is proposed to be taken, as contrary to that body's rules, practices, or precedents.

potential gross domestic product: The level of real gross domestic product that corresponds to a high level of resource (labor and capital) use. (Procedures for calculating potential GDP are described in *CBO's Method for Estimating Potential Output: An Update*, August 2001.) See gross domestic product, potential output, and real.

potential labor force: The labor force adjusted for movements in the business cycle. See business cycle and labor force.

potential output: The level of production that corresponds to a high level of resource (labor and capital) use. Potential output for the national economy is also referred to as *potential gross domestic product.* (Procedures for calculating potential output are described in *CBO's Method for Estimating Potential Output: An Update,* August 2001.) See potential gross domestic product.

present value: A single number that expresses a flow of current and future income (or payments) in terms of an equivalent lump sum received (or paid) today. The present value depends on the rate of interest used (the discount rate). For example, if $100 is invested on January 1 at an annual interest rate of 5 percent, it will grow to $105 by January 1 of the next year. Hence, at an annual 5 percent interest rate, the present value of $105 payable a year from today is $100.

price index for personal consumption expenditures (PCE price index): A summary measure of the prices of all goods and services that make up personal consumption expenditures. The Federal Reserve uses measures based on this index as its primary measures of inflation in conducting monetary policy, because they are more representative of current consumer spending patterns than the consumer price index. Also referred to as the chained price index for personal consumption expenditures. See consumption, consumer price index, and inflation.

primary deficit: See **deficit**.

private saving: Saving by households and businesses. Private saving is equal to personal saving plus after-tax corporate profits minus dividends paid. (BEA) Compare with personal saving.

productivity: Average real output per unit of input. *Labor productivity* is average real output per hour of labor. The growth of labor productivity is defined as the growth of real output that is not explained by the growth of labor input alone. *Total factor productivity* is average real output per unit of combined labor and capital services. The growth of total factor productivity is defined as the growth of real output that is not explained by the growth of labor and capital. Labor productivity and total factor productivity differ in that increases in capital per worker raise labor productivity but not total factor productivity. (BLS) See capital services and real.

program account: A budgetary account associated with a credit program that receives an appropriation of the subsidy cost of that program's loan obligations or commitments, as well as (in most cases) the program's administrative expenses. From the program account, the subsidy cost is disbursed to the applicable financing account. See credit subsidy and financing account; compare with liquidating account.

Real: Adjusted to remove the effects of inflation. *Real output* represents the quantity, rather than the dollar value, of goods and services produced. *Real income* represents the power to purchase real output. *Real data* at the finest level of disaggregation are constructed by dividing the corresponding nominal data, such as spending or wage rates, by a price index.

Real aggregates, such as real gross domestic product, are constructed by a procedure that allows the real growth of the aggregate to reflect the real growth of its components, appropriately weighted by the importance of the components. A *real interest rate* is a nominal interest rate adjusted for expected inflation; it is often approximated by subtracting an estimate of the expected inflation rate from the nominal interest rate. See inflation; compare with current dollar and nominal.

real trade-weighted value of the dollar: See **trade-weighted value of the dollar**.

receipt account: An account established within federal funds and trust funds to record offsetting receipts or revenues credited to that fund. The receipt account typically finances the obligations and outlays from an associated expenditure account. See federal funds, outlays, and trust funds; compare with expenditure account.

recession: A phase of the business cycle that extends from a peak to the next trough and that is characterized by a substantial decline in overall business activity—output, income, employment, and trade—for at least several months. As a rule of thumb, although not an official measure, recessions are often identified by a decline in real gross domestic product for at least two consecutive quarters. (NBER) See business cycle, gross domestic product, and real; compare with expansion.

reconciliation: A special Congressional procedure often used to implement the revenue and spending targets established in the budget resolution. The budget resolution may contain *reconciliation instructions,* which direct Congressional committees to make changes in laws under their jurisdictions that affect revenues or direct spending to achieve a specified budgetary result. The legislation to implement those instructions is usually combined into a comprehensive *reconciliation bill,* which is considered under special rules. Reconciliation affects revenues, direct spending, and offsetting receipts but usually not discretionary spending. See budget resolution, direct spending, discretionary spending, offsetting receipts, and revenues.

recovery: A phase of the business cycle that lasts from a trough until overall economic activity returns to the level it reached at the previous peak. (NBER) See business cycle.

rescission: The withdrawal of authority to incur financial obligations that was previously provided by law and has not yet expired. See budget authority and obligation.

revenues: Funds collected from the public that arise from the government's exercise of its sovereign or governmental powers. Federal revenues come from a variety of sources, including individual and corporate income taxes, excise taxes, customs duties, estate and gift taxes, fees and fines, payroll taxes for social insurance programs, and miscellaneous receipts (such as earnings of the Federal Reserve System, donations, and bequests). Federal revenues are also known as federal governmental receipts. Compare with offsetting collections and offsetting receipts.

risk premium: The additional return that investors require to hold assets whose returns are more variable than those of riskless assets. The risk can arise from many sources, such as the possibility of default (in the case of corporate or municipal debt) or the volatility of interest rates or earnings (in the case of corporate stocks).

Scorporation: A domestically owned corporation with no more than 100 owners who have elected to pay taxes under Subchapter S of the Internal Revenue Code. An S corporation is taxed like a partnership: It is exempt from the corporate income tax, but its owners pay individual income taxes on all of the business's income, even if some of the earnings are retained by the company.

saving rate: See **national saving** and **personal saving**.

savings bond: A nontransferable, registered security issued by the Treasury at a discount and in denominations from $50 to $10,000. The interest earned on savings bonds is exempt from state and local taxation; it is also exempt from federal taxation until the bonds are redeemed or reach maturity.

seigniorage: The gain to the government from the difference between the face value of minted coins put into circulation and the cost of producing them (including the cost of the metal used in the coins). Seigniorage is considered a means of financing and is not included in the budget totals. See means of financing.

sequestration: An enforcement mechanism established in the Balanced Budget and Emergency Deficit Control Act of 1985 that would result in the cancellation of budgetary resources available for a fiscal year. The mechanism enforced the discretionary spending limits and pay-as-you-go (PAYGO) procedures of that law, as amended. A sequestration of discretionary budget authority would occur in a fiscal year if the budget authority or outlays provided in appropriation acts exceeded the applicable discretionary spending limit for that year. A PAYGO sequestration would occur in a fiscal year if the total budgetary effect of laws that affect direct spending and revenues was not deficit neutral in that year. The discretionary spending limits and the sequestration procedure to enforce them expired on September 30, 2002. PAYGO and its sequestration procedure were rendered ineffective on December 2, 2002, when Public Law 107-312 reduced all PAYGO balances to zero. See appropriation act, Balanced Budget and Emergency Deficit Control Act of 1985, budget authority, direct spending, discretionary spending limits, fiscal year, outlays, pay-as-you-go, and revenues.

short-term interest rate: The interest rate earned by a debt instrument (such as a Treasury bill) that will mature within one year.

state and local government security (SLGS): A time deposit sold by the Treasury to issuers of state and local government tax-exempt debt to facilitate compliance with the Internal Revenue Code's *arbitrage provisions,* which restrict state and local governments from earning profits by investing bond proceeds in higher-yielding investments.

statutory tax rate: A tax rate specified by law. In some cases, such as with individual and corporate income taxes, the statutory tax rate varies with the amount of taxable income. (For example, under the federal corporate income tax, the statutory tax rate for companies with taxable income below $50,000 is 15 percent, whereas the rate for corporations with taxable income greater than $18.3 million is 35 percent.) In other cases, the statutory tax rate is uniform. (For instance, the statutory federal tax rate on gasoline is 18.4 cents per gallon for all taxpayers.) Compare with effective tax rate and marginal tax rate.

Subchapter S corporation: See **S corporation**.

subsidy cost: See **credit subsidy**.

surplus: The amount by which the federal government's total revenues exceed its total outlays in a given period, typically a fiscal year. See fiscal year, outlays, and revenues; compare with deficit.

Sustainable Growth Rate (SGR): The formula that determines updates to payment rates for physicians under the Medicare program. The SGR sets annual and cumulative spending targets for those payments. If total spending exceeds those targets, an across-the-board reduction is supposed to be made in future fees to bring spending back into line (both annually and cumulatively). However, since 2003, the Congress has overridden such reductions; the most recent provision is set to expire at the end of February 2010.

TARP: See **Troubled Asset Relief Program.**

Taylor rule: A rule for the conduct of monetary policy, specifically the setting of the federal funds rate on the basis of how much inflation differs from a target inflation rate and how much the unemployment rate differs from an estimated full-employment unemployment rate. In some formulations, the difference between gross domestic product and an estimate of potential gross domestic product is used instead of the unemployment rate. Named after John Taylor, an economist who proposed such a rule in 1993.

Tax Increase Prevention Act of 2007 (Public Law 110-166): This law provided relief from the individual alternative minimum tax for the tax year that ended December 31, 2007. See alternative minimum tax.

total factor productivity: See productivity.

trade balance: See net exports.

trade-weighted value of the dollar: The value of the U.S. dollar relative to the currencies of U.S. trading partners, with the weight of each country's currency equal to that country's share of U.S. trade. The *real trade-weighted value of the dollar* is an index of the trade-weighted value of the dollar whose movement is adjusted for the difference between U.S. inflation and inflation among U.S. trading partners. An increase in the real trade-weighted value of the dollar means that the price of U.S.-produced goods and services has increased relative to the price of foreign-produced goods and services. See inflation.

transfer payments: Payments made to a person or organization for which no current or future goods or services are required in return. Federal transfer payments include Social Security and unemployment benefits. (BEA)

Treasury bill: A security issued by the Treasury with a maturity of 28, 91, or 182 days. Interest on a Treasury bill is calculated as the difference between the purchase price and the value paid at redemption.

Treasury bond: A fixed-rate, interest-bearing security issued by the Treasury that matures in 30 years.

Treasury inflation-protected security (TIPS): A marketable security with a maturity of 5, 10, or 20 years issued by the Treasury that is designed to protect investors from inflation. The principal of a TIPS is linked to the consumer price index, and at maturity, the security pays the greater of the original or the adjusted principal. The security makes semiannual interest payments based on a fixed rate of interest and the adjusted principal amount.

Treasury note: A fixed-rate, interest-bearing security issued by the Treasury with a maturity of 2, 5, or 10years.

Troubled Asset Relief Program (TARP): A program that permits the Secretary of the Treasury to purchase or insure troubled financial assets. Authority for the program was initially set by the Emergency Economic Stabilization Act of 2008 at $700 billion in assets outstanding at any one time (the limit now stands at nearly $699 billion) and remains in effect until October 3, 2010. The TARP's activities have included the purchase of preferred stock from financial institutions, support to automakers and related businesses, a program to avert housing foreclosures, and partnerships with the private sector. See Emergency Economic Stabilization Act of 2008.

trust funds: In the federal accounting structure, accounts designated by law as trust funds (regardless of any other meaning of that term). Trust funds record the revenues, offsetting receipts, or offsetting collections earmarked for the purpose of the fund, as well as budget authority and outlays of the fund that are financed by those revenues or receipts. The federal government has more than 200 trust funds. The largest and best known finance major benefit programs (including Social Security and Medicare) and infrastructure spending (such as the Highway Trust Fund and the Airport and Airway Trust Fund). See budget authority, offsetting collections, offsetting receipts, outlays, and revenues; compare with federal funds.

Unemployment rate: A measure of the number of jobless people who are available for work and are actively seeking jobs, expressed as a percentage of the labor force. (BLS) See discouraged workers and labor force.

Unfunded Mandates Reform Act of 1995 (UMRA, Public Law 104-4): This law, parts of which are incorporated as Title IV of the Congressional Budget Act of 1974, was enacted to address concerns about federal statutes and rules that place requirements on state, local, and tribal governments or the private sector. Requirements not tied to conditions of assistance and those that add responsibilities in some large entitlement programs are defined in the act as federal mandates. UMRA requires Congressional committees, the Congressional Budget Office, the Office of Management and Budget, and agencies in the Executive branch to provide information about the nature and cost of potential federal mandates to assist the

Congress and agency decision-makers as they consider proposed legislation and rules. See Congressional Budget Act of 1974.

unified budget: The entire federal budget, which consolidates all on-budget and off-budget outlays and revenues. See off-budget, outlays, and revenues.

unilateral transfers: Payments from sources within the United States to sources abroad (and vice versa) that are not made in exchange for goods or services. Examples include a private gift sent abroad, a pension payment from a U.S. employer to an eligible retiree living in a foreign country, or taxes paid to the United States by people living overseas.

unobligated balances: The portion of budget authority that has not yet been obligated. When budget authority is provided for one fiscal year, any unobligated balances at the end of that year expire and are no longer available for obligation. When budget authority is provided for a specific number of years, any unobligated balances are carried forward and are available for obligation during the years specified. When budget authority is provided for an unspecified number of years, the unobligated balances are carried forward indefinitely, until one of the following occurs: the balances are expended or rescinded, the purpose for which they were provided is accomplished, or no disbursements have been made for two consecutive years. See budget authority, fiscal year, and obligation; compare with advance appropriation, forward funding, and obligation delay.

user fee: Money that the federal government charges for services or for the sale or use of federal goods or resources that generally provide benefits to the recipients beyond those that may accrue to the general public. The amount of the fee is typically related to the cost of the service provided or the value of the good or resource used. In the federal budget, user fees can be classified as offsetting collections, offsetting receipts, or revenues. See offsetting collections, offsetting receipts, and revenues.

Withholding: The deduction of taxes by an employer or other payor from wages or other taxable payments to be transmitted directly to a government. Federal tax withholding includes deductions for income taxes, as well as contributions to Social Security and Medicare (payroll taxes). When taxpayers file their tax returns at the end of the taxable year, they either pay the balance of unpaid tax liability or they receive any overpayment as a refund. Federal tax withholding is classified as revenue in the federal budget when received by the U.S. Treasury.

Yield: The average annual rate of return on an investment held over a period of time. For a fixed-income security, such as a bond, the yield is determined by several factors, including the security's interest rate, face value, and purchase price and the length of time that the security is held. The *yield to maturity* is the effective interest rate earned on a fixed-income security if it is held until the date on which it comes due for payment.

yield curve: The relationship formed by plotting the yields of otherwise comparable fixed-income securities against their terms to maturity. Typically, yields increase as maturities lengthen, and the rate determines the "steepness" or "flatness" of the yield curve.

Ordinarily, a steepening (or flattening) of the yield curve is taken to suggest that short-term interest rates are expected to rise (or fall). See short-term interest rate and yield.

The Budget and Economic Outlook: Fiscal Years 2010 to 2020

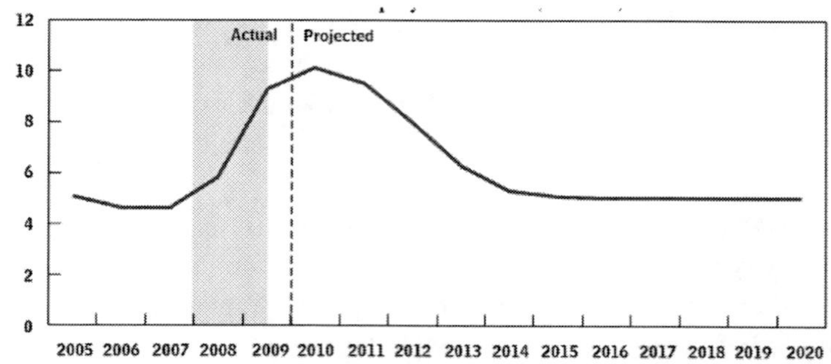

The Unemployment Rate (Percent).

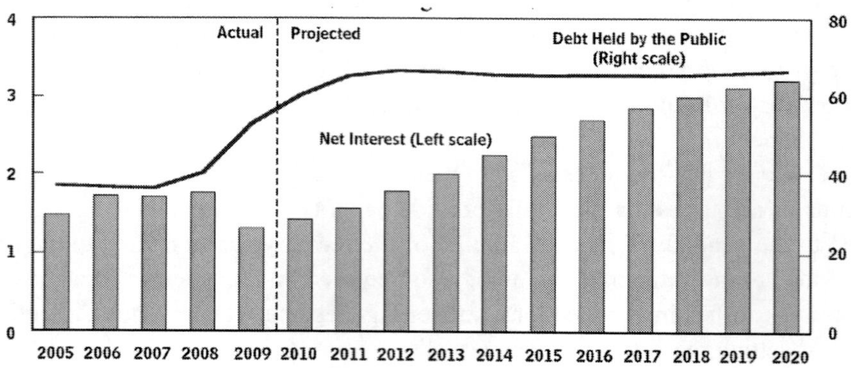

Debt Held by the Public and Net Interest Payments (Percentage of GDP).

End Notes

[1] Those provisions—most of which were originally enacted in the Economic Growth and Tax Relief Reconciliation Act of 2001, the Jobs and Growth Tax Relief Reconciliation Act of 2003, or the American Recovery and Reinvestment Act of 2009—are scheduled to expire at the end of December 2010. The assumption that those expirations will occur as scheduled accounts for about half of the total growth in revenues in dollar terms between 2010 and 2012 in CBO's baseline projections.

[2] In the federal budget, net interest primarily consists of the government's interest payments on debt held by the public, offset by interest income that the government receives from various sources.

[3] More details about the nation's long-term fiscal challenges can be found in Congressional Budget Office, *The Long-Term Budget Outlook* (June 2009).

[4] In 2009, the Treasury recorded $91 billion in net outlays related to Fannie Mae and Freddie Mac. That amount reflects cash infusions of nearly $96 billion from the Treasury to the two entities (for purchases of their preferred stock) partly offset by about $4 billion in dividends received on that stock. CBO's estimate of federal costs for Fannie Mae and Freddie Mac in 2010, $21 billion, is an estimate of subsidy costs that reflects the projected net present value of transactions undertaken by the two entities in 2010. In addition, net cash infusions are likely to be substantially smaller this year than they were last year. See Chapter3 for a more detailed discussion of the estimated budgetary impact of assistance to Fannie Mae and Freddie Mac. For

information about the methodology that CBO uses to construct its baseline estimates for the two entities, see Congressional Budget Office, *CBO's Budgetary Treatment of Fannie Mae and Freddie Mac,* Background Paper (January 2010).

[5] The Deficit Control Act provided some exceptions. For example, spending programs whose authorizations are set to expire are assumed to continue if they have outlays of more than $50 million in the current year and were established on or before the enactment of the Balanced Budget Act of 1997. Programs established after that law was enacted are not automatically assumed to continue. The Deficit Control Act also required CBO to assume that expiring excise taxes dedicated to trust funds would be extended at their current rates. The law did not provide for the extension of other expiring tax provisions, even if they have been extended routinely in the past.

[6] The average troop level of 200,000 in 2010 reflects an average of about 85,000 personnel in Afghanistan (as the number of troops deployed in that region climbs from about 70,000 at the end of 2009 to about 100,000 by the end of 2010) and an average of 115,000 personnel in Iraq (as the majority of U.S. troops there are withdrawn during the year).

[7] In 2010, troop levels in Afghanistan would be the same as under the first scenario, but the number of personnel in Iraq would drop less sharply, to an average of 150,000 rather than 115,000.

[8] That estimate includes increases in outlays for refundable tax credits, but it excludes any effects that the expiration of the tax provisions would have on the economy. CBO's baseline projections, in contrast, incorporate such macroeconomic effects.

[9] Information about foreign holders of Treasury debt should be viewed as approximate. In many cases, it is impossible to accurately determine the home country of a foreign holder of U.S. securities because intermediaries may be involved in the custody, management, purchase, or sale of the securities.

[10] The Treasury created the Supplementary Financing Program to help offset the expansion of the Federal Reserve's activities during the financial crisis. Funding raised by issuing Treasury bills was placed in an account held at the Federal Reserve. For more information, see Board of Governors of the Federal Reserve System, "Credit and Liquidity Programs and the Balance Sheet" (January 13, 2010), available at www.federalreserve.gov/monetarypolicy/ bst_frliabilities.htm.

[11] For more details on the fiscal situation after 2020, see Congressional Budget Office, *The Long-Term Budget Outlook* (June 2009).

[12] The natural rate of unemployment is an estimate of the rate of unemployment arising from sources other than fluctuations in the business cycle.

[13] The PCE price index is preferred by most analysts and emphasized by the Federal Reserve, because the weights it puts on the prices of different consumer goods and services are more up to date and representative than those of the consumer price index.

[14] The "central tendency" excludes the three highest and three lowest forecasts for each variable in each year.

[15] See the statement of Jon Greenlee, Associate Director, Division of Banking Supervision and Regulation, Federal Reserve, *Residential and Commercial Real Estate* (November 21, 2009).

[16] Analysts often gauge the Federal Reserve's preferred level of the federal funds rate on the basis of models of its past responses to inflation and recessions. Such models are now widely termed "Taylor rules." Most Taylor-rule specifications indicate that, if it were possible, the Federal Reserve's target federal funds rate would have been well below zero during the recession and would remain below zero currently.

[17] Growth was also boosted by legislation other than ARRA, including the extension of unemployment insurance benefits, credits for first-time home buyers (which were extended once by ARRA and again by the Worker, Homeownership, and Business Assistance Act of 2009), and the Car Allowance Rebate System (the CARS program), often referred to as "Cash for Clunkers."

[18] CBO selected low and high estimates of the effects of a given policy, on a judgmental basis, to encompass most economists' views about the effects of that type of policy. Those estimates are based on a previous analysis of the economic effects of ARRA. See Congressional Budget Office, "Estimated Macroeconomic Impacts of the American Recovery and Reinvestment Act of 2009," letter to the Honorable Charles E. Grassley (March 2, 2009).

[19] Similar but smaller automatic changes occur in state and local revenues and spending. In contrast with automatic stabilizers at the federal level, those at the state and local levels are largely offset by discretionary actions used to comply with balanced-budget rules. Those actions include reductions in state and local spending and increases in tax rates and various fees.

[20] See Chapter 4 for further discussion of the revenue effects of the expiration of AMT relief.

[21] Excess vacant units are measured as the difference between the actual number of vacant units—including units for sale or for rent, second homes, and units held off the market for various reasons—and an estimate of the number that would be vacant under normal market conditions. Vacant units are thought to better reflect the excess supply of housing than the total inventory of units for sale because occupied units for sale are part of both the supply of and the demand for housing.

[22] Since the middle of 2006, the price index for exports of nonagricultural goods has fallen by 3 percent relative to the price of imports of nonpetroleum goods; in comparison, in the previous 10 years, from 1996 to 2006, export prices rose faster than import prices.

[23] Some emerging economies have performed much better than the U.S. economy over the past year. In particular, in China, India, and Indonesia, real GDP growth slowed in 2009, but those countries never went into recession and are likely to post strong growth over the next few years. Other Asian economies that were in recession during 2008 and early 2009 have rebounded sharply, in part because of the continued strength of the Chinese economy. However, the United States does not send a large proportion of its exports to countries with such strong growth.

[24] Those figures are based on current official data and do not take into account the benchmark revisions scheduled for early February 2010. In its preliminary benchmark announcement, the Bureau of Labor Statistics indicated that the March 2009 employment level would probably be revised downward by about 800,000. Estimates of employment growth since then may also be revised.

[25] This discussion is based on Congressional Budget Office, *Policies for Increasing Economic Growth and Employment in 2010 and 2011* (January 2010).

[26] For a variety of views on this topic, see Federal Reserve Bank of Boston, Conference Series 53, "Understanding Inflation and the Implications for Monetary Policy: A Phillips Curve Retrospective" (June 2008), available at www.bos.frb.org/economic/conf/conf53/ index.htm.

[27] CBO's measure of labor income consists of the total compensation that employers pay their employees and 65 percent of proprietors' income (a commonly used estimate of the proportion of proprietors' income that represents compensation for the labor effort they put into the enterprise). Total compensation is the sum of wages and salaries and supplemental benefits, including employers' payments for health and other insurance premiums, their contributions to pension funds, and their share of payroll taxes for Social Security and Medicare.

[28] A closer approximation to the tax base that incorporates estimates of depreciation allowable under tax law—known as domestic book profits—follows a similar path to that of domestic economic profits. However, in the latter years of the projection period, its share of GDP does not fall appreciably below the share in the projection from last August.

[29] The American Recovery and Reinvestment Act of 2009 temporarily increased federal matching rates under Medicaid through December 2010.

[30] Medicare Part C (now known as Medicare Advantage) specifies the rules under which private health care plans can assume responsibility for, and be compensated for, providing benefits covered under Parts A, B, and D.

[31] Social Security benefits are indexed to inflation, as measured by the consumer price index for urban wage earners and clerical workers (the CPI-W). The Social Security Administration generally adjusts benefits paid in January of each year on the basis of the annual change in the CPI-W through the third quarter of the previous calendar year. If the resulting adjustment is negative, no cost-of-living-adjustment is made. The next cost-of-living adjustment is made when the CPI-W for the third quarter of the calendar year exceeds the CPI-W in the third quarter of the last year for which an adjustment was made.

[32] The amounts for the EITC and child tax credits apply only to the refundable portions of those credits and do not include their effects on revenues.

[33] For more information on Fannie Mae and Freddie Mac, see Congressional Budget Office, *CBO's Budgetary Treatment of Fannie Mae and Freddie Mac* (January 2010).

[34] The net cost recorded in the budget for the TARP, broadly speaking, is the purchase cost minus the present value of any estimated future earnings from holding the asset and the proceeds from the eventual sale of the asset. The present value is calculated using an appropriate discount factor that reflects the riskiness of the asset. Once the asset matures or is disposed of, adjustments are made to the original estimate of the subsidy cost to reflect actual cash flows.

[35] The law that created the TARP—the Emergency Economic Stabilization Act of 2008—specified that the program be recorded in the budget by calculating the present value of its anticipated costs, using an adjustment for market risk. Under standard accounting for credit programs in the federal budget, the original subsidy calculation may be increased or decreased by a "credit reestimate" in subsequent years, based on updated valuations of the present-value costs of the cash flows associated with those credit programs.

[36] For information on the President's proposal to replace federally guaranteed student loans with direct government loans, see Congressional Budget Office, "Analysis of the Subsidy Costs of Direct and Guaranteed Student Loans," letter to Senator Judd Gregg (July 27, 2009); also, see Congressional Budget Office, *Subsidy Estimates for Guaranteed and Direct Student Loans* (November 2005).

[37] Benefits under SNAP are adjusted annually according to increases in a market basket of food served at home. Under provisions of ARRA, however, maximum SNAP benefits were set at $688, about 17 percent higher than the maximum benefit at the time that legislation was enacted. Under ARRA, the maximum benefit will remain at that higher amount until inflation causes the unadjusted benefit to exceed the ARRA-mandated one. CBO estimates that the maximum SNAP benefit will remain at the amount stipulated by ARRA until 2019.

[38] The Medicare economic index tracks the costs of physicians' time and operating expenses. Most of the components of the index come from the Bureau of Labor Statistics. Changes in the costs of physicians' time are measured through changes in nonfarm labor costs. Changes in productivity also are factored directly into the index.

[39] Amounts discussed for Medicare are for gross spending and do not include the offsetting effects of premium payments. Those payments are set to cover about one-quarter of the costs for Part B, the Supplementary Medical Insurance program. Premiums also are paid under Part D, the prescription drug benefit program.

[40] Student loans and several other programs in that category are not included in that total because they are considered mandatory.

[41] Other income security programs, such as unemployment compensation and TANF, are not included in the total because they are included in mandatory spending.

[42] In this scenario, budget authority for some items (such as offsetting collections and payments made by the Treasury on behalf of the Department of Defense for TRICARE for Life) is not held constant at the 2010 amount.

[43] Debt held by the public does not include securities issued from the Treasury to certain federal programs. That intragovernmental debt is included as part of the measure of gross federal debt (see AppendixD).

[44] The provisions also affect revenues by influencing the broader economy (see Chapter 2). Although those effects are incorporated into baseline revenue projections, they are not identified separately in this chapter.

[45] Congressional Budget Office, *The Budget and Economic Outlook: An Update* (August 2009).

[46] According to projections made on the basis of current law, the number of taxpayers with AMT liability will dip temporarily in 2011, as will the amount of AMT receipts in 2012, because of increases in regular tax rates and other changes that result from the expiration of provisions originally enacted in EGTRRA and JGTRRA.

[47] For a more thorough discussion of the expanding scope of the AMT under current law and the types of taxpayers affected, see Congressional Budget Office, *The Individual Alternative Minimum Tax,* Issue Brief (January 15, 2010).

[48] For example, taxpayers with income below $150,000 can avoid penalties by making estimated payments and withholding amounts equal to their prior year's tax liability. Taxpayers with income above $150,000 can avoid penalties by paying at least 110percent of their prior year's liability.

[49] A capital gains realization is the increase in the value of an asset between the time it is purchased and sold.

[50] The scheduled return to higher tax rates on capital gains in 2011 also will alter the timing of realizations by encouraging taxpayers to sell assets that will generate taxable capital gains in 2010, before the rates go up, rather than waiting until 2011.

[51] Taxpayers are considered overwithheld for a year if their tax liability is less than the combined amount of income taxes withheld from their paychecks and any estimated taxes paid to the Internal Revenue Service in quarterly installments.

[52] That effect contributes to projected increases in individual income tax receipts that more than offset the decline in receipts from social insurance taxes.

[53] Tax law allows businesses to receive refunds in the current year for tax payments in past years by carrying back current-year losses for up to two years to offset earlier tax liability. WHBAA temporarily allowed all businesses to choose to carry back such losses for up to five years and to receive refunds in 2010. Businesses that take advantage of that provision will have fewer losses to use to offset future tax liability, and receipts will increase more in future years than they would have without the expanded carryback window. Tax law also allows businesses that experience losses during economic downturns to reduce their tax liability in future, profitable, years by carrying forward their losses during the downturn and deducting them from later taxable income. WHBAA did not change the carry-forward provision in current law.

[54] The provision generally allows corporations that buy back their debt in 2009 or 2010 for less than the issue price to defer for several years including the gain in taxable income.

[55] Although the provisions of the Balanced Budget and Emergency Deficit Control Act of 1985 that pertain to the baseline expired on September 30, 2006, CBO continues to follow that law's specifications in constructing its baseline.

[56] In years after 2010, a 5 percent surtax also will be imposed on wealth transfers between $10.0 million and $17.184 million, resulting in an effective marginal tax rate of 60 percent for transfers in that range.

[57] For a more comprehensive discussion of projections for estate and gift taxes as they are affected by changes in tax law, see Congressional Budget Office, *Federal Estate and Gift Taxes,* Issue Brief (December 18, 2009).

[58] The discount window usually extends short-term credit to depository institutions facing temporary shortages in liquidity.

[59] The estimates of extending the expiring provisions are consistent with the effects on the baseline of assuming that the provisions will expire (see Box4-1).

[60] A table, "Effects of Extending Tax Provisions Scheduled to Expire Before 2020," appears as a Web supplement to this report at www.cbo.gov.

[61] Refundable credits reduce a taxpayer's overall tax liability; if the credit exceeds that liability, the excess may be refunded, in which case it is classified as an outlay in the federal budget.

[62] When this report went to press, only rough preliminary estimates based on CBO's new economic forecast were available for the impact of extending certain provisions, including various individual income tax provisions of EGTRRA and JGTRRA that are scheduled to expire at the end of 2010 and changes to the exemption amount under the AMT that expired at the end of 2009. CBO will make the updated estimates from the Joint Committee on Taxation available when they are completed.

[63] See Table1-5 for the budgetary effects of selected policy alternatives not included in CBO's baseline, including the effects of reforming the AMT by indexing its higher exemptions and tax brackets for inflation. That policy change would reduce the number of taxpayers that might become subject to the AMT over time by more than would extending the AMT's exemptions at their 2009 amounts.

[64] ARRA (Public Law 111-5) was not the only legislation enacted in recent years in an effort to bolster the economy. Before ARRA, polices such as tax cuts in the Economic Stimulus Act of 2008 and two extensions of unemployment benefits tried to lessen the harm caused by the downturn. Legislative initiatives after ARRA included the Car Allowance Rebate System program (also known as Cash for Clunkers), an extension and expansion of the tax credit for first-time home buyers, and additional expansions and extensions of emergency unemployment benefits and health insurance subsidies for the unemployed. In addition to those legislative efforts, various actions have been taken by the Federal Reserve and other government agencies to support the financial, housing, and manufacturing sectors of the economy.

[65] See Congressional Budget Office, cost estimate for the conference agreement for H.R. 1, the American Recovery and Reinvestment Act of 2009 (February 13, 2009). The staff of the Joint Committee on Taxation estimated most of the revenue effects of ARRA. CBO's cost estimate did not address ARRA's economic impact; that is discussed in Congressional Budget Office, *Estimated Impact of the American Recovery and Reinvestment Act on Employment and Economic Output as of September 2009* (November 2009).

[66] About $3 billion of the higher outlays for unemployment benefits stemmed from an intergovernmental transfer; CBO did not show that transaction as having an effect on outlays, but it was recorded that way by the Administration. It is likely that what ended up being recorded as outlays from ARRA were actually state benefits that would have occurred regardless of ARRA's enactment.

[67] Refundable credits reduce a taxpayer's overall tax liability; if the credit exceeds that liability, the excess may be refunded to the taxpayer, in which case it is classified as an outlay in the budget. The largest refundable credit in ARRA is the Making Work Pay credit.

[68] The Worker, Homeownership, and Business Assistance Act of 2009 (Public Law 111-92) expanded the benefits available under the temporary program for emergency unemployment compensation; people who exhaust regular benefits can now receive as many as 53 weeks of additional benefits under the emergency program. Amendments to the Department of Defense Appropriations Act, 2010 (P.L. 111-118), extended that program for two months, through February 2010.

[69] Those projections were published in *The Budget and Economic Outlook: An Update* (August 2009).

[70] The Deficit Control Act specified that mandatory spending programs whose authorizations are set to expire should be assumed to continue if they have outlays of more than $50 million in the current year and were established on or before the date the Balanced Budget Act of 1997 was enacted. Programs established after that date are not automatically assumed to continue. The Deficit Control Act also specified that expiring excise taxes whose revenues are dedicated to trust funds should be assumed to be extended at their current rates. The law did not provide for the extension of other expiring tax provisions, even if they had been routinely extended in the past.

[71] The law that created the TARP—the Emergency Economic Stabilization Act of 2008—specified that the program should be recorded in the budget by calculating the present value of its anticipated costs, using an adjustment for market risk. Under standard accounting for credit programs in the federal budget, the original subsidy calculation may be increased or decreased by a "credit reestimate" in subsequent years, on the basis of updated valuations of the present-value costs of the cash flows associated with those credit programs. CBO's baseline anticipates that such reestimates of TARP costs will occur.

[72] In developing its projections, CBO assumes an interaction between CHIP and Medicaid. The former is capped, with funding available for two years; when funding to maintain coverage under the program is insufficient, states may provide services for some children through Medicaid. In its current projections, CBO estimates that states will spend less from CHIP authority in the near term than the agency assumed in August, leaving more funds available to be spent in later years. As a result, CBO estimates that states will cover fewer children under Medicaid in those years in which more CHIP funding is now estimated to be available.

[73] For an explanation of the relative costs of the direct and guaranteed student loan program, see Congressional Budget Office, *Subsidy Estimates for Guaranteed and Direct Student Loans* (November 2005).

[74] For more detail on CBO's August baseline estimates for Fannie Mae and Freddie Mac and on the methodology the agency uses to assess such costs, see Congressional Budget Office, *CBO's Budgetary Treatment of Fannie Mae and Freddie Mac* (January 2010).

[75] The profit measure, which derives from the national income and product accounts and most closely approximates the corporate income tax base, takes profits from current production on activity within the United States by U.S. and foreign firms (that is, domestic economic profits) and adjusts them to substitute estimates of past and

future tax depreciation for the depreciation that more closely matches the loss in value of capital in the production process.

[76] A conventional way to measure past variability is to use the standard deviation. In the case of GDP growth, CBO calculates the extent to which actual growth over 10-year periods differs from the post-World War II average. The standard deviation is the size of the difference that is exceeded about one-third of the time.

[77] A change in the rate of real growth would generally affect other economic variables, such as inflation and unemployment; however, CBO's rule of thumb does not include such effects.

[78] Medicare's payment rates for physicians' services are computed using a formula that compares annual spending with a target amount that partly reflects the growth of GDP.

[79] Congressional Budget Office, *The Budget and Economic Outlook: Fiscal Years 2008 to 2018* (January 2008).

[80] The Federal Financing Bank is a government entity that was established to centralize and reduce the cost of federal borrowing. In 2009, it issued $12 billion in securities to the Civil Service Retirement Fund.

CHAPTER SOURCES

The following chapters have been previously published:

Chapter 1 – This is an edited, reformatted and augmented version of Congressional Research Service publication, Report R41134, dated March 23, 2010.

Chapter 2 – This is an edited, reformatted and augmented version of the United States Congressional Budget Office, dated January 2010.

INDEX

D

E

F

G

M

N

O

P

R

S

T

U

V

W